LEARNER-CENTERED LEADERSHIP

Research, Policy, and Practice

Topics in Educational Leadership
Larry W. Hughes, Series Editor

Gaynor • Analyzing Problems in Schools and School Systems: A Theoretical Approach

Earle/Kruse • Organizational Literacy for Educators

Shapiro/Stefkowitz • Ethical Leadership and Decision Making in Education: Applying Theoretical Perspectives to Complex Dilemmas

Bizar/Barr (Eds.) • School Leadership in Times of Urban Reform

Brouillette • Charter Schools: Lessons in School Reform

Fishbaugh/Schroth/Berkeley (Eds.) • Ensuring Safe School Environments: Exploring Issues—Seeking Solutions

For more information on LEA titles, please contact Lawrence Erlbaum Associates, Publishers at www.erlbaum.com

LEARNER-CENTERED LEADERSHIP

Research, Policy, and Practice

EDITED BY

ARNOLD B. DANZIG
Arizona State University

KATHRYN M. BORMAN
University of South Florida

BRUCE A. JONES
University of South Florida

WILLIAM F. WRIGHT
Northern Arizona University

2007

LAWRENCE ERLBAUM ASSOCIATES, PUBLISHERS
MAHWAH, NEW JERSEY   LONDON

Lawrence Erlbaum Associates, Inc., Publishers
10 Industrial Avenue
Mahwah, New Jersey 07430
www.erlbaum.com

Cover design by Tomai Maridou

Library of Congress Cataloging-in-Publication Data

Learner-centered leadership : research, policy, and practice / edited by Arnold B. Danzig
… [et al.]
    p. cm. —
Includes bibliographical references and index.
ISBN 0-8058-5843-1 (cloth : alk. paper)
ISBN 0-8058-5844-X (pbk. : alk. paper)
1. School administrators—In-service training—United States. 2. Educational leadership—
United States   I. Danzig, Arnold Bob, 1948–

LB1738.5.P77 2006
371.2'011—dc22   2006011744
                                                                CIP

Books published by Lawrence Erlbaum Associates are printed on acid-free paper, and their bindings are chosen for strength and durability.

Printed in the United States of America
10   9   8   7   6   5   4   3   2   1

CONTENTS

ABOUT THE EDITORS ix

FOREWORD xi
  David C. Berliner

PART I—INTRODUCTION AND OVERVIEW OF LEARNER-CENTERED 1
    LEADERSHIP

1 LEARNER-CENTERED LEADERSHIP: NEW DIRECTIONS FOR SCHOOL 3
  LEADERSHIP IN A NATIONAL PERSPECTIVE
    Arnold B. Danzig, Kathryn M. Borman, Bruce A. Jones, and William F. Wright

PART II—HISTORICAL AND INTELLECTUAL UNDERPINNINGS 21
    OF LEARNER-CENTERED LEADERSHIP–POLICY
    SHIFTS AND HISTORICAL SHIFTS IN PROFESSIONAL
    DEVELOPMENT FOR PRINCIPALS

2 A CULTURE IN THE MAKING: LEADERSHIP IN LEARNER-CENTERED 23
  SCHOOLS
    Ann Lieberman, Beverly Falk, and Leslie Alexander

3 A LEARNER-CENTERED APPROACH TO LEADERSHIP PREPARATION 51
  AND PROFESSIONAL DEVELOPMENT
    Arnold B. Danzig, Gerald Blankson, and Gary Kiltz

4 CONCEPTUAL FOUNDATIONS FOR PRINCIPAL LEADERSHIP 73
    G. Thomas Bellamy, Connie L. Fulmer, Michael J. Murphy, and Rodney Muth

PART III—PROFESSIONAL DEVELOPMENT, CONTEXT   109
KNOWLEDGE, CURRICULAR REFORM,
AND ADMINISTRATOR DEVELOPMENT

5 LEADERSHIP FOR CURRICULUM CHANGE: SCHOOLS ENGAGED   111
IN "CLOSING THE GAP"
Lesa M. Covington Clarkson and Karen Seashore Louis

6 THE DEVELOPMENT OF LEADERSHIP IN MATHEMATICS: 131
CASES OF URBAN REFORM
James A. Middleton and Kay Coleman

7 ELIMINATING ISOLATION TO FOSTER LEARNER-CENTERED LEADERSHIP: 149
LESSONS FORM RURAL SCHOOLS AND RESEARCH UNIVERSITIES
Karen DeMoss, Carolyn J. Wood, and Richard Howell

8 KENTUCKY'S COLLABORATIVE MODEL FOR DEVELOPING SCHOOL   171
LEADERS FOR RURAL HIGH-NEED SCHOOLS:
PRINCIPALS EXCELLENCE PROGRAM
Tricia Browne-Ferrigno and Jane Clark Lindle

PART IV—RESEARCH AND PRACTICE ON SCHOOL   187
LEADERSHIP AND PROFESSIONAL DEVELOPMENT

9 LEADERSHIP FOR DATA-BASED DECISION MAKING: 189
COLLABORATIVE EDUCATOR TEAMS
Jeffrey C. Wayman, Steve Midgley, and Sam Stringfield

10 LEARNER-CENTERED LEADERSHIP IN "URBAN" CONTEXTS: 207
KEY ELEMENTS TO CONSIDER FOR PROFESSIONAL DEVELOPMENT
Bruce A. Jones and Nathan D. Jackson

11 MANAGING POLICY ISSUES IN CARRYING OUT SYSTEMIC REFORM: 221
LESSONS FOR PRINCIPALS FROM CHICAGO, EL PASO, MEMPHIS,
AND MIAMI
Kathryn M. Borman, Theodore Boydston, and William Katzenmeyer

PART V—SOCIAL JUSTICE AND URBAN REFORM ISSUES   239
IN PROFESSIONAL DEVELOPMENT FOR
LEARNER-CENTERED SCHOOL LEADERS

12 LEADERSHIP IN BORDER RURAL AREAS: 241
A PEDAGOGICAL AWAKENING OF A PRINCIPAL PREPARATION PROGRAM
Elsy Fierro and María Luisa González

13 USING STORY AND NARRATIVE TO ENHANCE THE PROFESSIONAL   251
       DEVELOPMENT OF LEARNER-CENTERED LEADERS
         Arnold B. Danzig and William F. Wright

14 MORAL ISSUES IN A TEST-DRIVEN ACCOUNTABILITY AGENDA: 275
       MORAL CHALLENGES FOR LEARNING-CENTERED LEADERSHIP
         Robert J. Starratt

       AUTHOR INDEX   291

       SUBJECT INDEX   301

About the Editors

Arnold B. Danzig is Associate Professor of Educational Leadership in the Division of Educational Leadership and Policy Studies at Arizona State University. He is principal investigator of a multi-year leadership development grant from the United States Department of Education, which applies the concept of learner-centered leadership in language and culturally diverse schools in urban settings.

Kathryn M. Borman is Professor of Anthropology and also affiliated with the Alliance for Applied Research in Education and Anthropology in the Department of Anthropology at the University of South Florida where she is involved with large-scale research projects supported by the United States Department of Education and the National Science Foundation.

Bruce A. Jones is the David C. Anchin Professor of Education and Director of the Anchin Research Center at the University of South Florida in Tampa. His research foci are educational leadership and public policy in K–12 and higher education. He holds a PhD in political science from Columbia University in New York.

William F. Wright is Professor and Chair of the Department of Educational Leadership at Northern Arizona University. He has served as teacher, coach, principal, and superintendent, before joining the University faculty. He is an author for the *Master Teacher*, and also a member of the faculty of the Master Teacher Academy.

FOREWORD

David C. Berliner
Regents' Professor
Arizona State University

I have always respected the uniquely American philosophy of pragmatism and often use it to think about new ideas and theories that I come across. At its root, pragmatism holds that intelligent organisms, in trying to survive the environments in which they find themselves, develop ideas, beliefs, and theories that are "true." These are not "true" in some absolute sense, but true in the sense that they work for those organisms. They work amidst the conditions in which the organisms find themselves.

So for an organism to survive, to live longer and live better, it needs to develop ideas, beliefs, and theories that are practical, useful, fitting to its circumstances. When we move from the general case of organisms interacting with their environments, to the particular case addressed by the scholars in this book, namely, administrators at their work, pragmatism offers a guide for judging which ideas about managing complex environments are to be preferred among those that abound. What school administrators need for survival are ideas and theories that work, ideas that allow school administrators to survive and thrive in their unique and complex environments. Given the inordinately high turnover rates of school administrators in the United States it is clear that if we judge administrative success by survival on the job, the traditional set of beliefs, ideas, and theories about management possessed by administrators do not lead to success. So more pragmatic theories are needed to guide administrators.

Pragmatic beliefs, ideas and theories have a special affinity to what has also recently been called evidence-based approaches to education. Since a pragmatic theory is one that works, evidence that this is so is required. In education the evidence obtained may not be from a randomized clinical trial, as medicine might demand, but credible evidence is required, nevertheless. In school administration the forms of evidence that an administrative theory might rely on have to do with satisfaction of teachers and other employees, increased staff retention, student growth along with student and parent satisfaction, administrator self-report, and so on.

But because administrators deal with adult humans in the interest of creating environments that help young humans grow well, and these young and malleable humans are the central focus of administrators' work, there must be a moral component to the theories and ideas administrators choose to live by. We know, for example, that some things that work, that allow administrators to survive longer, are abhorrent (e. g. the propagation of fear among teachers and students through threats of job loss or retention in grade). In fact, the philosophy of pragmatism holds that not every idea that works is to be preferred, rather, among the ideas that are presented to us, those that contribute to the betterment of society, that contribute to the common good, are the ideas that should be preferred over others.

And so I introduce the reader to Learner-Centered Leadership, a pragmatic idea that I have just learned about myself. The belief in, idea of, or theory of Learner-Centered Leadership (LCL) passes the tests I have mentioned above. First of all it is useful. But as important to me also is that it is broadly rather than narrowly useful, and it is also a generative theory. Many new ideas about the management of schools flow from adoption of a LCL approach. Second, there is convincing evidence to support a LCL approach to school administration. For example, there is now considerable agreement from New York and Pittsburgh, among other research on school system change, that there is considerable payoff from promoting ways for teachers to talk about children's learning and their own instruction. Leadership that fosters analysis of student and teacher learning pays off! Finally, LCL is a morally appropriate way to conceptualize the administrators' role in schools. Adoption of a learning perspective breaks lines of authority down in all the appropriate ways because it brings to the foreground the fact that we are all learners—students, teachers and administrators. Status differences are minimized when everyone is engaged in trying to make a successful learning community. The role of the administrator who adopts LCL is much less likely to be authoritarian and power-relationship oriented, and much more likely to be authoritative and outcome focused. This is likely to be good for a school system.

I recommend these chapters to readers because they present a big idea, sometimes forgotten in the artificial world of schooling that we civilized people have created. That big idea is that learning is a natural process, and as such, we shouldn't think of it merely as the product of the schools we work in, but the process by which students, teachers and administrators all accomplish the tasks of schooling. We have been given the skills to learn from our social groups and from other experience, and thus, perhaps, the best way to run a school is to remember to focus on this skill, this process, that makes us so unique.

If we set out to more consciously focus on the learning of the students, rather than their need to pass tests, their attendance, or their misbehavior we might develop a different kind of school climate than we customarily see. If we focus on the learning of the teachers, rather than their ability to keep order, turn in forms on time, or prepare their students for tests, we might have a staff that works smarter, enjoys work more, and readily accomplishes the managerial tasks entailed in classroom teaching. And if we focus more on the learning that each administrator takes from their daily portion of complexity, novelty, tragedy and triumph, then they too probably will learn to work smarter, enjoy work more, and lead a community that is engaged in growing better, together. What these various chapters do, each in their own way, is present the rational for such learning communities, and sometimes, as well, the plans for designing administrative training programs that might bring such communities about. There is little uniformity of approach here, but all chapters share in a common desire to have administrators run school systems in which there is no loss of the intrinsic motivation that students and teachers first brought to their classrooms. These chapters offer a leadership model that might well enhance the motivation of students to learn, and protect the passion of teachers to enable that learning, instead of having students and teachers display the resignation that seems common in our schools because the environment for each of them is felt to be repressive.

Throughout these chapters about LCL we see administrators trained to recognize a shift in their relationships with teachers and students from a power centered leadership to a human needs oriented kind of leadership. We see them training on real world problems of humans in organizations, and receiving less training in traditional theories of organizational management. We see administrators spending more of their training time learning through mentorship, and a bit less than through courses and books, establishing the very necessary condition for LCL, an appreciation of the wisdom of others. Harnessing the wisdom of practice is a characteristic of a practicing learner-centered leader. Creating communities of conversation and support in order that the wisdom derived from practice can be shared becomes one of the primary goals of a practicing learner-centered leader. It is these communities of conversation and support that allow for the new data driven models of school improvement to be successful. Without broadly based community discourse, the process of interpretation of school data in order to form action plans, often fails. Without discourse communities school data may stay inert, lifeless, and it may never become transformed into information upon which a community chooses to act. The actions taken stand a much better chance to be successful than were they mandated by leaders who had no communal sounding boards and advisors. A good deal of the education of LCL teaches why this is so. And the education of LCL includes ways to involve the broader community, even urban communities, in the process of making schools better places for its teachers and its students to spend their time.

The many ideas about LCL that run through these chapters reveal to me that the concept of LCL is more like a lens than a tight theory. Fitted with the LCL lenses I look at America's schools and training programs for administrators and ask whether the beliefs and ideas associated with LCL are present, and I find they are not. But this book could begin to change that. The authors make a convincing argument that there is a better way to run our schools—a pragmatic way—one that is useful and fits well into the school environment, one backed by convincing evidence, and one that is morally appropriate. I certainly am supportive of these scholars who provide us the LCL lens to use in thinking about how schools could be organized and managed, in comparison to the way our schools run now.

Phoenix, AZ
February, 2006

INTRODUCTION AND OVERVIEW
OF LEARNER-CENTERED LEADERSHIP

PART

I

INTRODUCTION AND OVERVIEW
OF LEARNER-CENTERED LEADERSHIP

1

LEARNER-CENTERED LEADERSHIP: NEW DIRECTIONS FOR SCHOOL LEADERSHIP IN A NATIONAL PERSPECTIVE

Arnold B. Danzig
Arizona State University

Kathryn M. Borman
Bruce A. Jones
University of South Florida

William F. Wright
Northern Arizona University

This book explores the concept *Learner-Centered Leadership* (LCL) relative to the professional development needs of school leaders. In this professional development context, the concept includes new knowledge and skills for aspiring and practicing school leaders. LCL implies a belief in democracy, and places responsibility for learning and development with multiple participants in educational settings: students, staff, teachers, and administrators. In this sense, LCL stands in opposition to the forces promoting organizational efficiency and standardization because establishing and maintaining a learner-centered atmosphere or climate in schools requires time and commitment.

The concept of LCL is especially relevant today because expectations for school leaders held by constituents and stakeholders invested in schools are quite different. The professional knowledge that teachers and administrators bring to bear, the community knowledge housed with children and families, and the political expectations of politicians and stakeholders send contradictory or conflicting messages to school leaders. At the same time, the demands of leading a complex organization and conducting the day-to-day operations of running a school undertaking fundamental change in how it does business easily result in school leaders expressing their frustration and exhaustion (Borman, Carter, Aladjem, & Le Floch, 2004). Current debates over the future of teacher and administrator leadership training and professional development recognize these disharmonies. The difficulty of finding high-quality candidates to enter and remain in leadership positions in schools indicates a continuing erosion of the quality of the work. Professional journals are filled with descriptions of new approaches to school leadership: distributed leadership and site-based management, data-driven decision-making and high-stakes accountability, curricular and instructional leadership, and cultural and organizational learning. The approach to school leadership is often determined by whether priority is given to (a) maintaining order and stability, (b) advancing technical approaches to skill development and career aspirations, or (c) promoting *school betterment*, a term Jeannie Oakes and her colleagues use to reference "the educative, socially just, caring, and democratic conditions that educators hope to create for their students" (Oakes, Quartz, Ryan, & Lipton, 2000, p. 316). One goal for this book is to help school leaders think about what is important about their work. The chapters that follow provide examples of learner-centered approaches for accomplishing this work.

LCL begins with a shift in the personal dispositions and professional norms of school leaders. For this shift to occur, learner-centered leaders need to be better educated in general, drawing on social science knowledge as well as ethical, critical, and legal reasoning (Bellamy, Fulmer, Murphy, & Muth, 2003; Murphy, 2002). LCL also recognizes the importance of craft knowledge that is part of leadership and decision making, as well as a tacit dimension to leadership that draws on prior experience in complex organizational settings, that is, schools. The co-editors hope that the themes raised in this book provide rich examples of leadership and leadership development for practitioners at different levels along the continuum from preparation to expert practice.

LCL: SOME KEY ELEMENTS

A key element discussed in all of the chapters included in this volume is the priority placed on learning. It is taken for granted that the managers and leaders of today's businesses understand the underlying principles of their products or services. For school leaders, this knowledge requires understanding of the basic and deeper principles related to learning in diverse educational settings. The knowledge and application of learning principles are frequently based on years of experience in the classroom, along with study of and reflection on principles of teaching and learning.

Learner-centered leaders understand themselves as learners. They recognize how motivation affects what is learned and how learning takes place. They are aware of how people learn and what facilitates the learning of children, youth, and adults.

Learner-centered leaders reject sanctions as the basic approach for motivating others to learn, and instead view freedom and autonomy as primary sources of learning. Learner-centered leaders recognize that learners need control over their own learning.

Learner-centered leaders understand that learning is social. Learning is influenced by social interactions, interpersonal relations, and communication with others. Learning is enhanced when the learner has an opportunity to interact and to collaborate with others, on meaningful tasks. Settings that encourage learning allow for social interactions, respect diversity, and encourage flexible thinking and social competence. People learn as they participate with a community of learners, interacting with that community and understanding and participating in its history, assumptions, and cultural values and rules.

Learning Occurs at Multiple Levels

A second theme evident in each of this volume's chapters relates to the multiple contexts in which people learn. Learning is defined, acquired, and used at the individual, organizational, and community levels. Each of the chapters reveals the complex nature of schools and accompanying challenges to improve learning. If the learning that occurs in schools is to go beyond individual learning, there must be organizational learning as well. By organizational learning, we mean to focus attention on how groups of people come together to share information, make decisions, and take actions related to individual and organizational goals (Schön, 1991; Senge et al., 1999; Weick, 1993; Weick & Roberts, 1993).

One component of organizational learning is a leader's ability to understand and give meaning to how the day-to-day activities of participants contribute to educational purposes. LCL is invested in defining purposes that touch on student and community learning. Learner-centered leaders translate guiding ideas into educational practices that engage all members of the community. As Lieberman, Falk, and Alexander point out in their chapter, LCL requires school leaders to be educators, problem solvers, crisis managers, change agents, enablers, consensus builders, and networkers.

LCL assumes that leaders also serve community ideals while recognizing that the community is a work in progress. This image of the principal as community builder encourages others to be leaders in their own right and to see to it that leadership is deeply distributed in the organization. Many of the chapters refer to issues related to leadership and democratic community, social justice and social conscience in rural and border communities, and are indicators of the relevance of LCL to concepts related to community. Focusing on community also presses school leaders to ask questions about community values, particularly values concerned with educational equity and social justice. A community committed to learning requires a process of working through differences in beliefs and opinions. If the examples presented in this volume are indicative of trends across the United States, school leaders of the future will be even more heavily involved in defining the purposes, identifying vision, and giving meaning to actions than the current generation of practitioners (Bennis, 2003; Weick & Roberts, 1993). These commitments involve greater attention to the people that inhabit schools and communities, and to the knowledge and values of students, parents, families, and communities. LCL is anchored in the competence to understand, articulate, and communicate the knowledge and values of multiple constituents and stakeholders. Collaboration requires new learning to make sense of conflicting norms and information, consider new ideas, and model democratic participation, which embraces differences. These attributes are essential in the repertoire of learner-centered leaders.

Learner-Centered Leaders Recognize Dilemmas of Administrative Practice

One challenge to the concept of LCL is that, when things go wrong, individuals, not organizations, are identified and held responsible. In this view, school principals are held accountable for school-site stability and student achievement under No Child Left Behind (NCLB), whereas teachers are expected to be in control of their classrooms. One result is that the norm of reciprocity prevails with a *quid pro quo* of arrangements, between administrators and school board, between principals and teachers, and between teachers and students. Too often, this leads to territorialism, where defending turf instead of building community is the norm. As indicated in the chapter by Borman et al., new learning about the culture of schools, and the role of leadership in building school culture is required if learning is to be nurtured. Otherwise, stakeholders will resist collaborating; building community will take a backseat to preserving individual control over respective domains.

Another challenge to LCL is learning to balance individuality with community and collaboration. Autonomy, time, nonaccountability, control over one's own clientele, a sense of personal accomplishment, discretionary decision making, and the control of space can all be rewards for individual performance. LCL recognizes the value of collaborative learning within and across organizational boundaries. The organization is not static and the source of social and environmental problems is not defined by the behaviors of individuals. Rather, the organization must adapt to the ever changing needs of individuals while individuals learn to adapt to their environments. LCL challenges leaders to better understand the assumptions and filters that inform their leadership and the tacit values that go into decision making (Vickers, 1995).

A related challenge of LCL is recognizing that the positional authority that comes from being a principal is not the same as the moral commitments and leadership skills required to create a learner-centered school. LCL gives priority to the autonomous learning that comes from professional networks and peers; it involves mentoring and coaching separate from the role of supervisor and evaluator. The traditional role expectation of the principal expects too much of one person—expert in content knowledge, authority on instructional pedagogy, and model for individual and organizational excellence. Learner-centered leaders open spaces and provide opportunities for others to empower themselves and to facilitate their own learning.

APPLICATIONS TO THE POLITICAL AND POLICY CONTEXT

The learner-centered approach to educational leadership is complicated by the current political demands for greater accountability and the press for increased individual and school test scores. Learner-centered leaders advance learning, rather than ever higher test scores, as the core concept around which other school efforts are measured. They resist the trend toward targeting those children most likely to show immediate test score gain. This priority given to learning distinguishes LCL from political leadership.

The contributions of this volume share several themes about leadership reform and professional development. Collaboration, teamwork, an appreciation for ongoing learning, the need to develop instruction that focuses on the development of critical thinking skills in children as opposed to rote memorization and regurgitation instructional are approaches argued in this volume. Unfortunately, the press to focus almost exclusively on test preparation stands in contradiction to approaches to leadership and school reform advocated by a number of policymakers in the public and private sectors. Through regulatory, fiscal, and (at the state level) mandate authority, policymakers exert enormous influence on the implementation of school reform agendas and professional development priorities that are ultimately developed by school districts. For example, state policymakers at the agency-level who operate from traditional viewpoints of schooling may not value the need for supporting leadership development in schools. These policymakers may believe that there is a greater need to narrowly focus on teachers' classroom instruction while viewing principal leadership as primarily as managing for results related to standards-based accountability systems and state assessments (Hess & Kelley, 2005). Budget allocations, state-sponsored workshops, and policy priorities may reflect this more traditional view in contrast to the broader focus on learner-centered approaches to schooling.

The private corporate and philanthropic sectors in recent years have placed a strong emphasis on the need for more student testing and teacher and administrator accountability sanctions for poor school academic performance. For example, the Ed Trust under Katie Haycock's capable leadership has been in the forefront of those calling for change under the guidelines of NCLB. Such organizations are demanding school leaders to tighten up what may have been viewed as relatively democratic governing and leadership structures to hold the feet of teachers and school staff to the fire regarding school performance. With this phenomenon, the press is for school leaders to be increasingly transactional and authoritarian as opposed to transformative and democratic. Leaders must issue edicts in a hierarchal manner for teachers and school staff to follow obediently or suffer the punitive consequences. This is all in contradiction to the philosophical and practical leadership notions that are advocated in this volume.

According to Jones (in press), at least four phenomena or trends during the past 25 years have contributed to the policies and practices just described. Each potentially holds consequences for how school leadership under the rubric of a learner-centered model will be manifest and subsequently institutionalized in school settings: (a) *the importance of formal education*; (b) *the bully pulpit function of the federal government in public education*; (c) *the intrusion of community elites* in education at a national level and the affairs of public schooling at a local level; and (d) the significance of *nationally driven school reform packages*.

The Growing Importance of Formal Education

With each passing decade, the importance of education has grown exponentially. Much more is now at stake regarding the education of children and the success that they attain as productive citizens in adulthood. Increasingly, education has become the single most important mechanism for achieving success in the global society. Once thought of as the world's premier education system, urban schools in the United States are now failing to help children achieve success (Cuban, 1990; Murphy & Beck, 1995). In the wake of this failure, the U.S. Census Bureau reports that average earnings progressively increase with each level of educational attainment. At the bottom of the income hierarchy are high school noncompleters, earning an average of $18,826. High school graduates earn an average of 45% more at $27,280, an overwhelming amount in comparison when compounded over a lifetime. The income discrepancy grows even wider for college graduates, who earn an average of $51,194—nearly double that of high school graduates and almost three times that of high school noncompleters.

The Growing Importance of the Federal Government's Bully Pulpit

The 1983 National Commission on Excellence in Education's *Nation at Risk Report* brought a level of federal involvement in education that is unprecedented in history. The report declared that "if an unfriendly foreign power had attempted to impose on America the mediocre educational performance that exists today, we might well have viewed it as an act of war. As it stands, we have allowed this to happen to ourselves" (p. 5). On the heels of the report, more than three fourths of the states feverishly began work on comprehensive state action plans for school improvement (Guthrie & Springer, 2004). At the national level, school reform efforts were driven by President G. H. W. Bush's *America 2000* initiative, President Clinton's *Goals 2000*, initiative and the current President G. W. Bush's *No Child Left Behind* initiative.

The NCLB initiative is viewed as the most activist involvement of the federal government in U.S. public education history (Emery & Ohanian, 2004; Sergiovanni et al., 2004). For the first time, the federal government garnered the authority to impose sanctions and penalties on school districts that fail to meet adequate yearly progress (AYP) as stipulated by the requirements of the NCLB legislation. These penalties include obligatory student transfer options at the district's expense, forced reallocation of district federal funding, potential principal and teacher dismissal at underperforming schools, and even external school takeover or closure (Corcoran & Goertz, 2005). The number of schools now subject to these penalties "has skyrocketed" (NEA, 2004).

The roots of NCLB trace back to the "Great Society" programs of Lyndon Johnson. In 1965, Congress passed the Elementary and Secondary Education Act (ESEA)— "the first federal statute that ... provided really substantial, precedent-setting amount of federal money to local schools so that better education could be provided to historically underserved student groups such as minority and low income students" (Popham, 2004, p. 14). The ESEA had positive results as achievement gaps narrowed between 1967 and 1988. However, achievement gaps (based on race and income) stopped narrowing and began to widen in 1988 (Chenoweth, 2004, p. 40).

In 1994, under the Clinton administration, Congress utilized the Reauthorization of the ESEA to insist for the first time that "federal money must not simply be spent on poor kids, as it had been since the first ESEA of 1965, but that it had to be used to bring poor kids up to state standards" (Chenoweth, 2004, p. 41). At the same time, Congress mandated that schools receiving federal funds must also demonstrate that they are teaching all students in concert with state standards in critical subject matter areas in-cluding mathematics, language arts, and, most recently, science. Because of noncom-pliance on the part of states, and lack of clarity concerning standards, NCLB (the 2001 Reauthorization of the ESEA) was designed to require each state to "1) set standards that it expects all children without major cognitive disabilities to meet; 2) have a way of measuring whether children meet those standards; and 3) demonstrate regular prog-ress toward the goal of having all students meet state standards by 2014" (pp. 41–42).

It is fair to say that NCLB has drastically changed the way that states, school dis-tricts, and schools operate. The mandate of NCLB prescribes a thorough focus on rais-ing student achievement as measured in testing and AYP requirements. Due to the accompanying financial leverage of this mandate, NCLB has become, arguably, the primary concern of educational professionals.

Although many district personnel may view NCLB as overly prescriptive, and as an intrusion into their policymaking purview, the threat of losing federal funds due to non-compliance is a powerful source of coercion. In much the same way as Congress utilizes the spending clause to coerce adherence to "most federal education policies," such as "Title VI (race, ethnicity, and national origin)" or "Title IX (gender)," Congress has uti-lized the spending clause to coerce adherence to the prescriptions of NCLB (McColl, 2005, p. 605). Concerning the term "coercion," McColl (2005) writes,

> As a matter of law, some courts may be reluctant to characterize the state's reliance on funds or the federal intrusion into state programs as "coercion," but it is certainly possible that NCLB will be vulnerable to this challenge. Indeed, states that have relied on Title I funds as part of a piecemeal strategy for serving at-risk children certainly have no realis-tic choice but to accept the conditions of the law. (pp. 608–609)

Because of this financial leverage, formal objections on the part of states and dis-tricts have had financial consequences (Bracey, 2004; McColl, 2005).

The Growing Intrusion of Community Elites

There has been an uncommonly large involvement of community elites from the business, philanthropic, and media sectors in urban schooling that is remarkably different from their past participation. Historically, community elite involvement (particularly by the business community) in urban school affairs was largely lim-ited to ceremonial events, such as teacher of the year banquets and/or adopt-a-school initiatives. However, since the release of the *Nation at Risk Report* and the declaration by President Ronald Reagan that the 1980s constituted the decade of *business–school partnerships*, businesses have been at the center of school deci-sion making regarding curriculum and instruction reform, professional develop-ment for teachers and administrators, hiring and firing of school staff, school board candidate selection and elections, and the establishment of school budget priori-ties (Jones & Otterbourg, 2000). At a national level, the private business and phil-anthropic sectors through the Business Roundtable Table (BRT) and affiliated business interest groups[1] actually authored the basic principles that under gird the *America 2000, Goals 2000,* and NCLB legislations of the past three presidential

---

[1]The National Alliance of Business, the Committee for Economic Development, the Conference Board, and the Business Coalition for Excellence in Education, to name a few.

administrations (Boyles, 2000; Cibulka, 2000; Emery & Ohanian, 2004; Jones & Otterbourg, 2000). According to Emery & Ohanian (2004),

> A high-ranking leader of the BRT admitted his commitment to beating up on public schools. ... According to this leader, "large organizations such as schools don't change because they see the light; they change because they feel the heat." (p. 38)

In the push for schools to adopt corporate, traditionally hierarchal models of leadership, urban school leaders who subscribe to shared or distributive leadership models of schooling that are characteristic of the *learner-centered community* concept do so at their own peril. In this regard, the corporate impact on schooling is potentially threatening and detrimental to teacher leadership models of school governance. Boyles (2000) reported, "For teachers, increasing business interests means increasing subordination and marginalization of their roles" (p. 7).

The Growing Significance of School Reform Packages

Since the release of the *Nation at Risk Report*, an extraordinary number of school reform packages have been produced by model developers who purport to know what schools and school districts need in the way of teacher and staff professional development, curriculum and instruction reform, and student and parent enrichment programming. Approximately $2.1 billion in contracts is awarded annually to the 40 most prominent school reform packages in the country (Jones, 2006). According to Jones (2004), "school districts have become (lucrative) bastions of experimentation for school reform advocates who proclaim to hold the magic cure for what ails school districts" (p. B6).

The issue of school reform in the context of formal comprehensive school reform (CSR) packages is really quite complex. Some states such as California have used funding streams including Title 1 funds to address poor school performance and channeled CSR funding to failing schools as a state-wide strategy to boost student performance. In other states including Pennsylvania and New Jersey, state takeover of failing schools has led to strategies that include adoption at the school level of CSR models. In New Jersey, state level takeover emanated from a series of legal decisions. The series of court decisions resulting from the *Abbott v. Burke* cases in New Jersey provide an example of ways state governance structures—in this case, the judicial system and the governor—may intervene in school reform. In New Jersey, "whole-school reform" efforts (as they were referenced in the Abbott rulings) became intertwined in a decades-long battle to address funding disparities among New Jersey school districts. The 1998 *Abbott v. Burke* ruling ("Abbott V") required the state commissioner of education "to implement whole-school reform ... as expeditiously as possible" in 30 of the most impoverished districts, and the Success for All (SFA) model was specifically cited as "the recommended version of whole-school reform for elementary schools." Other requirements of Abbott V included the establishment of full-day kindergarten and new technology programs and substantial new funds for school facilities. The Commissioner wrote that, "for the first time in more than a quarter century, there is consensus on an approach that clearly has demonstrated great potential to provide the state's poorest school children with the kind of education they deserve" (Klaghoz, 1998).

However, consensus regarding the potential efficacy of whole-school reform for Abbott districts dissipated in the years following the landmark ruling, resulting in Spring 2002 in a freeze on new funding for schools affected by the Abbott ruling. The following year, Governor James McGreevey formally asked the court to lift the order to implement whole-school reform in the Abbott districts. Ultimately, the Abbott parties entered into mediation, resulting in a new set of regulations, *Improving Learning and Literacy in Abbott Districts: Implementing Standards-Driven Instruction, Reforms, Programs and Services under Abbott v. Burke*, issued by the state Commissioner in September 2003. Under this set of regulations, elementary schools are still required to maintain a contract with an approved whole-school reform provider, with exceptions made for high-performing schools and those with an evidence-driven case that they would be better served by alternative reform strategies.

In her ongoing assessment of reform effects on outcomes in the Abbott districts, Erlichson notes that, whereas both Abbott districts and wealthier New Jersey districts are currently posting gains in student achievement, Abbott districts are making greater gains in language arts proficiency, gaining on average 24 points in contrast to the non-Abbott average of 15 points over the same 2-year period (Erlichson & Goertz, 2001). Erlichson and others have nonetheless been critical of New Jersey's implementation process, noting that promised funds from the state to support CSR implementation have been extremely slow in getting to Abbott schools. This delay (and other factors) compromised both the faculty buy-in process and sustainability of reform in these schools. The New Jersey Department of Education ultimately argued that whole school reform proved less effective than expected and sought to have the court order lifted. Through mediation, the parties agreed in 2003 to allow the highest performing schools to abandon their CSR models.

We have attempted here to provide a brief overview of several trends that provide the important policy background for understanding the focus in this volume on learner-centered leadership at the school level. The school principal and his or her administrative team and teachers constitute the critical link between federal, state, and district policies and the student learner. Without their total commitment to student learning, the enterprise is lost.

OVERVIEW OF THE CHAPTERS

This volume consists of 14 chapters that examine different aspects and applications of the LCL concept. The volume begins with a foreword by David Berliner. Professor Berliner is probably best known for his book *The Manufactured Crisis*, which explores themes in school reform with direct implications for school administration and professional development. Dr. Berliner's research and writing considers the significance and character of learning and directs readers to consider implications of learner-centered approaches as they relate not only to book learning but also to art, music, community service, and so on. Dr. Berliner's work asks principals and school administrators to consider what is it that they don't know about instruction. His foreword provides some historical, theoretical, and practical frameworks that situate the book.

The introductory chapter describes some of the key principles of LCL, introduces readers to the policy context for the chapters, and briefly summarizes the other sections and chapters of the book.

Section II provides historical and intellectual underpinnings for understanding LCL and professional development. The section begins with a chapter by Ann Lieberman and her colleagues. This chapter explicates the leadership dimensions for learner centeredness, with reference to school leadership. Lieberman revisits an earlier piece that she wrote on small schools in the early 1990s, to examine what learner-centered means in context of contemporary schooling. She adds an epilogue that contains two cases of practicing principals and shows how learner-centered ideas impact leadership and shape the environment for teachers and students.

This chapter is followed by a discussion of the conceptual foundations for understanding principal leadership by Thomas Bellamy and colleagues at the University of Colorado. Based on the work of the New School Leadership Project and a forthcoming book, *Reframing the Principalship: Knowledge, Practice, and Preparation*, this chapter describes a way of organizing and using the profession's knowledge to support leadership in schools. Key elements of the approach are (a) an accomplishment model for organizing knowledge and assessing local practice, (b) a conception of leadership practice across three domains (sustainable purposes, strategic focus, and effective action), and (c) a proposal for documenting craft knowledge through "annual cases." The chapter also illustrates the use of these conceptual tools in district-based efforts to support leadership development among teachers, a university leadership education program, and collaborative efforts to use annual cases for principals' professional development and sharing of craft knowledge.

The chapter provides important discussion of the tacit and craft knowledge of professionals (which has been largely unexplored and undervalued) and other knowledge bases brought to the forefront in the practice of principals. They argue that principal leadership is best understood as it engages the practical concerns that principals face on a daily basis. What is new about this work is the focus on school leadership practice, at the same time organizing knowledge (ethical and critical reasoning, legal reasoning, and social science research) to support practice.

The section concludes with a chapter by Danzig and his colleagues at the Arizona State University, which describes a leadership and professional development program implemented as part of a 3-year U.S. Department of Education School Leadership Grant "LCL for Language and Culturally Diverse Schools in High Needs Urban Settings." The chapter provides a practical example of the LCL concept and explores some of the dilemmas faced by school districts and by universities, as they collaborate to provide leadership training and professional development for aspiring, rising, and experienced school administrators.

The focus on LCL reflects renewed attention to the primary role of teaching and learning in the development of school leadership expertise. With a focus on learning, the need to create collaborative structures where trust, respect, and communication are promoted among the participants is deemed critical. In the early going, the project goal has been to develop the capacity for mentoring across districts. To create this capacity, the project has focused on building relationships among participants using a threefold process: formal workshops that introduce the districts and participants; informal gatherings that break down barriers and establish opportunities for networking; and a series of problem-solving initiatives called a team challenge that requires participants to work together, communicate, and cooperate to solve the challenging activities.

The LCL program illustrates how participants balance practical concerns related to leadership and learning with the deeper concepts from which practice is drawn. The willingness of project participants to jointly plan sessions, co-teach classes and workshops, facilitate interaction among administrators, provide mentoring within and between districts, and share practical and conceptual knowledge are explored in the chapter.

Section III explores LCL and connections to administrator professional development, content knowledge, and curricular reform. The opening chapter, "Curriculum Reform and School Administrator Development: A 'Bottom Up' Perspective," by Lesa Clarkson and Karen Seashore Louis, contends that synthesizing what we know about effective schools and school improvement provides a "backward map" that leads to both more effective content and to the production of problem-centered learning that is focused on how best to support teachers and effective instruction. This discussion examines, in detail, case material and teacher survey results from a recent study of schools implementing NSF-funded mathematics curriculum. This particular investigation significantly expands previous backward mapping efforts by focusing on what principals need to know and be able to do about (a) teachers' need for support in mediating relationships with parents in connection with curriculum reform, (b) providing specific support for "letting go" of past practices in teaching and assessment, and (c) supporting new classroom management strategies that are required by new curriculum reforms.

The chapter by James Middleton and Kay Coleman on the development of leadership in mathematics explores the real work of two urban school districts in Arizona in developing district-wide mathematics initiatives, which have had great impact on student understanding, student achievement, and skillful teaching. The work has been based on the development of capacity and leadership at the school site level as well as across all schools in the district. Case studies are used to make explicit the process and change over time at the classroom, school, and district level.

Their cases illustrate the process a successful urban elementary school district enacted, over a 9-year period, to develop a critical mass of teacher leaders in mathematics teaching and learning. It contrasts "Pyramid Schemes" for diffusion of innovation with that of developing local learning communities. Given the economics of professional development, and given the pressures of the No Child Left Behind Act, new models for leadership development are critical for deep and coherent educational improvement. Key learnings from the case underscore the need for teacher leaders to continue to practice their craft in the classroom, to utilize resources from higher education, and to plan for the long haul.

Karen DeMoss, Carolyn Wood, and Richard Howell at the University of New Mexico explore more rural themes in their chapter "Eliminating Isolation to Foster LCL: Lessons from Rural Schools and Research Universities." Their chapter addresses three areas of need among current New Mexico principals who aspire to leadership roles: instructional leadership, community leadership, and systems management skills. The primary goal of the project is to help administrators become proficient in managing the change process, facilitating the creation of a shared vision, and communicating support for that vision. A concerted effort is being made to create a "community of practice" consisting of three cohorts of current principals and assistant principals, and augmented by a cadre of veteran mentor principals called "Circuit Riders."

Their project team has faced a number of challenges in the first year, including a new governor with an educational reform agenda, a new legislative mandate to respond to the No Child Left Behind Act, and significant turnover by superintendents and principals in Northern New Mexico. Despite these obstacles, the project has engaged principals of the 26 school districts that make up the Northern New Mexico Network for Rural Education. The project team has developed an instructional model that emphasizes the community of learners concepts, cognitive coaching, and leadership skills. The results of first-year research and evaluation activities, and lessons learned in the application of a leadership agenda for rural principals, are discussed as part of the chapter.

The final chapter in this section by Tricia Browne-Ferrigno and Jane Clark Lindle explores "Kentucky's Collaborative Model for Developing School Leaders for Rural High-Needs Schools." This chapter focuses on a project entitled the Principals Excellence Program (PEP), a collaborative partnership between the University of Kentucky and Pike County School District. The overarching goal for the federally funded project was the design and refinement of a model for improved school leadership that ensures learning for at-risk students in rural school districts. Project objectives addressed recruitment, development, and retention as strategies to increase the pool of effective principals available to lead high-need schools in eastern Kentucky. The project was delivered as an interconnected series of seminar-workshops, field-based experiences, and structured reflections intended to develop a professional community of practicing and aspiring principals who have the desire to be change agents, the commitment to be lifelong learners, and the skills to be data-based decision makers and reflective practitioners. Continuously collected data informed and guided the actions by the project instructional team and district leadership teams throughout implementation. Formal data collection involving project participants included (a) a series of pre- and postsurveys, (b) a series of reflective questionnaires, and (c) focus-group interviews conducted by the principal investigator. The instructional teams visited schools where project-sponsored action research projects were conducted and talked informally with mentor principals about the field-based experiences; mentor principals also critiqued their experiences with PEP through completing surveys and reflective questionnaires and participating in focus-group interviews. WestEd selected PEP as one of six leadership development initiatives (among a group of approximately 50 nationally) to be featured in its School Leadership Innovation Guide. Data collected during the WestEd interviews with district leaders, instructors, mentor principals, and cohort members and quantitative data about district and school performance based on student achievement are also integrated into the assessment of project impact.

Section IV examines research and practice on school leadership and professional development. The first chapter in this section by Jeff Wayman and colleagues explores "Leadership for Data-Based Decision-Making: Collaborative Educator Teams." The authors look at the use of student achievement tests and other forms of assessment as a policy lever for effecting school change. They consider the underlying assumptions concerning student data sources used by education stakeholders to examine practice and make changes that will positively impact student outcomes. They find that school leaders are finding this a difficult charge, however—not only are educators typically unprepared to make effective use of these new sources of student data, but educators lack an organizational framework within which data can be created, evaluated, and related back to instructional activities. Consequently, school leaders are often overwhelmed by the prospect of transforming their schools into "data-rich environments."

A promising leadership practice in this area is the formation of collaborative teams to collectively explore student data. When functioning effectively, such teams offer members a safe forum to share and explore pedagogical frameworks, and engage in the process of effective goal-setting for school improvement. However, for collaborative instructional teams to be effective systemically, a number of organizational strategies need to be concurrently implemented, including strategic planning, goal setting, performance management, leadership development, curricular systems, and instructional practice development. Though research shows that collaborative teams often are successful, this research seldom discusses these supportive organizational strategies.

From an ongoing project designed to help school personnel utilize student data to improve education, the authors present data from schools that are using collaborative data teams to modify and improve educational practice. They discuss necessary systemic precursor elements and difficulties arising in implementation of data team cultures in large educational systems. Results from this study are used to compare and contrast the experiences of these schools, providing evidence for discussion of lessons learned through this process and recommendations for best practice.

Bruce Jones and Nathan Jackson's chapter, "Advanced Professional Development for School Administrators in Urban Settings," exemplifies the ideal in what is meant by "collaboration" in the spirit of the learner-centered model. Under the rubric of the *State Action Leadership Education Program* (SALEP), the *Urban School Leadership Consortium* (USLC) was established as the first leadership development initiative in the State of Missouri to bring two large urban school districts together to address school leadership needs in a joint fashion. Historically, the two urban districts (Kansas City, Missouri, and the St. Louis School Districts) worked in isolation of each other although many of the policy issues that the districts faced concerning student achievement and teacher and administrator efficacy were similar.

The emphasis on "urban" is critical to the authors because, typically, leadership development initiatives fail to take into account school context distinctions, such as, rural, suburban, and urban contexts. The authors contend that school leaders face different challenges and opportunities in each of these contexts that must be considered with the development and implementation of professional development programming. The chapter discusses the evolution of the USLC regarding its learner-centered conceptual frameworks and its emphasis on preparing urban school leaders to adopt participatory styles of leadership, work with multiple constituencies in the public and private sectors, and use technology for the advancement and improvement of school operations and administrator and teacher efficacy.

The final chapter in the section is by K. Borman and her colleagues, "Managing Policy Issues in Carrying out Systemic Reform: Lessons for Principals from Chicago, El Paso, Memphis and Miami." The chapter analyzes data from interviews with school district personnel including the superintendents (CEO in the case of Chicago), principals, and teachers. These findings have direct implications for the professional development of principals. The chapter provides case examples from the project to show how this can be accomplished and why it is important. First, principals should support teachers' work in aligning professional development with classroom practice and student assessment. Second, principals who were most effective in implementing reform were those who understood which community resources could provide the most support for their students' academic achievement. There was great variation among the four urban sites in this regard. In Memphis, for example, faith-based organizations were particularly effective in reaching students and their families to support student achievement in math and science. Finally, although each of the sites had high levels of child poverty and chronically low levels of student achievement, each site capitalized on district resources to support math and science teaching and learning.

Principals in school districts undertaking system-wide reform must juggle implementation of reform with accountability for its affect on student achievement. In carrying out this study of the impact of the National Science Foundation's Urban Systemic Initiative (USI) in four cities, a major focus of the work was on how national, state, and district policies supported or constrained the day-to-day roles and responsibilities of the 47 school principals participating in the research. The questions addressed by this chapter are designed to understand the importance of policies related to systemic reform including assessments, standards, and professional development. The authors explore how resources were mobilized among various constituencies such as schools, universities, business and industry, and community-based institutions and agencies. They sought to determine which community and district contextual characteristics were particularly important in affecting student outcomes.

The final section of the book appraises social justice and school reform issues with implications for professional development of school leaders. The opening chapter, by Elsy Fierro and María Luisa González, is "Leadership In Border Rural Areas (LIBRA): Transcending the Mexico/US Border: Approaches to a Pedagogical Awakening for Principal Preparation Programs." The authors suggest that principal preparation programs along the U.S.–Mexico border have traditionally followed the national trend focusing on a broad spectrum of educational leadership topics. Few principal preparation programs along this region have addressed the unique educational needs and strengths of students and their families living along the U.S.–Mexico border. Though significant educational needs and strengths of students and their families along this region have been well documented, little has been done to prepare future school administrators for the daunting task of leading a school along the U.S.–Mexico border, let alone school administrators who are encountering this growing population in nonborder states.

New Mexico State University, through its Project LIBRA grant (Leadership in Border Rural Areas), began to reform its principal preparation program to include issues unique to students and their families along the Mexico–U.S. border. Through Project LIBRA, 34 aspiring principals are being prepared through a curriculum that focuses on issues of race, ethnicity, gender, class, language, poverty, immigration, and healthcare. Traditional course content that formerly would have emphasized management skills and basic leadership skills is now incorporating a discussion and a critical analysis of these issues within the realm of instructional leadership.

The preparation described in Project LIBRA is setting precedence in creating a new generation of principals, a generation of principals who redefine educational leadership as it has been described through the mainstream literature. Principals along the borderlands must set the standard by educating ELL students and addressing the traditional sets of leadership dilemmas. They must also know how to work with language minority students and their parents, understand immigration issues and the differences among recent immigrants and U.S.-born Hispanic students, circumvent the limitations of poverty, and understand the political debates associated with policy and instructional practice associated with teaching English Language Learners.

An alternate model of professional development that uses story and narrative is described in the chapter, "Using Story and Narrative to Enhance the Professional Development of Learner-Centered Leaders," by Arnold Danzig and William Wright. This chapter describes an approach to professional development with the administrative team of a regional county school district using narrative and story. The narrative approach asked education leaders to explore their own stories, workplace experiences, and professional dilemmas, as they crafted stories of practice. The story is seen as a means by which professionals gain access to their own lives and values and provide a potential to grow from experience. During 2000–2001, the authors worked with the leadership team from a county accommodation school district in the southwestern United States. The authors met weekly with the leadership team of the district. Participants read and analyzed education-related stories and narratives. Participants worked in pairs to collect and write each other's stories.

The leadership team engaged in conversations concerning key commitments of the school leaders related to teaching and instruction, professional commitments, administrative standards, and other professional issues related to everyday concerns in their schools and districts. Three objectives informed the narrative approach to professional development: (a) for education leaders to demonstrate the power of personal biography and history to understanding organizational leadership roles, (b) for education leaders to delineate multiple perspectives people bring to the workplace and to identify some of their social and cultural influences, and (c) for education leaders to experience a model of knowledge construction for use in settings with teachers, parents, and students.

Danzig and Wright conclude that narratives and stories are designed first to externalize the otherwise internal and autonomous expertise process. The emphasis on self-knowledge and learning from experience requires the learner to examine closely how one becomes more expert. The process toward expertise is not linear with clear-cut starting and ending points, but an ongoing circle where reflection, application, and growth occur again and again. School life is increasingly complex and school leaders are facing ambiguous and ill-defined situations. School leaders need to examine their own beliefs about the complexity of teaching, learning, and school leadership, which combine abstract thought processes, concentrated study, and practice. The political context of the school district, however, may interrupt the learning that is required for its leadership team to be successful.

The volume concludes with Robert Starratt's chapter, "Moral Issues in the Test-Driven Accountability Agenda: Implications for Learner-Centered Ed Leadership Programs." This chapter takes up several ethical issues critical to the practice of high-stakes testing, namely the injustice involved in testing learners who have not had an opportunity to learn what is being tested, the injustice of testing students with limited English proficiency as though they were as linguistically proficient as the general population of students their age, and the injustice of testing special education students, when their teachers have not developed appropriate curricular materials that could prepare them for testing, in whatever modified form the testers might devise. Additional ethical issues involve the distortion of any appreciation of the complexity of learning and student knowledge by the easy claims of school authorities that these tests measure the essential or important things students are to learn, and the injustice of blaming teachers for low achievement scores, when they have not been given adequate time or resources to modify curriculum content, and whose complex work is reduced to the one dimension of preparing students for these tests.

The chapter then takes up a number of ways in which educational leaders, especially those who claim to be learner-focused leaders, can be helped to confront these ethical challenges within their own schools and school systems, and to form political coalitions to oppose these injustices.

REFERENCES

Bellamy, T., Fulmer, C., Murphy, M., & Muth, R. (2003). A framework for school leadership accomplishments: Perspectives on knowledge, practice, and preparation for principals. *Leadership and Policy in Schools, 2*(4), 241–261.

Bennis, W. (2003). *On becoming a leader* (Rev. ed.). Cambridge, MA: Perseus.

Borman, K., Carter, K. Aladjem, D., & Le Floch, K. (2004). Challenges To the future of comprehensive school reform. In C. T. Cross (Ed.), *Putting the pieces together: Lessons from comprehensive school reform research* (pp. 109–150). The National Clearinghouse for Comprehensive School Reform, Washington, DC.

Boyles, D. (2000). *American education & corporations: The free market goes to school*. New York: Falmer.

Bracey, G. W. (2004) *Setting the record straight: Responses to misconceptions about public education in the U.S.* (2nd ed.). Portsmouth, NH: Heinemann.

Chenoweth, K. (2004). 50 Years Later: Can current education policy finish the work that started with *Brown? Blacks Issues in Higher Education, 22*(9), 40–44.

Cibulka, J. G. (2000). Contests over governance of educational policy: Educational prospects for the new century. In B. A. Jones (Ed.), *Educational leadership: Policy dimensions in the 21st century* (pp. 3–20). Stamford, CT: Ablex.

Corcoran, T., & Goertz, M. (2005). The governance of public education. In S. Furman & M. Lazerson (Eds.), *The public schools* (pp. 25–56). New York: Oxford University Press.

Cuban, L. (1990). Four stories about national goals for American education. *Phi Delta Kappan, 72*(4), 264–271.

Emery, K., & Ohanian, S. (2004). *Why is corporate America bashing our public schools?* Portsmouth, NH: Heinemann.

Erlickson, B., & Goertz, M. (2001). *Implementing whole school reform in New Jersey: Year two.* New Brunswick, NJ: Rutgers University.

Guthrie, J. W., & Springer, M. G. (2004). A Nation at Risk Revisited: Did "Wrong" Reasoning Result in "Right" Results? At What Cost? *Peabody Journal of Education, 79*(1), 7–35.

Hess, F., & Kelly, A. (2005, Summer). The accidental principal. *Education Next,* 33–40.

Jones, B. A. (in press). African American school leadership in a "policy" context: A tornado of public and private influences. In L. Foster & L. Tillman (Eds.), *African American perspectives on leadership in schools: Building a culture of empowerment.* UCEA Press.

Jones, B. A. (2004, September 15). As I see it: Reform schools from the inside. *The Kansas City Star.*

Jones, B. A., & Otterbourg, S. (2000). School change business and the private push. In B. A. Jones (Ed.), *Educational leadership: Policy dimensions in the 21st century.* Stamford, CT: Ablex.

Klaghoz, 1998

McColl, A. (2005). Tough call: Is No Child Left Behind constitutional? *Phi Delta Kappan, 86,* 604–610.

Murphy, J. (Ed.). (2002). *The educational leadership challenge: Redefining leadership for the 21st century.* One Hundred-first Yearbook of the National Society for the Study of Education. Chicago: University of Chicago Press.

Murphy, J., & Beck, L. G. (1995). *School-based management as school reform.* Thousand Oaks, CA: Corwin.

NEA Today. (2004). *Test and Punish, 23*(3), 10–12.

Oakes, J., Quartz, K., Ryan, S., & Lipton, M. (2000). *Becoming good American schools: The struggle for civic virtue in education reform.* San Francisco: Jossey-Bass.

Popham, J. W. (2004). *America's failing schools: How parents and teachers can cope with No Child Left Behind.* New York: Routledge Falmer.

Schön, D. (1991). *The reflective turn.* Boston: Harvard University press.

Senge, P., Kleiner, A., Roberts, C., Ross, R., Roth, G., & Smith, B. (1999). *The dance of change: The challenges to sustaining momentum in learning organizations.* New York: Currency/Doubleday.

Sergiovanni, T. (2004, September). Collaborative cultures & communities of practice. *Principal Leadership.*

Vickers, G. (1995). *The art of judgment: A study of policy making.* Thousand Oaks, CA: Sage.

Weick, K. (1993). The collapse of sensemaking in organizations: The Man Gulch disaster. *Administrative Science Quarterly, 38,* 628–652.

Weick, K., & Roberts, K. (1993). Collective mind in organizations: Heedful interrelating on flight decks. *Administrative Science Quarterly, 38,* 357–381.

HISTORICAL AND INTELLECTUAL
UNDERPINNINGS OF
LEARNER-CENTERED LEADERSHIP–
POLICY SHIFTS AND HISTORICAL SHIFTS
IN PROFESSIONAL DEVELOPMENT
FOR PRINCIPALS

2

A CULTURE IN THE MAKING: LEADERSHIP IN LEARNER-CENTERED SCHOOLS

Ann Lieberman
The Carnegie Foundation for the Advancement of Teaching

Beverly Falk
The City College of New York

Leslie Alexander

This piece, written in 1993, was based on interviews and observations with the leaders of some of the first small public schools created in New York City. These individuals represent the first and second wave of small learner-centered schools (the first wave being the Central Park East schools, created in the late 1970s by the now-famous educator Deborah Meir; the second wave being a group of elementary and middle schools created in the image of Central Park East in the late 1980s and early 1990s). Today there is a third wave of new small schools, mostly high schools, proliferating around the country.

Pages 3 through 34 of this chapter were first published as "A Culture in the Making: Leadership in Learner-Centered Schools" by A. Lieberman, B. Falk, L. Alexander in *Creating New Learning Communities* (92nd yearbook of the National Society for the Study of Education, Part I, 1995). They are reprinted here with the permission of NSSE.

The work begun by the original small schools discussed in this chapter (often officially recognized only as programs or "alternatives") has moved today into the mainstream of education. At the elementary school level, the "learner-centered" focus has
been scaled up for widespread enactment throughout larger schools. The role of
teacher-director, discussed later, has all but disappeared. Leaders of these schools are
now principals or assistant principals and the schools are now officially established as
their own entities. Yet, the values of many who hold these roles remain remarkably
consistent with the values written about in our original piece. We revisit that piece now
to examine what "learner-centered" means in the context of contemporary schooling.
We add an epilogue containing two cases of principals today: one who leads The
Bronx New School in New York City, one of the elementary schools originally examined for this piece; another who leads High Tech Hi, a charter school network of secondary schools recently begun in California. Each in its way is representative of the
changing context as well as of the way learner-centered ideas have made their way into
schools being shaped by and shaping the environment for teachers and their students.

The need for leadership in the struggle to build and transform schools into places
where students can learn in challenging, meaningful, and purposeful contexts is the
subject of much discussion and many reports. Though there is a great deal of disagree-
ment as to how to go about reforming schools, one point on which there is agreement is
that leadership is critical to this process (Barth, 1990; Fullan, 1991; Patterson, 1993;
Poplin, 1992, pp. 10–11; Sergiovanni, 1992). Unfortunately, the discussion of leadership has not been sufficiently informed by the voices and experiences of those who
have been directly involved in reforming old schools and creating new ones. Yet it is
precisely by observing and listening to these voices that we can gain a clearer understanding of how schools change, how new ways of working are established, and how
these norms are "built into the walls" of schools through the subtle interchanges of everyday living and working.

This chapter attempts to address this need by giving voice to the experiences and
understandings of teacher-leaders who are (or have been) the directors of six public alternative elementary schools in New York City. These schools are all from seven to 19
years old and identify themselves as "learner-centered."[1] By "learner-centered" we
mean focusing on meeting the needs of learners in school organization, governance,
curriculum, and teaching. This definition is enacted through a number of commonly
shared characteristics: The schools are autonomous units, situated within larger
school buildings, and led by teacher-directors, not building principals. Their populations are small (anywhere from 200 to 300 students) and diverse (they reflect the socioeconomic, racial, and ethnic diversity of New York City). They are organized into
heterogeneous, multi-age classes and are structured to encourage and enhance collaboration among faculty, students, and students' families. Their classroom environments feature active involvement with materials and experiences, peer interaction,

---

[1]The elementary schools represented in this study are Central Park East1 (CEP1), Central Park East 2,
(CEP2), River East, P.S. 234, the Brooklyn New School, and the New Program at P.S. 261. They are all
members of the Center for Collaborative Education (CCE), the New York affiliate of the Coalition of Essential Schools, a national reform network of elementary and secondary schools that was created in 1985.

and an interdisciplinary approach to learning. Teachers function as facilitators and supporters of student learning rather than as transmitters of information.

The authors of this chapter felt uniquely situated to develop and to conduct this study. We are all former teachers who have, among us, experienced a variety of leadership roles. Our first author is a university professor who has been both a researcher and an educator of educators in a number of collaborative school–university partnerships. She currently is co-director of the National Center for Restructuring Education, Schools, and Teaching. Our second author is a former teacher-director who created and developed a learner-centered school similar to those discussed in this chapter and who, in her present role as a researcher and teacher educator, is involved in a variety of educational restructuring initiatives. And our third author is one of the teacher-leaders who was interviewed for this study. She is presently the founding director of a newly formed learner-centered New York City school.

As a result of these different experiences, all three of us have come to see firsthand the critical role that leadership can play in efforts to change schools and schooling. Unfortunately, however, it seems that the role of leadership is not well understood, although it is critically important. By studying the role of leadership, particularly as it plays out in learner-centered schools, we can enrich and deepen our understanding of the unique characteristics and practices of the teacher-directors who are part of the Center for Collaborative Education (CCE) schools.[2] We developed the following set of questions: How are values of "learner centeredness" played out in schools? How do leaders work within their schools to build community? How are norms and structures that keep a school focused on students' lives and their learning built and sustained? What does it take to build commitment and motivate teachers to become an inquiring community? How do leaders think about and act on their own individual interests and concerns while dealing with the collective work of running a school? How do they cope with the distractions of daily problems as they struggle to improve the quality of life and learning in the school?

To find answers to these questions we sought individual and group interviews with the school directors, made a series of observations in their schools, and studied the documents produced by the schools. These research efforts provided us with an opportunity to learn not only about issues of leadership, but also about how schools are created to focus on learners, and how norms, values, and practices are maintained through a succession of leadership and variations in style.

We begin our study with a brief history of these schools, recognizing that they have been built on a foundation of ideas strongly rooted in the past.

HISTORY AND CONTEXT

These learner-centered schools are philosophically rooted in the work of child-centered educators and theorists of the late 19th and early 20th centuries who believed that schools should be observant of children's interests and responsive to their needs, that

---

[2]The original leaders of these schools, as well as their successors, are represented in this study. The original leaders all continue, however, to engage in other leadership work. In two schools, retired directors are now involved in leadership roles in a preparatory program for urban school principals; two others are leaders in secondary schools; and one school has developed a form of shared leadership due to the particularities of the context.

the purpose of education was to create the conditions for student development and autonomy while establishing a pattern of support for continuous progress within a school community nurtured by a democratic ethic (Dewey, 1916, 1938, 1956; Froebel, 1885/1974). These ideas have been enriched and expanded over the years through the work of educators, researchers, and philosophers such as Caroline Pratt (1948), Jean Piaget (1969), Jerome Bruner (1966), Patricia Carini (1975, 1979), Maxine Greene (1978, 1984), LS.Vygotsky (1978), Eleanor Duckworth (1987), and Sue Bredekamp (1987). They were first developed and brought to life in the public schools of the United States by Lillian Weber, the founder of the City College Open Corridor/Workshop Center Advisory, in New York City in the 1960s and 1970s. The initiative she led was committed to enacting teaching practices and organizational structures that reflected understandings of child development. It grouped several primary-grade classrooms together along the corridors of selected public schools. The corridors not only defined the organizational structure of the programs; they were also literally used as learning centers. This arrangement encouraged activities emanating from inside the classrooms to flow out into the corridors. The teaching and learning that took place in these corridors helped to develop an increased awareness of the different kinds of contexts and resources that can nurture children's growth.

The practices developed in these corridors were also instrumental in stimulating thinking about how to apply understandings of teaching and learning not only to children, but to the adults charged with supporting their development. Corridor advisors assisted in this process. They were experienced teachers themselves who were knowledgeable about child development and sensitized to issues of adult learning, and who possessed a range of teaching strategies supportive of both teacher and student learning. They worked one day a week in each corridor program, always independent of the supervisory structure, providing teachers with continual opportunities to discuss and get feedback on their practice. They helped to support teachers to connect to their own interests, to engage in their own inquiry, and thus to experience themselves as learners. Weber explains:

> [The Workshop Center Advisory] was intended to be facilitating of teachers, to support them in a new teacher role, and to provide beginnings for people to break with the traditional isolation of teacher–teacher, teacher–child, and child–child.[3]

This pioneering work was in large part responsible for the emergence of a new view of the teacher's role and a new conceptualization of the nature of professional development. The teacher's role was being crafted as that of facilitator of student learning rather than simply a transmitter of information. Conceptions of professional development were changing from a deficit to a capacity-building model—making a shift from "training" teachers in the use of teaching packages and recipes to developing and supporting teachers' varied strengths through a process of collegial dialogue and reflection. Weber comments:

> The idea was to assist the teacher. The point was not to make someone over, but to be supportive of teachers' strengths in the direction of supporting children. [In the course of this

---

[3]Quotations that are not referenced are all from individuals interviewed from the CCE schools discussed herein.

initiative] the advisors continually tested out how things worked or didn't work. Questions evolved. "How do you get a pattern of support for children's motion forward given that each child is an individual?" Many questions were raised in the course of addressing this question. These inevitably led to battles on the institutional front.

The "institutional front" to which Weber refers was the national, test-driven, "back-to basics" movement of the 1970s (Olban, 1984), which developed during the same period in which the Open Corridor initiative was launched. At this time an emphasis on mastery of basic skills as a prerequisite for higher order thinking was competing with an emphasis on developing habits of ongoing student inquiry. This was reflected in a proliferation of teacher-proof, sequential, discipline-based curricula that were discouraging efforts to get teachers to create their own multidimensional, interdisciplinary studies.

Despite the setbacks to child-centered education caused by this clash with the back-to-basics movement, many of the practices that were being forged by Weber and her colleagues have since become commonly acknowledged standards of excellence in contemporary professional practice. Classrooms featuring informal arrangements, active involvement with materials and experiences, an inquiry-based orientation, interage and heterogeneous grouping, and authentic assessment of student work are being promoted and increasingly accepted today as an integral part of the movement for educational reform (Darling-Hammond, 1993; Oakes, 1985; Resnick, 1987).

CENTRAL PARK EAST: LEADERSHIP FROM WITHIN THE COMMUNITY

A powerful offspring of the Open Corridor/Workshop Center Advisory was the Central Park East Elementary School (CPE) created by Deborah Meier, an original participant in Weber's initiative.[4] A small elementary public school of choice, located in New York City's East Harlem neighborhood, CPE was designed to be a whole-school community that put understandings about child development into practice throughout the grades while thinking about and treating teachers in the same way that they were being asked to think about and treat their students. The schools intent was to create a racially and socioeconomically diverse community that would identify each individual's strengths and interests, support each student as a capable learner, and do this in an equitable manner. The original idea about school structure and governance was that there would be no formal leadership position so that all decisions could be made collectively and everyone could build the school together. All teachers were to work directly with the children, thus making it possible to have smaller classes. Three teachers, two aides,

---

[4]It is important to note that Weber's idea of a teacher advisory, as well as the values inherent in it, were critical to Central Park East's and later the Center for Collaborative Education's notion of a teacher-director. The efforts of this school and this organization to establish a learning community in which both students and teachers are jointly involved in inquiring how to support student and teacher learning all developed from Open Corridor practices. Although the formation of CPE has been written about elsewhere (Bensman, 1987), the formation of leadership *values* and *ways of working* has been assumed and perhaps taken for granted. However, the challenge to leadership inherent in the process of creating CPE is revealed in its struggles to develop as a school community that focuses on student needs and interests that rethinks student evaluation (an early precursor to performance assessments); that attempts to fully involve parents, families, students, and teachers in the life of the school; and that concomitantly develops a language and a culture shifting from a blame and deficit norm to one of development and collective responsibility for the school community.

and a paraprofessional made up the original adult community while the student community began with 35 children and eventually grew to 260.

Staff meetings, initially emphasizing egalitarian values, became the centerpiece for making decisions about the fledgling school. But by the end of the second year, budget cuts, district demands, and the unwieldy process of trying to make all decisions collaboratively resulted in the staff's realization that creating a separate position of "teacher-director" was indeed going to be necessary. Someone had to assume responsibility for protecting and nurturing the life of the school—representing the school to the district, pressing to keep the focus of the school on students' needs, and developing growing relationships with parents and families. This part of the CPE story reveals a view of leadership that grew out of the process of creating and defining a "democratic learning community." The teacher-director is "of" the community, an advisor rather than a supervisor, a keeper and developer of values of student-centered practice rather than a maintainer of the system, a creator of opportunities to learn rather than an enforcer of the status quo.

These values were deepened and extended over the years, not only at Central Park East Elementary School (which came to be known as CPE 1), but at the other small New York City public schools that were inspired by the CPE model. Though the conditions of each of these schools are unique, the schools share a set of core values and common assumptions about teaching, learning, and human development. Though this core encourages expression of individual differences and the building of cultures uniquely their own, it also binds them together in a larger community that offers them a historical perspective on the continuity of their struggle, support to know and do more, and a moral and material base for the difficult task of engaging in change.

CORE VALUES OF THE CENTER FOR COLLABORATIVE EDUCATION SCHOOLS

When visiting any of the Center for Collaborative Education schools, one is struck by how clearly their core values are evidenced in their policies and practices. We identify several of them here.

All Children Have the Capacity to Learn

Although there is much talk in school reform circles these days about all children having the capacity to learn, this axiom is not just rhetoric in the Center for Collaborative Education schools. It is indeed the philosophical foundation—the core of the core—on which the schools are built and organized. This belief is evident in school policies and structures, which provide equal learning opportunities and resources for all students, regardless of their differing experiences and abilities. Classrooms are heterogeneously grouped to include students who represent a span of ages, a range of racial and socioeconomic backgrounds, and a spectrum of individual strengths and talents (including special education students). Each student is supported to develop at his or her own pace and an attempt is made to provide everyone with the necessary resources for the realization of each individual's potential to the fullest extent possible.

Differences in abilities are provided for in a number of respectful ways. Students who require special learning supports (in chapter 1 or Resource Room Programs) are not isolated from the classroom or stigmatized by their need. In some schools, students with special needs are provided with a program of enrichment in their classrooms that allows participation by other interested students. For example, a Resource Room teacher in one particular school often connects her instruction to enjoyable cooking activities and, as a consequence, is frequently inundated with requests by regular education students to join in her projects.

Many of the schools support students' individual interests by providing opportunities for them to select from a range of different types of classes (extra dance, art, music, and sport classes are notable examples of these). In contrast to many schools—where both teachers and curricula are rationed to those whose academic success is most assured (Oakes, 1985)—*all* of the students in these schools are given access to high-quality teaching and to a "thinking curriculum" that provides all students with work that challenges them to develop the ability to use their minds well—to think critically and creatively, to engage in deep exploration of ideas and topics, and to acquire the skills and knowledge necessary for future school and life experiences. This is made possible because the schools provide professional growth opportunities for all teachers.

At the same time that student differences are addressed in these schools, a conscious effort is being made to develop a common standard of excellence for what and how students learn. This is being accomplished in variety of ways. One is the development of open-ended assignments that provide entry points for many different kinds of learners and that allow students to participate at a variety of difficulty levels. For example, when studying the New York City harbor, all second–third-grade students in one of the schools engaged in a core set of interdisciplinary experiences. In addition, however, some students—driven by their interests or their abilities—pursued other areas of study connected with the topic. Some engaged in historical research, some wrote stories that centered on the area of study, some built models of bridges or dioramas of the harbor utilizing a range of materials. No two students produced the same work or came away from the study with exactly the same information, but all were exposed to some basic ideas and information and some general principles of learning and inquiry.

Another way that a standard of excellence is being developed is through public demonstration of student learning that exposes students to a variety of levels of academic success and a variety of forms in which knowledge can be expressed. In many of the schools, units of study are often concluded by exhibitions or "museums" in which students display and explain their work to their classmates, schoolmates, family members, and school faculty. These demonstrations have included not only written reports but experiments, constructions, puppet shows, videos, musical performances, and art exhibits.

Still another way in which standards for learning and for student outcomes are developed is by providing students with regular opportunities for discussion of their different learning strategies. Such discussions take place at classroom meetings, small group forums, or individual conferences between teachers and students. One director describes how such discussions facilitate learning for the children in her school:

When a math problem is discussed at a classroom meeting, many strategies for learning will often be presented. Sometimes one person's strategy will open up an understanding for another. For example, at one meeting Hugh explained how he does multiplication by engaging in repeated addition. This was the only way that Manuel, who had been having a terrible time grasping the concept, seemed to be able to understand it. Although many of us had tried to help Manuel before, it wasn't until he heard and saw a fellow student's explanation that he was finally able to make the connection.

Honoring Diversity

The schools represented in this study all demonstrate a variety of ways in which they consciously acknowledge and demonstrate a respect for diversity—of cultures, language, gender, and socioeconomic background, as well as of various thinking styles, learning rates, and academic, social, and physical abilities. One of the directors of the schools notes the importance of this particular value: "Diversity is not an add-on, but a way of thinking here."

Support for diverse learning styles and strengths is evident everywhere in these schools. Students are often seen working side by side, utilizing their particular interests and strengths to enrich and extend the work of others as well as to create individual paths of entry into their own particular challenges. Two students involved in an animal research project in a fourth–fifth-grade classroom in one of the schools provide a good example of this. Both were deeply engaged in a study about cats and were exploring a variety of informational texts. We were informed by the teacher that one of the students was particularly able in reading and writing but inexperienced in and intimidated by visual art forms. The other struggled mightily with the printed form but was extraordinarily uninhibited and able to express his ideas through painting and drawing. As these two worked together, we saw each contributing to the research process in his area of strength—one provided the written text, the other provided the illustrations. Yet both were involved in analysis and discussion of the content, and both were utilizing research and problem-solving skills. The director of the school explained how they work to develop adaptive teaching: "It's about acknowledging that each [person] has different gifts, strengths, and concerns and then finding a way to utilize them."

In addition to respect for different learning styles, these schools also value cultural diversity. One can see it sprinkled throughout the learning environment—in the books the children read, the stories they write, the songs they sing, the foods they cook, the trips they take, and the conversations they have. One can see it in the composition of the school staffs, which reflect the diversity of their student populations. (Where this is not the case we were told that recruitment of teachers from diverse cultures and backgrounds is a number-one priority.) In addition, one can see it in the opportunities provided for families to be meaningfully involved in the life of the schools—family histories and cultural traditions are used as the starting point of many classroom studies; ethnic meals and artistic performances are a regular feature of the cultural lives of the schools; and home–school conferences and other forms of communication regularly solicit family languages, traditions, and knowledge about the learner to inform the teaching that takes place in the school. The views and voices of all the directors are clear and uncompromising in this regard. One director said,

"Everybody is special—the greater the variety, the richer a life for ourselves and the kids. School has to be all inclusive. It has to be a place where all are safe and respected—adults, parents, everyone."

Providing for the Needs of the "Whole Child"

Another value held in common by the Center for Collaborative Education schools is their respect for the needs—emotional, physical, artistic, and academic—of the "whole child." Children's needs are placed before bureaucratic considerations and guide both educational practice and policy. This is manifested in the details that comprise the quality of daily life for the children in these schools. The tone of voice and the gestures used by adults as they speak to children, the manner in which such daily routines as lining up for buses are conducted, the atmosphere at breakfast–lunch–recess, the way security guards and custodians interact with students, as well as how children who are sick or lonely are treated, all demonstrate the dignity and respect that is regularly accorded to children.

Care and concern are also exhibited for other aspects of children's lives traditionally considered outside the realm of the school's responsibilities. Physical health, mental health, and extracurricular needs are considered important and are addressed by the schools in a variety of ways: Some offer after-school programs and make arrangements for children to attend summer camps; some refer families to service providers for health-related issues; some provide childcare during evening meetings.

Another means of addressing children's needs, used by virtually all of the CCE schools, is the Descriptive Review (Prospect Archive and Center for Education and Research, 1980). This is a process in which school personnel collaboratively discuss issues, problems, or concerns of a child in a full and holistic way. The process is usually undertaken after school hours and begins with a description of a child, developed from documented observations over time collected by the child's classroom teacher. This description is followed by comments from those who participate in the review process. They offer suggestions for ways the teacher and school can best support the growth of the child.

> The perspectives through which the child is described are multiple, to ensure a balanced portrayal of the person, that neither overemphasizes some current "problem" nor minimizes an ongoing difficulty. The description of the child addresses the following facets of the person as these characteristics are expressed within the classroom setting at the present time:
>
> > The child's physical presence and gesture.
> >
> > The child's disposition.
> >
> > The child's relationships with other children and adults.
> >
> > The child's activities and interests.
> >
> > The child's approach to formal learning.
> >
> > The child's strengths and vulnerabilities. (pp. 26–27)

The kind of observation and discussion that takes place during the Descriptive Review offers understandings that set the tone for a learning environment that provides for the needs of the whole child and makes each child visible to the school community. This is especially powerful in schools that serve diverse communities and that are struggling to include all children in the ranks of successful learners. A director explains, "The value of an education will never be missed by visible and included children. They will be too excited by their own wonderful ideas to give up on learning."

Assessments in Support of Meaningful Teaching and Learning

The Descriptive Review process is related to still another core value of CCE schools: Assessments of student work are intricately connected to and supportive of meaningful teaching and learning. One of the original directors describes how this aspect of all of the schools has been woven into their structure from their inception:

> From the beginning, we realized we couldn't assess in this kind of setting in any traditional way. We had to have different assessment tools which could be used to report to teachers, families, and posterity. We had to develop ways to see the work and to watch kids grow over time.

Many kinds of assessments have thus been developed to provide information to teachers, families, and communities about the progress of students and of the schools as a whole. Some schools keep track of student growth through documented teacher observations collected over time. Some keep samples of student work in portfolios. Some have students demonstrate what they can do in research projects, scientific experiments, performances, exhibitions, or interdisciplinary tasks that resemble the problems of real-life situations. Many have students engaged in self-assessments and all schools report their learnings about students in detailed narrative progress reports sent home to families on a regular basis followed by lengthy home–school conferences in which student work is discussed and reviewed.

At present these practices, which focus on direct evidence of students' work gathered by teachers and interwoven into the teaching–learning process, are undertaken as an addition to the indirect evidence collected by external agencies through the norm-referenced standardized tests currently mandated in New York City and New York State. Involvement in both the internal and external assessment systems creates great tensions and problems for the schools. Not only is there not enough time for teachers to fulfill the requirements of these two very different systems, but there are significant differences in what the systems assess and in how they go about assessing it. All the directors of the CCE schools, however, expressed their optimism about the current flurry of reform taking place at all levels of the educational system. They see this phenomenon as public validation of the learning-centered assessment that has long been in use in their schools.

Viewing Everyone as a Learner

Another value held in common by the Center for Collaborative Education schools is that all of the members of their school communities–students, staff, and families alike–are viewed as learners and provided with continual growth opportunities. Students are encouraged to exchange ideas among themselves and with their teachers through small-group discussions, classroom meetings, and meetings of the whole school community. These model the process of "learning how to learn" and create an atmosphere encouraging of inquiry and problem solving.

Teachers and other school support staff are also provided with various opportunities for ongoing learning. Staff meet together in formal as well as informal meetings, including semiannual all-school retreats, where ideas and resources are exchanged to deepen understandings of children, of teaching, and of their own personal professional growth.

In addition, the family members of students are included in the learning environment of these schools. Two-way learning is at the heart of this relationship—teachers learning from families about their children and families learning from schools about education. This is enacted through a variety of communication forms: teacher curriculum letters and homework notes, director newsletters, phone calls to family members, narrative progress reports, and school–home conferences.

These continual ways in which members of the school community can connect and reconnect to being learners are facilitated by the work of the school directors. One of them explains, "Someone has to pull in the world so that teachers [and others] don't get ingrown. Someone needs to create opportunities to talk about why we do what we do, to rethink, to validate, to deal with ideas."

As directors do this, an atmosphere is created in their school that is respectful, trusting, and facilitating for the learning of both the children and the adults involved. The comments of one of the school directors reveal more about the how and why:

> We have based our theories about school on what we think to be true about human learning. Certain kinds of school environments speak to what's true about human learning and help it emerge so that in the process of teaching children, and talking about teaching children, and thinking about themselves as learners, teachers reconnect to who they are as learners.

A Democratic Learning Community

The embodiment of the aforementioned values results in a school culture and organization that promotes democratic values and that makes room for everyone to have a voice. The conviction is strong in the CCE community that schools should be organized in ways that allow students and adults to live their beliefs, not just to talk about them. This conviction is expressed by the words of the directors:

> [We want] to help children learn how to cooperate and how to respect the differences among them. We share a common belief in teaching about nonviolence, sexism, and racism.

These aspects of a living democracy have always been stressed in these schools. These beliefs are put into practice in the schools' organizational structures as well as in the development of their curricula. Culturally sensitive curricula are consciously developed that include the study of people and places from non dominant cultures and that utilize the experiences and resources of the schools' diverse communities. Students engage in neighborhood studies, in community service projects, and in work that connects their daily lives to the issues and problems of the world at large. In addition, conflict-resolution programs help them to develop problem-solving strategies. Student newsletters and surveys provide access to the views and concerns of their peers. (In one of the upper grade classes in the schools a survey was developed to elicit the views held by students and parents about homework so that assignments could be developed by the teacher to most effectively incorporate family concerns and ideas.)

School structures also speak to aspects of democratic living. These provide opportunities for families and teachers to participate in shaping the vision and work of the school. Many have been mentioned previously—Descriptive Reviews, faculty meetings, all-school retreats, parent meetings, conferences, progress reports, newsletters, and curriculum letters. One of the directors, who helped develop her school from its inception, explains how the vision of a democratic community, in which all participants have a say in decisions affecting their lives, has been a driving force of her school: "From the beginning, there was always the sense that these intelligent people should have a say in how the school worked."

HOW LEADERS LEAD IN LEARNER-CENTERED SCHOOLS: BALANCING CHALLENGES AND COMMITMENTS

Fashioning the role of teacher-director has particular meaning in CCE schools. The directors are required to simultaneously balance a variety of skills and abilities: administrative skills (overseeing paperwork, buses, schedules), political skills (educating and negotiating with stakeholders in the educational enterprise, both inside and outside of their schools), pedagogical understandings (providing ongoing professional development and support to teachers), and a vision for the future (anticipating and preparing for new developments). This multifaceted combination of attributes is difficult to find in any one individual and the directors readily acknowledge their limitations in this regard. But recognizing one's strengths and building on the particulars of personal and professional challenges seems part of the norm of these school communities. Statements by directors ranging from "I model decency" and "I know what I can't do" to "I never wanted to be a principal; I thought I would always be struggling and compromising" suggest the candor and integrity of the struggle to be "leaders *of* the community and representatives *from* the community." The strong value placed on the assumption that "everybody, absolutely everybody, is capable of having ideas, and making sense of the world and needs to be taken seriously" seems to be as much a credo for the directors as it is for other members of their communities.

The challenge of constructing a leaner-centered community is made greater in the case of these particular schools by the fact that the directors and schools are trying to do their work within the context of a routinized and standardized big-city school system. Directors are thus required to simultaneously develop a set of skills and responsibilities that can keep their organizations healthy and growing and another set of skills that can effectively maneuver the tensions and challenges posed by membership in the ranks of the public school bureaucracy.

Internal Challenges and Demands

In the course of their daily lives in schools, teacher-directors experience many situations that challenge their values, question their commitments, and test their educational understandings. The role of director calls on a host of leadership attributes and dispositions. It requires school leaders to simultaneously be educators, problem solvers, crisis managers, change-agents, enablers, consensus builders, and networkers as well as limit-setters and authority figures. As teacher-directors enact these sometimes contradictory roles, achieving a balanced performance tests even those with the strongest mettle: when to assert and when to hold back; when to intervene and how to do it right; when to deliberately lead and take a position and when to facilitate group struggle; how to handle conflict and how to make it productive; how to be accepting and respectful of differences while seeking to achieve overall agreement; how to be patient and supportive of strengths in the face of difficult problems; how to simultaneously advocate for teachers, children, and their families while maintaining the day-to-day functioning of a school.

Supporting the Growth of Teachers.   Directors facilitate and support teacher growth in much the same way that teachers are expected to do with children. As one director explains,

> What we model for kids, I try to model for adults. Good kindergarten practice is also good leadership practice. It's about acknowledging that each has different gifts, strengths, and concerns and then finding a way to utilize them. It's about giving teachers a sense of understanding, empathy, partnership, belonging. My personal understanding of learner-centered teaching has become my model of leadership.

Expanding on this idea, another director adds,

> I try to get to know each person by him/herself, as an individual. Then I find something I can relate to and support. I struggle against making judgments (the skill of observing and describing children helps a lot here). I can't let judgment get in the way of the forward movement of the teacher. It's important to always leave the teacher with respect.

Similar to the way learner-centered teaching takes place, the director functions as an observer, supporter, and reflector of individual and institutional memory for others ("Remember when you did that?") and as a keeper of teachers' questions and comments. The director often reflects these questions and answers back to the teachers, picking up pieces of the myriad experiences taking place in and out of the classroom, and using them as a reminder and a connection to larger ideas in the outside world. One teacher explains how this has helped her growth:

> The sharing that goes on in the classroom between myself and the kids is the same process that goes on between the director and the teachers. She often reflects back to us what has happened in our classrooms, helping us see to the positive things that have happened during the day rather than just the last crazy five minutes we are able to remember.

Building on strengths (a norm for students) is also the way directors support the learning and growth of adults. But there are delicate balances to maintain: how to nurture while also pushing forward by asking hard questions, raising new issues, and maintaining a standard of excellence for teaching; how to find a way to facilitate rather than dictate; how to assert leadership and assume responsibility while also building on the initiatives of others. These concerns are among the problems faced by all the directors:

> I have had many conflicts about the appropriate way to enact my role. I struggle with knowing when to exert authority and when to support the initiatives of others; how to be respectful of the views and feelings of others without losing the strength and integrity of a vision which supports student learning; how to balance differences in cultures and values and to incorporate aspects of these into the community to continually build common ground.

Perhaps most subtle, and yet most critical, is that directors must find ways to support teachers so that they can be supportive of the learning process and thereby support students and their families. Directors do this by taking care of paperwork; supervising buses, breakfast, lunch, and recess times; settling disputes among students; and attending to district demands. The assumption of these responsibilities (frequently considered unimportant and mundane) ultimately frees teachers to concentrate on their students. This dignifies the hard and intense work of teaching.

Providing Staff With Continual Learning Opportunities.   Directors of these learner-centered schools have a deep conviction that growth and learning are never-ending. One says, "Learning about learning is never finished. There is no end to the need to continue to deepen understanding."

Directors continually search for ways to deepen and sustain the culture of learner-centered education. They encourage teachers to try out new ideas—to teach a different grade level, to invest in new equipment, to attend classes or conferences, or to teach with other colleagues. They are aware that "staying fresh" in teaching is a major problem. Directors also struggle to bring new teachers into the fold—to orient them to learner-centered thinking and to help them develop effective teaching strategies. One director deliberately places new teachers alongside more experienced teachers in the classroom corridors so that they can learn from exposure to one another.

All of the directors have created structures to address the fact that "teachers, like students, need many different kinds of learning experiences." Directors provide opportunities for teachers to work with and support each other in a variety of ways: to visit each others' classrooms, to take trips together to other schools, to be involved in child study teams and Descriptive Reviews, to discuss professional books and articles, to meet on issues of common concern—issues of curriculum, world events, or special happenings in the community. These activities create an atmosphere that is described by one director as a "culture of extreme support" for individual as well as collective learning. One director explains,

> Our school is literally an institution of higher education. There are lots of opportunities for dialogue and conversation—both formal and informal. We have formal meetings—weekly grade meetings, monthly staff meetings. But the informal meetings every day after school are the best.

Teachers and staff in these learner-centered schools are thus continually engaged in talk about work, values, processes, ideas, and concerns. These conversations—facilitated by the directors—are the cornerstone of professional development through which staff members develop a powerful sense of collegiality, collaboration, and community.

Upholding the Vision and Values of the School.   As the years have gone by and the schools have evolved, a major challenge for teacher-directors has been the preservation of the core learner-centered values. Directors have struggled to find ways to maintain the original school communities' intimacy and zeal as they have grown in size and brought in new people. This has entailed developing ways to avoid insularity, self-satisfaction, and nonproductive conflict as well as creating mechanisms to connect to the outside world of ideas and people.

Another challenge that has arisen as schools have become more established is that the cohesiveness of the original communities has often become diluted. Several directors are currently experiencing this phenomenon in their schools. They report that as their schools have become increasingly successful, the parent bodies have become increasingly diverse. Families have joined the schools for a variety of reasons: some in search of a learner-centered philosophy, others in search of a school that is safe and well-equipped and has a caring staff or a "good" reputation.

Such a diversity of reasons for attending the schools brings diverse views about future directions and priorities. Sometimes teachers or families find that they have conflicts with the fundamental values of the schools. This presents an important challenge to school leadership—a challenge to educate and to build a base of support for learner-centered practices while being respectful of input and participation. Directors address this challenge by listening, evaluating, and responding to concerns in a way that incorporates professional knowledge about teaching and change. One director described a situation that highlights the need for these important skills and understandings:

> A parent objected to heterogeneous grouping out of a belief that it didn't best serve her child. She wanted the school to reconsider this practice for the community as a whole. I had to find a way to help her understand that some values are inviolable and form the basis of our school.

Realizing the Vision Through Empowerment of Others.   Underlying this seemingly endless array of ways that directors subtly or frontally lead is a vision that is educational, social, and fundamentally political in nature. Keeping this vision comprehensive is difficult. It necessitates being aware that, although one has the power to "push things through," it is not worth it. Instead, connecting to what people understand, want, believe, and are ready to do is the great challenge. As one director states, "It's not enough to have good ideas. Helping others to realize their good ideas and come together to create a common vision and then to jointly enact that vision is the real leadership challenge."

How to be a hub and be central to all aspects of the school while not being in the center, how to be the spokesperson for all the constituencies without demanding compliance to a singular view, and how to turn problems into possibilities are aspects of leadership style that become embodied in community belief and action. According to another director: "I try to empower people, have a calming effect, model decency, and help people listen to one another. I want to help people find solutions to problems, to see that problems are solvable." Creating these conditions calls on directors to handle dualities and to be closely connected to people, events, and the dailyness of school— but also, a director suggests, to have some distance: "I feel passionately for others but I also have common sense. I am a stabilizing factor in my school."

To keep a school community constantly open to struggle with and develop its ideals means that directors also need to be open to change: "I value each person but also want to challenge each person. I want us to be open to change—to expose ourselves and our classrooms to that. I want people to speak up, raise issues."

All of these examples give a sense of how, in attempting to put these ideas into practice, directors provide teachers with similar supports to the supports teachers provide to their students: "I needed to let them do what they needed to do. And I needed to figure out what they needed. But I found that the more respect and trust 1 gave to the staff, the more they gave the same to the kids."

When teachers and students feel efficacious in their work, this becomes the real meaning of "empowerment." This is not a slogan; it is the subtle means by which directors create the conditions for continuous growth for adults and students alike. When this happens, the momentum of change cannot be contained. It makes one director feel like shouting, "Hey, wait for me, I'm your leader!" (Barth, 1990, p. 170).

External Challenges

Though the internal growth of a school community presents challenges that pull directors in different directions, problems of the outside world also present particular challenges. Even though the reform community is articulate about the need for change—and these schools are indeed a testimony to its potential—the contexts in which these schools are embedded require special skills and abilities (political, practical, and pedagogical) of their leaders even as they are guided by their strong commitments and shared purposes (Darling-Hammond, 1993; McLaughlin & Talbert, 1993).

Working Within Contexts of Contradictory Values. These directors are charting the course of their schools in the context of district and system policies and politics that are often in conflict with their values. This creates great frustration for the directors, most particularly in the areas of curriculum and assessment. Curriculum mandates and standardized testing clash directly with the developmental and holistic practices that are fundamental to learner-centered schools. Though teaching and assessment in learner-centered schools are geared to the differing strengths and needs of students, the success of the schools and their practices is nevertheless measured through the use of standardized tests, known to do a notoriously poor job of reflecting students' strengths and differences (Darling-Hammond, 1991). This phenomenon places directors and their staff in an inextricable bind. They must simultaneously fulfill the requirements for survival in the established system and struggle to develop and maintain an "alternate" community that enacts, takes risks, and works to establish practices that question categorization of students, fragmentation of the school program, and a standardized conception of knowledge and learning.

Working With Limited Resources and Supports. Additional challenges faced by directors revolve around the necessity for reconfiguring how money is spent, what human and material resources are available, and how time is allocated in their schools. Schools are not currently given the resources to provide enough time for teachers to engage in the kind of observing, recording, reflecting, and reporting that is required for learner-centered teaching. They also do not receive the resources to provide teachers with adequate opportunities for professional growth. Though directors are frustrated by these limitations, they have found a number of ways to compensate for them: seeking financial supports from outside the school system, learning how to use networks external to the school, depending on a high level of commitment from their staffs.

A NETWORK OF COMMUNITY VALUES:
SUPPORT FOR LEADING AND LEARNING

The learner-centered schools described in this chapter are embedded in a network—the Center for Collaborative Education—that supports and gives meaning to their daily work. What happens in each individual school takes on a greater significance because it is part of a larger whole.

Although there has been little empirical study of educational networks and their effects on members, it has been suggested that there is a cohesive power in networks that represents "the strength of weak ties" (Granovetter, 1973). Instead of relying only on people who are friends (strong ties), networks provide a power and influence over people in organizations by connecting them to norms, values, and influences that occur indirectly (weak ties). Two examples illustrate the efficaciousness of networks.

One director spoke of how her attendance at a network meeting encouraged her to initiate implementation of authentic assessment in her school. Through discussion of the various possibilities for how the work of students could be assessed, she was able to see how these possibilities connected to all the other things that her school was doing. She left the meeting inspired to find a way to raise these issues at her school.

Another director attending an annual network meeting participated in a discussion about the importance of standard setting for the network elementary schools. This discussion, although very contentious, made her realize that the staff of her school could indeed benefit by looking more carefully at its practices and relating them to standards held by the school but not yet formally articulated.

These examples help us to understand the critical role that networks can play in supporting both personal and professional growth. The Center for Collaborative Education network supports directors not only in articulating educational values of learner-centeredness but in developing social values that suggest what democratic schools should be. This helps them make sense of the daily struggles against bureaucratic routine and the human crises that occur so frequently, giving energy and commitment to their work. Seeking help is not seen as a weakness, but rather a part of the personal and organizational expectations of the entire community.

Networking for knowledge building and support is thus a norm of learner-centered communities, one that nurtures and encourages collective discussion and problem solving around tough issues of diversity and curriculum, as well as differing cultural and pedagogical practices (Lieberman & McLaughlin, 1992). Commitment to the hard work of changing schools comes from a will and a motivation that cannot be imposed by policies from above, as it stems from a shared belief in ideals that provide meaning and direction in the face of seemingly intractable problems (McLaughlin, 1987).

REFRAMING LEADERSHIP

In some ways Center for Collaborative Education schools seem like other schools trying to deal with changing student and parent populations, and with the integration of new knowledge and approaches to learning and assessment. What makes these schools different is the ideals they share that find expression in the daily ness of their work and in the way that their leaders lead: providing perspective in the midst of confusion, solving problems and setting problem-solving norms, setting priorities among competing agendas, making conflict productive, gauging the temperature of the community and acting on its needs, being respectful of each other when placing blame is easier, taking care of things backstage while the teachers and students are on stage. Teacher-directors, although their styles and strengths differ, tend to be both passionate in their beliefs and optimistic about what these beliefs will enable them to accomplish. They measure their success by the extent to which they support the collective conscience of their own school communities as well as by the extent to which their ideas and practices influence and support the work and ideas of others.

In the traditional school, the principal is assumed to be the fount of pedagogical knowledge as well as the repository of power and control over all resources—both human and material. The principal holds power by virtue of her or his position. Meetings are most often for the principal to present his/her agenda. In fact, the traditional definition of a good school has often been that it is orderly and technically well-run. Though no one would dispute the need for an orderly and well-run school, in the Center for Collaborative Education schools, order is important if it is perceived as enabling for teachers and students. These members of the school community are not cut out of the decision-making process. Instead, the directors organize the schools so that all members have input into decisions critical to their lives and their work.

This change redefines the role of leadership and it is perhaps our most significant learning. In learner-centered schools the leaders are not only chosen *by* the community; they are themselves members *of* the community, and are also held directly accountable *to* the community. Leadership is centered around the enactment of the ideals that the community embraces, recognizing that it is an unfinished work, a culture continually in the making.

EPILOGUE

Case 1—Paul Smith, Principal of the Bronx New School: Protector and Translator of Learner-Centered Values in a High-Stakes Accountability Context[5]

Paul Smith is the principal of the Bronx New School (one of the second wave of small New York City schools). He is a direct descendant of the early small schools movement. Beginning his career as a classroom teacher at Midtown West, another second-wave learner-centered school, he later received an administrative credential after studying at the Bank Street College of Education's Principal's Institute with several of the early small schools' directors.

Paul is an advocate of the core values of learner-centered schools. A recent visit to the Bronx New School finds these values alive and well, albeit situated in a different context—both internally and externally—than the one in 1987 when the school was created. He approaches his work as a "ministry," demonstrating through his interactions with others that he cares deeply about the children, their families, and the school staff. He sees his role as a protector of the school's history and culture. However, he advocates the enactment of these values in ways that address the changed context of contemporary times.

It is Paul's belief that fitting into the context of current policies will ensure that the school's founding values endure. To do this he has to negotiate changes that include increased centralized district authority, which exerts ever-closer control over what takes place at his school; district-mandated curricula and pacing schedules; yearly high-stakes standardized tests, which effect whether students will be promoted from grade to grade; and a principal appraisal system based on students' performance on those tests. Other changes from the conditions of the school's early years are that Paul's position is no longer considered a "teacher-director" as it was when the school first opened. He now has the stature of a principal and the school is considered its own entity rather than a program in a school. Though this change has had little impact on his vision of leadership, it has left him more isolated because it has put an end to the informal network that was established by the first teacher-directors to nurture them through their early years.

Upholding Core Values.   Recent visits to the Bronx New School and interviews with Paul reveal that the core values of learner-centered schooling discussed in our 1993 article are still evident in the practices of the school. I found Paul to be a champion and model of these values.

Fundamentally he believes that all children can learn. This core value of learner-centered leadership and schooling was the foundation on which the Bronx New School was built. Speaking from his own experience as an "at risk" child who experienced teachers who made a critical difference in his life, he explained to me his belief that all children can think critically if provided with the right conditions. "We need

---

[5]Case 1 was written by Beverly Falk; Case 2 was written by Ann Lieberman.

to find ways to teach our children, to remove obstacles for them to think, and to put things in place to help them be independent, productive citizens of society."

Being *responsive to diversity*, another core value of learner-centered schools, is also very important to Paul. He believes in the power of education to transform lives and he makes this belief visible to the school community. School gatherings honor struggles to access this power. School bulletin boards are filled with the poetry and writings of educators and activists such as Langston Hughes, Martin Luther King, Jr., W. E. B. DuBois, and others whose work was devoted to the quest for equality. Issues of social justice are also consciously woven into schoolwide as well as classroom curricula. For example, a study of colonial America in the fifth grade was built around understanding the different perspectives that stem from differences in race, class, and gender; and a study of skin color was launched in a third grade class to address a racial slur overheard in the play yard.

Paul also works to ensure that diversity of learning style is supported in the school. Teachers carry on the tradition, established at the school's inception, of using performance assessments that provide them with information about the unique needs and abilities of each child. They then use this information to differentiate instruction. Paul does the same thing in his work with the teachers. He tries to figure out where they are in their practice and what they need to develop so that he can attend to their needs. "I try to recognize everyone's strengths. I try to work from peoples' strengths and differentiate the expectations of what they are to do. Teachers get stale if you do not respect their special needs—those of the senior as well as the novice teacher." So he moves a struggling classroom teacher out of the classroom to become instead a specialty teacher in her area of strength; or he finds ways that a master teacher who does not want to leave the classroom can play a leadership role with her colleagues.

Paul's goal is not only to provide for everyone's differing needs, but to help everyone be a *life-long learner* and to create a community of learners in the school, two other core values of learner-centered schools. "I want to help people want to keep being learners, to never settle and always get better at their practice. People are thinkers and growers if given the opportunity. When the original option schools were put together, they wanted to do better things for children. The people who came here to teach took time to look for a place that fit their style and was where they wanted to be. The people here are always looking for ways to learn. That's why they stay late and work hard. I try to assist them by treating them in the same way that I want them to treat the kids they teach. I want them to work from children's strengths, look for their successes, and always try to get the most from them."

Enacting Core Values.   One of the ways that Paul expresses these original core values of learner-centered schools is through the structures he has helped to maintain in the school as well as the new ones that he has created. Since its inception, meetings have played a big part of life in The Bronx New School—meetings for teachers, for children, and for families. Recognizing the importance of these gatherings to create the shared meanings and coherence that characterize a professional culture, Paul has made sure to allot time for them. He has set up the school schedule to ensure that there are weekly all-school meetings and daily classroom meetings for the children, regular meetings for the faculty, as well as regular family–community meetings. He has also instituted structures for the faculty that require additional meeting time during the day—grade level and cross-grade teams for each discipline. To do this Paul has used resources creatively so that he can hire specialty teachers to cover classes and so that he can pay teachers to attend after school professional development sessions. Paul sees his job as helping to educate others about what it means to be a professional community. "I am constantly reminding everyone of the value of meetings to maintain our focus on student learning." Staying in close touch with the children and their learning is another way that Paul stays focused on the learner-centered values he has pledged to uphold. He, like every other adult in the school, works with a small group of children who meet regularly in a book club to read a monthly selection Paul chooses for the whole school. This shared experience across all the grades helps to build community. In an interview, Paul talked about how he loves to be "in the company of children." Being engaged with the kids, talking and listening to them, being involved in their conversations, and helping them learn how to work together are, Paul says, "what helps me get up in the morning and come back to school every day."

Struggling With Leadership Challenges and Demands.   In all that he does, Paul struggles with how to be a good leader. The challenges are internal as well as external.

One challenge is inherent in the leadership role itself. Leaders ignite memories, attitudes, and behaviors in others that often have nothing to do with what the leader actually does but rather are simply a reaction to authority. Paul struggles with how not to take this personally. He works hard to understand adult development, to keep growing, to get beyond unwarranted responses to him, and to take responsibility for his own reactions.

Another leadership challenge for Paul is to find, in his work with the teachers, the right balance between push and support. He tries to model this so that they do the same with the children entrusted to their care.

> I want to help the teachers be all they can be and support them to do the same for children. Sometimes that requires going outside their comfort zone. Sometimes I have to say "you have to do more; it's not good enough." We have to let kids know what standards are and push them so that they can reach their potentials.

To do this Paul searches for ways to get teachers to get better at strengthening children's skills without compromising the school's core values of supporting the development of the whole child.

Working with the families of the school raises still other leadership challenges for Paul. Because families were co-founders of the school and their involvement has been central to the school's history, they feel as if the school is their own. They are heavily invested. They feel very empowered, sometimes without fully understanding the complexities of the bureaucratic mandates and requirements to which the school is subjected. Paul must negotiate how to educate families about these realities and how to balance the families' sense of empowerment with a respect for the constraints the school faces. He is especially sensitive about making sure that the families of *all* the children get involved in school matters and that they assist him in upholding the school's values in the midst not only of the contradictory values of contemporary demands, but also the limited resources provided to the school. Paul explains:

My main concern is that the good work we do here connects to results that the district understands. At the same time I want to work to change the system so that it better supports what we do here. And I have to do all of this with so little. I shouldn't have to do so much with so little. All I want is to do the best for the children. But to do this, I need to use different ways—different from the ways of the school administration and different from some of the ways of the school's past.

One example of how this tension plays out is in the school's recent transformation from multi-age classrooms to "looped" same-grade classes. Paul advocated for this change because of the pressures of imposed curricula, testing, and retention policies. He argued that moving to single grade classes could better help the children meet district demands, while instituting looping (teachers move up with their students to the next grade) combined with across-grade projects would still ensure that children could be well known by their teacher as well as maintain the sense of community so valued by the school. In this way, Paul tried to find a way to translate the founding values of the school into language and actions that the district could understand and the school community could support.

Continuities–Discontinuities.   Just as the leaders described in the piece earlier, Paul is a promoter of learner-centered values. However, because of the current high-stakes accountability climate, he must act as a protector of those values too. As he negotiates the demands of the outside world with the inside world of the school culture, he struggles to be a buffer between the teachers, the families, and the district. His challenge is to instill a larger vision that transcends the demands of both worlds. This involves protecting as well as creating school structures and practices that nurture the holistic development of all (students, their families, and the school's teachers). Though some of the details of the work differ from the work of the early learner-centered leaders, the essence of Paul's job remains the same: to be an enabler of growth and a constant reminder for everyone to stay focused on learning.

Case 2—Joe Feldman, Executive Director of High Tech Hi Bayshore: A New Director With a Solid Background and Beliefs in Learner-Centered Values, Structures, and Practices.[6]

Joe Feldman is in his 2nd week as the new principal, but has had over 5 years of experience with Hi Tech Hi in San Diego playing various roles. He has been there since the beginning. Now he is a new leader in a school that is being transformed into a Hi Tech Hi model replication housed in a new state of the art building in Redwood City.

Background and Formation of Hi Tech Hi.   Two big ideas have fueled the idea of high tech high schools, originally in San Diego and now in Redwood City (open as of September 2005). Business leaders were complaining that they could not get employees who were prepared to work in the new global economy and the investments that they have made in education were not yielding any change. Headed by Larry

---

[6]I interviewed Joe Feldman and asked him the same questions that had been asked in our original study on August 1, 2005.

Rosenstock (an educator), a business group and an education group met and created Hi Tech Hi together. Their idea was that it should have three design principles which would prepare students for the world of work. They are,

Personalization—small advisories, differentiated instruction.

Common intellectual mission—no tracking, group work, presentations, and project based assignments.

Adult-world connection—internships and public displays of what they do.

Teaching Vocational Skills Along With Academics.   With these design principles, the first high school was opened in 2000. Planning for the school started two years before in 1998. It was so successful that both parents and the business community pressed for a middle school and an international school on the same campus using the same principles. There are currently six schools in California with the idea of opening two to three schools a year in California.

Hi Tech Hi Bayshore

The first replication using these principles is High Tech Hi Bayshore opening September 2005 in Redwood City. The school will open with 200 students drawing from San Carlos High School. The school will start by using the design of Hi Tech Hi and the structures and practices that have been developed over the last five years in San Diego.

INSIDE HIGH TECH HI

The Structure of Teaching and Learning

Teachers in Hi Tech Hi each teach a double block of subjects—either the humanities or math and science. Two teachers have adjacent classrooms and share an office so that they can talk about the students and the curriculum. The blocks take up 5 hours of a 7-hour day. Each teacher teaches two blocks.

Talk Time

Classes are arranged so that teachers have the same prep time. There are meetings before school recognizing that it is easier to plan for what you can do than think about after school meetings where people are tired and ready to go home. Wednesdays are full staff meetings; Tuesdays and Thursdays are usually team meetings; Fridays there is professional development—all before school. School starts at 9 and ends at 4. This decision was made to accommodate adolescent development figuring that a later arrival would better meet the needs of student sleeping habits. Meetings are 8–9 AM for the adults.

Advisories

In advisories teachers talk with students about the progress they are making. They learn how to be better students and how to negotiate the relationships that are important for their success in school. As in Central Park East Secondary School, described previously, students lead conferences with their parents and their advisors, connecting school and home support, making the student a full partner.

LEADERSHIP AND BUILDING A PROFESSIONAL CULTURE

Leadership is critical in creating a professional culture. To create a professional community, teachers' time and energy needs protecting so that they can spend the majority of their time on teaching and learning. Principals make it their business to not interrupt classroom time. Teachers are not on committees. Classroom time is sacrosanct. Because of this noninterrupted time, students too get the message that school is about learning, about participation, and about developing the skills and abilities to eventually take their place in the world. And eventually teachers begin to trust the idea that the major focus of the school is the learning of students (and eventually their own learning as well).

Visible Signs of the Culture

Early in the year students' art work fills the school. Students are recognized at community meetings giving them an opportunity to participate vocally in the growing professional culture. The language of collaboration is used by students, faculty, and administration alike. Students (and teachers) work in teams and get used to collaborating with their peers. At the beginning of the year the school engages students in the *Ropes* course, which is becoming standard in many colleges to help students connect to each other and to build team spirit.

Leadership Responsibilities

Leadership is primarily about protecting teachers' time. Principals of these schools are constantly inquiring asking: How do you do that? What do you need? What do you want help with? Principals also concern themselves with facilitating the kinds of skills that students are learning (with adults), collaborating, learning to facilitate project-based learning, working in teams. Of course everything does not go smoothly and efficiently. As Voltaire taught us long ago *there is no such thing as perfection, nor should there be.* There are always tensions to be negotiated in a school. Often parents, teachers, and students want a strong person to make all the decisions. Sometimes principals push too hard and forget that they need to be selective and keep the pulse and trust of the group. New teachers need different supports than veterans. In High Tech Hi Bayshore (the new school) there will be some returning teachers and eight new teachers who need to be socialized into this new culture. Trust, skills, and the ability to both create and participate in this new professional culture will try both the experienced and novice teachers alike. Leaders of new schools sometimes feel that "they are 30,000 feet high and then down to one foot and in the process they must somehow maintain their equilibrium."

Learning From Small Schools

Given a new state of the art building, 60% new freshmen, a new curriculum, and a new organizational design, Hi Tech Hi has its work laid out for the students, teachers, and parents, as well as the leadership. These schools have learned from the earlier small schools about a focus on the learner and created structures and practices that are similar to the earlier small schools. There are advisories, blocks, teacher planning time, performance assessments, and real world work and in this sense there is an interesting continuity with the earlier small schools. But Hi Tech Hi has added some interesting nuances as well (all meetings before school, working in teams, consciously connecting school work to real world internships, partnering with the business community). But there are some important issues raised by the Hi Tech Schools as they seek to work with the business community in a rapidly changing global context.

CHARTERS, CHOICE, AND IMPROVING SCHOOLS

Hi Tech Hi Learning, the umbrella group for these schools intends to petition the state to spread these schools all over California.[7] If the petition is accepted other Charters will clearly have a strengthened position to spread freely throughout the state. This raises the very thorny issue of who is accountable for schools. Charters exist within districts, but are accountable to the State. Clearly local districts will lose control over public schools. Parents will complain that their tax dollars are being spent on these schools. But Hi Tech Hi advocates can claim that they are doing exactly what the public wants—offering good education to all students who are achieving. Charter school advocates claim that choice and competition is exactly what schools need. But is this a fair assessment of what we mean by competition? Do schools learn from each other by competing with them for resources? Is competition an appropriate way of transforming schools?

Struggling With the Contentious Issues

Hi Tech Hi Bayshore will be the first "replication" of a Hi Tech Hi School. This idea raises some important conundrums that the school change literature has been grappling with for years. What does it take to "replicate" good ideas and transport them to different contexts without losing the essence of the ideas? It would seem on the face of it that these schools have design principles and they also have practices and structures that relate to these principles. They have attended to values, practices, and the social organization of the school. Leadership in these schools is characterized by facilitating and providing the opportunity to reflect, inquire, and collaborate while keeping the school focused on student learning. We will clearly learn some important lessons from these schools, but we will have to also continue to question and struggle with how "choice" schools fit into the public education structure, whether other schools can learn from them, what the appropriate balance between the needs of the economy and

---

[7]Patel, Julie (2005) "Charter Group has Statewide Goal" in San Jose Mercury News, August 1.

the need to broadly educate can be, how schools of choice are financed and held accountable to the public, and whether these schools have found all the ingredients to "replicate" their successes in other contexts. Surely leadership and the building of a professional culture are key to their success. The debate is still on.

DIFFERENT APPROACHES TO DEALING WITH THE CURRENT CONTEXT

In our 1993 piece (above), the leaders were teacher directors. While today's leaders have the title of school principals, their work remains remarkably the same. All saw, and still see today, their role as providing structures that support student learning and that create community in their schools. What is different today is the changed context. Across the nation there is an increased systemwide press for standardization of school practices in response to widespread high-stakes accountability policies. However, there are also some opportunities for freedom from many of these system requirements that have been created by recently established charter school structures supported by the business community's growing interest in preparing students for the realities of the 21st-century world.

The two leaders highlighted in this Epilogue are dealing with different aspects of the new context. The Bronx New School is situated in the midst of the curriculum and pedagogical mandates emanating from high-stakes accountability policies. Its leader's challenge is to meet the demands of the system while keeping alive the legacy of traditions and strong values deeply rooted in its parent as well as teacher community. To do this, he must negotiate a delicate balance between a new heightened focus on student outcomes emanating from the current climate and a focus on the nurturing of student processes that is the tradition of the past. He has to figure out how to deal with these tensions on his own, because his school is the only one of its kind in his district. High Tech High, on the other hand, is situated in the midst of a growing charter school network. Even though it is a newly created school, because its network has already shown some success and has the support of the business community, its leader has some credibility that he can lean on and he has some freedom from many of the pressures currently experienced by regular public schools. His school must produce, but they have a lot of catche rooted in their approach and their promise to meet the demands of the contemporary global society. His challenge is to create a new professional community and to create new ways to meet the expectations for his school community while not alienating the school from its larger community where it physically resides.

Though the specific contexts of these two schools differ, both leaders advocate for values and practices that remain consistent with those of the early learner-centered schools. As they do this, their work is shifting where the accountability lies. Is it the district who should be responsible? The individual school? The State? In the process, they are constructing and redefining the characteristics of leaders in the third wave of learner-centered schools.

All of this raises important questions. Will the schools that were started years ago be able to maintain their integrity and their community in the face of the constraints of the new accountability context? Will the newly created charter schools be able to uphold learner-centered values within a new entrepreneurial frontier? As a new generation of leaders unfolds it will be important to see how (or if) learner-centered leadership and its professional cultures can survive (or thrive). As the core values of learner-centered leadership become embedded in a new group of small schools, we will learn just how robust these ideas are and how they adapt to the rapidly changing context.

REFERENCES

Barth, R. (1990). *Improving Schools from within*. San Francisco: Jossey-Bass.

Bensman, D. (1987). *Quality education in the inner city: The story of the Central Park East schools*. New York: Community School District 4.

Bredekamp, S. (1987). *Developmentally-appropriate practice*. Washington, DC: National Association for the Education of Young Children.

Bruner, J. (1966). *The process of education*. Cambridge, MA: Harvard University Press.

Carini, P. (1975). *Observation and description: An Alternative methodology for the investigation of human phenomena*. Grand Forks, ND: North Dakota Study Group on Evaluation.

Carini, P. (1979). *The art of seeing and the visibility of the person*. Grand Forks, ND: North Dakota Study Group on Evaluation.

Cuban, L. (1984). *How teachers taught: Constancy and change in american classrooms*. New York: Longman.

Darling-Hammond, L. (1991). The implications of testing policy for educational quality and equality. *Phi Delta Kappan, 73,* 220–225.

Darling-Hammond, L. (1993). Reframing the school reform agenda: Developing capacity for school transformation. *Phi Delta Kappan, 74,* 753–761.

Dewey, J. (1916). *Democracy and education*. New York: Macmillan

Dewey, J. (1938). *Education and experience*. New York: Macmillan.

Dewey, J. (1956). *The child and the curriculum*. Chicago: University of Chicago Press.

Duckworth, E. (1987). *The having of wonderful ideas and other essays*. New York: Teachers College Press.

Froebel, F. (1974). *Education of man*. Englewood Cliffs, NJ: Appleton-Century-Crofts. (Original work published 1885)

Fullan, M., & Hargreaves, A. (1991). *What's worth fighting for: Working together for your school*. Toronto, Canada: Ontario Public School Teachers' Federation.

Granovetter, M. S. (1973). The strength of weak ties. *The American Journal of Sociology, 78,* 1360–1380.

Greene, M. (1984). How do we think about our craft? *Teachers College Record, 86*(1), 55–67.

Lieberman, A., & McLaughlin, M. W. (1992). Networks for educational change: Powerful and problematic. *Phi Delta Kappan, 73,* 673–677.

McLaughlin, M. W. (1987). Learning from experience: Lessons from policy implementation. *Educational Evaluation and Policy Analysis, 9*(2), 171–178.

McLaughlin, M. W., & Talbert, J. E. (1993). *Contexts that matter for teaching and learning: Strategic opportunities for meeting the nation's educational goals*. Stanford, CA: Center for Research on the Context of Secondary School Teaching.

Oakes, J. (1985). *Keeping track: How schools structure inequality*. New Haven, CT: Yale University Press.

Patterson, J. L. (1993). *Leadership for Tomorrow's schools*. Alexandria, VA: Association for Supervision and Curriculum Development.

Piaget, J., & Inhelder, B. (1969). *The psychology of the child*. New York: Basic Books.

Poplin, M. (1992). The leader's new role: Looking to the growth of teachers. *Educational Leadership, 49*(5), 10–11.

Pratt, C. (1948). *I learn from children*. New York: Simon & Schuster.

Prospect Archive and Center for Education and Research. (1986). *The Prospect Center documentary processes: In progress*. North Bennington, VT: Author.

Resnick, L. B. (1987). *Education and learning to think*. Washington, DC: National Academy Press.

Serbiovanni, T. J. (1992). *Moral leadership: Getting to the heart of school improvement*. San Francisco: Jossey-Bass.

Vygotsky, L. S. (1978). *Mind in society*. Cambridge, MA: Harvard University Press.

3

A LEARNER-CENTERED APPROACH TO LEADERSHIP PREPARATION AND PROFESSIONAL DEVELOPMENT

Arnold B. Danzig
Gerald Blankson
Gary Kiltz
Arizona State University

This chapter begins with a theoretical overview that highlights some of the basic psychological principles associated with learning. The section explores connections between learning principles and leadership, and extends the discussion to adult learning and professional development. The section concludes by contrasting learner-centered leadership with instructional leadership and raises other challenges to the concept of learner-centered leadership (LCL).

LEARNER-CENTERED PSYCHOLOGICAL PRINCIPLES

The theoretical framework for this section draws from the literature on adult learning theory (Knowles, 1980; Merriam, 2001a, 2001b), learner-centered psychological principles (American Psychological Association [APA], 1997), adult learner autonomy (Pierce & Kalkman, 2003), learning as a social activity situated in personal and professional contexts (Guskey, 2000; Hansman, 2001; Lave & Wegner, 1991), and organizational learning. The American Psychological Association Work Group on

School Redesign and Reform (APA, 1997) uses the term *learner-centered psychological principles* to explore many of the factors related to how people learn. A brief summary of these principles suggests that successful learners reflect on how they think and learn, and then use this information to choose fitting strategies, methods, and goals for themselves. Successful learners monitor progress and make adjustments either to methods or goals when a problem arises. When instructing learners, methods that tap high-order meta-cognition enhance learning and personal responsibility (APA, 1997).

Motivation and Learning

Motivation affects learning. The APA guidelines report that motivation to learn is connected to perceptions of novelty and difficulty, to relevance, and to personal choice and control. Motivation affects what is learned and how it is learned. Motivation is related to individuals' emotional states, beliefs, interests and goals, and habits of thinking. The APA guidelines also highlight the importance of *intrinsic motivation* to learning. Curiosity, flexibility, insightful thinking, and creativity are major indicators of the learners' intrinsic motivation to learn; intrinsic motivation is in large part a function of meeting basic needs to be competent and to exercise personal control. Intrinsic motivation is facilitated on tasks that learners perceive as interesting, personally relevant and meaningful, appropriate in complexity and difficulty to the learners' abilities, and on tasks in which learners believe they can succeed. Intrinsic motivation is also facilitated on tasks that are comparable to real-world situations and meet needs for choice and control (APA, 1997).

Learning Autonomy and Social Context

Learning is social. Learning is not static or void of context; it is learned and rehashed in social contexts. Learning is influenced by social interactions, interpersonal relations, and communication with others. Learning is enhanced when the learner has an opportunity to interact and to collaborate with others on instructional tasks. Learning settings that allow for social interactions, and that respect diversity, encourage flexible thinking and social competence. Hansman (2001) described teaching writing to adults as a way to understand learning in social context. Her work on situated learning takes into account social context. Citing Lave and Wegner (1991), she argued that people learn as they participate with a community of learners, interacting with the community and understanding and participating in its history, assumptions, and cultural values and rules. She believes that communities of practice are self-organized with selected groups of people who share a common purpose and desire to learn what each other knows. They can exist in larger organizations and are based on mutual engagement, joint enterprise, and shared repertoire.

What sorts of social experiences build learning autonomy? Pierce and Kalkman (2003) discussed several techniques to build learning autonomy. Learners confront prior knowledge and multiplicity of views of peers through *direct reflection*. Learners make studying strategies an explicit part of the learning through *action learning*. Learners use and reflect on how these strategies might work on other problems or in other circumstances. *Choice* in problem selection is cited as an important factor to motivation. *Social interaction* is also cited as a component of the learning experience. The evaluation of learning autonomy is then based on how learners develop their own ideas on the topic, and also how they exchange ideas with others and collaborate.

EXTENDING LEARNING PRINCIPLES TO ADULT LEARNERS AND PROFESSIONAL DEVELOPMENT

The extension of learning principles to adult learners emerges from a number of core assumptions posited by Knowles (1980). Learners feel a need to learn. The learning environment is characterized by physical comfort, mutual trust and respect, mutual helpfulness, freedom of expression, and acceptance of differences. Learners perceive the goals of a learning experience to be their goals. Learners accept a share of the responsibility for planning and operating a learning experience, and therefore have a feeling of commitment toward it. Learners participate actively in the learning process and the learning process is related to and makes use of the experience of the learners. Finally, learners have a sense of progress toward their goals.

Adult Learning and Professional Development

The best examples of professional development reflect a method of embedding new knowledge into the existing roles, processes, and structures of schools (Guskey, 2000). Understanding the processes by which adults learn and develop is the key component for research and development of professional development practices for teachers and school leaders.

The determinants of effective professional development for teachers provide some guidance for understanding professional development of school principals and administrators. Data from a longitudinal study on the effects of professional development on teachers' instruction (Desimone, Porter, Garet, Yoon, & Birman, 2002) indicate that professional development is more effective in changing teachers' classroom practice when it has four features: (a) collective participation of teachers from the same school, department, or grade; (b) active learning opportunities; (c) coherence—activities are consistent with teachers' goals, are based on their previous knowledge, and are followed up with activities built on the activities teachers attended; (d) reform activities—substitute traditional workshops or conferences by teacher study groups, teacher networks, mentoring, internships, and resource centers.

From Teacher to Administrator Professional Development

A research brief by the American Educational Research Association on professional development (Holland, 2005) summarizes the movement of teacher professional development from a focus on generic teaching skills (class time, grouping, classroom management, assessing comprehension) to a focus on subject matter and student learning.

There has also been a shift in thinking about adult learning and professional development related to school administration. Over the years, three different philosophical orientations have guided the professional development of educational administrators: (a) traditional–scientific management, (b) craft, and (c) reflective inquiry (Fenwick & Pierce, 2002). The administrator in the traditional view is the passive recipient of new knowledge delivered in group settings by consultants or experts. The craft model exposes the principal to knowledge from seasoned administrators whom she or he shadows in internships and field experiences. The third approach, reflective inquiry, encourages the principal to generate knowledge through a process of systematic inquiry and the source of knowledge is in self-reflection and engagement. Networking, mentoring, reflective reading, and writing are key components of this approach (p. 3). The models of leadership and professional development explored in this book are most closely aligned with this third approach. Reading roundtables, small and large group meetings with administrators across districts, sunrise storytelling, action learning projects, are all examples which focus on the leader as learner, and components of the LCL program explored in the second part of the chapter.

BUILDING AN LCL PROGRAM: LCL FOR LANGUAGE AND CULTURALLY DIVERSE SCHOOLS IN HIGH NEEDS URBAN SETTINGS

Since October 2002, the College of Education at Arizona State University, in collaboration with the Southwest Center for Educational Equity and Language Diversity and four diverse, urban school districts in the Phoenix area, has been working to implement LCL and professional development programs for school leaders. A 3-year grant from the United States Department of Education's *School Leadership Program* has provided the opportunity to create the LCL program for language and culturally diverse schools in high needs, urban districts.

The intention of the federal grant program is to assist high need local educational agencies in developing, enhancing, or expanding their innovative programs to recruit, train, and mentor principals and assistant principals (United States Department of Education, 2002). The LCL project collaborates with four participating school districts in (a) recruiting and training aspiring, rising, and experienced school administrators; (b) building the knowledge, skills, and competencies of novice principals and assistant principals based on current research through meetings, workshops, institutes, reading roundtables, and action learning projects; and (c) encouraging promotion and retention of novice and expert school administrators through participation in professional development and mentoring activities (Danzig, 2002; Danzig et al., 2004; Kiltz, Danzig, & Szecsy, 2004).

COMMITMENT AND COLLABORATION IN IDENTIFICATION, RECRUITMENT AND SELECTION OF PARTICIPANTS

From the beginning, the LCL program has involved collaboration between ASU and the four districts. The project sought participants from three distinct groups: Group 1—prospective administrators, Group 2—rising administrators, and Group 3—accomplished administrators. District superintendents served as project liaisons until permanent district liaisons were identified and selected by each of the collaborating school districts.

As indicated, the program goal was to create and develop a pipeline of well-trained and accomplished school administrators to serve urban schools; this required the identification, recruitment, and selection of participants by each district. Rough guidelines for desired participant characteristics were developed by the project team, with participating districts responsible for recruitment. This process of district selection is significant and provides a way of rewarding and guiding promising staff. During one of the project team meetings (November 13, 2002) the following nomination and selection criteria and procedures were developed by the liaisons and other team members.

1. Each district liaison is to have list of names and packets to ASU by December 3, 2002.
2. Group 1 participants should be teachers and emerging leaders who want to pursue a career in educational administration. Group 1 packets should include three pieces of information: (a) individual letter of nomination from the district, (b) resume or vita, and (c) letter of interest and potential contribution to M.Ed/Certification program in Ed. Admin.
3. Letter will be sent by ASU to each of the participants inviting them to apply to Graduate College after acceptance into the program by the Educational Administration Admissions Committee.
4. Educational administration faculty will recommend admission to Graduate College.

There was agreement by the project team (district liaisons and university personnel) that nontraditional leaders need to be identified in nontraditional ways. It was explicit in these discussions that participants reflect the diversity of the community in these high-needs, urban school districts. Along with this, a comprehensive list of other criteria was discussed and agreed to by the project team. Nominations were to include the following characteristics:

1. Risk takers.
2. Successful teachers in classroom with demonstrated effective instruction.
3. Teachers who enjoy being in the classroom.
4. Effective in classroom-management skills.
5. Demonstrate self-direction and initiative.
6. Have ability to work within established standards and structures.
7. Loyal to the district.
8. Stewards of school district and community.
9. Smart people.
10. Have the ability to communicate effectively.
11. Have the ability to prioritize.
12. Resilient.
13. Individuals in the beginning stage of formal training in educational administration.
14. Consideration for traditionally overlooked persons.

Based on interviews, there was variability in the degree to which each of the school districts followed these guidelines in selecting participants for Group 1 and each used a different process in making these decisions. With careful attention, however, all four of the participating districts identified minorities often underrepresented in school administration. Participants from these groups had specific needs and were each engaged in varying program activities. Beginning in 2005, a new cohort was recruited from these four districts and extended to other urban districts.

THE LCL PROGRAM FOR PROSPECTIVE ADMINISTRATORS

During the 3 years of the LCL program, 27 prospective administrators completed a program leading to the master's degree in educational administration and administrative certification. In December 2004, the 27 students graduated with a master's in Educational Administration and the necessary coursework for principal certification.

This group consisted of practicing teachers interested in pursuing a program in educational administration at Arizona State University. While entering a master's program is not uncommon for those seeking to step into administrative roles, LCL emphasized the importance of relationships and collaboration to learning. The group entered the master's program as a cohort. They attended classes and completed course work together. This process lends itself to developing longstanding relationships.

Commitment to Collaboration

Traditionally, graduate courses are developed and taught by university faculty, based on national and state standards. For the LCL program, new courses were developed and older courses revised. This collaboration between school district administrators and education faculty resulted in some revised courses with new titles and new courses in the program. Two new courses were created by university faculty: (a) *concepts of LCL* and (b) *sociology of teaching and learning*. Three courses were revised around learner-centered concepts and co-taught by university faculty and district administrators from one of the four participating districts: (a) *competency and performances of administrators* was revised under a new title of *leadership & personal knowledge,* (b) *school-community relations* was revised to *family-school-community connections*, and (c) *introduction to research* was revised as *student testing, data and the evaluation of learning*. A new capstone course and capstone project replaced a multiple choice–information recall comprehensive exam. The capstone project required that students write a reflective paper on the learning that took place over the course of study, and developing a portfolio documenting learning experiences and impact on the job. This course was also co-taught by a tenure track faculty member and a clinical faculty member, a former school superintendent of one of the larger Phoenix area school districts. The combination of new courses, new course titles with revised content, and co-teaching of courses by faculty and practitioners, changed the knowledge base around core concepts of LCL and applications. The LCL program for prospective administrators built on an existing master's program framework, while at the same time, made significant changes to overall curriculum and structure of its delivery.

Figure 3.1 lists the matrix of courses offered in the LCL master's certification program.

Program Participants

As stated earlier, the first LCL cohort consisted of teachers identified by four urban school districts, working toward a master's degree in educational administration and administrative certification. In December 2004, the 27 students graduated with a master's degree in education administration and the necessary coursework for state principal certification. Table 3.1 lists participants and completers, by gender and ethnicity.

The LCL program began a second cohort in January 2005. The second cohort includes 17 teachers from six different districts. The course of study is the same as first LCL cohort. Table 3.2 provides information related to gender and ethnicity in this second cohort.

LEARNING ON THE JOB—
PROFESSIONAL DEVELOPMENT FOR RISING ADMINISTRATORS

Group 2, rising administrators, were part of the professional development program. Over the course of 1st year, the grant moved from building relationships, to developing a capacity for action plans, implementation, and mentoring. In the 2nd and 3rd years of the project, the LCL program used a four stage process of mentoring as the foundation of professional development for school administrators involved in the project. Those

Spring 2005	1ˢᵗ Summer Session 2005	Fall 2005	Spring 2006	1ˢᵗ Summer Session 2006	Fall 2006
EDA 501 Competency Performance: *Leadership, Communication & Personal Knowledge* Mondays 1/24/-3/14/05 4:40 – 9:30 PM ASU Downtown	EDA 548 Family-School-Community Connections 5/16-6/2/05 Monday, Tuesday & Thursday 4:00-8:30 pm ASU Downtown Center	EDA 526 Instructional Supervision & the **Principalship** Mondays 4:40 – 9:30 PM ASU Downtown Center	EDA 591 Sociology of Teaching and Learning Mondays 4:40 – 9:30 ASU Downtown Center	EDA 591 State & Local Finance: *Resources for School Improvement & Reform* M, T, Th 4 PM– 8:30 PM ASU Downtown Dates - TBD	EDA 511 School Law: Legal Issues for Schools in Urban Settings Mondays 4:40 – 9:30 ASU Downtown Center
EDA 591 Concepts of Learner-Centered Educational Leadership: *How People Learn* Mondays 3/21-5/9/05 4:40 – 9:30 PM ASU Downtown Center	COE 505 American Education System: **Issues in Urban Education** 6/13-6/30/05 Monday, Tuesday & Thursday 4:00-8:30 pm ASU Downtown Center	EDA 584 *Internship I* To Be Arranged	EDA 684 *Internship II* To Be Arranged	COE 501 Intro. To Research and Evaluation: *Student Testing, Data, and the Evaluation of Learning* M, T, Th 4 PM– 8:30 PM ASU Downtown Dates - TBD	EDA 691 Evaluation & Assessment of School Change: Capstone and Comps Mondays 4:40 – 9:30 PM ASU Downtown Center

Figure 3.1   LCL master's certification in Educational Administration—Course Matrix (October 2004).

TABLE 3.1

Participant Information (Prospective Administrators-Cohort I) - May 2005

Program Participation	Number of Participants	Gender	Ethnicity
Entering	34	25 Female (73%) 9 Males (27%)	7 African American (20%) 16 Caucasians (47%) 11 Hispanics (33%)
Completing	27	19 Females (70%) 8 Males (30%)	5 African Americans (18.5%) 12 Caucasians (44%) 10 Hispanics (37%)

TABLE 3.2

Participant Information (Prospective Administators-Cohort II) - June 15, 2005

Program Participant	Number of Participants	Gender	Ethnicity
Entering	17	10 Females (59%) 7 Males (41%)	3 African Americans (18%) 7 Caucasians (41%) 7 Hispanics (41%)

stages are (a) developing relationships that create the capacity for mentoring, (b) negotiating the mentoring relationship through action and mentoring plan processes, (c) embedding mentoring through action plan implementation, and (d) reflecting on the learning that occurs over the course of the mentoring experience.

These stages incorporate important principles of learner-centeredness referenced in previous sections. The relationships create socially situated spaces and tie into identified concerns and job-related interests. Mentors are selected by the rising administrators and not assigned. Action plans are developed based on individual preferences and on the context of schools and districts.

Forty-six rising administrators have participated in professional development activities, of which 34 are currently enrolled. Nine participants left, for various reasons. One of these individuals was initially chosen as a rising administrator and moved during the first semester to the prospective administrator group. Another rising administrator moved to the accomplished administrator group. Five participants received new positions in other districts. Two participants had other priorities that caused them to leave the LCL program (see Table 3.3).

Action Learning Plans

One theme of professional development in the LCL program was the development of action learning plans, implemented by the rising administrators. The purpose of these action learning plans was to outline a series of actions that would help rising administrators improve professionally and strengthen their school as a learning community. The project team wanted to create a process that allowed for flexibility in the content

TABLE 3.3

Participant Information (Rising Administrators - June 15, 2005)

Rising Administrator Participation	Total Population	Gender	Ethnicity
Total Enrolled (Year One and Two)	46	27 Females (59%) 19 Males (41%)	7 African American (15%) 1 Asian American (2%) 26 Caucasian (57%) 11 Hispanic (24%) 1 Native American (2%)
Current Participation	34	20 Females (59%) 14 Males (41%)	6 African American (18%) 1 Asian American (3%) 17 Causasian (50%) 9 Hispanic (26%) 1 Native American (3%)

of the plan. As a result, participants were able to focus on an individual professional development plan, a school-level initiative or program, or an action research project as the foundation of the action learning plan. Table 3.4 provides a breakdown of the number of each type of action plan. Specific information on each of the action plans is provided in the annual performance reviews (Kiltz & Danzig, 2003, 2004, 2005). In analyzing these action goals, 21 focus on new program implementation on campus, 8 are action research projects, and 4 are geared toward professional growth opportunities for the individual administrator. In terms of categories for the action goals, Table 3.5 provides a breakdown of the educational categories that are covered by the action

TABLE 3.4

Breakdown of Action Plans by Type (June, 2005)

Type	Number of Action Plans
Implementation of New Programs	21
Action Research	8
Personal Professional Development	4

TABLE 3.5

Action Goals in Relation to Educational Categories (June 2005)

Category	Number of Action Plans That Fall Into This Category
Academic Intervention	2
Literacy	5
Parent Involvement	4
Professional Growth	4
Student Behavior/Discipline	10
Teacher Quality/Teacher Development	8

plans. These categories provided a way to organize rising and mentor administrators together for formal conversations and workshops.

To support the rising administrators in the implementation of action plans, four levels of professional development activities were provided: (a) summer book discussions and reading roundtables that focused on the action plan categories, (b) formal workshops, (c) district level team meetings, and (d) monthly one-on-one mentoring between a novice administrator and a matched accomplished administrator. Each is summarized below.

Summer Book Discussions

The summer book discussions evolved from online book discussion in the 1st year into face-to-face roundtable discussions usually hosted over breakfast or lunch. Rising administrators were asked to select at least two book discussions in which to participate over the summer. The sessions were hosted by university faculty, district administrators, and combinations from both groups. Books were selected by the project team and included both university and district suggestions. The idea was also to use the reading roundtable to support the action learning plans that were being implemented by the rising administrators. The number of participants in each of the discussions is listed in Table 3.6 and Table 3.7. Though the books were not necessarily chosen because they are about learner-centered principles, the process of selecting books from the personal and professional interests of participants is a learner-centered principle.

Reading sessions hosted by district administrators were generally better attended than those hosted by university professors. Interest in and relevance of the book title, location and time of the sessions, and the desire to participate with a specific facilitator likely affected who participated in the book discussions.

Formal Workshops

The second level of activities that LCL program hosted was a series of workshops for rising administrators, which were developed and facilitated by the accomplished administrators, university professors, and outside experts. First-year workshops met monthly on Saturdays and focused on team building, mentoring, curriculum leader-

TABLE 3.6
Reading Roundtable Participation (Summer 2004)

Book Title Participated	Number Enrolled	Number
Making the Grade	9	6
Good to Great	15	14
Dealing with Difficult Teacher	16	16
Leadership Without Easy Answers	4	2
Laws of Leadership	10	8
Getting Below the Surface	5	3
Why Don't They Learn English	7	4

TABLE 3.7

Reading Roundtable Participation (Summer 2005)

Book Title	Enrolled	Participated
What Great Principals Do Differently	17	15
Building Background Knowledge for Academic Achievement	15	13
The Wounded Leader	14	13
Journal Articles in School Law	18	9
On Common Ground: The Power of Professional Learning Communities	12	8
Hopeful Girls, Troubled Boys: Race and Gender Disparity in Urban Education	4	2
Dividing Classes: How the Middle Class Negotiates School Advantage	1	0

ship, and exemplary programs going on at each of the participants school districts. In year 2, programs were moved to weekday evenings with focus on workplace learning, and in year 3 a combination of weekends and evenings were scheduled for meetings and workshops.

Early on in the program, participants indicated that they did not want the professional development activities to be dominated by theory or university perspectives alone. Instead, they articulated the desire for a sharing of information and collaboration among program participants, districts leadership teams, and university partners. The rising and accomplished administrators told us that, if learning was to take place, they wanted to collaborate on the agendas, projects, workshops, and meetings.

To illustrate, in 2004–2005 the LCL program sponsored three formal workshops for the rising administrators, in fall, winter, and summer. The first workshop explored themes related to student achievement and high stakes testing. Accomplished administrators and faculty facilitated multiple breakout sessions that explored research and policy on student testing, as well as tips, templates, and strategies, related to high-stakes testing. Rising administrators were also asked to apply workshop information to their individual action learning projects. A bibliography of information was prepared in advance of the session, and facilitators met to discuss the significance of reading and applications to schools. Articles and citations were also posted on the LCL Web site.

The title of the Winter Institute was "School, Family, and Community Connections." Each participant had the opportunity to attend two out of four sessions during the institute. The topics of the four sessions were parent involvement and participation in learning, development of plans to encourage business partnerships, community partnerships and resources for families, and communication and involvement with parents of students in special education. Planning teams for the sessions included a combination of ASU faculty and mentor administrators from the four districts. Each district had at least one representative on each of the planning teams. A faculty member from ASU also served on each of the teams to represent the university. The planning teams met at least twice to determine content and strategies for the workshop.

The final institute sponsored by the LCL project was the Summer Institute in June 2005. This session consisted of a day and a half of activities in a joint partnership with the Southwest Center of Education Equity and Language Diversity. The title of the Summer Institute was "Class, Ethnicity, and Family: What Really Matters." During the 1st day of the Institute, three speakers presented information. Dr. Annette Lareau presented a perspective on family based on recent research that she has conducted. Dr. Kris Gutierrez presented a perspective on culture based on research that she has done. Finally, Dr. Josue Gonzalez gave a presentation entitled "Class: Creating and Maintaining Social Pecking Orders." After each of the individual presentations, participants had the opportunity to relate the research to current practices in small breakout sessions. These sessions were facilitated by LCL mentors.

On the second day of the Summer Institute, novice administrators had the opportunity to share progress and data related to their action plans. These presentations were done in district teams so that novice administrators received feedback on their plans from district colleagues who could continue to help with the extension of action plans into the 2005–2006 school year. District liaisons facilitated these sessions. After sharing action plan progress, novice administrators had the opportunity to meet with other rising administrators who were implementing similar types of action plans. Using mentors who had particular expertise in each of the categories as facilitators, novice administrators attended one of six different groups depending on the topic of their action plan: academic intervention, literacy, parent involvement, professional growth, student behavior–discipline, and teacher quality–professional development. Participants were able to discuss successes and challenges and exchange information to improve action plans for the following year.

The final activity during the 2nd day of the Summer Institute was a celebration. The celebration included acknowledging the district superintendents and liaisons who were critical to the successful implementation of the LCL program in each of the districts. Certificates of appreciation were also given to each of the participants. ASU faculty members were applauded for their willingness to work cooperatively with the districts.

District Level Meetings

The third level of activities provided to novice and accomplished administrators consisted of a series of five district level meetings over the course of the school year. Each district liaison developed the agenda for the meetings with the corresponding participants. ASU faculty members served as participants but were not active planners of the activities in these sessions. Each district used the meetings for different purposes. One of the districts used it as an opportunity to conduct book discussions with their school leaders. Another district used the meeting as an opportunity to check in with novice administrators and mentors to see if the team could solve any developing issues associated with the action plans. The third district used it as an opportunity to informally chat about issues that were happening in the schools and district. The final district used the meetings as a chance to develop a district-wide professional development plan for administrators. If nothing else, the district level meetings provided space and time to reflect on the practice of school leadership.

One-on-One Mentoring

The final level of activities consisted of monthly one-on-one mentoring between rising and accomplished administrators. The specific nature of these interactions was determined by the mentoring teams and formalized in a mentoring plan. Based on data collected, the one-on-one mentoring component was the most difficult to fulfill due to conflicts with time and proximity. To get a sense of the effectiveness of the one-on-one component of the mentoring model, interviews were conducted with four mentoring pairs (one from each district).

Four related themes emerged in the interviews with novice administrators: (a) the action plan process provides for focused professional development for school administrators; (b) participants need to be able to select mentors based on needs and goals that they identify; (c) participants need formalized time to network and reflect with other administrators on the action plan in order for it to be successfully implemented; and (d) participants need to see the immediate connection between workshops and daily practice in order to view it as a meaningful learning experience.

COMMITMENT TO MENTORING AND COACHING: GROUP 3 ACCOMPLISHED ADMINISTRATORS

Thirty-two accomplished administrators currently participate in the LCL program as mentors and co-instructors. The project team recruited and selected a total of 36 individuals into this group. Over the past year and a half, the program lost four mentors (one to a career change, two to new jobs in different districts, and one to retirement). Participation of the accomplished administrators, by gender and ethnicity, are listed in Table 3.8.

Mentoring

As indicated in previous sections, mentoring was one of responsibilities of the accomplished administrators who participated in the program. Accomplished administrators also participated as co-instructors of courses, hosts of reading roundtables, planners of workshop sessions, facilitators for meetings, group sessions, and leaders of workshop breakout sessions.

TABLE 3.8
Participant Information (Accomplished Administrators - June 15, 2005)

Experienced Administrator Participation	Total Population	Gender	Ethnicity
Total enrolled (Year one and two)	36	20 Females (56%) 16 Males (44%)	9 African American (25%) 20 Caucasian (55%) 7 Hispanic (20%)
Current participation	32	19 Females (59%) 13 Males (41%)	8 African American (18%) 18 Caucasian (56%) 6 Hispanic (19%)

Interviews with accomplished administrators, who also served as mentors, revealed multiple themes related to leadership and professional development: (a) the action plan process brought structure and purpose to the mentoring experience, allowing for tangible benefits at the schools; (b) mentors also learned and grew professionally as a result of the opportunities to network and converse with colleagues; and (c) time is an issue in providing the type of in-depth mentoring that is engaging and meaningful, but the mentors plan on continuing to serve in this capacity.

The common themes that emerged from the interviews include the following:

- Purposeful mentoring requires trust, respect, ethics, communication, and confidentiality. This theme is supported in the literature related to effective mentoring (Hay, 1995; Johnson, 1997; Robbins & Alvy, 2004; Shea, 1994; Zepeda, 2003).
- Mentoring must include effective communication that embraces listening and constructive feedback (Harkins, 1999; Lovely, 2004; Starratt, 2003).
- The blend of university and school district personnel to develop curriculum and workshops decreases the gap between theory and practice and promotes the use of research-based best practices.
- Developing structured action plans for novice administrators is a valuable professional development experience.
- Time is the greatest barrier. Finding "time" to participate in the LCL Saturday project activities was difficult, but the activities were rewarding.
- Most of the participants interviewed perceived participation in the LCL project promoted significant professional growth. The action plan process allowed novice administrators to observe mentors "modeling" effective leadership in the work environment.
- A significant number of the participants believed the LCL project provided the opportunity for valuable networking and affirmed that they were not alone (Lovely, 2004).
- Most of the participants interviewed believed the mentor–novice administrator relationship would continue beyond the end of the LCL project.

To sum, the overall goal of the purposeful mentoring component of the LCL program appeared to be successful. Purposeful mentoring involved continuous growth and innovation related to school-specific goals and strategies that are outlined in a formalized plan of action. Supportive, positive relationships between mentors and those being mentored were developed to engage in critical conversations that led to professional growth and improved practice. There was a connection among theory, research, and literature related to strategic innovation that occurred at school sites. Professional development was embedded into daily practices of administration. Professional development was blended into a formal action plan based on assessment of individual needs, reflection, and critiquing one's leadership.

INDICATIONS AND IMPLICATIONS OF PROGRAM EFFECTS AND OUTCOMES

A survey was administered the week of April 29, 2004, to the cohort of prospective administrators in the LCL program. The survey asked whether the coursework prepared participants for internships, their overall satisfaction with courses, the perceived responsiveness of their district, and the respondents' willingness to participate in a follow-up session. The survey provided immediate feedback and program information used for program design.

Evidence of Course Relevance and District Support for Prospective Administrators

Ninety-one percent of respondents strongly agreed or agreed with the statement "I feel the coursework in the LCL master's–certification program prepared me for my first internship experience." More than 95% strongly agreed or agreed with the statement "I am satisfied with the courses that I have taken as part of LCL master's–certification program." Most of the respondents either strongly agreed (50.0%) or agreed (36.4%) with the statement "I feel my work in the LCL program is being supported in my district." In response to the question, "What additional learning experiences would you recommend to help you prepare for the second internship?" recommendations for the following learning areas were noted.

- Interpersonal relationships.
- Conflict resolution.
- Templates to document hours, opportunities.
- Additional content related to curriculum and instruction.
- Implementation of a vision.
- Case studies of dilemmas and conflict of practice and policy.
- Broader perspective of the principal's role.
- Information on the experiences of principals.
- Shadowing of administrators.

Finally, respondents were asked "Would you be interested in participating in follow-up sessions during the spring of 2005, after you have completed the LCL program?" A total of 90.9% of the respondents indicated an interest in participating in follow-up sessions after completion of their program.

After graduation, the LCL program sponsored two workshops for the 27 prospective administrators in Spring 2005. The workshops were geared toward helping the participants make the transition from the classroom to administration. One of the workshops provided strategies to prepare for the state certification exam. The second workshop provided an opportunity for participants to talk to directors of personnel from each of the four districts to get tips and strategies on completing an application and interviewing.

A focus group was conducted after graduation with the 27 students. These data as well as other program information data provide evidence of a commitment to self-study, learning, and reflection, attributes of LCL.

Indications of District Buy-In: Administrator Promotions

During this professional development program, 34 LCL program participants received promotions. As of June 30, 2005, five prospective administrators moved from teaching to assistant principal positions. With the rising administrators, five moved from intervention specialists to assistant principal positions and 18 participants moved from assistant principal to principal positions. Three of the accomplished administrators moved from the principal position to assistant superintendent positions. Three other accomplished administrators moved from the principal to district level director positions. Table 3.9 provides a summary of the information.

Greater Importance Placed on Learning Role Definitions of Rising Administrators

In the 1st year of the program, rising administrators completed the TELSA—*Training and Educational Leader Self Assessment* instrument (United States Department of Energy, 1998) to assess professional development needs.

Eighteen months later, 19 of these administrators retook the TELSA (at the end of the 2nd year of the program). Though the results and changes are not statistically significant and cannot be attributed solely to the program, they are supportive of project goals. In completing the TELSA administrators must assess the difficulty, importance, and frequency of tasks within 10 general leadership categories. The consistent change that is evident in the table is in the importance given to leadership tasks related to instruction. These tasks related directly to leadership and learning, rather than budgeting, crisis, or staff-related duties. This finding is significant because the focus of the program is on LCL and linking leadership to instruction. The results are listed below.

The LCL program focused attention on leaders as model learners. Learner-centered leaders need to drive learning by modeling processes of reflection, rejuvenation, and improvement through learning. The positive scores in Table 3.11 indicate greater recognition of the importance of instruction to rising administrators. Most of the rising administrators were assistant principals, and much of their daily action is associated with discipline and crisis management. As new assistant principals, they may have anticipated that less time would be spent dealing with these crises. As they gained knowledge and experience, they came to realize the importance of instruction.

An indicator of participation and effectiveness of LCL activities is the feedback that was received from participants during workshops and institutes. Table 3.12 provides the average scores in eight categories. Participants rated each of these categories using a Likert-type scale of 1 to 4 (1 = *not at all satisfied*; 2 = *somewhat satisfied*; 3 = *mostly satisfied*; 4 = *very satisfied*). The final average score given in the table is based on the feedback results from 23 workshops that were held between February 2003 and June 2005. The av-

TABLE 3.9
Promotion (Participants within each group) (June 15, 2005)

Group	Yr 1	Yr 2	Yr 3	Total
Prospective Administrators	0	1	4	5
Rising Administrators	9	5	9	23
Accomplished Administrators	3	1	2	6

TABLE 3.10

TELSA Average Results (Rising Administrators, February 1, 2003)

Category	Difficulty	Importance	Frequency	Sum
Lead analysis design and development	2.84	3.46	4.1	10.4
Lead implementation of instruction	2.24	4.2	2.93	9.37
Lead evaluation of instruction	2.39	3.69	3.66	9.74
Lead staff development	2.48	4.01	3.46	9.95
Learner-related duties	1.86	4.49	2.2	8.55
Staff-related duties	2.42	4.43	3.32	10.17
Budget & other admin. duties	2.83	4.2	3.9	10.93
Communication skills	1.83	4.0	2.58	8.41
Self-development	2.34	4.55	1.6	8.49
Crisis management	2.09	4.58	3.87	10.54

Use the following scale to interpret total scores.

Score of 3-7-No formal training or development necessary-address your specific needs through reading and/or coaching from a mentor.

Score of 8-11-Initial formal training and development necessary (train one time). Take a college or commercial training course. Attend a seminar.

Score of 12-15-Initial and on-going formal training and development necessary. Take a college or commercial training course, attend a seminar. Follow up with refresher courses and seminar

TABLE 3.11

Average Difference in Pre/Post Scores on TELSA (N=19)

Category	Difficulty	Importance	Frequency	Sum
Lead analysis design instruction	-0.3530	.095	-0.114	-0.372
Implement instruction	-0.1920	.053	-0.312	-0.451
Lead evaluation of instruction	-0.5460	.047	-0.361	-0.86
Lead staff development	-0.37	-0.307	-0.332	-1.009
Learner duties	-0.204	-0.534	-0.248	-0.986
Staff duties	-0.702	-0.671	-0.298	-1.671
Budget, other admin. duties	-0.534	-0.496	-0.268	-1.298
Communication	-0.191	-0.219	-0.001	-0.411
Self development	-0.501	-0.4610	.118	-0.844
Crisis management	-0.287	-0.3950	.299	-0.383
Average change	-0.388	-0.2888	-0.1517	-0.436

TABLE 3.12

Results From Feedback Forms (Based upon feedback from 23 workshops
held between February 2003 and June 2005)(Average Response Rate-72%)

Question	Average Rating
Overall Satisfaction	3.6
Build Understanding	3.56
Comfortable Facilities	3.78
Organization and Value of the Information	3.6
Achieve Desired Objectives	3.6
Build Relationships	3.67
Progress with Mentoring	3.52
Action Plans	3.7

erage participant response rate with the feedback forms was 72%. Overall, the scores reflect a general satisfaction with the content of the LCL activities and the processes used to facilitate mentoring and professional development for participating administrators.

Another indicator of participation is the average attendance rates of the participating districts at LCL activities and workshops. Table 3.13 provides a comparison of Year One (February 2003–January 2004) and Year Two (February 2004–January 2005) attendance rates for the four districts involved in LCL activities. A concerted effort was made by the liaisons to increase participation and the rates indicate the success of their efforts.

POINTS TO PONDER

A mentoring model is a way to foster learning for professional development, and as a way to build university-district and interdistrict collaboration. Research has shown the importance of mentoring for prospective administrators who are in the process of learning through internships (Crow & Matthews, 1998; Daresh & Playko, 1992; Martin, Wright, Danzig, Flanary, & Brown, 2005) as well as rising administrators who may be in their first years in administration (Daresh, 2001; Daresh & Playko, 1997). In ideal circumstances, mentoring provides the wisdom that comes from experience, while promoting for reflection and autonomy of action.

TABLE 3.13

Average Rate of Attendance by District-Years One and Two (in percent)

District	Year One	Year Two
Alhambra	73	76
Creighton	64	73
Phoenix Union	60	70
Roosevelt	58	74

Effective mentoring relationships require a level of trust, respect, ethics, and communication (Hay, 1995; Johnson, 1997; Shea, 1994). To engage in intense dialogue about difficult and complicated issues in meaningful ways, participants must establish a level of trust including the insurance that confidences will not be betrayed. Along with this, the participants must respect opinions and experiences that each brings to the mentoring relationship. Without this mutual respect, learning may not occur as a result of the dialogue and mentoring. Finally, mentoring is about effective communication that embraces listening and providing constructive feedback. This does not mean that ideas and opinions should not be challenged. On the contrary, a mentoring relationship encourages shifting of thoughts, roles, and ideas. At times, this requires confrontation, but if the relationship is built on trust, respect, and ethics, then the result of this confrontation will be administrative learning and professional development. To ensure that the appropriate foundation is set to engage in these difficult conversations, relationships need to be formed that reflect trust, respect, and communication.

CONCLUSION

During the past 18 months, the LCL program has been focusing on the building of relationships so that participants have the capacity to embed the mentoring model into their daily practices. Although the four districts are in close proximity with each other, they historically have done little interdistrict planning or sharing of resources and expertise. One of the goals of the grant project has been to ensure that interdistrict collaboration occurred. For this reason, it was important for the project team to begin breaking down barriers that may have existed at the very beginning of the grant project. The goal was to accomplish this through a three-fold process: formal activities and workshops that introduced each district and its administrators including needs and expectations; informal activities that broke down personal barriers and developed a pattern of networking; and participation in activities that focus on team building. The three elements provided a comprehensive plan for building interdistrict relationships that create the capacity for effective mentoring.

The second part of this chapter describes the LCL program and some of the preliminary results for participants. The LCL program is composed of multiple goals and activities. Participants meet with peers and with mentors on a regular basis. There are district-wide meetings with opportunities to share information and seek help when needed. There are also cross-district meetings, workshops, and institutes that have been developed collaboratively among the participating mentors and the university project team. Mentoring, action planning, book study groups, and workshops all sought to maintain autonomy, tie into current work, and encourage social learning and principles of LCL. All activities and action are built around this view of leader as learner.

REFERENCES

American Psychological Association. (1997). *Learner-centered psychological principles: A framework for school redesign and reform.* Retrieved October 13, 2004, from http://www.apa.org/ed/lcp.html

Bransford, J., Brown, A., & Cocking, R. (1999). *How people learn: Brain, mind, experience, and school.* Washington, DC: National Academy Press.

Crow, G., & Matthews, L. J. (1998). *Finding one's way: How mentoring can lead to dynamic leadership.* Thousand Oaks, CA: Corwin.

Danzig, A. (2002). *Learner-centered leadership for language and culturally diverse schools in high need urban settings.* Grant Application to USDoE, Office of Innovation and School Improvement un NCLB, Title II, Subpart 5, Section 2151, School Leadership. Arizona State University, Tempe, AZ.

Danzig, A., Kiltz, G., Osanloo, A., Szecsy, E., Wiley, T., Boyle, C., et al. (2004). Creating an environment for learner centered leadership in schools: First-year rationales, experiences, and findings from the learner centered leadership grant project. In C. Carr & C. Fulmer (Eds.), *Educational leadership: Knowing the way, going the way, showing the way 2004 NCPEA yearbook.* Lanham, MD: Scarecrow Education.

Daresh, J. (2001). *Leaders helping leaders: A practical guide to administrative mentoring.* Thousand Oaks, CA: Corwin.

Daresh, J., & Playko, M. (1992). *The professional development of school administrators: Preservice, induction, and inservice applications.* Boston: Allyn & Bacon.

Daresh, J., & Playko, M. (1997). *Beginning the principalship: A practical guide for new school leaders.* Thousand Oaks, CA: Corwin.

Desimone, L., Porter, A., Garet, M., Yoon, K., & Birman, B. (2002). Effects of professional development on teachers' instruction: Results from a Three-year Longitudinal Study. *Educational Evaluation and Policy Analysis, 24*(2), 81–112.

Fenwick, L., & Pierce, M. (2002, December). *Professional development of principals.* Washington, DC: ERIC Clearinghouse on Teaching and Teacher Education,

Guskey, T. (2000). *Evaluating professional development.* Thousand Oaks, CA: Corwin.

Hansman, C. A. (2001). Context-based adult learning. In S. B. Merriam (Ed.), *The new update on adult learning theory #89* (pp. 43–51). San Francisco: Jossey-Bass.

Harkins, P. (1999). *Powerful conversations: How high impact leaders communicate.* New York: McGraw-Hill.

Hay, J. (1995). *Transformational mentoring: Creating developmental alliances for changing organizational cultures.* New York: McGraw-Hill.

Holland, H. (2005). Teaching teachers: Professional development to improve student achievement. *Research Points: Essential Information for Education Policy, 3*(1), 1–4.

Johnson, H. (1997). *Mentoring for exceptional performance.* Glendale, CA: Griffin.

Knowles, M. (1980). *The modern practice of adult education: From pedagogy to andragogy.* Englewood Cliffs, NJ: Cambridge Adult Education.

Kiltz, G., Danzig, A., & Szecsy, E. (2004). Learner centered leadership: An emerging mentoring model for the professional development of school administrators. *Mentoring & Tutoring, 12*(2), 135–153.

Kiltz, G., & Danzig, A. (2003, 2004, 2005). *Learner-centered leadership for language and culturally diverse schools in high need urban settings: Annual performance reports-years one, two, and three.* Tempe, AZ: Arizona State University.

Lave, J., & Wenger, E. (1991). *Situated learning: Legitimate peripheral participation.* New York: Cambridge.

Lovely, S. (2004). Scaffolding for new leaders; coaching and mentoring helps rookie principals grow on the job and gain confidence. *School Administrator, 61*(6).

Martin, G., Wright, W., & Danzig, A., Flanary, R., & Brown, F. (2005). *School leader internship* (2nd ed.). Larchmont, NY: Eye On Education.

Merriam, S. (2001a). Andragogy and self-directed learning: Pillars of adult learning theory. In S. B. Merriam (Ed.), *The new update on adult learning theory #89* (pp. 3–14). San Francisco: Jossey-Bass.

Merriam, S. (2001b). Something old, something new: Adult learning theory for the twenty-first century. In S. B. Merriam (Ed.), *The new update on adult learning theory #89* (pp. 93–96). San Francisco: Jossey-Bass.

Pierce, J., & Kalkman, D. (2003). Applying learner-centered principles in teacher education. *Theory Into Practice, 42*(2), 127–132.

Robbins, P., & Alvy, A. (2004). *The new principal's fieldbook: Strategies for success.* Virginia: Association for Supervisors and Curriculum Development. *39*, 78–79.

Shea, G. (1994). *Mentoring: Helping employees reach their full potential.* New York: American Management Association.

Starratt, R. (2003). *Centering educational administration: Cultivating meaning, community, responsibility.* Mahwah, NJ: Lawrence Erlbaum Associates, Inc.

United States Department of Education. (2002). *Application for grants under the school leadership program.* Washington, DC: United States Department of Education.

United States Department of Energy. (1998). *TELSA—Training and educational leader self assessment.* Carlsbad, CA: Author.

Zepeda, J. (2003). *The principal as instructional leader: A handbook for supervisors.* New York: Eye on Education.

4

Conceptual Foundations for Principal Leadership

G. Thomas Bellamy
University of Washington, Bothell

Connie L. Fulmer
Michael J. Murphy
Rodney Muth
University of Colorado at Denver

As principals confront challenges of school leadership, they depend on both their tacit, craft knowledge (Polanyi, 1962) developed over a career in schools as well as the more formal knowledge that is shared among members of the school-leadership profession. Rather than drawing solely on their experiences to achieve desired results, principals need to rely more on the profession's shared knowledge because of the challenges and increasing complexity of problems of practice.

As pressures for immediate accountability for student learning have intensified in recent years, school leaders have been criticized for not using scientific research in their strategic and daily decisions, for not relying more on the results of educational and social sciences to guide practice (Shavelson & Towne, 2002). Such criticism is not new and has been a theme for many years as the profession has invested in development and organization of knowledge to support practice (Griffiths, 1959; Thompson, 1993).

However, many individuals have pointed out that good reasons may exist for the limited use of research-based knowledge. Hills (1978), for example, was among the first to note that university discipline-based research is not very useful to administrators who must wrestle with daily problems of practice. Most professions, he argued, organize scientific knowledge around problems that practitioners face, allowing them to draw easily on the knowledge to address a particular problems. Similarly, Merton (1967) observed that social science theories are mostly descriptive, of the "middle range," and incomplete as prescriptions for action in problem situations.

Still others have noted that the problems that principals face require more than the technical solutions that are offered through positivist research paradigms (Donmoyer, 2001; Griffiths, 1991; Lincoln & Guba, 1985). The problems that school leaders address most often reflect normative judgments about what is important about schooling, and the actions taken have moral consequences that resonate throughout the school community (Sergiovanni, 1996). Consequently, though principals need the support that professional knowledge can offer as they confront contemporary challenges of school leadership, that knowledge will be useful only if it is inclusive of both normative and technical elements and if it is organized around practical challenges as Hills (1978) and others endorse.

As part of a larger effort to explore the links between knowledge and practice in school leadership, we propose in this chapter a way to organize professional knowledge for school leadership that is directly linked to a reconceptualization of leadership practice. By doing so, we hope to stimulate greater use of professional knowledge by practitioners and greater interest in knowledge structure among our colleagues in universities and professional associations. Elsewhere, we have focused on principal leadership in the context of cumulative annual cycles in the life of a school and asked how the craft knowledge that emerges from this leadership might be collected, codified, and shared more systematically (Muth, Bellamy, Fulmer, & Murphy, 2004). Here, we supplement this holistic view of leadership with an analytical approach that focuses on separate components of a principal's role and the knowledge that supports these components.

Our suggestions for organizing knowledge around discrete components of principals' work builds on Hills' (1978) recommendation to structure knowledge around problems of practice and on several previous efforts to implement these recommendations (Forsyth & Tallerico, 1993; Thompson, 1993). What is new in our approach is our simultaneous proposal for a way of thinking about school leadership practice and a way of organizing knowledge to support that practice.

PRINCIPAL PRACTICE AS STEWARDSHIP FOR SCHOOL ACCOMPLISHMENTS

The work of school leadership can be usefully viewed as *fostering and sustaining school conditions* that at once enable expected student learning and express community values about what constitutes effective schools. These school conditions—such as the climate that students experience, the instruction that they receive, the organizational support that teachers experience, or the partnership with families that the school maintains—serve as intermediate results that link the daily work of school leadership with the goals that schools are expected to achieve.

School goals are complex, and this is reflected in the nature of the conditions that principals strive to sustain. Communities and their elected leaders have ambitious expectations for *what students should learn*, and they also have strong feelings about *what schools should be an do*, because children do much of their growing up in school. School conditions need to support both; that is, schools need to provide instrumental support for learning and to adapt to normative community expectations about schooling.

We call these school conditions *accomplishments* to highlight their important implications for leaders. Pulled from literature on human performance in organizations (Gilbert, 1978), the term *accomplishment* describes the conditions, or results, that are achieved through organizational processes. The accomplishments deriving from these processes reflect theories of action (Merton, 1967) about how to achieve goals by influencing the conditions over which some control can be exerted. In essence, then, organizational accomplishments address the question, "What conditions or intermediate results are most important in achieving the profit, esteem, learning, funding, status, sustainability, or other essential outcomes that an organization most wants to achieve?"

The concept of an accomplishment contains two perspectives that seem particularly useful when thinking about school leadership. First, accomplishments differentiate the conditions that result from a leader's or some other organizational actions from the actions themselves. These conditions then are evaluated as worthy or good based on *success criteria*, which define the desired, or quality, features of an accomplishment. For example, when a principal says that the school climate should be welcoming for all students, focused on academic achievement, and characterized by close student–teacher relationships, he or she is describing success criteria for the accomplishment, *student climate*.

Second, our accomplishment perspective encourages an eclectic and pragmatic approach to realizing accomplishments according to their success criteria. When success criteria for school accomplishments reflect community values and expectations, achieving those criteria is more important than adherence to any particular approach. Thus, to realize accomplishments in a variety of school conditions, school leaders need a deep repertoire of alternative strategies and approaches to the important accomplishments in a school's annual cycles.

Taken together, these two ideas—success criteria for quality results supported by a broad repertoire of action strategies—suggest that *principals lead by defining values and goals*, to establish success criteria for school accomplishments, *and by taking action*, to achieve the success criteria so defined. In this view, means and ends constantly interact in school leadership, and principals approach each aspect of their work with attention to what values should inform success criteria and what strategies will best achieve those criteria.

This way of thinking about school leadership raises three questions that our professional knowledge ultimately must address: (a) What accomplishments, or school conditions, are important enough to require principal attention? (b) What success criteria, or features of these accomplishments, support both student learning and community values for school success? (c) What leadership strategies and actions could be helpful in reaching those success criteria in different school circumstances? Thus, if professional knowledge is organized pragmatically and usefully, then it will focus explicitly on problems of practice.

THE FRAMEWORK FOR SCHOOL LEADERSHIP ACCOMPLISHMENTS

The Framework for School Leadership Accomplishments (FSLA) defines a set of school conditions that school leaders attempt to create, maintain, or improve in their schools through which they enable student learning and express community values (Bellamy, 1999; Bellamy, Fulmer, Murphy, & Muth, 2003). Though many alternate conceptualizations are possible, the FSLA defines a comprehensive and economical set of school conditions that require systematic attention from school leaders. Each set of conditions requires leadership to define success criteria and to support needed action. It is important to note that these school conditions are not actions, values, or success criteria, because these are embedded in the definition of accomplishments.

The FSLA (see Fig. 4.1) consists of nine accomplishments organized to reflect paths of influence on student learning. Four accomplishments frame the *environment for learning* in a school and affect learning by influencing the direction and

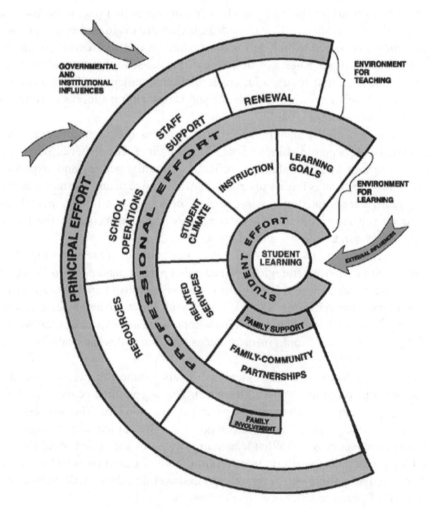

Figure 4.1.   Framework for School Leadership Accomplishments (Adapted from Bellamy, 1999; Copyright G. T. Bellamy. Used with Permission.).

level of student effort. Four other accomplishments reflect the *structure of a school environment for teaching* and affect student learning by influencing the level and focus of professional effort. A ninth accomplishment, *family–community partnership*, affects student learning by influencing both student effort and professional effort. Each of these accomplishments is linked to student learning through one or more intermediate results, shown in the shaded portions of the figure, which illustrates dependence on the effort of teachers, family members, and students themselves. The open space to the right of Fig. 4.1 symbolizes the many influences on *student learning, student effort, family involvement, family support,* and *professional effort* over which the school exerts little or no influence. For example, the economic status of the community and its recreational opportunities or the attractiveness of television that may compete with studying are all important influences on student learning but are largely outside professional control.

To clarify the FSLA, we briefly explain each accomplishment and then rationalize each one—why it is important in promoting valued student learning—and outline current research and strategies associated with each accomplishment. In Tables 4.1–4.9, we supplement this short discussion with illustrations of how professional knowledge can be organized by asking two questions: (a) what constitutes quality in the accomplishment and (b) what action strategies are potentially useful in a principal's pursuit of excellence in the accomplishment?

The Environment for Learning

The environment for learning includes those aspects of the school that have a direct influence on student learning. The accomplishments, which are directly adjacent to student learning and impact *student effort*, cluster in the first tier of the figure: the nature of the *learning goals* that are defined, the quality of the *instruction* that is provided, the *climate* that is sustained for students, and the *related services* that are provided. The fifth accomplishment in the learning environment, *family–community partnerships*, affects student learning indirectly, primarily through the support that students receive outside the school.

Student Effort. Student effort is the intermediate result that the five accomplishments associated with the school's learning environment are intended to influence. Student effort yields student learning; whereas school professionals seek to influence the level and direction of student effort, they cannot control it.

Student effort—showing up, paying attention, studying, trying hard—evolves from discussions of student engagement (Marks, 2000; Steinberg, 1996). Student effort emphasizes student work in learning (Schlechty, 1990), though not excluding other aspects of engagement, such as psychological connection. Most current measures of student effort rely on student responses to questionnaires, although other measures, like attendance, tardiness, and homework-completion rates, further depict student effort.

Learning Goals Defined. Learning goals are the formal statements used by school professionals to define what students are expected to learn—the intended curriculum. Learning goals encompass content standards, exit outcomes, and graduation requirements and refer to the knowledge that students are expected to demonstrate. They also frame both educational destinations and milestones, shaping what is taught and learned and providing the basis for assessments of learning (Beane, 1995).

Knowledge supporting the definition of success criteria for this accomplishment includes the implications of various curriculum ideologies (Eisner, 1992), legal requirements like those related to individualized program planning for children with disabilities, discussions of nonacademic learning goals (Goble & Brooks, 1983; Solomon, Watson, & Battistich, 2001), and critical perspectives on curriculum and its impact on marginalized students (Apple, 1999; Simon, 1992). Knowledge supporting a principal's action repertoire includes, for example, strategies for developing performance goals for various content standards (Marzano & Kendall, 1996) and aligning these expectations with various grade and developmental levels (Bereiter & Scardemalia, 1992), criteria for evaluating textbooks (Tanner, 1988), and approaches to leading local curriculum deliberations (Reid, 1978). Table 4.1 illustrates examples of the professional knowledge that supports principal leadership for the learning goals accomplishment.

Instruction Provided.   In many ways, the concept of instruction is inseparable from that of curriculum: The learning goals actually implemented are always mediated by the actions and priorities of individual teachers and students. Instruction involves interactions among teachers, students, and subject matter. To define instruction as an accomplishment involves specifying the results that are expected from these interactions, rather than the associated behaviors and processes. From this perspective, instruction constitutes the tasks or assignments expected of students, together with the social and physical context supporting task completion. As Doyle (1983, 1992) suggested, instruction involves three essential components:

> (1) a goal or end state to be accomplished, (2) a problem space or set of conditions and resources (e.g., information, tools) available to accomplish the task; and (3) the operations (thoughts and actions) involved in assembling and using resources to reach the goal state. (1992, p. 504)

Of course, the nature of the tasks—their relationship with desired goals, their cognitive demands, their relationship to students' current understandings—determine their effectiveness in promoting desired learning. These features comprise important aspects of the success criteria for this accomplishment.

Table 4.2 provides examples of professional knowledge supporting the instruction accomplishment. To establish success criteria, principals can draw on theory and research related to the cognitive demands of various instructional tasks (Bransford, Brown, & Cocking, 2001), debates and research on the use of incentives (Cameron & Pierce, 1994; Kohn, 1993), and research and critical perspectives on differential student treatment by gender and race in typical classrooms (Sadker & Sadker, 1982; Scott & McCollum, 1993). Knowledge supporting a principal's action repertoire includes, for example, the competing theoretical frameworks about teaching and learning (Richardson, 2001), research on and meta-analyses of instructional strategies (Marzano, 2003; Wang, Haertel, & Walberg, 1993), classroom assessment techniques

TABLE 4.1

Examples of Professional Knowledge Related to the Learning Goals Accomplishment

	Ethical and Critical Reasoning	Legal Reasoning	Social Science Research	Craft Knowledge
Knowledge supporting definition of success criteria	Knowledge of debates regarding the proper emphasis on moral education and character development in the school's curriculum (Molnar, 1997). Understanding of critical perspectives on curriculum that reflect concerns of cultural and linguistic minorities, gender, and disability groups (Apple, 1999; Biklen & Pollard, 1993; Noddings, 1992; Payne, 1998).

Understanding the implications of various ideologies for judgments on curriculum quality (Cibulka, 1999; Eisner, 1992). | Authority of school districts to define curriculum within a standard of educational purposes and reasonableness (Alexander & Alexander, 2003). | Research on the impact of curriculum exposure and achievement (Brewer & Stasz, 1996; Gamoran, Porter, Smithson, & White, 1997; McDonnell, 1995).

Knowledge of research and theory related to curriculum structure and design (Goodlad & Su, 1992; Wiggins & McTighe, 1998). | |
| Knowledge supporting principal's action repertoire | Skills for leading local curriculum deliberations and justifying curriculum decisions (Reid, 1978; Scheffler, 1958).

Knowledge of advocacy for inclusion of indigenous cultures and languages in the curriculum (Nee-Benham & Cooper, 2000). | Knowledge of content standards adopted in state and district policy (Marzano & Kendall, 1996).

Process requirements for setting goals for children with disabilities through the Individualized Educational Program (Rothstein, 2000). | Knowledge for enhancing learning and transfer through use of contrasting cases (Bransford, Brown, & Cocking,, 2001; Englemann & Carnine, 1982). Understanding typical sequences in children's content-domain knowledge development for evaluating curriculum sequences (Bereiter & Scardemalia, 1992). | Skills in developing and evaluating effective benchmarks and performance goals associated with state and district standards (Marzano & Kendall, 1996).

Leadership strategies for focusing the school on curriculum goals (Glatthorn, 2000). |

TABLE 4.2

Examples of Professional Knowledge Related to the Instruction Accomplishment

	Ethical and Critical Reasoning	Legal Reasoning	Social Science Research	Craft Knowledge
Knowledge supporting definition of success criteria	Knowledge about the moral choices that are embedded in normal classroom interactions (Campbell, 2001; Oser, 1994) Knowledge of descriptive research and critical prespectives regarding differential treatment of various student groups in instructional interactions (Sadker & Sadker, 1982; Scott & McCollum, 1993; Sleeter & Grant, 1993). Knowledge of the implications of various religions, political affiliations, and cultures regarding what is and is not an appropriate educational experience (Gaddy, Hall, & Marzano, 1996; Spring, 2002).	Federal requirements for participation of students with disabilities in assessment programs (Lashley, 2002)	Knowledge of classroom conditions that effect learning (Danielson, 1996; Marzano, 2003; Wang, Haertel, & Walberg, 1993). An understanding of contemporary conceptualizations of how people learn and the implications of this knowledge for teaching (Bransford et al., 2001). Knowledge of research and theory on student motivation (Ames, 1992; Hidi & Harackiewicz, 2000; Wigfield, Eccles, & Rodriguez, 1998)	

Knowledge supporting principal's action repertoire	Knowledge of culture norms (cultural proficiency) and implications for classroom practice (Lindsey, Robbins, & Terrell, 1999).	An understanding of task assignment structures and how these can support task performance and learning (Doyle, 1992)	Knowledge of practical strategies for classroom rules, procedures, and organization (Doyle, 1986; Brophy, 1996).
		An understanding of nationally recognized and locally used assessments (Blythe, Allen, & Powell, 1999; Marzano, Pickering, & McTighe, 1993; Payne, 1997; Wiggins, 1993).	Knowledge of classroom startup activities (Wong & Wong, 1990).
		Knowledge of strategies for grouping students for instruction and adapting instruction for heterogeneous groups (Gay, 2000; Gersten & Baker, 2000; Miramontes, Nadeau, & Commins, 1997; Tilton, 1996).	
		Knowledge of formative assessment and instructional strategies that affect student learning (Bangert-Drowns, Kulik, Kulik, & Morgan, 1991; Black & Wiliam, 1998; Creemers, 1994; Good & Brophy, 1997; Marzano, Pickering, & Pollock, 2001; Rosenshine & Stevens, 1986).	
		Knowledge of programs and strategies for classroom behavior management (Baer, 1998; Burden, 1995; Everston, 1980).	
		Knowledge of effective instructional strategies and assignments for particular subjects and grade levels (Cunningham & Allington, 1999; West & Staub, 2003; Zemelman, Daniels, & Hyde, 1998).	

(Blythe, Allen, & Powell, 1999; Wiggins, 1993), and adaptations for students with diverse backgrounds and skills (Miramontes, Nadeau, & Commins, 1997).

Student Climate Sustained.   Learning goals and instruction frame only part of how students experience school life. Informal and social aspects of the school, or climate, also affect the effort that students spend and the learning that results. Student climate is variously described as the personality, feel, tone, atmosphere, character, and mood of a school. From an accomplishment perspective, student climate is the sum of a school's explicit and implicit messages to students about what is important as these are perceived and understood by individual students. Because students generally are able to describe what is important in their schools and classes (Anderson, 1982), their perceptions affect their beliefs, attributions, and motivations (Maehr & Fyans, 1989) and school attendance (Moos, 1978) and, thus, their learning (Walberg, Rasher, & Singh, 1977).

For success criteria, principals can draw on legal reasoning associated with nondiscrimination requirements and special protections associated with discipline of children in special education, many critical analyses of how school environments affect students from poor and minority communities (Delpit, 1995; Lomotey, 1990), and research on how various peer groups create opportunities and constraints for their members (Steinberg, 1996). A principal's action repertoire includes research and theory on student motivation (Wigfield, Eccles, & Rodriguez, 1998), alternative approaches to classroom and school-wide behavior management systems (Sugai & Horner, 2002), and knowledge of strategies for managing extracurricular activities (Otto, 1982). Table 4.3 provides examples of the professional knowledge that supports principal leadership for the student–climate accomplishment.

Related Services Provided.   Schools provide a variety of noninstructional services for students that are intended to support the student's educational goals. Though related service comes from special education legislation, where it refers to those services that are necessary for children to benefit from a school's educational program, most schools provide services to other children as well, and we broadly view related services to include transportation, school breakfast and lunch programs, college-preparation advising, special programs to reduce use of illegal drugs, speech and language therapy, and so on. From an accomplishment perspective, related services are the supports provided to students that help them benefit from instruction.

Success criteria for this accomplishment include program standards and codes of ethics recommended by various professional associations (American Psychological Association, 1981; American Speech-Language-Hearing Association, 2003; Moyers, 1999), research on effective practices in various professions (Thompson, 2002), and legal requirements associated with service eligibility. A principal's action repertoire is supported by research and theory on assessment of service needs and models for delivery of special services (Allensworth, Lawson, Nicholson, & Wyche, 1997; Damico, 1987; Garden & Liebemann, 1989; Miller, 1989). Table 4.4 includes examples of the professional knowledge that can help principals provide leadership for the related services accomplishment.

TABLE 4.3

Examples of Professional Knowledge Related to the Student Climate Accomplishment

	Ethical and Critical Reasoning	Legal Reasoning	Social Science Research	Craft Knowledge
Knowledge supporting definition of success criteria	Understanding of values that underlie the student communities proposed for various school designs (Boyer, 1995; Edison Project, 1994). Knowledge of critical analyses of how school environments affect students from poor and minority communities (Delpit, 1995; Lomotey, 1990).	Knowledge of student rights and discipline, freedom from harassment, and so on (LaMorte, 1999; Stein, 1999). Understanding of constraints on free speech in student activities and publications (Stewart, 1989). Knowledge of responsibility for supervision before, during, and after school hours (LaMorte, 1999). Understanding limits on religious expression by faculty/students (Fischer, Schimmer, & Kelly, 1995).	Knowledge of student climate characteristics that promote student learning (Edmonds, 1982; Joyce, Hersh, & McKibben, 1983; Levine & Lezotte, 1990). Knowledge of research on the importance of students' sense of belonging (Osterman, 2000)	
Knowledge supporting principal's action repertoire	Knowledge of strategies for implementing values of caring and justice (Beck, 1993; Noddings, 1999).	Knowledge of due process rights: disciplinary suspension, expulsion, and transfer of students (McCarthy, Cambron-McCabe, & Thomas, 2004). Knowledge of the effects of peer group membership on students' experience of school climate (Steinberg, 1996). Knowledge of strategies to assess and influence school cultures (Peterson & Deal, 1999; 2002).	Knowledge of behavior-management systems that include clear expectations/ defined roles for teachers, the principal, and others (Baer, 1998; Sugai & Horner 2002; Nelson & Martella, 1998). Knowledge of strategies for creating economically and culturally inclusive school climates (Cushner, McClelland, & Safford, 1996)	Knowledge of strategies for and effects of extracurricular activities (Otto, 1982).

TABLE 4.4

Examples of Professional Knowledge Related to the Related Services Accomplishment

	Ethical and Critical Reasoning	Legal Reasoning	Social Science Research	Craft Knowledge
Knowledge supporting definition of success criteria		Knowledge of legal foundations and constraints for delivery of related services (Fischer & Sorenson, 1996)	Knowledge of the potential impact of community organizations on youth development and the strategies that make these organizations successful (McLaughlin, 2000).	Professional association standards for delivery of related services (American Psychological Association, 1981; American Speech-Language-Hearing Association, 2003; Moyers, 1999).
Knowledge supporting principal's action repertoire		Knowledge of assessment and eligibility requirements and associated processes associated with special education and related services (Burnette, 2000; Gorn, 1997).	Knowledge of research-based practices and professional practice recommendations in the various related services (Thomas & Grimes, 2002; Thompson, 2002). Knowledge of strategies for integrating education, health, and social services (Casella, 2002; Eilers, 2002).	Knowledge of strategies for coordinating school and community services (Cibulka & Kirtek, 1996). Knowledge of organizational models for delivery of special services (Allensworth, Lawson, Nicholson, & Wiche, 1997; Damico, 1987; Garden & Liebemann, 1989; Miller, 1989).

The Environment for Teaching

The quality of the environment for learning depends on the effort of the school's staff. Consistently striving for excellence in the learning environment for all students requires extraordinary commitment. Schools and their principals provide direct support for professional effort through four accomplishments clustered in the second tier of Figure 4.1. Schools (a) obtain resources to support their operations, (b) allocate those resources to support daily operations, (c) provide supports for the staff, and (d) establish processes for organizational change and renewal. The fifth accomplishment, family–community partnerships, influences professional effort indirectly, through the initial impact of parent involvement in the school. The quality with which these accomplishments are realized affects the level and focus of professional effort, which in turn influences the environment for learning, and, ultimately, student effort and learning.

Professional Effort.   Like for most organizations, the motivation and skills of a school's employees is critical to the work necessary to achieve its goals. Schools rely on their ability to influence professional effort, because the difference between very successful schools and others is often the extraordinary effort that teachers commit to instruction and relationship-building with students and parents.

The accomplishments associated with a school's environment for teaching influence many aspects of professional effort (McLaughlin, Talbert, & Bascia, 1990): (a) teacher motivation, reflecting personal willingness to exert energy on school tasks and goals; (b) conception of task, including an understanding of the many responsibilities associated with student achievement; (c) enthusiasm over subject matter, or the excitement that teachers communicate to students about their subjects; and (d) sense of efficacy, the teacher's belief that he or she can make a difference. Though important, the school environment represents only one of many influences on these aspects of professional effort. Also influential are the larger organizational and professional contexts: district and state policies associated with teaching, the community's expectations, affiliation with professional organizations, and, of course, a variety of individual circumstances.

Resources Mobilized.   All schools depend on fiscal, human, and material resources to reach their goals, and school leaders typically must seek these resources from the school district, community, families, and other sources. To garner resources that the school can apply to meet its purposes, principals complete budget proposals, recruit volunteers, write grants, request needed services, and so on. In essence, this accomplishment is about the school's external communications about its needs, plans, programs, and resources.

Many schools must now recruit students and parents. Choice, open enrollment, charters, vouchers, and home schooling all create alternatives for families when they believe that a particular school is not the best situation for their child. Enrollment management is an important part of how a school sustains its resource base, because school funding often depends on the number of students served. Consequently, the resources mobilized accomplishment includes such areas as orienting new parents, school tours, and other marketing strategies.

Table 4.5 illustrates various sources of professional knowledge supporting leadership for the resources accomplishment. Knowledge that can help principals define success criteria includes legal requirements associated with federal and state programs that offer school funding and the controversies about the impact of increased funding on school quality (National Research Council, 1999). To develop action repertoires, principals draw, for example, on knowledge of program planning (Kaufman, Herman, & Watters, 1996), grant writing (Bauer, 1999), volunteer programs (Brown, 1998), school–university partnerships (Goodlad, 1988), and school marketing (Holcomb, 1993; Warner, 1994).

School Operations Organized and Supported.   To support daily operations with the resources that they have, schools use a variety of organizational structures, policies, job assignments, schedules, and plans. These details of school operations create the work of the school, clarifying (a) what is to be done; (b) who will do it; (c) when it will be done; (d) where the work will be located; (e) what equipment, information, and supplies are available to support it; (f) what standards exist for performance; (g) who will evaluate the work; and (h) what help is available. Viewed this way, school-operations management is an important part of the overall leadership of the school (Leithwood, 1994), not just a separate and less important management function. Support for school operations includes allocation of physical, human, fiscal, and information resources.

For success criteria, principals can draw on foundational knowledge that helps them mediate conflicts about allocation of time, talent, equipment, and funds. Important knowledge includes both critical perspectives on how school-operations decisions such as tracking affect various student groups (Oakes, 1985) and legal requirements associated with maintenance of and access to school facilities. Knowledge supporting a principal's action repertoire includes such topics as school scheduling models (Canady, 1988), research and theory on organizational structuring, and craft knowledge on use of paraprofessionals in schools (French, 2001; Skelton, 1997). Table 4.6 provides examples of the professional knowledge that support principals' leadership for the operations accomplishment.

Staff Supported.   Schools make long-term investments in teachers and other staff and then depend on these individuals' work as the primary means of achieving organizational goals. This accomplishment includes the implicit and explicit messages that teachers receive from the principal and school about what is expected, together with the social and administrative support that they receive to meet those expectations. Schools and their principals work toward this accomplishment through activities associated with a broad range of human-resource functions, including staff supervision, evaluation, and professional development, along with strategies to foster strong cultures, shared values, and high motivation. Different views of the nature of teacher work and characteristics of schools as organizations lead to contrasting approaches to these human resource functions. Broad agreement, however, underscores the functions that are important influences on teacher commitment (Firestone & Pennell,

TABLE 4.5

Examples of Professional Knowledge Related to the Resources Accomplishment

	Ethical and Critical Reasoning	Legal Reasoning	Social Science Research	Craft Knowledge
Knowledge supporting definition of success criteria	Knowledge of competing values associated with school resource development such as efficiency, effectiveness, equity, and adequacy (Odden & Picus, 2004)	Knowledge of major state and federal programs, their budgets, and the associated requirements (U.S. Department of Education, 2000a; 2000b). Knowledge of state systems for financing schools (Odden, 1999)	Knowledge of features of effective branding and related communications (Holcomb, 1993; Warner, 1994	Knowledge of available programs and resources, including organizations making grants to schools.
Knowledge supporting principal's action repertoire	Knowledge current practices, controversies and critical perspectives concerning equity in the distribution of resources to schools and programs (Arnold, 1998; Picus, 2000)	Knowledge of the financial responsibilities of principals as public employees (Guthrie, 1980; Swanson & King, 1997).		Knowledge of effective grant writing (Bauer, 1999). Knowledge of recruitment, marketing, and community-relations strategies (Gallagher, Bagin, & Kindred, 2001; Warner, 1994). Knowledge of how to sustain partnership with business, universities, and other organizations (Firestone & Fisler, 2002; Goodlad, 1988). Skills in volunteer management (Brown, 1998). Knowledge of various planning, budgeting, and accounting systems (Herman & Herman, 1997; Kaufman, Herman, & Watters, 1996; Meyers, 1999).

TABLE 4.6

Examples of Professional Knowledge Related to the School Operations Accomplishment

	Ethical and Critical Reasoning	Legal Reasoning	Social Science Research	Craft Knowledge
Knowledge supporting definition of success criteria	Knowledge of critical and empirical investigations of the impact of tracking, inclusion, and other grouping strategies (Oakes, 1985).	Knowledge of legal requirements associated with access to and maintenance of school facilities (LaMorte, 1999). Understanding standards of care that apply to various job assignments in schools (Fischer, Schimmel, & Kelly, 1995; Fischer & Sorenson, 1996).	Research on the importance of instructional time and the implications for school schedules (Levine & Lezotte, 1990; Scheerens & Bosker, 1997). Knowledge of the micro-politics of school environments (Blase, 1989; Blase & Blase, 1998).	Understanding of accreditation standards associated with scheduled time and teacher expertise in various subjects (North Central Association Commission on Accreditation and School Improvement, 2001). Knowledge of potential benefits or organizing schools into small learning communities (Meier, 1996).
Knowledge supporting principal's action repertoire			Knowledge of strategies for assigning and supervising paraprofessionals (French, 2003; Skelton, 1997). Knowledge of possible relationships between school structures and development of professional learning communities (Halverson, 2003).	Understanding of various scheduling models and the instructional goals and school purposes they support (Canady, 1988). Knowledge of facility and equipment management strategies (Castaldi, 1987; Kowalski, 2002). Knowledge of strategies for aligning resources with school goals (Odden & Archibald, 2000).

1993; Rosenholtz, 1989) often receive insufficient attention in the press of principals' daily responsibilities (Osborne & Wiggins, 1989).

Success criteria for the accomplishment are informed by contrasting perspectives on schools as technical and professional workplaces (Rowan, 1990), proposed standards for professional development (National Staff Development Council, 1995), and characteristics of leadership to enhance social capital and community (Smylie & Hart, 1999). Knowledge to support a principal's action repertoire includes topics like adult learning theories (Knowles, 1984; Merriam & Caffarella, 1991), models for teacher supervision and their conceptual foundations (Oja & Reiman, 1998), organizational communications research and theory (Shockley-Zalabak, 1999), and strategies for building cohesive school cultures (Deal & Peterson, 1990). Table 4.7 outlines examples of the profession's knowledge that support leadership toward the staff support accomplishment.

School Renewal Supported. To reach their accomplishments in ways that promote learning for all students, school professionals must constantly accommodate new students, parent expectations, required tests and curricula, technologies, school board policies, and program possibilities. Although schools are structured in ways that make change difficult (Sarason, 1982, 1990), stakeholders face continuing challenges to adapt to new expectations, adopt new practices, and adjust to new political realities.

Organizational change can require staff to give up familiar strategies in which they are very competent for new procedures that require a period of vulnerability and learning (Evans, 1996). Change can be stymied by cultural norms that are not apparent until threatened (Bolman & Deal, 1991). When successful, school renewal can create conflict and uneven acceptance (Hall & Hord, 1987). Renewal, without an overall strategy for adopting changes, can lead to pessimism and alienation. Clear organizational change processes that include feedback and improvement cycles appear related to teachers' commitment (Bacharach, Bamberger, Conley, & Bauer, 1990), expectations (Little, 1982), and involvement (Mohrman, Lawler, & Mohrman, 1992). Consequently, this accomplishment involves the processes and structures that a school has in place to provide itself feedback on its effectiveness, set goals for improvement, support implementation of new procedures, and evaluate results.

Table 4.8 illustrates areas of professional knowledge that inform leadership toward the school-renewal accomplishment. To define success criteria, principals can draw on knowledge about standards for quality improvements in organizations (Baldridge National Quality Program, 2002), alternative ways of framing the challenges of school improvement (Louis, Toole, & Hargreaves, 1999), and research on effective strategies for adoption of innovations (Hall & Hord, 1987). A principal's action repertoire is supported, in this case, by knowledge about human factors in the change process (Evans, 1996), strategies for data analysis and display (Barnhardt, 1998), and knowledge of action research strategies for organizational change (Lytle & Cochran-Smith, 1994).

Family and Community Partnerships Sustained

The school's partnership with families and communities is a part of both the environment for learning and the environment for teaching, because it has the potential to in-

TABLE 4.7

Examples of Professional Knowledge Related to the Staff Support Accomplishment

	Ethical and Critical Reasoning	Legal Reasoning	Social Science Research	Craft Knowledge
Knowledge Supporting Definition of Success Criteria	Knowledge of discussions of ethical dimensions of staff leadership (Begley, 2001). Knowledge of critical perspectives on teachers' work (Acker, 1995; Apple, 1986).	Knowledge of the legal foundations of collective bargaining and the content of local labor agreements (Murphy & Cresswell, 1980). Knowledge of the legal rights and responsibilities of teachers and other school staff with regard to freedom of expression, academic freedom, and professional conduct (Fischer et al., 1995; LaMorte, 1999).	Knowledge of research on factors that contribute to success of professional development (Garet, Porter, Desimone, Birman, & Yoon, 2001; Loucks-Horsley & Matsumoto, 1999). Knowledge of leadership features and characteristics that promote development of social capital and professional community (DuFour & Eaker, 1998; Smylie & Hart, 1999).	Knowledge of proposed standards for staff development, (U. S. Department of Education, 1995; National Staff Development Council, 1995).
Knowledge supporting principal's action repertoire	Understanding of the political, moral, and social issues that are inherent in teacher supervision and support (Ingersoll, 2003; Smyth & Garman, 1989).	Knowledge of procedural steps in handling personnel actions (Lawrence, Vachon, Leake, & Leake, 2001).	Knowledge of adult learning theories and approaches (Knowles, 1980, 1984; Merriam & Caffarella, 1991). Knowledge of strategies for sustaining strong cultures in schools (Bolman & Deal, 1991; Deal & Peterson, 1990; Ott, 1989). Knowledge of strategies and research on shared decision-making in schools (Conley, 1991; Murphy & Beck, 1995; Mohrman, Cohen, & Mohrman, 1995). Knowledge of strategies for influencing and supervising instruction (Blase & Blase, 1994, 2000; Danielson & McGreal, 2000; Glickman, Gordon, & Ross-Gordon, 2001; Hoy & Hoy, 2003; Oja & Reiman, 1998). Knowledge of strategies and norms that foster teacher collegiality and collaborative work (Barth, 1990; Blase & Blase, 2001; Louis, Marks, & Kruse, 1996; Schmuck & Runkel, 1994; Smylie & Hart, 1999. Knowledge of organizational communications research and theory (Shockley-Zalabak, 1999).	Knowledge of models and techniques for professional development (Gordon & Nicely, 1998; Journal of Staff Development).

Table 4.8

Examples of Professional Knowledge Related to the School Renewal Accomplishment

	Ethical and Critical Reasoning	Legal Reasoning	Social Science Research	Craft Knowledge
Knowledge supporting definition of success criteria	Knowledge of the critical and ethical bases of competing school purposes (Goodlad, 1996; Larson & Murtadha, 2002; Noddings, 1999). Understanding of professional codes of ethics and related debates (Shapiro & Stefkovich; 2001).	Knowledge of student and parent rights regarding confidentiality of data and records (Essex, 1999). Knowledge of state and local requirements for school improvement planning processes.	Results of school-based management and whole school reform evaluations (Berends, Bodilly, & Kirby, 2002; Conley, 1991; Murphy & Beck, 1995; Wohlstetter & Mohrman, 1993). Knowledge of the results of meta analyses and research summaries indicating the likely effects of various interventions (Lipsey & Wilson, 1993; Marzano, 2003; Scheerens & Bosker, 1997)	Understanding of current standards for quality improvements in organizations (Baldridge National Quality Program, 2002). Knowledge of innovative programs and practices that help to define possible school improvement visions and goals (e.g., Educational Leadership).
Knowledge supporting principal's action repertoire	Knowledge and skills for leading deliberations about school goals (Patterson, Grenny, McMillan, & Switzer, 2002; Reid, 1978). Knowledge associated with creating decision processes that are inclusive of diverse cultures and viewpoints (Onikama, Hammond, & Koki, 1998).		Knowledge about human factors and change process in organizations (Evans, 1996; Hargreaves, Earl, Moore, & Manning, 2001). Knowledge of research on school change strategies, including innovations, action research, professional development, and change implementation. (Fullan, 1985; Hall & Hord, 1987; Loucks-Horsley, Hewson, Love, & Stiles, 1998; Lytle & Cochran-Smith, 1994; McLaughlin et al., 1990). Knowledge of strategies for successful site-based management and decision-making (Beck & Murphy, 1996; Mohrman, Cohen, & Morhman, 1995; Robertson, Wohlstetter, & Mohrman, 1995).	Knowledge of strategies to increase participation and engagement of parents, students, teachers, and others in school decisions (Epstein, 2001). Knowledge of strategies for continuous quality improvement in schools and other organizations (e.g. American Association of School Administrators, 1991). Knowledge about design and use of school data systems that generate feedback about school and student performance (Barnhardt, 1998; Johnson, 2002).

fluence both student effort and professional effort. Though activities supporting families and community members are typically an integrated whole, the things that families and community members choose to do as a result of partnership expectations are different as they support student and professional effort.

Intermediate Results.   Family and community partnerships support student effort and learning through two intermediate results. Parent and community support involves the influences outside the school that contribute to or detract from student academic effort (Hale & Jackson, 1984). Children and adolescents spend the vast majority of their time at home and in other community settings, and the influences present in those settings have much to do with their academic effort and learning. Family and community support can promote student effort outside of school in many ways, including setting standards for school performance (Clark, 1993), collaborating with the school in solving problems (Henderson, 1987), approaching parenting in an authoritative way (Baumrind, 1978), establishing homework routines and reading to their children (Tizard, Schonfield, & Hevinson, 1982), creating a rich and positive language environment (Hart & Risley, 1995), and limiting television viewing (Steinberg, 1996).

The second intermediate result through which the family and community partnership affects schools is parent and community involvement. This includes a wide array of activities through which parents and community members support professional effort through their engagement in the school. Involvement can include, for example, volunteering in the school, participating in school councils, as well as encouraging and supporting teachers' work. Parents and community members can give stability to school programs by participating in school decisions, supporting the principal's staff recruitment and retention efforts, and assisting with special events.

Family and Community Partnerships Sustained.   To promote both involvement and support, this accomplishment comprises the full range of strategies through which school personnel share responsibility for child growth and learning with families and other community groups. Even though communication with parents is an essential component of these partnerships (Epstein, 2001; Rich, 1987), this accomplishment focuses on the results that are achieved through communication, including all of the influences exerted by parents and other community members to help children succeed in school. Work toward this accomplishment includes everything that school personnel do to encourage and assist parents to provide basic services to their children, serve as teachers in the home, and collaborate to solve learning difficulties. This professional work also includes strategies to engage parents in the operation of the school as volunteers and participants in discussions of school plans.

Table 4.9 provides examples of the knowledge areas that support leadership for the family–community partnership accomplishment. For success criteria, principals can use knowledge about cultural norms among different ethnic and economic groups (Lynch & Hanson, 1998), standards for family involvement programs (National Parent Teacher Association, 1998), research and theory on family systems, and legal requirements associated with family privacy. The principal's action repertoire is supported by knowledge about family involvement programs (Coleman, 1998), strategies for coordination of school and community services (Cibulka & Kirtek, 1996),

TABLE 4.9

Examples of Professional Knowledge Related to the Family-Community Partnership Accomplishment

	Ethical and Critical Reasoning	Legal Reasoning	Social Science Research	Craft Knowledge
Knowledge supporting definition of success criteria		Knowledge of legal constraints related to student records and privacy (Essex, 1999).		Knowledge of the standards for parent involvement proposed by the National Parent Teachers Association (1998).
Knowledge supporting principal's action repertoire	Understanding of economic, cultural and religious differences that can affect how parents prefer to and are able to share responsibilities with schools (Chavkin, 1983; Lopez, Scribner, & Mahitivanichcha, 2001; Onikama et al., 1998).	Understanding of the due process rights of families of children with disabilities (Boyle & Weishaar, 2001).	Skill in mediation and resolution of conflicts among school staff, family members, and the community (Girard & Koch, 1996; Whitaker & Fiore, 2001). Knowledge of strategies for programs like family literacy and parenting support (Brooks, Gorman, Harman, Hutchinson, & Wilkin, 1996; Morrow & Young, 1997).	Knowledge of programs and strategies for supporting parents and involving them is schools (Coleman, 1998; Epstein, 2001; Tangri & Moles, 1987). Knowledge of the structure, funding, and responsibilities of various social service, public safety, juvenile corrections, and health agencies with which a school might collaborate to increase student adjustment and achievement.

models for shared decision making in school governance (Carnegie Council on Adolescent Development, 1989), and programs like family literacy and parenting support
(Brooks, Gorman, Harman, Hutchinson, & Wilkin, 1996; Morrow & Young, 1997).

Principal Effort

Principal effort is a major factor affecting the quality of teaching and learning environments. Many studies cite principal leadership as a primary factor in a successful school
(Levine & Lezotte, 1990). Though district administrators and policymakers attempt to
influence principal effort in many ways, personal effort is directly under the control of
principals themselves. As a matter of personal and professional development, principal effort can be enhanced by factors similar to those emphasized by McLaughlin et al.
(1990) for teachers:

1. Conception of task, or development of a comprehensive understanding of the
    role and its expectations. The FSLA can serve as a mental model to help develop
    such a conception of task.
2. Sense of efficacy, or the degree to which a principal sees that he or she can influ-
    ence important aspects of the school. Having a well-organized personal knowl-
    edge base and a framework for categorizing new information can help, and the
    FSLA can serve as such a framework.
3. Motivation, or the positive effort that principals exert in their work. In this re-
    gard, honing emotional intelligence (Goleman, Boyatzis, & McKee, 2002)
    might provide a means of supporting positive motivation.

Principal effort also can influence (a) the principal's connection to and understanding of the school's community; (b) the correspondence between a principal's own values and those of the community, so that it is possible to lead from a set of explicit core
beliefs; (c) an understanding of the specific challenges facing the school; and (d) confidence that her or his knowledge and preparation matched the unique challenge
presented by the school.

RESEARCH SUPPORT FOR FSLA ACCOMPLISHMENTS

The FSLA is an evolving conception. As knowledge about relationships between school
conditions and student learning continues to develop, the list of major accomplishments
and their particulars should evolve. Further, the way that accomplishments themselves
are defined should evolve as a product of improvements in professional knowledge.

Meta-analyses of research on how various interventions affect student learning
should validate any model focused on student learning. The FSLA and its categories
reflect what is known currently about how schools influence learning. A selection of
significant positive effects associated with interventions that are related to the FSLA
accomplishments is shown in Table 4.10.

Though differences in methodologies and statistics make it difficult to compare effect sizes across studies, Cohen (1998) provided a useful rule of thumb for categoriz-

TABLE 4.10

Selected Effect Sizes Associated With Accomplishments in the FSLA

Accomplishment	Type of Intervention	Effect Size	Source
Learning goals defined	Acceleration programs for gifted students	Large	Frasier, Walberg, Welch, & Hattie (1987)
	Modern vs. traditional math curriculum	Small	Lipsey & Wilson (1993)
	New vs. traditional science curriculum	Small	Lipsey & Wilson (1993)
	Content coverage	Small	Scheerens & Bosker (1997)
Instruction provided	Identifying similarities and differences	Large	Marzano (1998; 2000)
	Computer-based instruction	Large	Lipsey & Wilson (1993)
	Reinforcement	Large	Frasier et al. (1987)
	Summarizing and note taking	Large	Marzano (1998; 2000)
	Reading training	Large	Frasier et al. (1987)
	Cues and feedback	Large	Frasier et al. (1987)
	Setting goals and providing feedback	Medium	Marzano (1998; 2000)
	Cooperative programs	Medium	Lipsey & Wilson (1993)
	Generating and testing hypotheses	Medium	Marzano (1998; 2000)
	Graded homework	Medium	Frasier et al. (1987)
	Activating prior knowledge	Medium	Marzano (1998; 2000)
	Diagnostic/prescription	Small	Frasier et al. (1987)
	Individualized instruction	Small	Frasier et al. (1987)
	Tutoring	Small	Frasier et al. (1987)
	Individualized instruction (math and science)	Small	Lipsey & Wilson (1993)
	Student tutoring	Small	Lipsey & Wilson (1993)
	Principal involvement in curriculum, instruction, and assessment	Small	Walters, Marzano, & McNulty (2003)
	Principal knowledge of curriculum, instruction, and assessment	Small	Walters et al., (2003)
Student climate sustained	Class morale	Medium	Frasier et al. (1987)
	Pressure to achieve	Small	Scheerens & Bosker (1997)
	School climate	Small	Scheerens & Bosker (1997)

(continued on next page)

TABLE 4.10 (continued)

Accomplishment	Type of Intervention	Effect Size	Source
Related services provided	Primary prevention programs in schools	Medium (a)	Lipsey & Wilson (1993)
	Cognitive behavioral modification strategies with children	Small (a)	Lipsey & Wilson (1993)
	Counseling and guidance programs in high school	Small	Lipsey & Wilson (1993)
	Remedial and developmental language programs	Small	Lipsey & Wilson (1993)
Family and community partnerships sustained	Home instruction supported by school-based programs	Medium	Lipsey & Wilson (1993)
	Home interventions	Medium	Frasier et al. (1987)
	Parent effectiveness training	Small (a)	Lipsey & Wilson (1993)
	Parent involvement	Small	Scheerens & Bosker (1997)
Resources mobilized	outreach (principal is advocate/spokesperson for school to all stakeholders)	Small	Walters et al., (2003)
School operations organized and supported	Situational awareness (the principal is aware of details and undercurrents in the school and uses this information to address current and potential problems)	Medium	Walters et al., (2003)
	Instructional Time	Small	Frasier et al. (1987)
	Small vs. large class size	Small	Lipsey & Wilson (1993)
	Between and within class ability grouping	Small	Lipsey & Wilson (1993)
	Mainstreaming vs. segregated special education programs	Small	Lipsey & Wilson (1993)
	Order (the principal establishes a set of operating procedures and outlines)	Small	Walters et al., (2003)
	Discipline (the principals protects teachers form issues and influences that would detract from their instructional focus)	Small	Walters et al., (2003)
	Resources (the principal provides teachers with materials and professional development necessary for the successful execution of their jobs)	Small	Walters et al., (2003)

Staff supported	Feedback to teachers about individual academic performance of students	Medium	Lipsey & Wilson (1993)
	Input (the principal involves teachers in the design and implementation of important decisions and policies	Medium	Walters et al., (2003)
	Intellectual stimulation (the principal ensures that faculty and staff are aware of the most current theories and practices and makes the discussion of these a regular aspect of the school's climate)	Medium	Walters et al., (2003)
	Culture (the principal fosters shared beliefs and a sense of community and cooperation)	Small	Walters et al., (2003)
	Communication (the principal establishes strong lines of communication with teachers and among students)	Small	Walters et al., (2003)
	Affirmation (the principal recognizes and celebrates school accomplishments and acknowledges failures)	Small	Walters et al., (2003)
	Monitoring	Small	Witziers, Bosker, & Kruger (2003)
	Ideals (the principal communicates and operates from strong beliefs about schooling)	Small	Walters et al., (2003)
	Flexibility (the principal adapts leadership behavior to the needs of the current situation and is comfortable with dissent)	Small	Walters et al., (2003)
School renewal supported	Change agent (the principal is willing to and actively challenges the status quo)	Medium	Walters et al., (2003)
	School leadership	Small	Scheerens & Bosker (1997)
	Defining and communicating a mission	Small	Witziers et al., (2003)
	Focus (the principal establishes clear goals and keeps those goals in the forefront of the school's attention)	Small	Walters et al., (2003)
	Optimizer (the principal inspires and leads new and challenging innovations)	Small	Walters et al., (2003)

(a) Effect sizes designated with "(a)" are computed using dependent variables in addition to academic achievement and may overestimate effects on achievement.

ing the average effects as small, medium, or large. As might be expected, interventions associated with accomplishments in the environment for learning have larger effects than those associated with the environment for teaching, but all the accomplishments have positive and statistically significant relationships with student learning. Even small statistically significant effects are important, particularly as schools are under pressure for all students to achieve proficiency on content standards and state tests.

A NOTE ABOUT ORGANIZING PROFESSIONAL KNOWLEDGE

Organizing knowledge around various components of a school leader's role offers complementary perspectives on professional knowledge and its link with practice. Knowledge organized around school accomplishments appears to be directly related to the principal's dual responsibility of (a) defining quality accomplishments and (b) implementing leadership strategies to achieve desired outcomes. Knowledge that is organized around these two practical challenges for principals may make such knowledge more accessible to principals in their work and more easily applied in the rapid-paced context of life in schools.

Principals' work involves attention to the parts of a school that advance student learning as well as stewardship for the whole enterprise over successive annual cycles. Principals' work, then, requires constant learning as a school community creates and recreates itself in response to its unique challenges, relationships, opportunities, and constraints each school year. The resulting knowledge—often tacit—developed in and through practice, contextualized in a particular school environment, also is important as principals learn to address increasingly complex expectations. Elsewhere, we have proposed an annual case of school leadership (Muth et al., 2004) as a means of documenting and sharing the narrative knowledge that results from the holistic leadership of schools during annual cycles. We see the development and use of annual cases as a vital and necessary complement to the continuous improvement and wider availability of the knowledge outlined in Tables 4.1–4.9 and already organized around the accomplishment model that we propose.

ACKNOWLEDGMENTS

G. Thomas Bellamy, Vice Chancellor for Academic Affairs, University of Washington, Bothell; Connie L. Fulmer, Associate Professor, Administrative Leadership and Policy Studies, University of Colorado at Denver and Health Sciences Center; Michael J. Murphy, Professor Emeritus, University of Colorado at Denver and Health Sciences Center; Rodney Muth, Professor, Administrative Leadership and Policy Studies, University of Colorado at Denver and Health Sciences Center.

REFERENCES

Acker, S. (1995). Gender and teachers' work. In M. Apple (Ed.), *Review of research in education* (Vol. 21, pp. 99–162). Washington, DC: American Educational Research Association.

Allensworth, D., Lawson, E., Nicholson, L., & Wyche, J. (Eds.). (1997). *Schools and health: The nation's investment.* Washington, DC: National Academy Press.

Alexander, K., & Alexander, D. (2003). *The law of schools, students, and teachers.* St. Paul, MN: West.

American Association of School Administrators. (1991). *Total quality schools.* Arlington, VA: Author.

American Psychological Association. (1981). Guidelines for delivery of services by school psychologists. *American Psychologist, 36,* 670–681.

American Speech-Language-Hearing Association. (2003) *ASHA code of ethics* (Revised January 1, 2003). Retrieved September 14, 2003, from http://professional.asha.org/

Ames, C. (1992). Classrooms: Goals structures, and student motivation. *Journal of Educational Psychology, 84,* 261–271.

Anderson, C. (1982). The search for school climate: A review of the research. *Review of Educational Research, 52,* 368–420.

Apple, M. (1986). *Teachers and texts.* New York: Routledge.

Apple, M. (1999). *Power, meaning, and identity: Essays in critical educational studies.* New York: Peter Lang.

Arnold, M. (1998). Three kinds of equity. *American School Board Journal, 185*(5), 34–36.

Bacharach, S., Bamberger, P., Conley, S., & Bauer, S. (1990). The dimensionality of decision participation in educational organizations: The value of a multidomain approach. *Educational Administration Quarterly, 26*(2), 126–167.

Baer, G. (1998). School discipline in the United States: Prevention, detection, and long term social development. *School Psychology Review, 27*(1), 14–32.

Baldridge National Quality Program. (2002). *Educational criteria for performance excellence.* Gaithersberg, MD: Author.

Bangert-Drowns, R., Kulik, C., Kulic, J., & Morgan, M. (1991). The instructional effects of feedback in test-like events. *Review of Educational Research, 61*(2), 213–238.

Barnhardt, V. (1998). *Data analysis for comprehensive schoolwide improvement.* Larchmont, NY: Eye on Education.

Barth, R. (1990). *Improving schools from within: Teachers, parents and principals can make the difference.* San Francisco: Jossey-Bass.

Bauer, D. (1999). *The principal's guide to winning grants.* San Francisco: Jossey-Bass.

Baumrind, D. (1978). Parental disciplinary patterns and social competence in children. *Youth and Society, 9,* 239–276.

Beane, J. (1995). *Toward a coherent curriculum.* Alexandria, VA: Association for Supervision and Curriculum Development.

Beck, L. (1993). *Reclaiming educational administration as a caring profession.* New York: Teachers College Press.

Beck, L., & Murphy, J. (1996). *The four imperatives of a successful school.* Thousand Oaks, CA: Corwin.

Begley, P. (2001). In pursuit of authentic school leadership practice. *International Journal of Leadership in Education, 4,* 353–366.

Bellamy, T. (1999). *The whole school framework: A design for learning.* Des Moines, IA: New Iowa Schools Development Corporation.

Bellamy, T., Fulmer, C., Murphy, M., & Muth, R. (2003). A framework for school leadership accomplishments: Perspectives on knowledge, practice, and preparation for principals. *Leadership and Policy in Schools, 2*(4), 241–261.

Bereiter, C., & Scardemalia, M. (1992). Curriculum and cognition. In P. Jackson (Ed.), *Handbook of research on curriculum* (pp. 517–542). New York: Macmillan.

Berends, M., Bodilly, S., & Kirby, S. (2002). *Facing the challenges of whole school reform*: New American schools after a decade [MR-1498-EDU, 2002]. Santa Monica, CA: RAND.

Biklen, S., & Pollard, D. (1993). Sex, gender, feminism, and education. In S. Biklen & D. Pollard (Eds.), *Gender and education.* Ninety-Second Yearbook of the National Society for the Study of Education, Part 1. Chicago: University of Chicago Press.

Black, P., & Wiliam, D. (1998). Assessment and classroom learning. *Assessment in Education: Principles, Policy, and Practice, 5*(1), 7–74.

Blase, J. (1989). Teachers' political orientation vis-vis the principal: The micropolitics of the school. In J. Hannaway & R. Crowson (Eds.), *The politics of reforming school administration* (pp. 113–126). New York: Falmer.

Blase, J., & Blase, J. (1994). *Empowering teaches: What successful principals do.* Thousand Oaks, CA: Corwin.

Blase, J., & Blase, J. (1998). *Handbook of instructional leadership: How really good principals promote teaching and learning.* Thousand Oaks, CA: Corwin.

Blase, J., & Blase, J. (2000). Effective instructional leadership: teachers' perspectives on how principals promote teaching and learning in schools. *Journal of Educational Administration, 38*(2), 130–141.

Blase, J., & Blase, J. (2001). *Empowering teachers: What successful principals do* (2nd ed.). Thousand Oaks, CA: Corwin.

Blythe, T., Allen, D., & Powell, B. (1999). Looking together at student work. New York: Teachers College Press.

Bolman, L., & Deal, T. (1991). *Reframing organizations: Artistry, choice, and leadership.* San Francisco: Jossey-Bass.

Boyle, J., & Weishaar, M. (2001). *Special education law with cases.* Boston: Allyn & Bacon.

Boyer, E. (1995). *The basic school: A community for learning.* Ewing, NJ: Carnegie Foundation for the Advancement of Teaching.

Bransford, J., Brown, A., & Cocking, R. (Eds.). (2001). *How people learn: Brain, mind, experience, and school.* Washington, DC: National Academy Press.

Brewer, D., & Stasz, C. (1996). *Enhancing opportunity to learn measures in NCES data.* Santa Monica, CA: RAND.

Brophy, J. (1996). *Teaching problem students.* New York: Guilford.

Brooks, G., Gorman, T., Harman, J., Hutchinson, D., & Wilkin, A. (1996). *Family literacy works.* London: Basic Skills Agency.

Brown, D. (1998). *Schools with heart: Volunteerism and public education.* Boulder, CO: Westview.

Burden, P. (1995). *Classroom management and discipline.* New York: Longman.

Burnette, J. (2000). *Assessment of culturally and linguistically diverse students for special education eligibility.* Reston, VA: ERIC Clearinghouse on Disabilities and Gifted Education, Council for Exceptional Children, 2000.

Cameron, J., & Pierce, W. (1994). Reinforcement, reward, and intrinsic motivation: A meta-analysis. *Review of Educational Research, 64,* 363–423.

Campbell, E. (2001). Let right be done: Trying to put ethical standards into practice. *Journal of Education Policy, 16,* 395–412.

Canady, R. (1988). A cure for fragmented schedules in elementary schools. *Educational Leadership, 46*(2), 65–67.

Carnegie Council on Adolescent Development. (1989). *Turning points: Preparing America's youth for the 21st century.* Washington, DC: Author.

Casella, R. (2002). Where policy meets the pavement: Stages of public involvement in the prevention of school violence. *International Journal of Qualitative Studies in Education, 15,* 349–373.

Castaldi, B. (1987). *Educational facilities: Planning, modernization, and management* (3rd ed.). Boston: Allyn & Bacon.

Chavkin, N. (Ed.). (1993). *Families and schools in a pluralistic society.* Albany: State University of New York Press.

Cibulka, J. (1999). Ideological lenses for interpreting political and economic changes affecting schooling. In J. Murphy & K. Louis (Eds.), *Handbook of research on educational administration* (2nd ed., pp. 163–182). San Francisco: Jossey-Bass.

Cibulka, J., & Kritek, W. (Eds.). (1996). *Coordination among schools, families, and communities: Prospects for educational reform.* Albany: State University of New York Press.

Clark, R. (1993). Homework-focused parenting practices that positively affect student achievement. In N. Chavkin (Ed.), *Families and schools in a pluralistic society* (pp. 85–106). Albany: State University of New York Press.

Cohen, J. (1988). *Statistical power analyses for the behavioral sciences* (2nd ed.). Hillsdale, NJ: Lawrence Erlbaum Associates.

Coleman, P. (1998). *Parent, student, and teacher collaboration.* Thousand Oaks, CA: Sage.

Conley, S. (1991). Review of research on teacher participation in school decision making. In G. Grant (Ed.), *Review of research in education* (Vol. 17, pp. 225–265). Washington, DC: American Educational Research Association.

Creemers, B. (1994). *The effective classroom.* London: Cassell.

Cunningham, P., & Allington, R. (1999). *Classrooms that work: They can all read and write* (2nd ed.). New York: Longman.

Cushner, K., McClelland, A., & Safford, P. (1996). *Human diversity in education: An integrative approach* (2nd ed.). New York: McGraw-Hill.

Damico, J. (1987). Addressing language concerns in the schools: The SLP as consultant. *Journal of Childhood Communication Disorders, 11*(1), 17–40.

Danielson, C. (1996). *Enhancing professional practice: A framework for teaching.* Alexandria, VA: Association for supervision and Curriculum Development.

Danielson, C., & McGreal, T. (2000). *Teacher evaluation to enhance professional practice.* Princeton, NJ: Educational Testing Service.

Deal, T. E., & Peterson, K. D. (1990). *The principal's role in shaping school culture.* Washington, DC: U. S. Department of Education.

Delpit, L. (1995). *Other people's children: Cultural conflict in the classroom.* London: Falmer.

Donmoyer, R. (2001). Paradigm talk reconsidered. In V. Richardson (Ed.), *Handbook of research on teaching* (4th ed., pp. 174–197). Washington, DC: American Educational Research Association.

Doyle, W. (1983). Academic work. *Review of Educational Research, 53,* 159–199.

Doyle, W. (1992). Curriculum and pedagogy. In P. Jackson, (Ed.), *Handbook of research on curriculum* (pp. 486–516). New York: Macmillan.

DuFour, R., & Eaker, R. (1998). *Professional learning communities at work: Best practices for enhancing student achievement.* Reston, VA: Association for Supervision and Curriculum Development.

Edison Project. (1994). *Partnership school design.* New York: Author.

Edmonds, R. (1982). Programs of school improvement: An overview. *Educational Leadership, 40*(3), 4–12.

Eilers, A. (2002). School-linked collaborative services and systems change: Linking public agencies with public schools. *Administration and Society, 34,* 285–309.

Eisner, E. (1992). Curriculum ideologies. In P. Jackson (Ed.), *Handbook of research on curriculum* (pp. 302–326). New York: Macmillan.

Englemann, S., & Carnine, D. (1982). *Theory of instruction: Principles and applications.* New York: Irvington.

Epstein, J. (2001). *School, family, and community partnerships: Preparing educators and improving schools.* Boulder, CO: Westview.

Essex, N. (1999). *School law and the public schools.* Boston: Allyn & Bacon.

Evans, R. (1996). *The human side of school change: Reform, resistance, and the real-life problems of innovation.* San Francisco: Jossey-Bass.

Evertson, C. (1980). Effective classroom management at the beginning of the school year. *Elementary School Journal, 81,* 219–231.

Firestone, W., & Fisler, J. (2002). Politics, community, and leadership in a school-university partnership. *Educational Administration Quarterly, 38,* 449–494.

Firestone, W., & Pennell, J. (1993). Teacher commitment, working conditions, and differential incentive policies. *Review of Educational Research, 63,* 489–525.

Fischer, L., Schimmel, D., & Kelly, C. (1995). *Teachers and the law* (4th ed.). White Plains, NY: Longman.

Fischer, L., & Sorenson, G. (1996). *School law for counselors, psychologists, and social workers* (3rd ed.). White Plains, NY: Longman.

Forsyth, P., & Tallerico, M. (1993). *City schools: Leading the way.* Newbury Park, CA: Corwin.

Frasier, B., Walberg, H., Welch, W., & Hattie, J. (1987). Synthesis of educational productivity research. *International Journal of Educational Research, 11,* 145–252.

French, N. (2001). Supervising paraprofessionals: A survey of teacher practices. *Journal of Special Education, 35*(1), 41–53.

French, N. (2003). *Managing paraeducators in your school: How to hire, train, and supervise non-certified staff.* Thousand Oaks, CA: Corwin.

Fullan, M. (1985). Change processes and strategies at the local level. *Elementary School Journal, 85,* 391–421.

Gaddy, B., Hall, W., & Marzano, R. (1996). *School wars: Resolving our conflicts over religion and values.* San Francisco: Jossey-Bass.

Gallagher, D., Bagin, D., & Kindred, L. (2001). *The school and community relations.* Seventh Edition. Boston: Allyn & Bacon.

Gameron, A., Porter, A., Smithson, J., & White, P. (1997). Upgrading high school mathematics instructions: Improving learning opportunities for low-achieving, low-income youth. *Educational Evaluation and Policy Analysis, 19,* 325–228.

Garden, K., & Liebermann, J. (1989). State of the art in routing and scheduling. *School Business Affairs, 51*(4), 28, 30–31.

Garet, M., Porter, A., Desimone, L., Birman, B., & Yoon, K. (2001). What makes professional development effective? Results from a national sample of teachers. *American Educational Research Journal, 38*(4), 115–145.

Gersten, R., & Baker, S. (2000). What we know about effective instructional practices for English language learners. *Exceptional Children, 66,* 454–471.

Gilbert, T. (1978). *Human competence.* New York: McGraw-Hill.

Girard, D., & Koch, S. (1996). *Conflict resolution in the schools.* San Francisco: Jossey-Bass.

Glatthorn, A. (2000). *The principal as curriculum leader: Shaping what is taught and tested.* Thousand Oaks, CA: Corwin.

Glickmam, C., Gordon, S., & Ross-Gordon, J. (2001). *Supervision and instructional leadership: A developmental approach* (5th ed.). Needham Heights, MA: Allyn & Bacon.

Goble, F., & Brooks, B. (1983). *The case for character education.* Otawa, IL: Green Hill.

Goleman, D., Boyatzis, R., & McKee, A. (2002). *Primal leadership: Realizing the power of emotional intelligence.* Cambridge, MA: Harvard Business School Press.

Good, T., & Brophy, J. (1997). *Looking in classrooms* (7th ed.). New York: Longman.

Goodlad, J. (1988). School-university partnerships for educational renewal: Rationale and concepts. In K. Sirotnik & J. Goodlad (Eds.), *School-university partnerships in action* (pp. 3–31). New York: Teachers College Press.

Goodlad, J. I. (1996). Democracy, education, and community. In R. Soder (Ed.), *Democracy, education, and the schools* (pp. 87–124). San Francisco, CA: Jossey-Bass.

Goodlad, J., & Su, Z. (1992). Organization of the curriculum. In P. Jackson (Ed.), *Handbook of research on curriculum* (pp. 327–346). New York: Macmillan.

Gordon, S., & Nicely, R. (1998). Supervision and staff development. In G. Firth & E. Pajak (Eds.), *Handbook of research on school supervision* (pp. 801–841). New York: Macmillan.

Gorn, S. (1997). *What do I do when: The answer book on special education law.* Horsham, PA: LRP.

Griffiths, D. E. (1959). *Administrative theory.* New York: Appleton-Century-Crofts.

Griffiths, D. E. (Guest Ed.). (1991). Special Issue: Nontraditional theory and research. *Educational Administration Quarterly, 27*(3).

Guthrie, J. (Ed.). (1980). *School finance policies and practices.* First Annual Yearbook of the American Education Finance Association. Cambridge: Ballinger.

Hale, J., & Jackson, M. (1984). Effective schools and effective parent involvement. In J. Lyday & L. Winecoff (Eds.), *Effective schools: A guide for boards, central office administrators, principals, teachers, parents, and community educators.* Charlottesville, VA: Mid-Atlantic Consortium for Community Education. (ERIC Document Reproduction Service No. ED 302 906.)

Hall, G., & Hord, S. (1987). *Change in schools: Facilitating the process.* Albany: State University of New York Press.

Halverson, R. (2003). Systems of practice: How leaders use artifacts to create professional community in schools. *Education Policy Analysis Archives,* 11(37). Retrieved January 15, 2004, from http://epaa.asu.edu/epaa/v11n37/

Hargreaves, A., Earl, L., Moore, S., & Manning, S. (2001). *Learning to change: Teaching beyond subjects and standards.* San Francisco: Jossey-Bass.

Hart, B., & Risley, T. (1995). *Meaningful differences in the everyday experiences of young American children.* Baltimore: Paul H. Brookes.

Henderson, A. (1987). *The evidence continues to grow: Parent involvement improves student achievement.* Columbia, MD: National Committee for Citizens in Education. (ERIC Document Reproduction Service No. ED 315 199)

Herman, J. J., & Herman, J. L. (1997). *School-based budgets: Getting, spending, and accounting.* Lancaster, PA: Technomic.

Hidi, S., & Harackiewicz, J. (2000). Motivating the academically unmotivated: A critical issue for the 21st century. *Review of Educational Research, 70*(2), 151–179.

Hills, J. (1978). Problems in the production and utilization of knowledge in educational administration. *Educational Administration Quarterly, 14*(1), 1–12.

Holcomb, J. (1993). *Educational marketing: A business approach to school-community relations.* Lanham, MD: University Press of America.

Hoy, A., & Hoy, W. (2003). *Instructional leadership: A learning-centered guide.* Boston: Allyn & Bacon.

Ingersoll, R. (2003). *Who controls teachers work? Power and accountability in America's schools.* Cambridge, MA: Harvard University Press.

Johnson, R. (2002). *Using data to close the achievement gap: How to measure equity in our schools.* Thousand Oaks, CA: Corwin.

Joyce, B., Hersh, R., & McKibben, M. (1983). *The structure of school improvement.* New York: Longman.

Kaufman, R., Herman, J., & Watters, K. (1996). *Educational planning: Strategic, tactical, operational.* Lancaster, PA: Technomic.

Knowles, M. (1984). *The adult learner: A neglected species* (3rd ed.). London: Gulf.

Kohn, A. (1993). *Punished by rewards.* Boston: Houghton Mifflin.

Kowalski, T. (2002). *Planning and managing school facilities* (2nd ed.). Westport, CT: Bergin & Garvey.

LaMorte, M. (1999). *School law: Cases and concepts.* Boston: Allyn & Bacon.

Larson, C., & Murtadha, K. (2002). Leadership for social justice. In J. Murphy (Ed.), *The educational leadership challenge: Redefining leadership for the 21st century* (pp. 134–161). Chicago: University of Chicago Press.

Lashley, C. (2002). Participation of students with disabilities in statewide assessments and the general education curriculum. *Journal of Special Education Leadership, 15*(1), 10–16.

Lawrence, E., Vachon, M., Leake, D., & Leake, B. (2001). *The marginal teacher: A step by step guide to fair procedures for identification and dismissal.* Thousand Oaks, CA: Corwin.

Leithwood, K. (1994). Leadership for school restructuring. *Educational Administration Quarterly, 30,* 498–518.

Levine, D., & Lezotte, L. (1990). *Unusually effective schools: A review and analysis of research and practice.* Madison, WI: National Center for Effective Schools Research and Development.

Lincoln, Y. S., & Guba, E. G. (1985). *Naturalistic inquiry.* Beverly Hills, CA: Sage.

Lindsey, R., Robbins, D., & Terrell, R. (1999). *Cultural proficiency: A manual for school leaders.* Thousand Oaks, CA: Sage.

Lipsey, M., & Wilson, D. (1993). The efficacy of psychological, educational, and behavioral treatment. *American Psychologist, 48,* 1181–1209.

Little, J. (1982). Norms of collegiality and experimentation: Workplace conditions of school success. *American Educational Research Journal, 19,* 325–340.

Lomotey, K. (Ed.). (1990). *Going to school: The African-American experience.* Albany: State University of New York Press.

Loucks-Horsley, S., Hewson, P., Love, N., & Stiles, K. (1998). *Designing professional development for teachers of science and mathematics.* Thousand Oaks, CA: Corwin.

Loucks-Horsley, S., & Matsumoto, C. (1999). Research on professional development for teachers of mathematics and science. The state of the scene. *School Science and Mathematics, 99,* 258–271.

Louis, K., Marks, H., & Kruse, S. (1996). Teachers' professional community in restructuring schools. *American Educational Research Journal, 33,* 757–798.

Louis, K., Toole, J., & Hargreaves, A. (1999). Rethinking school improvement. In J. Murphy & K. Louis (Eds.), *Handbook of research on educational administration* (2nd ed., pp. 251–276). San Francisco: Jossey-Bass.

Lopez, G., Scribner, J., & Mahitivanichcha, K. (2001). Redefining parental involvement: Lessons from high-performing migrant-impacted schools. *American Educational Research Journal, 38,* 253–288.

Lynch, E., & Hanson, M. (1998). *Developing cross-cultural competence* (2nd ed.). Baltimore: Paul H. Brookes.

Lytle, S., & Cochran-Smith, M. (1994). Inquiry, knowledge, and practice. In S. Hollingsworth & H. Sockett (Eds.), *Teacher research and education reform*. Ninety-Third Yearbook of the National Society for the Study of Education, Part 1. Chicago: University of Chicago Press.

Maehr, M., & Fyans, L. (1989). School culture, motivation and achievement. In M. Maehr & C. Ames (Eds.), *Advances in motivation and achievement* (Vol. 6, pp. 215–247). Greenwich, CT: JAI.

Marks, H. (2000). Student engagement in instructional activity: Patterns in the elementary, middle, and high school years. *American Educational Research Journal, 37*(1), 153–184.

Marzano, R. (1998). *A theory based meta-analysis of research on instruction*. Aurora, CO: Mid-continent Research for Education and Learning. (ERIC Document Reproduction Service No. ED 427 087)

Marzano, R. (2000). *A new era of school reform: Going where the research takes us*. Aurora, CO: Mid-continent Research for Education and Learning. (ERIC Document Reproduction Service No. ED454 255)

Marzano, R. (2003). *What works in schools: Translating research into action*. Alexandria, VA: Association for Supervision and Curriculum Development.

Marzano, R., & Kendall, J. (1996). *Designing standards-based districts, schools, and classrooms*. Alexandria, VA: Association for Supervision and Curriculum Development.

Marzano, R., Pickering, D., & Pollock, J. (2001). *Classroom instruction that works. Research-based strategies for increasing student achievement*. Alexandria, VA: Association for Supervision and Curriculum Development.

McCarthy, M., Cambron-McCabe, N., & Thomas, S. (2004). *Legal rights of teachers and students*. Boston: Pearson.

McDonnell, L. (1995). Opportunity to learn as a research concept and a policy instrument. *Educational Evaluation and Policy Analysis, 7*, 305–322.

McLaughlin, M. (2000). *Community counts*. Washington, DC: Public Education Network.

McLaughlin, M., Talbert, J., & Bascia, N. (Eds.). (1990). *The contexts of teaching in secondary schools: Teachers realities*. New York: Teachers College Press.

Meier, D. (1996). *The power of their ideas: Lessons for America from a small school in Harlem*. Boston: Beacon.

Merriam, S., & Caffarella, R. (1991). *Learning in adulthood: A comprehensive guide*. San Francisco: Jossey-Bass.

Merton, R. K. (1967). *On theoretical sociology: Five essays, old and new*. New York: Free Press.

Meyers, R. (Ed.). (1999). *Handbook of government budgeting*. San Francisco: Jossey-Bass.

Miller, L. (1989). Classroom-based language intervention. *Language, Speech and Hearing Services in Schools, 20*, 153–169.

Miramontes, O., Nadeau, A., & Commins, N. (1997). *Restructuring schools for linguistic diversity*. New York: Teachers College Press.

Mohrman, S., Cohen, S., & Mohrman, A. (1995). *Designing team-based organizations*. San Francisco: Jossey-Bass.

Mohrman, S., Lawler, E., & Mohrman, A. (1992). Applying employee involvement in schools. *Educational Evaluation and Policy Analysis, 14*, 347–360.

Molnar, A. (Ed.). (1997). *The construction of children's character*. Ninety-Sixth Yearbook of the National Society for the Study of Education, Part 2. Chicago: University of Chicago Press.

Moos, R. (1978). Educational climates. In H. Walberg (Ed.), *Educational environments and effects* (pp. 79–100). Berkeley, CA: McCutchan.

Morrow, L., & Young, J. (1997). A family literacy program connecting school and home: Effects on attitude, motivation, and literacy achievement. *Journal of Educational Psychology, 89*, 736–742.

Moyers, P. (1999). *The guide to occupational therapy practice*. Bethesda, MD: American Occupational Therapy Association.

Murhpy, J., & Beck, L. (1995). *School-based management as school reform*. Thousand Oaks, CA: Sage.

Murphy, M., & Cresswell, A. (1980). *Teachers, unions and collective bargaining*. Berkeley, CA: McCutchan.

Muth, R., Bellamy, G. T., Fulmer, C. L., & Murphy, M. J. (2004). A model for building knowledge for professional practice. In C. Carr & C. L. Fulmer (Eds.), *Educational leadership: Knowing the way, going the way, showing the way* (pp. 83–103). 2004 Yearbook of the National Council of Professors of Educational Administration. Lanham, MD: Scarecrow Education.

National Parent Teacher Association. (1998). *National standards for parent/family involvement programs.* Washington, DC: Author.

National Research Council. (1999). *Making money matter: Financing America's schools.* Washington, DC. National Academy Press.

National Staff Development Council. (1995). *Standards for staff development.* Oxford, OH: Author.

Nee-Benham, M., & Cooper, J. (2000). *Indigenous educational models for contemporary practice: In our mother's voice.* Mahwah, NJ: Lawrence Erlbaum Associates, Inc.

Nelson, J., & Martella, R. (1998). The effect of teaching school expectations and establishing a consistent consequence of formal office disciplinary actions. *Journal of Emotional and Behavioral Disorders, 6*(3), 153–162.

Noddings, N. (1992). *The challenge to care in schools: An alternative approach to education.* New York: Teachers College Press.

Noddings, N. (1999). Care, justice, and equity. In M. Katz, N. Noddings, & K. Strike (Eds.), *Justice and caring: The search for common ground in education* (pp. 7–20). New York: Teachers College Press.

North Central Association Commission on Accreditation and School Improvement. (2001). *Standards and criteria for elementary, middle level, secondary, and unit schools.* Tempe, AZ: Author.

Oakes, J. (1985). *Keeping track: How schools structure inequality.* New Haven, CT: Yale University Press.

Odden, A. (1999). *Improving state school finance systems: New realities create need to re-engineer school finance structures* (CPRE Occasional Paper Series OP-04). Madison: University of Wisconsin.

Odden, A., & Archibald, S. (2000, November). The possibilities of resource allocation. *Principal Leadership, 1*(3), 26–32.

Odden, A., & Picus, L. (2004). *School finance: A policy perspective* (3rd ed.). Boston: McGraw-Hill.

Oja, S., & Reiman, A. (1998). Supervision for teacher development across the career span. In G. Firth & E. Pajak (Eds.), *Handbook of research on school supervision* (pp. 463–487). New York: Macmillan.

Onikama, D., Hammond, O., & Koki, S. (1998). *Family involvement in education: A synthesis of research for pacific educators.* Honolulu, HI: Pacific Resources for Education and Learning.

Osborne, W., & Wiggins, T. (1989). Perceptions of tasks in the school principalship. *Journal of Personnel Evaluation in Education, 2,* 367–375.

Oser, F. (1994). Moral perspectives on teaching. In L. Darling-Hammond (Ed.), *Review of research in education* (Vol. 20). Washington, DC: American Educational Research Association.

Osterman, K. (2000). Students' need for belonging in the school community. *Review of Educational Research, 70,* 323–367.

Otto, L. (1982). Extracurricular activities. In H. Walberg (Ed.), *Improving educational standards and productivity* (pp. 217–227). Berkeley, CA: McCutchan.

Patterson, K., Greeny, J., McMillan, R., & Switzer, A. (2002). *Crucial conversations: Tools for talking when stakes are high.* New York: McGraw-Hill.

Payne, R. (1998). *A framework for understanding poverty.* Highlands, TX: RFT.

Peterson, K., & Deal, T. (1999). *Shaping school culture.* San Francisco: Jossey-Bass.

Peterson, K., & Deal, T. (2002). *The shaping school culture fieldbook.* San Francisco: Jossey-Bass.

Picus, L. (2000). *How schools allocate and use their resources.* Eugene, OR: ERIC Clearinghouse on Educational Management.

Polanyi, M. (1962). *Personal knowledge: Towards a post-critical philosophy.* Chicago: University of Chicago Press.

Reid, W. (1978). *Thinking about the curriculum.* London: Routlege and Kegan Paul.

Rich, D. (1987). *Schools and families: Issues and action.* Washington, DC: National Education Association. (ERIC Document Reproduction Service No. ED 312 061)

Richardson, V. (Ed.). (2001). *Handbook of research on teaching* (4th ed.). Washington, DC: American Educational Research Association.

Robertson, P., Wohlstetter, P., & Mohrman, S. (1995). Generating curriculum and instructional innovations through site-based management. *Educational Administration Quarterly, 31,* 375–404.

Rosenshine, B., & Stevens, R. (1986). Teaching functions. In M. Wittrock (Ed.), *Handbook of research on teaching* (3rd ed.). New York: Macmillan

Rosenholtz, S. (1989). Workplace conditions that affect teacher quality and commitment: Implications for teacher induction programs. *Elementary School Journal, 89,* 421–439.

Rothstein, L. (2000). *Special education law.* White Plains, NY: Longman.

Rowan, B. (1990). Commitment and control: Alternative strategies for the organizational design of schools. In C. Cazden (Ed.), *Review of research in education* (Vol. 16, pp. 353–389). Washington, DC: American Educational Research Association.

Sadker, M., & Sadker, D. (1982). *Sex equity handbook for schools.* New York: Longman.

Sarason, S. (1982). *The culture of school and the problem of change* (2nd ed.). Boston: Allyn & Bacon.

Sarason, S. (1990). *The predictable failure of educational reform.* San Francisco: Jossey-Bass.

Scheerens, J., & Bosker, R. (1997). *The foundations of educational effectiveness.* New York: Elsevier.

Scheffler, I. (1958). Justifying curriculum decisions. *School Review, 66,* 461–472.

Schlechty, P. (1990). *Schools for the 21st Century: Leadership imperatives for educational reform.* San Francisco: Jossey-Bass.

Schmuck, R., & Runkle, P. (1994). *The handbook of organizational development in schools and colleges* (4th ed.). Prospect Heights, IL: Waveland.

Scott, E., & McCollum, H. (1993). Making it happen: Gender equitable classrooms. In S. Biklen & D. Pollard (Eds.), *Gender and education.* Ninety-Second yearbook of the National Society for the Study of Education, Part 1 (pp. 174–190). Chicago: University of Chicago Press.

Sergiovanni, T. J. (1996). Moral leadership. Getting to the heart of school improvement San Francisco: Jossey-Bass.

Shapiro, J., & Stefkovich, J. (2001). *Ethical leadership and decision making in education: Applying theoretical perspectives to complex dilemmas.* Mahwah, NJ: Lawrence Erlbaum Associates.

Shavelson, R., & Towne, L. (2002). *Scientific research in education.* Washington, DC: National Academy Press.

Shockley-Zalabak, P. (1999). *Fundamentals of organizational communication. Knowledge, sensitivity, skills, values.* New York: Longman.

Simon, R. (1992). *Teaching against the grain.* South Hadley, MA: Bergin & Garvey.

Skelton, K. (1997). *Paraprofessionals in education.* Albany, NY: Delmar.

Sleeter, C., & Grant, C. (1993). *Making choices for multicultural education: Five approaches to race, class, and gender.* New York: McMillan.

Smylie, M., & Hart, A. (1999). School leadership for teacher learning and change: A human and social capital development perspective. In J. Murphy & K. Louis (Eds.), *Handbook of research on educational administration* (2nd ed., pp. 421–443). San Francisco: Jossey-Bass.

Smyth, J., & Garman, M. (1989). Supervision as school reform: A "critical" perspective. *Journal of Education Policy, 4,* 343–361.

Solomon, D., Watson, M., & Battistich, V. (2001). Teaching and schooling effects on moral/prosocial development. In V. Richardson (Ed.), *Handbook of research on teaching* (4th ed., pp. 566–603). Washington, DC: American Educational Research Association.

Spring, J. (2002). *Political agendas for education: From the religious right to the green party* (2nd ed.). Mahwah, NJ: Lawrence Erlbaum Associates.

Stein, N. (1999). *Classrooms and courtrooms: Facing sexual harassment in K-12 schools.* New York: Teachers College Press.

Steinberg, L. (1996). *Beyond the classroom: Why school reform has failed and what parents need to do.* New York: Simon and Schuster.

Stewart, M. (1989). The First Amendment, the public schools, and the inculcation of community values. *Journal of Law and Education, 18,* 23–92.

Sugai, G., & Horner, R. H. (2002). Introduction to the special series on positive behavior support in schools. *Journal of Emotional & Behavioral Disorders, 10*(3), 130–135.

Swanson, A., & King, R. (1997). *School finance: Its economics and politics.* New York: Longman.

Tangri, S., & Moles, O. (1987). Parents and the community. In V. Richardson-Koehler (Ed.), *Educators' handbook: A research perspective* (pp. 1–82). New York: Longman.

Tanner, D. (1988). The textbook controversies. In L. Tanner (Ed.), *Critical issues in curriculum* (pp. 122–147). Eighty-Seventh Yearbook of the National Society for the Study of Education, Part I. Chicago: University of Chicago Press.

Thomas, A., & Grimes, J. (Eds.). (2002). *Best practices in school psychology VI*. Washington, DC: National Association of School Psychologists.

Thompson, R. (2002). *School counseling: Best practices for working in the schools*. New York: Routledge.

Thompson, S. (Ed.). (1993). *Principals for our changing schools: Knowledge and skill base*. Lancaster, PA: Technomic.

Tilton, L. (1996). *Inclusion: A fresh look*. Shorewood, MN: Covington Cove.

Tizard, J., Schonfield, W., & Hevinson, J. (1982). Collaboration between teachers and parents in assisting children's reading. *British Journal of Educational Psychology, 51*(1), 1–11.

U.S. Department of Education. (1995). *Building bridges: The mission and principles of staff development*. Washington, DC: Author.

U.S. Department of Education. (2000a). *The teacher's guide to the U. S. Department of Education*. Washington, DC: Author.

U.S. Department of Education. (2000b). *Promising initiatives to improve education in your community: A guide to selected U.S. Department of Education grant programs and funding opportunities*. Washington, DC: Author.

Walberg, H., Rasher, S., & Singh, R. (1977). An operational test of a three-factor theory of classroom social perception. *Psychology in the Schools, 14*, 508–513.

Wang, M., Haertel, G., & Walberg, H. (1993). Toward a knowledge base for school learning. *Review of Educational Research, 63*, 249–294.

Warner, C. (1994). *Promoting your school*. Thousand Oaks, CA: Corwin.

Waters, T., Marzano, R., & McNulty, B. (2003). *Balanced leadership: What 30 years of research tells us about the effect of leadership on student achievement*. Aurora, CO: Mid-continent Research for Education and Learning.

West, L., & Staub, F. (2003). *Content-focused coaching: Transforming mathematics lessons*. Portsmouth, NH: Heinemann.

Whitaker, T., & Fiore, D. (2001). *Dealing with difficult parents and with parents in difficult situations*. Larchmont, NY: Eye on Education.

Wigfield, A., Eccles, J., & Rodriguez, D. (1998). The development of children's motivation in school contexts. In D. Pearson & A. Iran-Nejad (Eds.), *Review of research in education* (Vol. 23, pp. 73–118). Washington, DC: American Educational Research Association.

Wiggins, G. (1993). *Assessing student performance: Exploring the purposes and limits of testing*. San Francisco: Jossey-Bass.

Wiggins, G., & McTighe, J. (1998). *Understanding by design*. Alexandria, VA: Association for Supervision and Curriculum Development.

Witziers, B., Boskers, R., & Kruger, M. (2003). Educational leadership and student achievement: The elusive search for an association. *Educational Administration Quarterly, 39*, 398–425.

Wohlstetter, P., & Mohrman, S. (1993). *School-based management: Strategies for success*. New Brunswick, NJ: Rutgers University.

Wong, H., & Wong, R. (1990). *The first days of school*. Sunnyvale, CA: Harry K. Wong.

Zemelman, S., Daniels, H., & Hyde, A. (1998). *Best practice: New standards for teaching and learning in America's schools* (2nd ed.). Portsmouth, NH: Heinemann.

PROFESSIONAL DEVELOPMENT, CONTEXT KNOWLEDGE, CURRICULAR REFORM, AND ADMINISTRATOR DEVELOPMENT

5

LEADERSHIP FOR CURRICULUM CHANGE: SCHOOLS ENGAGED IN "CLOSING THE GAP"

Lesa M. Covington Clarkson
Karen Seashore Louis
University of Minnesota

Over the last decade the challenges to educators working in urban schools have been numerous and often conflicting. Schools are confronted with changing demographics, a sense that student engagement and public faith in urban education is declining, and problems of attracting and retaining high-quality faculty and administrators to work in an embattled and poorly funded professional setting. In addition, curriculum and instruction challenges, which are the context by which we are framing this chapter, appear overwhelming.

In the past few decades, serious energy has gone into a wide range of reports that delineate the problems facing school and provide clear images of excellence. There is strong motivation to act on these reports at national, regional, and local levels, and many countries are enacting educational reform efforts that demand improvement. Moreover, there are an increasing number of well-documented and research-based programs based on what we know about content and student learning, that have demonstrable potential.

This chapter engages in a post hoc analysis of efforts to improve curriculum and teaching in two settings. Through "backward mapping" of both the results and process of implementing new curricula funded by the National Science Foundation, we point to the generation of energy for change at the school level. Our analysis is directed toward the theme of this book—learner-centered leadership—because it focuses on how *all* individuals in the school are involved in learning when efforts are made to shift practice in fundamental ways.

We look at learning-centered leadership from the ground up, beginning with a clear challenge in urban schools: students who have difficulty with grade-level mathematics content. Our approach stands in contrast to many current school improvement initiatives, including government-sponsored reform models, which emphasize the direct connection between teacher skills and student achievement. Clearly creating stronger content and improved instruction is at the core of school improvement (Newmann & Wehlage, 1995), but attention to the role of teacher and administrator leadership in guiding these efforts is often left to chance, and the voices of students are heard even more rarely. In examining the implementation of a new mathematics curriculum, we focus less on the specifics of how teachers acquire new knowledge and practices than on the way in which the social structure of the school is arranged to promote success. At the heart of our inquiry is our effort to understand the relationship between teachers' personal learning to improve their work with high-poverty urban children, and the role of teacher and principal leadership in that process. In addition, we also look at how the children's responses create reflective learning opportunities for adults, as communication about mathematics learning becomes a more widely shared component of the school. In other words, learner-centered leadership starts in the classroom.

We focus on how the efforts that the schools made to transform their mathematics teaching involved initial steps toward becoming "learning organizations" in which teachers and students are responsible for their own learning, and principals are challenged to become apprentices at the side of those that they ostensibly lead. What we see in the schools is not only a struggle to develop a *process* of collective learning, rather, based on our retrospective view, it is learning that is implicitly guided by the three anchors for a "new administrative leadership" outlined by Murphy (2001): *school improvement* (real change in student learning), *democratic community* (distributing responsibility and influence throughout the school), and *social justice* (creating opportunities for all participants to benefit equally from the public resources of schooling).

In framing our analysis, we draw on a number of different research perspectives. First we look briefly at the literature on the relationship between school and reform, student achievement and leadership. More specifically, we turn to the emerging literature on participatory and distributed leadership and the way in which the school's culture and climate affect active leadership from those other than the principal, including the role of formal and informal teams. Finally, we framed our work in the context of what is known about how schools move toward real instructional change.

LEADERSHIP, REFORM, AND STUDENT ACHIEVEMENT

Over the past two decades scholars have increasingly examined the relationship between leadership and school reform or innovation (Fullan, 1982; Fullan &

Stiegelbauer, 1994; (Leithwood, Louis, Anderson, & Wahlstrom, 2005). The underlying assumption—confirmed by research—is that leadership, whether from teachers or administrators, is a key factor in determining whether schools adapt to new conditions and work effectively with their students (Murphy, 2001). With the current state and national emphasis on accountability for student achievement, attention to the role of leadership has increased in the media as well as in the scholarly literature.

Many of these investigations begin with a "top down" focus: they define a leadership position or set of leaders, and then look for their impact on school improvement or school effectiveness (Bista & Glasman, 1998; Hallinger, 1996; Hallinger, & Heck, 1998; Teddlie & Reynolds, 2000).[1] Here the assumption is often that the authoritative or designated leader's action creates the conditions that permit other people in the organization to succeed or fail. Other investigations, especially qualitative case studies, look at improvement (or implementation) and map backward to find the effects of a principal or a leadership team (Hess, 1999; Louis & Miles, 1990). In this research we take the latter path, beginning with efforts to change classroom practice and student achievement through particular innovations—the *Connected Mathematics Project* (CMP) in urban middle schools and *Everyday Math* in an urban elementary charter school—and looking for the ways in which leadership affects the desired outcomes.[2]

Sources of Leadership

We also follow the emerging literature that emphasizes the indirect effects of distributive leadership rather than authoritative positional leadership (Murphy, 2001). There are a variety of ways in which more diffuse leadership effects can be examined. Spillane and his colleagues, for example, argue that "distributed leadership" is a practice that involves cognitive engagement with the school's social and situational context (Spillane, Halvorson, & Diamond, 2001), a perspective that is reflected in the work of others, not only in the United States (Pounder, 1995), but in other countries (Carter, 2002; Harris, 2002). Whereas most of these investigations have focused on high schools or elementary schools, middle schools are increasingly engaging in collaborative or distributed leadership practices (Clark & Clark, 2002). In this chapter we focus on both elementary and middle school contexts.

School culture or climate is an important intervening variable that helps to account for the effects of leadership behavior on innovation and student achievement, and leadership behaviors are often associated with more-or-less positive relationships among both adults and children (Hoy, Hannum, & Tschannen-Moran, 1998). Many have investigated the effects of school leadership on the teacher culture of the school, particularly on the propensity of teachers to engage in professional dialogue (Louis, Marks, & Kruse, 1996; Scribner, Cockrell, Cockrell, & Valentine, 1999) and to be open to innovation (Leithwood & Louis, 1998; Muijs, Harris, Chapman, Stoll, & Russ, 2004). Creating teacher teams, usually as a result of the initiative or support

---

[1]Though there have been few investigations of principal impact specific to middle schools, the principal-focused approach is apparent in this literature (Cooney, Moore, & Bottoms, 2002).

[2]These curricula are two of the most widely used National Science Foundation (NSF) mathematics curricula that are aligned with the National Council of Teachers of Mathematics (NCTM) standards.

of the principal, is one strategy that has often been used in elementary and middle schools to foster teacher leadership for innovation and improvement, but the results of such structural changes have been mixed. Formal teams may have limited effects on student achievement (Hackmann, Petzko, Valentine, Clark, & Nori, 2002; Supovitz, 2002) and may even undermine collaboration on a school-wide basis (Kruse & Louis, 1997). Instead, both researchers and practioners are focusing more on developing semiformal teamwork and collaboration in efforts to raise achievement—a culture of teamwork rather than a team structure (Chrispeels & Martin, 2002; Kanthak, 1995; Strahan, Cooper, & Ward, 2001). By *semiformal* we mean that groups of teachers rather than formal teaching teams chose to work together on a project relating to curriculum and instruction.

Professional development is typically a hallmark of evidence-based curriculum and instruction programs, particularly those sponsored by federal agencies. Quality professional development such as that delivered in these programs has been found, in other studies, to foster teamwork, innovation, and changes in practice (Disimone, Porter, & Garet, 2002). Not surprisingly, greater emphasis is being placed on whole-school or school-focused professional development, which is based on the principle of creating communities of conversation and support among teachers who work together. There is also consensus that professional development must consistently reinforce the basic focus on teaching and learning. This brings us back to the notion of instructional leadership, or at least a focus on curriculum, instruction, and classroom practice as the center of change (Spillane & Louis, 2002).

Change and Leadership Focusing on the Classroom

We begin with a number of assumptions. The first assumption is that reducing the achievement gap reduces the differential opportunity to learn. In other words, all students would be provided a rigor curriculum. Unless teachers have renewed curriculum and teach differently, it is hard to see how the achievement gap that characterizes most schools will be closed, and as Murphy points out, leaders at all levels in schools must accept their responsibility for creating a more just and equitable system. Nowhere is this more evident than in mathematics instruction, which, along with reading, has been the focus of major efforts to develop and "scale up" new ways of teaching less-advantaged students. In K–8 schools, much of the effort has been devoted to developing curricula that is challenging for all students. This effort to eliminate (or reduce) tracking is based on research that suggests that a differentiated curriculum contributes to the achievement gap of SES groups and ethnic groups (Hoeffer, 1995; Tate, 1997).

The second assumption is that students have an important role for student-centered leadership to be successful. In spite of the increasing emphasis on distributed–participatory leadership in fostering classroom change and student achievement, the focus of inquiry has been limited to adults (Rury, 2002). Students are generally viewed as passive actors in the school organizational innovation literature, where "stakeholders" are teachers, school administrators, parents, and policymakers (Sarason, 1996). Efforts to create participatory processes that include students are often transient, because they lack broad consensus around underlying organizational principles (Oakes, Quartz, Ryan, & Lipton, 2000). This perspective is in sharp contrast to research on instruction, which emphasizes the important role of students in guiding teachers' decisions (White, 1986; Windschitl & Sahl, 2002). Mathematics students are not just objects on which teachers act, but co-participants in the teaching–learning process (Franke & Kazemi, 2001). Though acknowledging that the schools in our research had few mechanisms to involve students on a formal level, we believe that the study of leadership and reform that pays no attention to the student voice is a problematic gap in the literature.

CURRICULUM AND LEADERSHIP CHANGE IN TWO SETTINGS

This chapter draws data from two different settings. The first setting is an urban school district whose middle schools had implemented CMP for 3 years and the second setting is an urban elementary charter school that started using Everyday Mathematics as a curriculum identified as closely aligned with the state's mathematics standards.

Setting 1: Urban Public Middle Schools

The analysis in this chapter is a secondary exploration of data collected from a larger study, whose purpose was to investigate the 3-year effects of Connections Mathematics Project (CMP) on the mathematics achievement of middle school students (Covington Clarkson, 2001). Quantitative data were collected from student records to compare the achievement of CMP students to the achievement of traditional curricula students, in general. The initial analyses suggest that students in CMP were not outscored by students in a traditional program, but that the achievement gap between African American and Caucasians students was smaller. Moreover, African American students in CMP outscored African American students in traditional curricula. The analysis below focuses on the effects of CMP on the social structure of classrooms and schools rather than student outcomes, although we briefly summarize the student achievement findings.

Method. The study design employed both qualitative and quantitative methods in a comparative study of classrooms and students in five schools located in an urban, Midwestern school district. The district in question was an ideal setting to look at leadership and reform. The superintendent at the time was regarded, both nationally and locally, as an exemplary proponent of curriculum reform, but also an advocate for site-based decision making. Information about the NSF funded model mathematics curriculum was available to all schools, and the district funded the extensive staff development activities that were intended as part of the implementation process. Schools were not, however, *required* to adopt the CMP model by a specific date.

Four schools were included in the study because they met the criterion of having school-wide implementation of CMP in Grades 6, 7, and 8 for 3 years by the beginning of the data collection (2000), and the teachers had participated in the district's staff development activities as well as having been supported by a mentor teacher. A comparison school was also sampled that met the criteria of having taught only traditional mathematics curricula in all three middle-level grades for 3 years.[3]

Data Collection.   Quantitative data relating to student demographics (race, SES, and ESL family background) and prior achievement (fifth-grade math and reading scores on the district's standardized tests) for those students who had experienced CMP/no CMP for 3 years were available for all schools. Classroom observations were conducted in eligible eighth-grade classrooms; if there was more than one eighth-grade math teacher, the teacher who was considered by the principal to be the "best implementer" of CMP was selected. Interviews were conducted with the five teachers and with a sample of the teachers' students ($N = 13$). Students were selected to maximize diversity in ability, gender, and ethnicity, although those who spoke no or very limited English were excluded. Principals in all five schools were also interviewed, as well as the district's mathematics specialist. Teachers and students were asked similar questions about perceptions of the pedagogy (the how) and the activities (the what) of mathematics lessons.

Data Analysis and Results.   Student eighth-grade results on the state's test of mathematics achievement while controlling for the available demographic characteristics were used in the analysis. As indicated previously, only students who met the strict criteria of exposure for 3 years/no exposure for 3 years were included. Regression models were run for the full sample, and separately for African Americans and Caucasians.[4] Because of the small number of interviews, the qualitative data were analyzed using "old fashioned" manual coding. Analyses focused on triangulating teacher and student perceptions of the classroom and its effectiveness in teaching and learning mathematics. For the purposes of this chapter, classroom observations were used primarily to examine communication and interaction patterns rather than the correspondence of teacher behavior to the expectations of CMP.

Findings from the quantitative data can be summarized simply: Overall, there was no significant difference in the mathematics achievement of middle school students in CMP when compared to that of middle school students in a traditional program. This chapter, however, refocuses our attention on interviews and observations to measure "success" that is not easily determined by the state's standards-based testing.

The qualitative data collected from interviews and classroom observations can be summarized in the following major findings substantiated with short vignettes form the observations and/or the voices of the students and their teachers.

- More mathematics interaction in CMP classrooms.

  Adams (CMP) teacher: *"They usually give all the input from the warm-up, you know, they give me the answers, so we're interacting there. During the class*

---

[3]Few comparison schools were available because of the district's support for a reformed mathematics curriculum.

[4]The focus of this analysis was on African Americans because the sample size was sufficient for us to consider the "closing the gap" issue. In the larger study analyses were also conducted with other ethnic and racial minority groups.

TABLE 5.1
Summary of Findings From Study 1

Achievement

> CMP students demonstrated algebraic reasoning skills at the same level as the traditional students and demonstrated conceptual understanding through use of multiple strategies at a higher level than the traditional students.

> Activities in the math class left a deeper impression on students and those impressions were more positive than those students who did not have activities in their math class.

School social structure

> CMP promoted communication between students as well as between students and teachers and between students and family members.

> CMP teachers have more opportunities for professional development experiences than traditional mathematics teachers. Principal involvement made a difference in implementation.

Community social structure

> Students in CMP classrooms interacted more mathematically than students in traditional classrooms and the quality of the mathematics as well as the quality of the interactions were better in CMP classrooms.

> CMP students had more opportunities to learn mathematics than traditional students. Additionally, ethnic minority students in CMP classrooms had more opportunities to learn mathematics than ethnic minorities in traditional classrooms.

time, I'm always walking around and asking them if they're getting it or if they're not, what's going on, so we're interacting in that way. And I guess, when they explain the summary, they're not only explaining it to the class but they're explaining it to me ... During the pair work, they are expected to talk."

Communication in the CMP classroom was not only allowed, but it was encouraged in all of the CMP classrooms. Each of the CMP classes demonstrated a variety of communication experiences for students. The students were consistently working in pairs or in small groups. Students also presented strategies and solutions to the whole class. Teachers were talking with students individually, facilitating pairs with guiding questions, and helping small groups during explorations.

- More opportunities to learn mathematics in CMP classrooms, especially for ethnic minority students.

The CMP lesson provided more opportunities for students to learn mathematics in the following ways. First, all students were provided the opportunity to learn "worthwhile" mathematics. Every student attending a CMP site was enrolled in a CMP mathematics class. There was no tracking into different levels of mathematics based on previous performance. Second, CMP students interacted with other students in their mathematics class. Communicating about mathematics allowed students to articulate their mathematical reasoning to peers. Third, interactions with the teacher further enabled students to communicate or justify their mathematical ideas while also allowing teachers to informally assess and provide feedback to students.

Observations and the teacher interviews suggest that students had different opportunities to learn mathematics based on the curriculum. One teacher indicated that CMP was the type of math where a variety of students had the opportunity to learn mathematics.

> Adams (CMP) teacher: *"They're from the [disability] program, but they asked if they could be linked up with CMP. One worked well for them. And I also had some ADHD students last year and it worked very well. So they ask if they could come in and just be in my math class but they aren't in any of the other classes. So they come just for [CMP]."*

Communication patterns also provided different opportunities for certain groups of students. In the traditional classroom, the teacher usually initiated any interaction between the teacher and the students. The teacher called on students to answer lower order questions throughout the observations, but never once called on an African American student. Noteworthy, the African American students in the traditional classroom had the farthest proximity to the teacher and rarely interacted with the teacher. Similarly, African American students did not volunteer to respond either.

The CMP classroom provided a different opportunity for interaction between the teacher and the students as well as between the students. Teachers consciously elicited responses from most students, which commonly included students of color. Students continually interacted with each other during exploration periods in most cases. Positive student interaction patterns were also evidenced in each of the CMP classrooms. Time on task, that is, engagement of students, also provided opportunities for students to learn mathematics.

- More communication between students as well as between students and teachers in CMP classrooms, and more communication about math between students and family members.

Generally, most CMP students indicated that they spoke to their teachers about math at some time. In addition, students indicated that they spoke to other students as well as family members about mathematics.

CMP students generally had positive comments about the interaction opportunities that occurred in their classrooms. They also shared positive comments about their teacher as they indicated that they liked that the interactions that they had with their teacher:

> Cara (CMP): *"... if we don't know it, [the teacher] explains it as much as she possibly can, so you can get it."*

> Justin (CMP): *"I like the way that [the teacher] helps us because, you know, [the teacher's] good at it. And even if we're not the best students all the time, [the teacher's] pretty good at making sure we understand."*

> Matt (CMP): *"[The teacher's] a really nice teacher and [the teacher] will like let us talk and stuff as long as we stay on the subject of math [until] we're done."*

Students talked to other students about math, too. Conversations happened in the classrooms as well as in the halls. Students talked in pairs or small groups inside the classroom while conversations outside of the classroom most likely occurred in pairs. These interactions were usually concerning homework problems or upcoming material.

> Vang (CMP): *"If I have a problem and I'm stumped on that problem, I'll ask them if they know it or [to] help me on it."*

Most students also indicated that they spoke to a parent, guardian, and/or sibling regarding their math. The conversations usually revolved around assistance with homework. Vang, a CMP student from Jackson, indicated that help was not available at home "...because [the parents] don't get it, because they're from another country." Even still, she felt as though her parents were supportive of the curriculum,

> Vang (CMP): *"...since we're doing something that they don't know, you know, they think that's really cool and it's good for us, you know, because we're getting more education than they have, so it's good."*

In more than one case, it was mentioned that the conversations developed into comparisons about math that CMP students were doing and the math that their parent and/or guardian experienced in eighth grade.

> Audrey (CMP): *"I talk about it with my guardian, my aunt, and my cousins ... If you compare what they did when they were in eighth grade with the math that we're learning now, and the differences. We've had lots of conversations about that. In the middle of me doing my homework, if I don't understand something, then we'll compare what they did to what I do now"*

• More active and positive recall of mathematics instruction in CMP classrooms.

Students were asked what they remembered about their sixth- and/or seventh-grade math class(es). Most CMP students remembered "doing" activities. Their comments describe a positive experience in mathematics across each of the CMP sites. The students were also asked what they would remember about their eighth-grade math class in a few years. Most CMP students responded that they would remember the activities.

> Justin (CMP): *"I remember the 'park project' ... It was fun once I got the hang of it. The major problem I had with it was I didn't know what the squares, how long to make all the squares."* (referring to sixth-grade CMP) *... I'll remember] how to do equations ... I'm good at equations. I didn't pass into geometry quite, but I'm good at equations."*

> Matt (CMP): *"I'll remember something that I just learned this year ... how to find out the tax and take like 20% off sales and stuff."*

Several students indicated that they liked working in groups and "doing activities and stuff." Audrey was insightful when she stated,

> Audrey (CMP): *"that instead of like getting fifty problems ... the CMP books actually have a goal behind them. [You] learn instead of sitting there trying to memorize your times tables ... it's more of a real life experience ... because a lot of the problems [are taken] from real life situations so [that] you understand how to work through stuff like that in later years."*

- Equivalent algebraic reasoning skills and greater conceptual understanding in the CMP classrooms. at the same level as the traditional students and demonstrated conceptual

Thomas A. Romberg (1998), University of Wisconsin, states that one of the goals of reform mathematics is for students to be able to use algebraic representations by the end of eighth grade. Students should develop this skill through the use of informal models and strategies as they move toward formal representations. To this end, students were asked to solve a problem that would demonstrate their algebraic reasoning skills. At the conclusion of each student interview, students were asked to think out loud as they were solving the problem. The students recorded their work and their solutions on the paper.

The student responses seemed to present three different groups of learners: students who completed the pattern correctly and derived the correct algebraic formula, students who completed the pattern correctly even though they derived an incorrect formula, and students who used methods other than a formula. CMP students used a larger variety of strategies (drawing, tables, pattern recognition, counting, and calculators) than traditional students and a higher percentage of CMP students were able to create algebraic representation, that is, a formula. CMP students were able to exhibit conceptual understanding of a recursive relationship through their written and verbal cues.

- CMP teachers have more opportunities for professional development and more networking with other teachers than traditional mathematics teachers.

All four of the CMP teachers in the study had participated in 80 hours of initial training in CMP pedagogy and mathematics content. These teachers also indicated that they participated in follow-up training sessions that were offered throughout their 1st year of teaching CMP. Each teacher used the mentor services provided by the district as well. Three of these CMP teachers are becoming involved in training new CMP teachers in the district. All talked about both the skills learned and the network of peers as major factors in their ability to change their practice.

- Principal involvement made a difference in implementation.

Principals were involved in the implementation of CMP to varying degrees. Most principals took a hands-off approach. That is, most did not attend any of the summer training sessions and even fewer participated in the follow-up sessions held through out the year. One principal supported teachers by providing an additional planning period for the teachers who had multiple preparations of CMP. The planning period was a common one so that teachers could collaborate in their planning. Three years later, the common planning period no longer exists but each teacher has taught each of the grade levels at least once and one teacher currently has only one grade level preparation.

Classroom observations indicated that the common planning period was effective for teachers to navigate through the curriculum, plan lessons, and test ideas. Teachers in this setting demonstrated the best lessons that were observed as a part of this study. They used instruction time efficiently and students responded positively. Students were also performing well on the basic skills test. In fact, close to 100% of the students passed this standardized test in mathematics on their first attempt.

> Adams (CMP) teacher: *"We plan together. Because we were given a math prep this quarter because we got a little burnt out last quarter during the elective time. Because we were teaching all three levels, our principal thought it would be nice and [the principal] worked it out that we could have a common prep time with the math teachers from 9:00 to 9:40."*

Setting 2: Urban Elementary Charter School

The results from the CMP middle school project intrigued us, and prompted an additional investigation of leadership, informal teaming, and implementation in a second setting, in which the first author was providing technical assistance with another NSF-sponsored program, *Everyday Math*.

Marshall Elementary School (MES) is an urban charter school with an Afrocentric focus. The school originated more than a decade ago in the home of the founders as a preschool. It later developed into a private elementary school for several years before becoming a public charter school. The founders decided that as a charter school they would be better able to serve a more socioeconomically diverse group of students. Presently, the school has approximately 350 students in kindergarten through the sixth grade. Ninety-nine percent of the students are African American and 70% of the student population qualify for free or reduced meals as determined by the federal guidelines. This study examined the affects of the new mathematics curriculum on student achievement as measured by the state No Child Left Behind assessment as part of the technical assistance provided by the first author. However, because of the relationship established with the staff members of the small school, the author was also able to gain access as a "participant observer" to study the issues raised in the first setting in more depth.

Method. This study design examined student achievement data, but this analysis relies more heavily on the first authors' journal entries during the 1-year period in which she "lived" in the school community.[5] The timeline of events and key activities are described in the data collection section.

In addition to the access provided by the participant observation role, Marshall was also an ideal choice for this research because of its distinct leadership style. Because

---

[5]More details about this study will be available in a forthcoming paper by Covington Clarkson.

this school had a history of being operated as a family business first and then as a private school, the leadership was, perhaps naturally, authoritative in nature. Moreover, the school had experienced significant student success with a highly structured and closely supervised reading program, but had minimal success with the previous mathematics program that was more traditional and teacher driven.

Data Collection: The State of the School Before ...   In December of 2001, math instruction was observed and the curriculum was examined. Most of the instruction was inconsistent with the NCTM standards. Primary teachers used one curriculum whereas intermediate teachers used another. Even more alarming was the fact that a student's math experience was not dependent on the state standards but rather on the skills the teacher identified as being important along with the curriculum's scope and sequence. At this time, the first author completed an alignment study of the curriculum's scope and sequence and the state standards. This study revealed that the curriculum did not sufficiently support the state standards. All of the strands—number sense; space, shape, and measurement; and data and probability—were not addressed before student's participated in state testing. Topics that were slighted in the curriculum included: collecting, representing, and analyzing data, creating and reading tables; creating line and bar graphs. In addition, students had no experiences with mathematical reasoning. Teachers were not aware of what student were required to know for the test and therefore could not adequately prepare students. A complete overhaul of the mathematics curriculum was proposed, and the school's director endorsed this approach.

Analysis and Results.   Data analysis included both an examination of improvements in mathematics test scores of the students over a 5-year period and a content analysis of the journal entries made by the first author. Table 5.2 summarizes the main findings of the analysis:

- Mathematics achievement increased in both tested grades.

State testing in Grades 3 and 5 provided data in both reading and math. Historically, Marshall Elementary students had performed above the state average in reading but struggled in mathematics in both grades. After the curriculum alignment, professional development experiences for teachers, and additional time for basic skills, the data provided significant evidence that student achievement improved almost immediately, and that these improvements were sustained. In Fig. 5.1, the scores for 2000 and 2001 represent preintervention scores. By 2002, after only preliminary planning and minor curriculum adjustments, 43.4% of the third graders were proficient and 43.59% of the fifth grade also scored in levels three, four, or five even after minor adjustments to the content and curriculum. After a year of school-wide strategic planning and systematic coordination, 54.76% of the fifth grade and an overwhelming 84.5% of the third grade were identified as proficient because they scored in levels three, four, or five on the state NCLB assessment in math. Although each year's scores consist of different groups of students, the school believes that students know and can do more, and expect that their students will continue to perform well on the state assessment.

Table 5.2

Summary of Findings in Setting 2

Achievement

> Mathematics achievement increased in grade five and significantly increased in grade three.
>
> Curricular alignment provided students with opportunities to learn mathematics that the state identified as grade level skills.

School social structure

> The new curriculum required and subsequently provided more professional development opportunities.
>
> Additional time was carved out of the schedule to focus on basic skills for students who were behind.
>
> The school director's involvement gave a sense of urgency to the implementation process.

Community social structure

> The overall plan provided teachers with opportunities to communicate within and across grade levels, and to make collective decisions.
>
> The school director's leadership style transformed not only in mathematics discussions but also in discussions about reading and language arts programs.

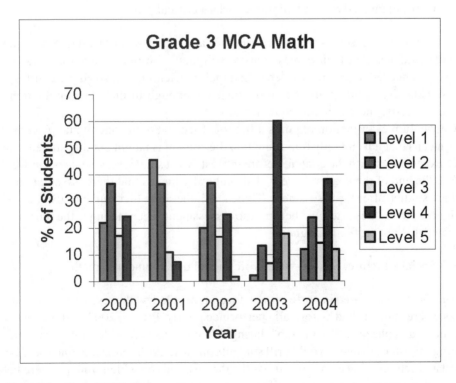

Figure 5.1. Grade 3 MCA Math.

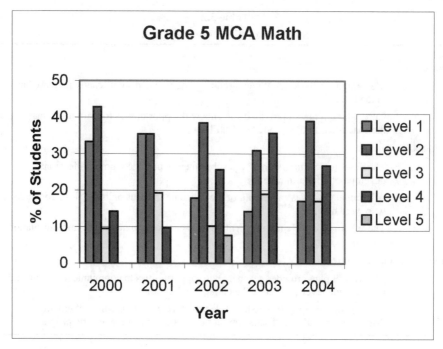

Figure 5.2.   Grade 5 MCA Math.

- Curriculum analysis and alignment was a critical process.

Though this step seems trivial, curriculum alignment was essential. States must provide evidence that their assessments are aligned with their standards. Likewise, this school needed to provide evidence that their curriculum is also aligned with standards. This alignment should be comprehensive enough to include examination of standards, tests, and curricular content and vocabulary.

Curriculum examination requires a flexible focus on both content and placement. This means that it is not only important that the content is taught but that students also have experiences with the content before the test. Most state assessments occur weeks before the end of the academic year. This naturally means that there are some topics that are studied after the assessment. Thus, it is imperative that students also have experiences with these topics before the assessment even though the curricular placement is not perfectly aligned.

- Social structure: School-wide professional development in math.

Teachers participated in professional development led by the researcher on content areas where students had historically performed poorly. Prior to 2002, test preparation was more a haphazard "boot camp" during 4 to 6 weeks before the state assessment. During this time, teachers would drill students on basic skills. Now the time was designated as a school-wide effort to address the three strands on which students were to be assessed. Each week focused on a different content area, such as data representation or measurement. Specific grade level skills were identified and taught during the weeks.

Although the situation was not ideal, the spring assessment suggested that the concentrated school-wide effort was effective even within a limited amount of time (3-month period). This effort was merely a "band-aid fix" for a much larger systemic problem.

During the spring of 2002, *Everyday Math* was selected as the school-wide mathematics curriculum. Teachers received initial training on the last day of the 2001–2002 academic year. August brought more professional development and the start of grade level meetings. Each team met with the researcher once a week for pacing and content updates during the first semester. In addition, more time was allocated to mathematics. A new math specialist was hired and taught all four sections of math for grades 5 and 6.

Later professional development for teachers included two important phases. During the first phase, teachers studied the mathematics standards, test specifications, and sample problems. This phase provides direction for instruction. The purpose of the second phase of professional development is to deepen teacher content knowledge and to give them a language for working together, removing their dependence on an outside professional developer. Both phases prepare teachers to provide students with opportunities to learn the mathematics of the grade level assessments.

- Participatory decision making around math curriculum.

Once the curriculum alignment was completed, it was necessary to select a high-quality curriculum that was more closely aligned with assessment goals. Though there is no perfectly aligned curriculum, many commercial publishers tout their alignment to the NCTM standards. But states are assessing *their* standards, which are increasingly grade level and skill specific, and they specify when this specific knowledge will be tested. Still, curricular goals need to be aligned with the NCTM standards. NCTM standards provide students with a mathematics background that will prepare them for more opportunities—mathematical, educational, and economic, irrespective of state tests. Teacher meetings, which were frequently attended by the principal, addressed the need to adjust NCTM and state standards in implementing *Everyday Math*.

- Shifting the school's schedule to accommodate a new focus.

Participation did not stop with the selection of the curriculum, however. The school began to examine its organization to better manage the tension between meeting NCTM and state norms. This tension is particularly stressful in schools like MSE. Not only does staff have to think about the dual alignment between state and NCTM standards, but they must also address the fact that their students are behind and lack developmental skills from previous grades. In urban school settings, student turnover (both within and between years) means that developmental issues cannot be fully resolved with effective curriculum and instructional planning. Students who are behind in mathematics are responsible for their grade-level skills, which are usually developmental and dependent on skills from previous grades. Simply put, to make up for the deficient skills, underperforming students needed more time and more time was allocated for math instruction.

In the fall of 2002, a sample state assessment was administered. Areas of strengths and weaknesses were identified. Systematically, the school schedule was reorganized to provide more time for mathematics instruction. In the past, MES students began their day with 90 min of reading, and math happened at different times during the day for each class. Now each kindergarten through fourth-grade class had math as the second block of the day. Because the math specialist taught all four sections from grades 5 and 6, these students continued to have at different times. Fifth-grade classes, however, were held earliest in the day because this was a state testing year. Fifth-grade students were more diverse in their math proficiency so an additional 15-min block of time was added to their schedule (it replaced the morning meeting) to focus on basic skills. The math specialist, the director, the classroom teachers, and the researcher also met weekly to assess the progress of the fifth-grade students. "Math Camp" was offered during spring break even though attendance was low. Math Night introduced parents to the new curriculum and the ways they could help their students at home.

- Shifting from authoritarian to distributed leadership.

Much of the work focused on improving the school's curriculum and teachers' ability to deliver it. The introduction of Everyday Math meant a critical shift, but most of the interventions emphasized working with teachers and the school leaders, as a group, to establish a new set of norms for how curriculum evolves. This process contrasts dramatically with the origins of the reading program, which was "invented," polished, and consistently transmitted by the school's founders, and provided a core identity for the school—but reexamining it was not encouraged. Teachers were not permitted to question the efficacy of the reading programs, and they were encouraged to leave the school if they disagreed with the founders' overall purpose and practice in this area. Because reading achievement in MSE was above the city's average for low-income minority students, there was little basis for challenging the norm of authoritarian leadership. Mathematics reform, on the other hand, took a different route.

POINTS TO PONDER

The overarching purpose of the NCTM *standards* is to raise the mathematics achievement of all students. *Standards*-based curricula like CMP and *Everyday Math* incorporate "new" pedagogy to teach "new" mathematics content that is based on mathematics understanding and reasoning as well as procedures and "math facts" (National Advisory Committee on Mathematical Education, 1975). In spite of support from national bodies, including the National Council for Teachers of Mathematics and the National Science Foundation, this shift has been slow, as local boards and school administrators seemed to go along with this "business as usual." On the other hand, shifts in mathematics content, pedagogy, scope, and conversations surrounding them in part is due to *No Child Left Behind*.

The three components that Murphy (2001) described as the new anchors for administrative leadership—school improvement, democratic community, and social justice—provided the foundation for the body of this thesis. These findings, consistent with the new anchors for leadership described by Murphy, are summarized in Table 5.3.

TABLE 5.3

Findings Disaggregated by Murphy's Components of New Administrative Leadership

	School Improvement	*Democratic Community*	*School Justice*
Students	Students demonstrated consistent growth in mathematics achievement: *both settings*	Students demonstrated increased mathematics communication in the classroom and outside the classroom: *setting 1*	More students had more opportunities to learn mathematics especially underrepresented students: *both settings*
Teachers	Teachers had more opportunities for professional development: *both settings*	Teachers had more opportunities to plan with their peers. *both settings*	Teachers accepted less tracking of students into lower groups: *setting 1*
Informational leadership teams	School leaders became more involved in curriculum and instructional issues: *variable in setting 1; pre-existing in setting 2*	Leadership style shifts from authoratative to participatory: *setting 2*	Teachers and principals understood the importance of exposing all students to "real world" mathematics; *both settings*
School improvement focus	School improvement efforts focused on "the gap" in *both settings*	More democratic organization is an unanticipated outcome of curriculum change: *both settings*	African American students had increased mathematics achievement: *both settings*

- School improvement.

CMP and *Everyday Math* provided an avenue for school improvement in the following ways. Teachers were afforded more opportunities for professional development experiences and students continued to demonstrate consistent growth in mathematics achievement when tested with traditional standardized assessments. Though these studies focused on the experiences of the students, it is also important to recognize the professional development opportunity for teachers in both settings. Professional development experiences are an important part of successful implementation of curricular reform. It is even more important when the reform is in elementary or middle school mathematics because of the large numbers of teachers who were trained as generalists and are serving as mathematics teachers with little or no formal education beyond high school mathematics. Professional development experiences provided teachers in both settings with more mathematics content knowledge and also prepared teachers to implement the lessons. Teachers and, in turn, students appeared to benefit from the professional development experiences.

- Democratic community.

The anchor of democratic community was evident through the communication opportunities. Students in setting 1 were talking to other students, to teachers, and to family members. Moreover, teachers in both settings had chances to talk to each other and share ideas especially when principals granted additional planning time. Administrative leadership was key to providing teachers with a schedule that increased the likelihood of peer communication and planning.

Democratic community was further evident in the transformation of leadership style. Though the authoritative leadership style was a traditional part of the school culture at MSE, unknowingly participatory leadership emerged in this setting.

- Social justice.

The opportunity to learn quality mathematics for all students established the foundation for social justice. The data suggest that there are aspects of CMP that are effective in middle school classrooms and most of these can best be described as increasing the opportunity to learn. All students experienced challenging mathematics. African American students, specifically, demonstrated mathematical achievement that was not evident under traditional curricula. Opportunity to learn was also evident from the curricular alignment of *Everyday Math* to the state standards. MSE students were now better prepared for the state assessment simply because they had experiences with the content of the math assessment.

In conclusion, no curriculum can alter the combination of the participants and the demographic circumstances that they bring to the classroom. But CMP did change what happened in the mathematics classroom once they met. These studies found stronger and more positive relationships between the students and the teachers; it also found a learning environment that was aligned with NCTM standards and focused on problem solving, communication, mathematical reasoning, and strategy development. Succinctly, these studies found democratic communities where school improvement was inevitable because of the increased social justice through innovative administrative leadership.

REFERENCES

Bista, M., & Glasman, N. (1998). Principals' leadership, antecedence, and student outcomes. *Journal of School Leadership, 8*(2), 109–136.

Carter, K. (2002). Leadership in urban and challenging contexts: Investigating EAZ policy and practice. *School Leadership and Management, 22*(1), 41–59.

Chrispeels, J. H., & Martin, K. J. (2002). Four school leadership teams define their roles within organizational and political structures to improve student learning. *School Effectiveness and School Improvement, 13*, 327–365.

Clark, S. N., & Clark, D. C. (2002). Collaborative decision making; a promising but underused strategy for middle school improvement. *Middle School Journal, 33*(4), 52–57.

Cooney, S., Moore, B., & Bottoms, G. (2002). Preparing all students for high school. *Principal, 81*(3), 40–41.

Covington Clarkson, L. M. (2001). *The effects of the Connected Mathematics Project on middle school mathematics achievement.* PhD dissertation, Minneapolis, MN: University of Minnesota.

DiSimone, L., Porter, A., & Garet, M. (2002). Effects of professional development on teachers instruction: Results from a three-year longitudinal study. *Educational Evaluation and Policy Analysis, 24*(2), 81–112.

Franke, M., & Kazemi, E. (2001). Learning to teach mathematics: Focus on student thinking. *Theory into Practice, 40*(2), 102–109.

Fullan, M. (1982). *The meaning of educational change*. New York: Teachers College Press.

Fullan, M., & Stiegelbauer, S. (1994). *The new meaning of educational change*. New York: Teachers College Press.

Hackmann, D., Petzko, V., Valentine, J., Clark, D. C., Nori, J., & Lucas, S. (2002). Beyond interdisciplinary teaming: Findings and implications of the NASSP national middle level study. *NASSP Bulletin, 86*(632), 33–47.

Hallinger, P. (1996). School context, principal leadership, and student reading achievement. *Elementary School Journal, 96,* 527–549.

Hallinger, P., & Heck, R. (1998). Exploring the principal's contribution to school effectiveness: 1980–1995. *School effectiveness and school improvement, 9*(2), 157–191.

Harris, A. (2002). Effective leadership in schools facing challenging contexts. *School Leadership and Management, 22*(1).

Hess, F. (1999). Understanding achievement (and other) changes under Chicago school reform. *Educational Evaluation and Policy Analysis, 21*(1), 67–83.

Hoeffer, T. B., Rasinski, K. A., & Moore, W. (1995). *Social background differences in high school mathematics and science coursetaking and achievement* (NCES 95-206). Washington, DC: U.S. Department of Education.

Hoy, W., Hannum, J., & Tschannen-Moran, M. (1998). Organizational climate and student achievement: A parsimonious and longitudinal view. *Journal of School Leadership, 8,* 336–359.

Kathak, L. M. (1995). Teamwork: Profile of high schieving schools and their leaders. *Schools in the Middle, 5*(2), 27–30.

Kruse, S., & Louis, K. S. (1997). Teacher teaming in middle school: Dilemmas for school-wide community. *Educational Administration Quarterly, 33,* 261–289.

Leithwood, K., & Louis, K. S. (Eds.). (1998). *Organizational learning in schools*. Lisse, NL: Swets and Zeitlinger.

Leithwood, K., Louis, K. S., Anderson, S., & Wahlstrom, K. (2005). *How leadership influences student learning*. Retrieved July 2005 from http://www.wallacefoundation.org/WF/KnowledgeCenter/KnowledgeTopics/EducationLeadership/HowLeadershipInfluencesStudentLearning.htm

Louis, K. S., Marks, H., & Kruse. (1996). Teachers' professional community in restructuring schools. *American Educational Research Journal, 33,* 357–398.

Louis, K. S., & Miles, M. B. (1990). *Improving the urban high school: What works and why*. New York: Teachers College Press.

Murphy, J. (2001). Reculturing the profession of educational leadership: New blueprints. In J. Murphy (Ed.), *Challenges of leadership: Yearbook of the National Society for the Study of Education*. Chicago: University of Chicago Press.

Muijs, D., Harris, A., Chapman, C., Stoll, L., & Russ, J. (2004). Improving schools in socioecononucally disadvantaged areas—A review of research evidence. *School Effectiveness and School Improvement, 15*(2), 149–175.

Newmann, F. M., & Wehlage, G. G. (1995). *Successful school restructuring: A report to the public and educators*. Madison, WI: Center on Organization and Restructuring of Schools, Wisconsin Center for Education Research, University of Wisconsin.

Newmann, F., Smith, B., Allensworth, E., & Bryk, A. S. (2002). Improving Chicago's schools: School instructional program coherence. *ERS Spectrum, 20*(2), 38–46.

Oakes, J., Quartz, K. H., Ryan, S., & Lipton, M. (2000). *Becoming good American schools: The struggle for civic virtue in educational reform*. San Francisco: Jossey Bass.

Pounder, D. (1995). Leadership as an organization-wide phenomenon: Its impact on school performance. *Educational Administration Quarterly, 31,* 564–588.

Rury, J. (2002). Democracy's high school? Social change and American secondary education in the post-Conant era. *American Educational Research Journal, 39,* 307–336.

Sarason, S. (1996). *Revisiting "The culture of the school and the problem of change."* New York: Teachers College Press.

Scribner, J. P., Cockrell, K. S., Cockrell, D. H., & Valentine, J. W. (1999). Creating professional communities in schools through organizational learning: An evaluation of a school improvement process. *Educational Administration Quarterly, 35*(1), 130–160.

Spillane, J. P., Halverson, R., & Diamond, J. B. (2001). Investigating school leadership practice: A distributed perspective. *Educational Researcher, 30*(3), 23–28.

Spillane, J., & Louis, K. S. (2002). School improvement processes and practices: Professional learning for building instructional capacity. In J. Murphy (Ed.), *Challenges of leadership: Yearbook of the National Society for the Study of Education.* Chicago: University of Chicago Press.

Strahan, D., Cooper, J., & Ward, M. (2001). Middle school reform through data and dialogue—Collaborative evaluation with 17 leadership teams. *Evaluation Review, 25*(1), 72–99.

Supovitz, J. (2002). Developing communities of instructional practice. *Teachers College Record, 104,* 1591–1626.

Tate, W. F. (1997). Race-ethnicity, SES, gender, and language proficiency trends in mathematics achievement: An update. *Journal of Research in Mathematics Education, 28,* 652–679.

Teddlie, C., & Reynolds, D. (2000). *The international handbook of school effectiveness research.* New York: Falmer.

White, P. (1986). Self-respect, self-esteem, and the school: A democratic perspective on authority. *Teachers College Record, 88*(1), 95–106.

Windschitl, M., & Sahl, K. (2002). Tracing teachers use of technology in a laptop computer chool: The interplay of teacher beliefs, social dynamics and institutional culture. *American Educational Research Journal, 39*(1), 165–205.

6

THE DEVELOPMENT
OF LEADERSHIP IN MATHEMATICS:
CASES OF URBAN REFORM

James A. Middleton
Arizona State University

Kay Coleman
Cartwright Elementary School District

Even a cursory glance at current reforms in mathematics education and other content areas reveals that one of the primary mechanisms for managing staff development, infusing innovation across the system, and sustaining reform efforts is the identification and training of teacher-leaders. The notion of a teacher-leader is not new to education. The notion of a principal, in fact, comes from the idea of a "principal teacher" who provides vision and direction for a school faculty. More recently, as schools and school districts have become large corporate structures, the notion of a teacher-leader has become differentiated from the administrative role of the principal or district administration.

The reforms and funding for professional development in the Johnson era during the 1960s created large numbers of institutes and projects with specific focus on content or particular approaches to pedagogy. Since those times, professional development has become more and more focused, requiring the education of staff with expertise in the areas of interest in which the education system wanted to move. By and large, these innovations relied on a pyramid model of diffusion—a trainer of trainers model—to scale up the number and quality of experiences throughout large, particularly urban, school systems. The residue of these models often doesn't last for a very long time when the source of funding for the teacher-leader position (primarily soft money) ends. Nevertheless, we can trace the invention of the curriculum specialist position, often at a district level, as a direct result of the simultaneous growth of districts, coupled with the increased need for content-specific teacher training. This position remains critical for the diffusion of innovation in large urban school districts, as the (former) teacher who occupies this role serves to broker the mandates of administration with the professed needs of teachers, and serves as a point-of-contact between teachers in the field, and the budgetary and executive bureaucracies of the system (Middleton & Webb, 1994).

Aside from the curriculum specialist, little personnel money is slated to maintain the release time, professional development experiences, and support structures of teachers identified as instructional leaders. And so, these teachers go back full-time to the classroom, doing great work personally, but the entire structure of the professional development program collapses with no personnel to perform the tasks of instruction, mentoring, and curriculum development. A more effective program for scale-up involves a broad constituency of teachers developing together over a long period of time. Instead of the trainer-of-trainers model, which assumes that leaders are knowledge disseminators, models that assume a cognitive coaching or team leader role seem to be more effective over the long haul in influencing student achievement. Under such models, leaders emerge broadly distributed when departments or grade-level teams grapple with issues of student learning and how their own practices can contribute to that learning (e.g., Kennedy, 1999).

The purpose of this article is to describe an innovative approach to teacher professional development that makes heavy use of teacher-leaders but that does not assume a trainer-of-trainers model. The case we are reporting is a medium-to-large urban, elementary school district (Grades K–8). We develop our model for the reader narratively, by recounting the development of innovations as their need arose over the course of 9 years of sustained effort. This effort needs to be underscored up front, as it represents the collective toil of a teaching cadre and building-level and district-level administration as they attempted to reform mathematics curriculum, teaching, and assessment over 9 years of concentrated effort.

WHY DEVELOP TEACHER-LEADERS?

Given the inability of most trainer-of-trainer models of leadership development to sustain innovation over the long haul, it becomes necessary to answer the question, "Why develop teacher-leaders at all?" It turns out there are a number of critical reasons why a local colleague, who is a peer at the building or grade level, is a more credible and more effective staff developer, in the long run, than either an outside expert or an expert at the administrative level of a district. These reasons center around the place of a teacher in the local community (both school and surrounding environs), and the place of administration (particularly in the current politics of urban school districts).

Sustained Reform Over Time

As alluded to earlier, one of the key failures of systemic reform efforts is the ability to institutionalize and sustain the initiated reforms beyond the typical 5-year lifespan of most federal projects. If continued activity is in fact a goal, there must be some administrative structure that (a) embeds the key learnings incurred in the professional development project in the building and grade levels and that (b) provides a feedback loop regarding the success of the reforms to the project as a whole. With the size of modern districts constituting multiple schools with potentially hundreds of teachers, some personnel that have direct access to each classroom on a regular basis are required to staff such an administrative structure. When faced with the further constraint on the limited number of people with the subject-matter expertise, expertise in a particular strategy for reform, and legitimacy in the eyes of practitioners, the pool of potential people to make up this staff is limited to teachers and a few experts at the district level and perhaps at local higher education institutions. A final constraint, cost, predicates that the structure for sustained activity in systemic reform be made up of current district employees—teachers.

Moreover, the development of local experts who have an investment in the community and institution is more likely to afford continued activity than is hiring a set of paid consultants from the outside. Teachers by and large live and work in, or at least have a professional investment in, the communities within which their schools are located. And, though teacher mobility across districts is becoming more and more of a staffing problem, there are still large numbers of teachers who remain in district for extended periods of time, sustaining the institutional knowledge of the reform beyond the life of external funding.

Transcending the Revolving Door Administrator

Though acknowledging teacher mobility to be a difficult problem, the bigger problem in school leadership today is the tendency for high-level administration to leave office in 3- to 5-year cycles (Middleton & Webb, 1994). When teachers are faced with new mandates, policies, procedures, and personalities regularly, they tend to perform their duties *in spite of* administration. Teacher-leaders, who are less likely to move than administration, can provide a more stable infrastructure on which to hang systemic reform than, say, superintendents and principals.

Embeddedness in the Community

High-quality teachers have the legitimacy to enact reforms that may at first be controversial by virtue of their connectedness with parents. Both the fact that teachers may encounter multiple children from the same family year after year, and their presence in community affairs, make them key brokers of information about reform and key advocates for the district.

Authority by Virtue of Experience

Though there are numerous cases of young, "wet behind the ears" teachers becoming leaders, our experience is such that we would characterize this as the exception rather than the rule. The level of experience working in classrooms with the same characteristics as others in the school or districts is taken seriously by teachers, and they hold a healthy skepticism of any new reform proposed by someone who hasn't actually tried to implement it under authentic conditions of teaching. Moreover, as the community becomes more attuned to the difficulties new teachers experience during their first few years in the classroom, the natural leadership (both good and bad) that an experienced teacher can exert over the inexperienced colleague is powerful. It seems profitable, then, to harness this natural apprenticeship, identify good role models, and support them with high quality experiences, tools, and materials. This influence may also be important for experienced teachers who are new to a school and who could use information about curriculum, available technologies, district expectations and philosophy, and school culture.

Capability for Moving Administration

As we speak of influence, the potential impact of teacher-leaders on the coherence and consistency of service in the district, given the increased mobility of administrators, cannot be understated. In numerous districts we have worked with, the core leadership among the teaching cadre remains stable across multiple administrations that often bring competing agendas that may countermand any current direction of reform. Teacher-leaders, as successful agents of reform, have been approached by new administrators for guidance in the implementation of new policies, for identification of appropriate sites for action, and for communication of new directions to the general district faculty. In some instances, initiative by the teachers in the district may actually provide impetus for administration to change or enact new policies, curriculum cycles, or priorities for professional development.

BASIC ASSUMPTIONS

The literature on leadership development defines leadership in simple, no-nonsense terms, as establishing direction for an organization, and influencing others to move in that direction (McNamara, 1999). Leadership development in K–12 school systems, then, can be defined as *the stimulation of the intellectual capacity of a district, aligned towards programmatic change*. Inherent to this definition is the belief that the capacity for leadership exists in all organizations, indeed, in all individuals in an organization. The key to widespread assumption of leadership responsibilities aligned to curricular reform is an *institutional priority towards the development of local expertise in all content areas*. Particularly in elementary schools, the model of the generalist teacher has not allowed teachers to become distinguished professionally from each other, to develop deep expertise in any one area of interest, or concomitantly, to take on the role of a leader in driving change in curriculum. Instead, curricular reform has been driven by textbook adoption cycles, state and local legislation, or administrator fiat.

It is clear from this bottom-up approach that the style of leadership we are focusing on is that of the democratic, participatory leader—one who empowers his or her team to direct themselves, providing information and resources as needed to maintain a coherent positive reform direction (e.g., Barth, 2001). Authority in such systems is driven by intellectual resources, knowledge, and vision, and different leaders emerge to assist the team at moments when their particular expertise can be brought to bear.

Moreover, this model assumes that teachers-as-leaders do not exist on their own, but in a community of learners, devoted to better understanding content, pedagogy, and the institutional context within which their practices must be imbedded. Broadly defined, the community(ies) of learners we are describing are coordinated around a common topic of interest within mathematics education (e.g., Cognitively Guided Instruction, Statistics in the Middle Grades, Collaborative Action Research on Geometry, to name a few), *and* these topical organizations are connected at a higher level of organization to disciplinary societies (e.g., National Council of Teachers of Mathematics), with their opportunities for enhanced professional development in the form of conferences, meetings, readings and publication, and higher education with its opportunities for degree programs, academic coursework, mentorship, and research projects.

Lastly, this model is developed in reaction to and stands in contradistinction to the current anti-intellectual movement in public education. Disciplined practical knowledge is assumed to be coherent, deriving on the best empirical evidence available. It is also assumed to be generative, continuously striving for improvement. It is also assumed to be theoretical, tied to a body of knowledge that explains *how* and *why* actions lead to particular forms of behavior and knowledge. This emphasis does not lessen the need for the "wisdom of practice"; rather it provides a structure by which this wisdom can be recognized and stimulated.

The remainder of this article chronicles the history and practices of leadership development in the Jefferson Elementary School District in urban Phoenix, Arizona. It describes major dilemmas facing teachers, administration, and parents as they grappled with changing demographics, administration, and curricular mandates. It also describes major opportunities that arose as a result of the district brokering relationships with Universities and Federal agencies. In the end, we provide musings on what worked and why, such that the intellectual residue of our work results in a plausible model of leadership development that can be transported to other districts facing similar pressures and opportunities.

HISTORY OF REFORM IN JEFFERSON

Demographic Description of Jefferson

The Jefferson Elementary School District is a Pre-K–8 public district located in the central corridor of Phoenix, Arizona. It serves approximately 5,000 students in seven schools. The ethnic breakdown is 3% Asian, 5% African American, 19% Hispanic, 5% American Indian, and 68% White. Based on trend data it is predicted that the district will have at least as many minority students as White students by 2007. Roughly 13% of the students are English Language Learners with 15 primary languages other than English represented. Free and reduced lunch rate is about 41% overall with the percentage varying between schools from 12% to 75%. The spectrum of poverty and racial–ethnic mix is not uniform across schools. Schools in the north of the district are more White and affluent. Schools in the south of the district tend to serve high poverty areas with a large percentage of minority and ELL students.

When this work began in 1994 Jefferson had a proven track record for student achievement as measured by norm-referenced standardized tests. The students in the district consistently scored above average compared to students across the county, state, and nation. In the early 1990s, prior to the initiatives in both mathematics and literacy, the district suffered a drop in ranking from which they were still trying to recover. There was a real understanding that, if the achievement levels did not rise, the affluent parents in the northern part of the district would pull their children from the public school system and educate them in private schools.

Chronology

In the early 1990s the curricular infrastructure of the district was largely lacking. There was no written curriculum for any content area and so it became clear to both administration and existing teacher-leaders that the core content areas needed to have curriculum frameworks and assessments developed. During these years the content taught in teachers' classes was textbook driven and new textbooks were purchased on an ongoing basis with the selection process being highly influenced by publishers who made direct contact with teachers.

In 1993 a new superintendent was hired. The following year he hired a new assistant superintendent (Coleman), whose job was to reverse the academic and instructional program decline with a focus on learning for all students. One of the first actions the new administration initiated was to have an external organization conduct a curriculum management audit and to begin to work with teachers who were interested in learning more about mathematics and literacy, which would be the focus of the initial curriculum development. Though this article centers on the work in mathematics and the development of leadership in that content area, contextually, it is important to understand that similar work was ongoing in literacy.

Beginning Work: Setting the Stage for Reform

To identify potential leaders for the effort, an invitation was sent out to all teachers to apply for the Mathematics Task Force. The application process was new to the district and not easily accepted. There were teachers who refused to apply because they viewed themselves as "the leaders" in mathematics and they questioned who this "new person" (i.e., the associate superintendent) was and what right she had to ask this of them.[1] Coleman felt that the process of application was important as it would begin to

---

[1] At least one of the strongest leaders in the district refused to apply in the initial stages of the reform effort. Her subsequent conversion will be treated later.

establish a professional context for the work to come. Ultimately all teachers who applied were accepted to the task force. In schools not represented, principals were instrumental in encouraging involvement of teachers interested in mathematics.

The task force began work in earnest with 3-hour meetings after school every other week for the academic year. This task force began its work by familiarizing itself with the latest research and background in the psychology of learning mathematics, Standards for Curriculum, Teaching, and Assessment, and in pedagogy specific to mathematics content. The group read the latest compendia of research, with chapters assigned to different members. They discussed the findings, and brought in experts in mathematics and mathematics education for specific instruction for the full year. Middleton was a new professor at ASU and agreed to help nurture the intellectual growth of the group, as did Nora Ramirez of the Maricopa Community College District, an educator active in the National Council of Teachers of Mathematics, and a leader in state mathematics reform.

Some of the reading was considered tortuous by the teachers, to the point that some members came to Coleman in tears believing that they could not think at that high of a level. Two teachers dropped out of the group because of the intellectual challenge. As a group these teachers had not had this type of challenge in understanding professional literature since graduate school, which for some, was many years prior. Further, only one teacher in the group was even familiar with the NCTM Standards (1989), which was at that time, new and revolutionary on the national scene. Middleton recommended Grouws' *Handbook of Research on Mathematics Teaching and Learning* (1992) along with articles on Cognitively Guided Instruction (Carpenter, 1985) and other pertinent mathematics articles. The practical work in exploring a new way of thinking about math instruction was facilitated by purchasing materials from the NCTM and Marilyn Burns. Teachers were asked to use these materials in their classrooms as replacement units—a kind of priming of the pump. Fortunately, Phoenix was the site of the NCTM regional conference that fall and all task force members were invited to attend and bring several colleagues and their principal with them.[2] This was a great opportunity for everyone to get a glimpse inside the bigger world of mathematics. It was at this point that a decision was made by Coleman to send task force members and their colleagues to the national NCTM conference on an annual basis if finances permitted.

During that year (1994–1995) the task force also was released for 6 full days (beyond regular staff development days) in which special speakers were invited to share insights into reform mathematics. The university partnership with Middleton was forged during this year (see also Middleton, Sawada, Judson, Bloom, & Turley, 2002). The work continued through the first month of Summer 1995 with the express purpose of designing what the curriculum outcomes would be for each grade level. Middleton spent every afternoon of that month with the task force following his own teaching of courses at the University in the morning. A love–hate relationship developed as Middleton pushed the task force members to think deeply about mathematics and student learning. The argument that was fostered in this summer work set the norms for

---

[2]A recurring theme throughout our reform efforts is that of *taking advantage of opportunities*. When an opportunity to learn arose, generally the district found ways to say "yes" and provide some level of support for teachers to attend meetings, purchase materials, or become involved in University projects.

professional interaction in the group that still exists today. Briefly, mathematics and mathematics education topics are open for skepticism and critique, and any recommendation for reform must be justified by an understanding of how it enhances the coherence of the curriculum, stems from best practices in teaching, and impacts children's mathematical thinking.

By the end of June the group had created a curriculum guideline and comprehensive set of standards for student learning, assessment, and teaching in the district. Although the group had been anxious to examine published curriculum materials, Coleman asked them to do the thinking about a coherent continuum of the curriculum first—generating the guidelines. The completion of these curriculum guidelines allowed the task force to then begin to look at curriculum materials, and they went forward from there to select a pool of possible materials, including NSF-sponsored curricula and some traditional materials, to begin a pilot test the coming school year.

Piloting New Curricula

To ensure buy-in and a reasonable pool of data from which to make decisions, the group of pilot teachers included all the task force members plus another 30 volunteers from across the district. Training in the specifics of the curricula took place prior to the school year, starting with publishers and relying heavily on task force members to support their colleagues in this important step. The pilot year was eventful because much of the material that is now taken for granted as quality instructional tools was still in prepublication form (e.g., *Mathematics in Context; Connected Mathematics Project; Investigations in Number, Data, and Space*).

In particular, the frustrations dealing with publishers began early in just procuring materials and training, and continued throughout the pilot year. Coleman, in a leap of frustration, phoned the authors of the materials directly and thus began a strong relationship with the authors and their institutions, which have provided varying levels of support throughout the implementation. In the pilot year, all pilot teachers met twice per month, much in the same way that the task force had done in the 1st year. Sessions were organized around discussion of what students were doing, what was going on in classes, and defining the problems teachers were having in implementation. Based on teachers' needs consultants were brought in to help them in their next steps.

At this point it became clear that this adoption was going to be like no other before, for the district and for Coleman. Strong opinions about what set of materials to adopt, for what children, and at what schools had the potential to diffuse the momentum gained in the Mathematics Task Force, and to diffuse the coherence of children's instructional experiences across the grade span. It was clear that the capacity for leadership needed to be developed *at the school level* so that teachers and principals had someone with a strong knowledge base to support the implementation of the reform programs that were adopted at the end of 1995–1996, thus, the birth of Mathematics Teacher-Leaders (MTLs).

Building-Based Mathematics Teacher-Leaders

Coleman went to the Task Force and discussed the idea of creating a group of building-based Mathematics Teacher-leaders (MTLs). The model was based on work that she had been involved with for several years in developing Literacy Teacher-Leaders and had already instituted in the district. From the beginning the group knew that the model would be different and that they would develop its structure as they went. The search began for someone who could support the MTLs on a monthly basis. A decision was made to bring a consultant in from California, Cynthia Garland, who had a strong background in *Math Their Way* (Baratta-Lorton, 1976) and *TERC Investigations* (TERC, 1997) for the MTLs in Grades K–5.

During the third year (1996–1997) all second- through fourth-grade teachers began implementation of the newly adopted curriculum and materials. Teachers were offered a full-week workshop in the summer to support the implementation. Two MTLs were identified at each building and they served as resources to their colleagues. They were selected primarily from members of the Math Task Force with input from the principals. Initially they helped with materials and organization and facilitated six early release days for staff development during the year. These sessions were organized as grade level groups across the district. They also offered voluntary study groups that met twice a month for each grade level with the purpose of helping support the implementation of the new materials. Many of the MTLs offered classroom demonstrations, peer coaching, and other mentoring opportunities on an informal basis based on their readiness to support their colleagues in these ways. Much was asked of the MTLs during this time.

Training for the K–5 MTLs started during that year, with a consultant spending one-half day monthly in each K–5 MTL's classroom focused on observing and asking hard questions of them regarding children's thinking, and helping to build their knowledge base in the classroom with kids. Principals were asked to shadow the consultant when she was on campus to build their own content knowledge around mathematics. During the time she was in district each month the consultant also ran a full-day seminar for the K–5 MTLs and their principals specifically on school-based reform and their own leadership in that reform. This served as an important learning experience in grounding the MTLs in the work that was coming. The work with MTLs in Grades 6–8 was more informal because there was difficulty locating an available consultant with a high level of expertise in the specific curriculum materials they had adopted (the *Connected Mathematics Project* was still in prepublication form). These MTLs were asked to attend the workshops with the K–5 consultant, but this frustrated them because it was not directly applicable to their own level of content or particular student characteristics. Attending national conferences also played into the ongoing training of all MTLs.

The Need for Seed: Grantsmanship

During the 4th year, 1997–1998, the expectation was for the entire district to engage in full implementation for the new mathematics curriculum K–8. The consultant support of MTLs was eliminated at their request. They felt that they no longer needed a consultant to work with them. They asked that the funds be shifted to the school sites to plan for their own use. In hindsight this was a poor decision, especially considering that all teachers had now moved to full implementation of the new curricula materials and the need for support was, in fact, intensified. This change caused the professional growth of the MTLs to level off for that year. Many teachers attended conferences that year and traveled around the country in search of mathematics support. It was evident that the level of support (e.g., ongoing and particularized to their own dilemmas) would not be found in the larger world of mathematics education, but instead truly needed to be institutionalized inside the school. At the same time it was apparent that there was no funding for MTLs to have release time to support their colleagues as had been the case for literacy teacher-leaders. So the search began to find external funding to support our efforts.

During the 5th year, 1998–1999, Coleman wrote grant proposals seeking funding to support the further development of the MTLs. By the summer of 1999 a planning grant had been secured from the National Science Foundation.

That 6th year, 1999–2000, was a rich year in terms of growth for the MTLs. With seed money, consultants from across the country were brought in to work alongside the MTLs in their classrooms, helping them to reflect deeply about their practice. Also during that year, a full proposal for a 4-year Local Systemic Initiative ($1.5 million) was funded by the NSF. This source of revenue allowed for the training of the MTLs to continue in earnest, including the implementation of required mathematics coursework in Algebra and Geometry for all classroom teachers in the district, as well as providing for half-time release from the classroom for the MTLs.

Half-time release was a critical innovation. Results from other Systemic Initiatives showed that, when leaders are released from their classroom duties full-time, they begin to lose credibility with their peers (i.e., they are no longer *teachers*). Moreover, because teacher-leaders are not able to think deeply and diagnostically about children's learning due to moving from class to class and focusing on facilitating adult learning, their own development can stagnate, and the very teachers they are helping can outstrip them in knowledge and ability (Middleton et al., 2002). So, by releasing MTLs half-time, they were able to work with their teachers with fidelity, and still maintain their own reflective practice and legitimacy in the eyes of their peers. This strategy also had the advantage of being politically salable, and financially expedient.

Current Status: Taking Advantage of Opportunities

In 2000 because of the kind of structure the district had enacted, a number of opportunities afforded themselves. Chief among these was the establishment of relationships with Research and Development projects at a number of Universities with national reputations. Primary-grades teacher-leaders became heavily involved in the Cognitively Guided Instruction project centered in the University of Wisconsin and UCLA. Teachers became part of a larger group of teachers in the urban core, doing research on children's mathematical thinking, and its relationship to their practice. Involvement in this project generated a common set of understandings about the importance of using children's thinking as the basis for instructional decision-making.

In the middle grades, much less innovation had occurred for the first few years of reform. It was only when attention moved from general implementation of curricula to specific issues of content, namely modern algebra (Middleton, 2003), geometry (Flores, 2002), and statistics (McClain, 2002) that the middle grades teacher-leaders became a coherent group and broader reform was enacted.

An example of this cohesion came when researchers from Vanderbilt University approached the district with a project in reasoning about data. The deal they presented was to work with a cadre of middle school leaders, helping them develop understanding of data visualization and statistical reasoning, and assisting them in changing their teaching practice. Kay McClain, the principal researcher from Vanderbilt, visits the district once per month for a week, providing seminars and visiting teachers' classrooms. As a result of this work, teacher-leaders are engaged in publishing papers based on their practice and incorporating other middle grades teachers in grade-level teams. The algebra and geometry work resulted in two of the teacher-leaders taking over the instruction from Middleton and ASU colleague Alfinio Flores, and offering graduate courses in modern Algebra and Geometry.

Outcomes: Student Achievement

Any leadership development effort would be satisfied if it resulted in the recognition of identified leaders in the larger community of educators. Certainly, recognition provides teachers with confirmation that their hard work has status among their peers and among those most knowledgeable about the content and instruction. Over the course of the Jefferson experiment, four of our teacher-leaders have been chosen as presidential awardees in a national competition sponsored by the National Science Foundation. Only two teachers per state are awarded this honor each year in mathematics. Part of this distinction stems from the attention we have placed on nominating quality teachers and support provided for the preparation of their applications. Nevertheless, it confirms that our leaders are indeed leaders by strictest definition.

Of course, all this work amounts to nothing at all if it doesn't result in some demonstrable changes in student achievement. We are happy to say that, longitudinally, our efforts have resulted in grade-by-grade improvement in student achievement, and a general longitudinal change across all grade bands on the mathematics portion of the Stanford Achievement Test (see Table 6.1). We find these results heartening for two reasons. First, though the stated goals of the reform effort were to fundamentally redesign the curriculum, instruction, and assessment practices of the district, it was recognized from the beginning that curriculum, instruction, and assessment are tools to effect student learning. Second, given the changing demographics of the district—moving from a solidly middle class constituency to a diverse, inner-city constituency with sharply increasing rates of poverty—our efforts have proven to impact children at all levels in the district. When achievement gains mirror gains in poverty, our attention to equity can be seen as both well-intentioned and effective.

TABLE 6.1
Stanford (9) Mathematics Achievement Results by Grade 2000-2003

Beginning Grade Level	Year Tested			
	2000	2001	2002	2003
2	54	67	70	69
3	58	56	71	73
4	63	63	72	75
5	63	55	69	73
6	63	62	68	76
7	67	56	64	73
8	61	61	74	69

KEY LEARNINGS

With the background and chronology of our efforts documented, we now present some key learnings from our experiences. We have attempted to present these at a level that is useful for administrators in other districts with similar goals.

Teacher-Leaders Are a Great Idea

Teacher-leaders enable curricular reforms to propagate at the building level. If the building is the unit of systemic reform, then teacher-leaders, *supported* by administration, are the mechanism by which a culture of reform is enacted (Institute for Educational Leadership, 2001). Our system would have fallen apart if the MTLs were not strong and willing to assume the leadership role across the district.

Changes in Practice Precede Changes in Beliefs

The reason that curriculum writing and adoption were a fruitful first step in our process of reform was that, from a central administration perspective, it is easier to change practices (i.e., what people do) than to change people's belief systems (e.g., Middleton, 1999). It was assumed that, with study and support augmenting this practical change, teachers' belief systems would begin to change and that this would start a cycle of perpetuation. For some of our MTL members, the evidence of student learning and attitude constituted a conversion experience, moving them from a more lecture-oriented approach to instruction using texts as authoritative mathematical documents, to a more facilitative approach, using texts as tools for students' learning. Others were already searching for something. They thought they understood reform, and used the language of problem-solving and such. However, without the development of the MTL community, being challenged to implement high-quality mathematics tasks, and assess students' thinking more deeply, their reform practices remained at more or less a surface level (e.g., Koellner, Bote, & Middleton, 1998). For both of these types of teachers, the actual implementation of new models preceded their change in attitude toward what mathematics reform was.

Develop Partnership With the Local University

Leadership development as we have defined it is about building intellectual capacity. Universities are a source of information, new models, and practices that can be adopted *given an ongoing collaborative* relationship. One-shot staff development sessions or workshops are ineffective (Gamoran, Secada, & Marrett, 2000). It is long-term hard work that breeds successful reform (Middleton et al., 2002). Without the relationship established with Arizona State University (and subsequently the University of Wisconsin and Vanderbilt), our own work would not have resulted in the same level of success.

Teacher-Leaders Must Still Teach

We found the part-day release model to be valuable for building and maintaining teacher leadership over the 9 years of our reform efforts. This model keeps the MTLs fresh in their own understanding of student learning and teaching. It helps them maintain their credibility with their colleagues by facing the same challenges daily with students that all teachers face. Moreover, fiscally, it is more tenable than the full-time release model.

One innovation that has been employed by Jefferson and by other districts in the surrounding area is that of hiring and training long-term subject-matter specific substitute teachers. These people can be recent retirees who do not wish to leave teaching entirely, recent graduates from teacher education programs who wish to receive explicit training in mathematics teaching and learning to bolster their marketability, and content experts in business and industry, hired as "special presenters." Their role is to ensure that there is no drop-off in level of quality instruction when teachers are released for staff development. These "Math Wizards," as we called them, learned the intricacies of the curriculum deeply, worked with teachers' students regularly to establish a relationship and knowledge of students' learning, and met weekly to bolster their own understanding of mathematics teaching and learning. The additional advantage this program served was to identify potential new hires for the district and cull the "cream of the crop" each year.

Teacher Leadership Is Dependent on District Leadership

Teacher-leaders need an instructional leader at the district level who is willing to both challenge and support their continual learning. Our implementation was dependent on an administrator (Coleman) who was deeply involved in curriculum and instruction issues, and who understood the model and how to make it work. It is unclear whether this model would have been sustained had the administration not had both the attitude and the knowledge it did. Our MTLs also needed an ongoing relationship with educators with more expertise in mathematics than they had (e.g., in the University or other institution of higher education). Because our reform was content driven, this is a plausible and necessary condition for success. The use of a consultant or external expert to coach MTLs was a good move in our case. It should never have been taken away for the year that it was. The consultant's time in the MTLs' classrooms observing and asking probing questions about student thinking and teachers' practice helped build the knowledge base *and the relevant criteria* by which their own success could be judged and improved.

The strength of administrative leadership cannot be overstated. These are the people that can lead the changes, sabotage the changes, or get out of the way and let others lead the changes. Teacher leadership is needed at the building level but cannot take the place of a strong and knowledgeable principal who is willing to learn with the teachers and teacher-leaders. One successful strategy from our experience is to use teacher-leaders to conduct administrative training on what to look for in reforming classrooms. As stated in our beginning assumptions, administrators look to teacher-leaders for information regarding school culture, implementation of curriculum, and teaching practice. It is important to take advantage of this natural proclivity.

Also in our case, the district was small enough that the superintendent could visit every classroom at least once per year. This impressed on all teachers the need to continually refine their practice.

Multiple Tiers of Leadership Must Be Developed

As our teacher-leaders grew intellectually, so did their colleagues in the district at large. With the majority of district and external funds going to support identified MTLs, the needs of this second tier of innovators met with some diminishing returns. In response to this, an application process was made for new teachers to be brought into the leadership system. Funds were not available for the same level of release, but the courses, institutes, and conference attendance benefits of leadership were afforded to this emergent group. Although this system is new to our efforts, we project that it will allow for continual renewal of the leadership role at every school. The process of application for second-tier leaders has the same reasoning as that for first-tier leaders. Although it is important to take all comers—that is, all who are interested—in the second tier, it must also be structured so that not everyone will want to be involved at that level. For purely pragmatic reasons, though all teachers can be leaders in the emergent process of reform, not all teachers can be *identified* leaders with a role defined in district policy (Barth, 2001); it is important to make the application process for this level formal. This identifies the risk takers and identifies those who really want to become involved (and weeds out simple opportunists).

Consider the use of grade-level content study groups. In our case the ability of leaders to meet with an entire faculty in a grade level to co-plan, review materials, and share advice were the first steps that helped teachers begin to look at the MTLs as leaders. This was a case of servant leadership in that these study groups were organized around the content needs of the teachers and not a formal set of experiences brought to them. In this regard it has much in common with other job-embedded staff development models (Loucks-Horseley, Hewson, Love, & Stiles, 1998). The most effective rule of thumb for organizing these meetings (and in tying more formal staff development experiences to daily practices) involved looking at student work. When teachers bring student work samples to a discussion, the mutual analysis and troubleshooting from their peers is critical to teachers opening their minds to change in practice (Driscoll & Bryant, 1998).

Broadening the Network

Aside from local University connections, there is a wealth of opportunities for leadership enhancement through involvement in professional societies. Sending MTLs to national and regional conferences was as key to their growth as was the year of reading. The MTL group is now presenting at professional meetings across the country. The networking at a national level certainly helped the MTLs become more confident and competent as experts. Now with the second tier leadership in place, the dilemma becomes how to afford supporting release time and travel expenses for a growing number of leaders.

Dealing With Resistance

Acclimating teacher-leaders to the fact that there will be resistance is critical. Resistance will appear from established leaders who have a different agenda. Resistance will come from teachers who don't want to change. Resistance will come from principals who are not informed deeply about how and why the reforms are beneficial for student learning. The key to dealing with resistance is to get to the point of understanding where the resistors are coming from. What is their belief system and values that support their resistance? Understanding the sources of resistance allows the system to generate strategies for dealing with it in a way that does not alienate, but incorporates resistors' compatible values into the professional development activities.

Our best example of this is of a strong teacher-leader who, at the beginning of the reform effort, sought to prove that what we were trying to accomplish would not (a) work or (b) constitute solid mathematics. Understanding this and providing opportunities for her to learn more, deeper mathematics and to implement this in her classroom resulted in this teacher becoming the poster child for reform to the point where she teaches graduate courses in mathematics education (algebra and geometry) in conjunction with University partners. The respect her fellow teachers in her middle school accorded her ensured that the whole school was able to change their beliefs about the reform efforts.

In hindsight, the title of math teacher-leader caused some issues and should be rethought. For some resistant teachers the title was a problem because of the term leader. "Math coach" or another less differentiated role name is softer and probably more palatable to other teachers as well as more descriptive of the actual work.

CONCLUSIONS

In an earlier publication the first author described the notion that a system as complex as a public school district should have as a goal, coherence at all levels of the system, from classroom teacher to superintendent (Middleton et al., 2002). The goals of the reform, even if they are fluid and evolving, must be understood by all, and their place in the overall support structure must be embraced. To a great extent the Jefferson case embodies this principle. The superintendent, assistant superintendent, principals, teacher-leaders, and classroom teachers were able to speak the same language of reform, recognize high quality practice, and assist each other in enhancing their knowledge and skills. Moreover, they were able to sustain their trajectory of reform over 9 years, some of them quite turbulent. The best testament to the institutionalization of the changes in Jefferson are illustrated in the fact that over half of the MTLs identified in the system have emerged over the course of the reform, increasing the number of leaders beyond the initial 12 and transcending the inevitable turnover due to retirement, promotion, and mobility. The final test of this institutionalization occurred in 2001 when Coleman, the assistant superintendent, left the district for opportunities in another system. Despite the move of the originator of the reform effort, and its chief supporter among administration, the MTLs took it upon themselves to continue their work and to train up a new assistant superintendent. In a recent meeting of an advisory board from the NSF, the participants agreed that the district has not "backslid" in any demonstrable fashion, but indeed, has continued to improve despite tighter budget constraints.

We leave the reader with five rules of thumb gleaned from our experiences. First, go into the program assuming that people are doing the best they can at the time, given their prior knowledge and the history of the district and its culture. Teachers want children to learn. Administrators want to help teachers. The question then becomes, "how can we change the system to stimulate our employees to take leadership and begin to engage in best practices?" In our case there was a vacuum where a curricular structure should have been. Rather than working directly on practice, engaging the most active teachers in designing a curriculum they could own and implement allowed for the most powerful influences on the practices of the schools' faculty—to own the process and attempt to persuade others to own it, too.

Second, assume that the potential for leadership exists within each school. In doing so, your reform efforts will take the form of capacity building as opposed to dogmatic mandates for change. Our MTLs were developed to provide support for their colleagues—building capacity for the generation of a new kind of community of learners across the district leadership.

Third, move from mandate-driven reform to collaborative-driven reform. Granted, there are mandates for curriculum, instruction, and assessment coming from the state and federal levels, and pressures from parent groups as well. The caveat then is that the curriculum and assessment system the teacher leadership designs must align in important ways with these mandates (given they are tenable and actually will help children). Part of our work in ensuring that this took place was to both create the initial study sessions on state and national standards and to insist on including standards-based materials in the curriculum adoption process.

Fourth, Content Knowledge Counts! You can't teach anything if you are not first a student of the discipline. This maxim holds for art and music, physical education and history, literacy, science, and mathematics. Teachers must be continuously upgrading their knowledge of content *and* their knowledge of how students learn that content. In doing so, they will pick up tools for teaching, an understanding of how the content plays out across the curriculum and the developmental appropriateness of their practices. In our case, the development of algebra, geometry, and statistics courses allowed content learning to be foregrounded, whereas the background within which the content was delivered—the pedagogy—illustrated best practices in teaching that very content. To make implementation strategies explicit, the content of the courses was developed by studying the curriculum materials teachers were using, and creating experiences whereby the mathematics of those materials was developed in a deeper and more connected manner (Middleton, 2003).

Lastly, find ways to say "YES." At the beginning of the project, leaders approached administration with requests to change their curriculum, to gain more understanding. District leadership said "yes" to these requests, but in a way that coordinated activity both with teachers' goals and with the larger goals of the administration. Both needs were served and the buy-in that this philosophy established continues even to this day, 10 years later.

ACKNOWLEDGMENTS

The research reported in this manuscript was supported, in part, by grants from the National Science Foundation (9911849) and the United States Department of Education (P336B990064). The opinions expressed are solely those of the authors and do not reflect the opinions of the National Science Foundation or the United States Department of Education.

REFERENCES

Baratta-Lorton, M. (1976). *Mathematics their way: An activity center mathematics program for early childhood education.* Menlo Park, CA: Addison-Wesley.

Barth, R. S. (2001). Teacher leader. *Phi Delta Kappan, 82*(4), page numbers.

Carpenter, T. P. (1985). How children solve simple word problems. *Education and Urban Society, 17,* 417–425.

Carpenter, Fennema, E., Peterson, P. L., Chiang, & Loef, M. (1989). Using knowledge of children's mathematical thinking in classroom teaching: An experimental study. *American Educational Research Journal, 26,* 499–531.

Driscoll, M., & Bryant, D. (1998). *Learning about assessment, learning through assessment.* Washington, DC. National Research Council.

Flores, A. (2002). A rhythmic approach to geometry. *Mathematics Teaching in the Middle School, 7,* 378–383.

Gamoran, A., Secada, W. G., & Marrett, C. B. (2000). The organizational context of teaching and learning: Changing theoretical perspectives. In M. T. Hallinan (Ed.), *Handbook of the sociology of education* (pp. 37–63). New York: Kluwer.

Grouws, D. A. (1992). *Handbook of research on mathematics teaching and learning.* New York: Macmillan.

Institute for Educational Leadership. (2001). *Leadership for student learning: Redefining the teacher as leader.* Washington, DC: Author.

Kennedy, M. M. (1999). Form and substance in mathematics and science professional development. *NISE Brief: Reporting on Issues of Research in Science Mathematics Engineering and Technology Education,* (3)2, 1–8.

Koellner, K. A., Bote, L. A., & Middleton, J. A. (1998). *Cycles of transformation in assessment practices in a Cognitively Guided Instruction Classroom.* Paper presented at the Annual Meeting of the American Educational Research Association, San Diego, CA.

Loucks-Horsley, S., Hewson, P., Love, N., & Stiles, K. E. (1998). *Designing professional development for teachers of science and mathematics.* Thousand Oaks, CA: Corwin.

McClain, K. (2002). Teacher's and students' understanding: The role of tools and inscriptions in supporting effective communication. *Journal for the Learning Sciences, 11*(2 & 3), 217–249.

McNamara, C. (1999). *Field guide to leadership and supervision for nonprofit staff.* Minneapolis, MN: Authenticity LLC.

Middleton, J. A. (1999). Curricular influences on the motivational beliefs and practice of two middle school mathematics teachers: A follow-up study. *Journal for Research in Mathematics Education, 30,* 349–358.

Middleton, J. A. (2003). *An epistemic fidelity approach to content: Developing teachers' content understanding in algebra.* Paper presented at the Research Presession of the Annual Meeting of the National Council of Teachers of Mathematics, San Antonio, TX.

Middleton, J. A., Sawada, D., Judson, E., Bloom, I., & Turley, J. (2002). Relationships build reform: Developing partnerships for research in teacher education. In L. English (Ed.), *Handbook of international research in mathematics education* (pp. 409–431). Mahwah, NJ: Lawrence Erlbaum Associates, Inc.

Middleton, J. A., & Webb, N. L. (1994). Collaboration and Urban School Systems. In N. L. Webb & T. A. Romberg (Eds.), *Reforming mathematics education in America's cities* (pp. 105–128). New York: Teachers' College Press.

NCTM. (1989). *Curriculum and evaluation standards for school mathematics.* Reston, VA: Author.

NCTM. (1991). *Professional standards for teaching mathematics.* Reston, VA: Author.

TERC. (1997). *Investigations in Number, Data, and Space.* Cambridge, MA: Author.

7

Eliminating Isolation to Foster Learner-Centered Leadership: Lessons from Rural Schools and Research Universities[1]

Karen DeMoss
Carolyn J. Wood
Richard Howell
University of New Mexico

Principal professional development increasingly has been championed as a key mechanism for improving school cultures, student outcomes, and leadership retention (Barth, 1990; DuFour, DuFour, Eaker, & Karhanek, 2004; Glickman, 2002; Lambert, 2002, 2003; Tucker & Codding, 2002). Sparks (2002), however, stated that even though we know a great deal about the elements that lead to effective staff development, "professional development as it is experienced by most teachers and principals is pretty much like it has always been—unfocused, insufficient, and irrelevant to the day-to-day problems faced by front line educators" (p. i). Rather than actually improve the skills of principals, staff development tends to emulate "sit and git," one-shot presentations by popular motivational speakers or "experts" from various specialties in

---

[1]The authors would like to acknowledge Ann House and Meave Stevens-Dominguez for contributions to the background information included in this chapter.

education. Consequently, the participants in this type of professional development tend to be relatively "passive recipients of information rather than active participants in solving important educational problems" (chap. 8, p. 2).

The newer, and according to Peterson and Kelley (2002), more effective processes of professional development for principals include proactive approaches in which peers interact through a "long-term set of experiences ... with continuing ... practice and coaching, [experiences that are] closely linked to participants' work and to the needs of current practitioners, schools, and districts" (pp. 341, 343). Interestingly, substituting "professional development" in Lambert's 1998 definition of "leadership" provides an excellent description of this newer type of learner-centered professional development:

> [Professional development] is about learning together, and constructing meaning and knowledge collectively and collaboratively. It involves opportunities to surface and mediate perceptions, values, beliefs, information, and assumptions through continuing conversations; to inquire about and generate ideas together; to seek to reflect upon and make sense of work in the light of shared beliefs and new information; and to create actions that grow out of these new understandings. Such is the core of [professional development.]. (pp. 5–6)

Though supporting such principal development can prove demanding in any circumstances, some contexts heighten the challenges. Principals with limited educational or management experience, leaders credentialed with minimal requirements, work environments where it is difficult to retain high quality leaders—all these can make the goal of supporting principal professional development for learner-centered schools more difficult. Such is the case in northern New Mexico, where 80% of districts report having insufficient numbers of candidates for their principal positions, and candidates who do apply are often underqualified, according to superintendents (DeMoss et al., 2005). Sadly, the difficulties of staffing do not stop with recruitment. Principal retention in the northern portion of the state is poor, with a turnover rate of nearly 300% in the past decade, or more than three principals on average per school, with many schools facing principal changes almost yearly (DeMoss et al., 2005; Winograd, Feijoo, Thorstensen, Jacobus, & Hughes, 2004). Of course, the devastating effect of such transience is a lack of consistency and stability, which all schools rely on to a certain extent to be able to move ahead with any type of sustained change process.

In addition to issues of recruitment and retention, principals who serve the north find themselves faced with a host of challenges. According to nationwide analyses by the Rural School and Community Trust, New Mexico ranks "first in rural child poverty, second in percentage of rural minority students, and third lowest in rural per capita income" (Beeson & Strange, 2003). New Mexico overall ranks 5th in percent of students with special educational needs (National Center for Educational Statistics, 2005a), 49th in 4th grade mathematics achievement (National Center for Educational Statistics, 2005b), 43rd in per pupil instructional expenditures (National Center for Educational Statistics, 2005c), 2nd in percent of students with limited English proficiency (National Center for Educational Statistics, 2003), 4th in percent of students eligible for free and reduced lunch (National Center for Educational Statistics, 2003). Coupled with these realities is the fact that the vast northern New

Mexico area, whose school districts host between 200 and 4,800 students, is geographically isolated. For many, the nearest midsized town with amenities such as grocery stores is 100 miles away.

In brief, the disincentives that many school leaders are feeling nationwide (Farkas, Johnson, Duffett, Foleno, & Foley, 2001) are compounded by isolation in northern New Mexico. The area faces a dire need for professional development that supports principals in the particularly demanding work of constructing rich learning environments and creating workplaces that foster long-term shared commitments to their schools' goals. The set of leadership challenges in the north both raises the stakes attached to the need for quality professional development and helps explain why staff with Lead New Mexico (LeadNM), the project discussed in this chapter, experienced cynical attitudes among principals in early stages of the grant.

LeadNM was a federally funded effort to provide sustained professional development designed to help principals in the northern portion of New Mexico address the challenges the region faces. LeadNM sought to develop and enhance school leaders' knowledge and skills to promote school improvement through the creation of rich professional learning communities. A key assumption of the grant was that reducing the isolation of these school leaders would be a necessary precondition both to increasing their skills for addressing their schools' challenges and to boosting their satisfaction with their work. What follows is an account of the processes and changes that the grant facilitated towards that end.

The chapter draws on LeadNM evaluation data, including monthly participant reflections, interviews with over 30 participants, and observations of meetings, to chronicle the learning processes that supported principals' movement toward Learner-Centered Leadership (LCL). The chapter is organized in three major sections. First, the introductory material sets the stage of the grant, explaining the major tenets behind the work. The second section explores the learning from the grant and is divided into five areas: (a) reduction of isolation, (b) designing professional development to meet individual principal needs and broader project goals, (c) development of community, (d) breakthroughs into new learning about leadership, and (e) evidence of change in leadership practices. The final section provides a discussion of implications from each of those subsections and offers resources for further reading.

LeadNM: CONTEXT AND GOALS OF THE GRANT

The University of New Mexico's Educational Leadership Program, in partnership with the Northern New Mexico Network for Rural Education and the University's distance education arm, received a federally funded grant, LeadNM, to support professional development for principals in schools in rural northern New Mexico. In planning the grant, principals and superintendents in the Network had made it clear that the isolation they faced was a critical barrier to improving leadership: formal professional development opportunities were rare; support systems for principals were nonexistent; basic information of all sorts was lacking. Moving forward on larger issues of school improvement would have to be met by first addressing the key issue of isolation.

What literature existed on the effects of isolation supported these tenets. Authors approach the issue of principal isolation from multiple perspectives (Ackerman &

Maslin-Ostrowski, 2002; Hancock & Lamendola, 2005; Holloway, 2004; Lashway, 2003, *Networks and clusters*, 2000; Rogers & Babinski, 1999; Wagner, 2001), but all comment on the necessity of prioritizing two key issues that principals have reported in multiple data-gathering activities: (a) the practical, day-to-day problems and demands of "school management," and (b) the experiential sharing and contact with others in similar situations. In every case, the research supports a movement toward the creation of collaborative environments in which principals are provided opportunities to "share experiences with colleagues as a preferred activity" (Holloway, 2004).

When principals do not have such collaborative opportunities, the effects are reflected in the kind of principal turnover and job mobility faced in northern New Mexico. One of the few empirical explorations of principal isolation documented that principals left alone to find their own way in new positions were likely to leave their jobs: Nine out of 10 new rural principals had left their positions within 2 years (Morford, 2002, reported in Lashway, 2003). This type of induced mobility is common to the Northern Network, where transience between northern districts has become a ritualized process; internal movement among the 28 districts is commonplace and expected on a yearly basis.

Accordingly, the grant was structured to address isolation in three ways. First, and key to the overall goals of the grant to foster improved school leadership, was the development of professional learning communities among network principals. Project personnel facilitated monthly cohort meetings focused on the connections between leadership and learning for five different groups comprised of 15–20 principals each. A total of 80 principals traveled from remote contexts to sites within their regions once a month for day-long cohort meetings. This component of the grant was designed to reduce isolation by bringing together practicing principals around issues of leadership and learning. Second, districts identified teachers who were strong candidates for principal preparation; these individuals were supported in principal licensure coursework, and they were also members of the monthly cohorts. This component of the grant had two intents: to broaden the range of participants at the cohort table, reducing the felt isolation between teachers and principals, and to create a pool of principal applicants who were already inducted into the professional learning community of northern New Mexico principals. Finally, educators who had deep roots in the north were engaged as traveling mentors called "circuit riders," who helped principals troubleshoot issues at their sites and served as a source for information about federal initiatives and policy mandates from the state. This component of the grant was designed to reduce both physical and informational isolation principals experienced at their sites.

The overriding goal of all of these structural opportunities was the same: to support principals in developing the skills and understandings necessary to foster rich learning communities within their school sites. Principals who have the skills to create a positive tone and high expectations in a school provide the foundations for school quality (Bottoms & Moore, 2004; Educational Research Service, 2000; Leithwood, Louis, Anderson, & Wahlstrom, 2004; Sebring & Bryk, 2000). Some of the classic studies on how, exactly, principals influence school performance present the leader's role as one of promoting and sustaining schools as organizations with cultures that support students' achievement (Borger, Lo, Oh, & Walberg, 1985; Darling-Hammond & McLaughlin, 1995; Newmann, 1996). To create such cultures, the norms, attitudes, beliefs, behaviors, and values—those complex patterns that are deeply ingrained in the very core of the school—must change (Barth, 2002; Fullan, 2002). The grant theorized that, if principals could experience a shift in their own attitudes through the development of a professional learning community, not only would isolation as a primary impediment be addressed, but leaders would begin to see new ways to meet the needs and goals at their sites.

SUPPORTING LEARNING IN LEADNM

Isolation: More Than a Physical Reality

During the course of the grant, researchers identified four distinct types of principal isolation. The first was akin to the isolation found in the literature about teachers, focusing on the simple aloneness of the work (Ackerman & Maslin-Ostrowski, 2002; Hancock & Lamendola, 2005; Holloway, 2004; Lashway, 2003; Rogers & Babinski, 1999; Wagner, 2001). This facet of isolation develops from the very structure of schooling in the United States: Classrooms generally house only one teacher, and schedules provide little time for interactions with other adults. Principals face this same endemic feeling, perhaps even surpassing teachers' isolation, according to Lashway (2003): "Unlike new teachers who can usually find an empathetic colleague just down the hall, principals literally have no peers in their building. The isolation can be magnified when they receive little feedback from supervisors." In geographically remote northern New Mexico, many principals found feedback to be rare, and few even had assistant principals with whom to talk. As one participant in the study put it simply, "The principalship can be lonely."

The second type of isolation grew out of both the singularity of the role of principal and the realities of rural areas. Because of the geographic isolation of these small rural communities, schools and districts not only found themselves "out of the loop"; sometimes there was no "loop" at all. Limited funds generated from small student bodies dictated that one person wear several hats: The principal was often also the district technology coordinator, the curriculum specialist, even, in a few instances, the sole teacher in a school. These realities translated to a limited range of expertise from which to draw; as one administrator noted, "We can't make the changes we need just locally because we only have three principals, and they are all pretty much new. We needed others' help, others' experience to guide us." Sometimes the need for other colleagues to support change went beyond sheer numbers. Depending on the philosophical orientations of school or district staffs, participants found that the new ideas they were exploring through the grant were not always welcomed, a reality expressed by one participant this way: "There was no one in the district to talk with." This particular type of isolation ultimately related to principals' role definition. Principals agreed that the role of school leaders needed to be reconceptualized as educational contexts changed, but to do so alone was an almost insurmountable prospect. They had, as had their predecessors, instead focused almost exclusively on traditional role definitions of principal as building manager and discipline arbitrator. To facilitate new conceptions of the role of principals required addressing this role isolation, engendered by both the rural context and the nature of the position of principal as the only designated head in a school.

The third type of isolation was informational. Grant planners had understood that Network principals often felt they were the last to know about federal and state initiatives and mandates; indeed, "circuit riders" were built into the grant in part to address information gaps. Still, despite expecting rural leaders to be relatively uninformed, project staff found the degree of unawareness striking. Educators were not acquainted with some of the most basic policies affecting schools. District staff did not understand adequate yearly progress as mandated by the No Child Left Behind Act and defined by the state. Principals did not understand their roles in teacher professional development and evaluation as mandated by the State's new licensure system. Teachers did not understand what the new, mandated criterion-referenced tests were all about. As one participant noted, "Without this kind of help [the assistance of the circuit riders], we'd be in the caves; we'd be in the boonies. We're geographically out there, and they [the State Public Education Department staff] don't give us a lot of information." Circuit riders found the bulk of work requested of them focused on bridging this informational isolation.

The fourth type of isolation, psychological, was far more critical from principals' perspectives. The work that occurred to address psychological isolation through the interactions within cohort learning communities proved the most powerful change mechanism for principals. Participant reflections were nearly universal in noting that assuaging their sense of isolation was a major benefit of the cohort. In some ways, what we are calling "psychological isolation" may be a result of the combined effects of the other three realities of isolation, where work isolation, role definition, and informational isolation combine to create a sense of being completely alone. Early data even indicated that principals had come to believe that no one else faced the kinds of issues they did. Despite widespread media attention regarding the challenges schools across the nation have, they found it "surprising" that others faced what they did; they had felt "alone," "unique," and "hopeless" prior to their LeadNM cohort experiences. One of the participants expressed how this sense of aloneness can negatively affect a principal's ability to move forward productively: "It's so nice to have meetings with other principals because it's nice to find out you're not by yourself. You feel isolated. Sometimes, then, for me, the next step is to feel overwhelmed."

Isolation and its diminishing effects were apparent throughout the 2 years of data gathering, in particular as new members joined the cohorts from time to time. Principals in their self-reflections and interviews repeatedly referred to the initial reduction of their isolation as a primary benefit of the grant, even after they had clearly moved beyond the limiting effects of those isolated feelings. More pervasive than any other kind of data, principals' reports on their initial sense of isolation led researchers to conclude that not only was the goal of reducing isolation a necessary structural component of working in remote rural areas, but it also was perhaps a deeper-seeded phenomenon in the experience of the principalship than the literature implies.

Designing Professional Development to Meet Principal Needs

Perhaps as a respite from the sense of aloneness in their work, principals had looked forward to the first group meeting for LeadNM. During the grant's initial year, principal participants were supported to attend a 3-day Summer Institute. Included in the

Institute were modules that paralleled key content in the university's preservice and doctoral coursework. The content explored cutting edge research on effective school leadership, and the workshops provided breakout sessions and small group discussions, a good beginning for breaking down isolation in the developers' minds. The planning had specifically sought to engage principals in content related to current school issues, to offer opportunity for discussion, and to ensure that new learning opportunities were provided to participants.

However, despite the intentional planning involved in the Institute, feedback from participants was clear: School leaders did not want opportunities to learn new information, information they summarily, even derogatorily, termed "theoretical." Rather, they said they needed and wanted time to talk with others about their day-to-day issues. They most appreciated their informal time together and the breakout sessions, where observers noted that conversations often were not specifically oriented toward the task at hand. In summing up the event, one veteran principal said,

> After you've been out in the real world slugging it out and you've been sued by the ACLU and you've had to restrain parents and you're restraining children and you're facing all these other things, I don't want somebody telling me how it *should* be.

Project staff went back to the drawing board, with 2 months' planning time before the first cohort meetings for the fall.

The challenge was to balance principals' stated needs—those two needs expressed throughout the literature of addressing practical problems of school management and of sharing experiences with other similarly situated professionals—with the intent of the grant to develop a learning community focused on issues of leading and learning. No one wanted the cohort sessions simply to provide a brief break from work with no substantive change or growth as a result. Facilitators and Principal Investigators were concerned about how to avoid cohort meetings becoming nothing more than a monthly release valve for the pressures principals were under. Project staff settled on a two-part approach to meet both principals' stated desire to hold discussions contextualized around their daily work and the broader goals of the grant to support changes in principal attitudes and actions about their leadership. Each approach resulted in different dynamics of principal learning: The first built community; the second challenged leaders to more deeply question themselves, their assumptions, and their practices.

Creating Community Through Sustained, Focused Conversation

It was clear that the principals wanted to base discussions on realities from their own sites. To increase the relevance of any "new" approaches to which they might be exposed, they wanted the exemplars to be grounded in their professional lives, using their current problems. Of course, the quandary was that facilitators could not provide the content of the problems principals were facing, save in a generalized, hypothetical, perhaps even "theoretical," way. Thus, the challenge was set: how to focus an entire day's agenda around unknown content that would arrive as principals entered the door.

The retooling of both the content and delivery of the LeadNM activities was designed to provide a safe, relevant, and participatory environment in which principals' work became the focus around which at least half of all discussions revolved. (The other half revolved around readings, described in the following section.) To ensure that the discussions were targeted, the staff drew on a combination of work from the Critical Friends Groups (CFGs) from the Coalition of Essential Schools and work by the National School Reform Faculty, to which the key facilitator belonged.

The processes used in Critical Friends Groups are based on adult learning principles and tend to focus on developing collegial relationships, promoting meaningful dialogue, encouraging reflective practice, and helping participants to rethink their practices. Rather than assign blame for problems occurring within the school or with a particular teacher or student, CFGs encourage participants to present a problem to a group of trusted peers who, in turn, examine the issue from a number of perspectives while providing support, honest critical feedback, and new insights to the person who has requested their assistance. According to Evans and Mohr (1999), who have extensive experience with the Annenberg Institute for School Reform, the work in CFGs is based on seven complex beliefs that mirror the dilemmas faced daily by principals:

1. Principals' learning is personal and yet takes place most effectively while working in groups.
2. Principals foster more powerful faculty and student learning by focusing on their own learning.
3. While we honor principals' thinking and voices, we want to push principals to move beyond their assumptions.
4. Focused reflection takes time away from "doing the work," and yet it is essential.
5. It takes strong leadership to have truly democratic learning.
6. Rigorous planning is necessary for flexible and responsive implementation.
7. New learning depends on protected dissonance. (p. 31)

To address these dilemmas, CFG members use agreed-on guidelines called protocols to help each other "tune" their practices. They analyze issues associated with student work, as well as with school, classroom, district, and community interactions. The protocols support a range of goals, from building trust to helping people make difficult decisions. For example, a protocol called "peeling the onion" helps participants appreciate the complexity of problems by probing to peel away layers of a problem to better understand and deal with the deeper issues beneath the surface. Another example is the "consultancy" protocol, in which the presenter first provides a detailed description of a current dilemma, then group participants talk among themselves as if the presenter were not there, analyzing the dilemma and proposing new ideas, perspectives, and approaches. By helping participants focus on the question raised by the presenter rather than on the presenter as a person, the protocol assists everyone to assume a nondefensive and nonjudgmental stance in dealing with dilemmas they face in their professional lives.

The cohort groups were not made up of leaders who all knew one another, yet almost immediately participants were willing to share their stories, offer advice, and work together using the protocols. The tenor of the interactions closely reflected this example of a new principal, whom we'll call Joe. Joe volunteered to share his issue using a variation of a consultancy protocol. The facilitator began the session asking whether Joe was honestly open to new thinking about the issue, and when he replied that he was, he shared his problem. Moving from descriptions of teachers being late for meetings to laments about parents not bathing and feeding children to problems with faculty not fulfilling their duties, Joe spoke for several minutes, clearly frustrated with his situation. Several minutes into his presentation, the facilitator requested that he focus on a specific element, group, or instance with which he would like help; after a few more false starts, he decided he was most frustrated by teachers not acting professionally in the course of their jobs, from missing meetings to not following rules.

The next portion of the protocol gave guidance to cohort members about what to do. First, there were 3 minutes for clarifying questions—Who? What? When? Where? How? Cohort members asked how many of the teachers were irresponsible, whether there was a split in experience that identified them, how often such behaviors occurred, whether there was a handbook that explained their responsibilities, whether the concerns were related to instructional quality, and if concerns included noncertified staff or just teachers. Next, the protocol asked listeners to say something they had heard Joe say. The group exhibited openness and honesty during this process, as each of these statements from different cohort members demonstrates:

> I heard you say you want to know how to teach or allow them to be responsible. I heard you say that this is something you are trying to implement that the past administration didn't implement. I heard you say you have problems with one third of your staff. I heard you say your staff is dumb and not doing what they should do. I heard you say you haven't identified the needs. I heard you say you are frustrated that staff can't even do minimal requirements. I heard you say this was a goal established by staff, but they are not taking part in it. I heard you say the expectations you want from your staff were what you required from your students when you were a teacher. I heard you say you are tired of excuses. I heard you say you are disappointed in one third of your staff because they are not living up to either their or your expectations. I heard you say the problem falls into mostly clerical issues since the majority are good teachers. I heard you say that this is the way you live your life yourself; it matters to you personally. I heard you say you assumed these teachers knew how to handle these duties.

Then Joe had a chance to clarify any misunderstandings. He found none, though, on hearing a recap of what he had said, he was a bit surprised at how harsh he had sounded.

The next portion of the protocol allowed the cohort to reflect on what the situation might mean at a deeper level for Joe's larger goals. Respondents believed that Joe was letting a small group destroy what he was trying to do; that he was bringing a personally held value into his interactions in ways that created mental roadblocks for himself but didn't change anything; that his way of "managing the problem" was getting in the way of true leadership; that the accountability pressures he felt might be heightening the situation; that if he really was convinced this was a big problem, he needed to be willing to act on it, not just get upset about it.

Joe again had an opportunity to reflect on the comments, agreeing that folks had assessed the situation "pretty straight." The facilitator moved to the next portion of the protocol, which suggested that listeners come up with probing questions. The group offered such questions as the following for Joe's contemplation: "Are there any personality issues between you and the people you're frustrated with?" "Is there a reason you wouldn't opt to restructure the clerical issues so that they didn't loom so large?" "Are these issues really impacting children, or are they just bothersome to you?"

Joe's time with those questions and similar follow-ups in the protocol brought him some newfound space to think differently about the issues that he had so passionately presented as problematic. In the end, he confessed that he didn't want to be seen as "a bad guy," so he had let things slide—things that then put him in tough spots, like either overlooking teachers' tardiness, which could lead to inequity and hard feelings among those who were on time, or being "the heavy" about rules with those who were lax. He didn't like it and didn't know how much to "bend" his personal preferences for the good of the whole. Also, the things he valued, like punctuality and organization, were clearly more important to him than to most of the staff, so he didn't always act on what he wanted, and he got frustrated as a result. In the end, his comment was, "I didn't think it was that much of a dilemma until I thought about it." He left with a plan to approach the situation in a low-key way, working from the clear sense of professional responsibility the majority of the staff exhibited.

Throughout the cohorts' experiences, protocols such as this were the mediating mechanism to help link the realities of principals' school sites with the development of the learning community. The protocols assisted participants in discussing a variety of goals, in depersonalizing situations, and in exploring difficult areas. Aside from the necessary condition of actually convening these geographically dispersed cohort groups over a sustained timeframe, the protocol conversations were the key component for developing their professional communities, as one principal captured:

> I feel better knowing that we all share the same issues and the need to resolve the problems through collaboration with each other.

It was clear from the data that having colleagues to talk with opened possible avenues for thinking about how to improve their schools. Time and again, participants spoke of "sharing ideas" to "solve problems." Cohort protocol discussions provided "solutions and a plan to move forward"; "ideas about how to go about accomplishing things you have had a hard time accomplishing"; "proven strategies to help me guide my staff and school through day-to-day challenges." Principals not only felt better about their newfound hope from these conversations, but many noted early on that these discussions had improved their skills, as this participant shared: "Being part of this group and sharing ideas, methods, strategies for dealing with issues has helped me become a better leader."

Learning About Self and Leadership by Questioning Assumptions

Breaking down the barriers of isolation using participants' personal dilemmas within a professional learning community and following the guidelines provided through the protocols clearly offered principals much-needed support for coping with pressures they faced in their schools. However, many of the early self-reports of changes they implemented at their school sites were still removed from actions that might reflect significant changes in their leadership styles. Early on, participants reported handling district demands differently, using new techniques to manage priorities within the principal role, passing information to staff that would clarify points of uncertainty, and establishing norms for their meetings with staff. Though each of these managerial shifts could improve working environments, none necessarily accomplished moving schools toward a primary focus on building a community dedicated to fostering learning at all levels: student, teacher, and principal.

Creating a safe space for participants to experience the potential power of moving a school toward leadership focused on learning required opportunities for principals to become the learners rather than the "knowers." To accomplish this goal, project personnel wanted to incorporate exploration of some of the knowledge base on leadership into the cohort experiences. However, based on early feedback, presentations to the group had been consciously limited to occasional informational sessions on new policy mandates. Instead of "sit and git" experiences about leadership research, facilitators provided a range of readings that tapped into what principals had brought up as key issues in their work. The cohort received such articles as Schmoker's (2004) "Tipping point: From feckless reform to substantive instructional improvement," Wagner's (2001) "Leadership for learning: An action theory of school change," and Elmore's (2002) "Hard questions about practice." Examples of longer readings, in which the cohorts expressed interest by the second year, included DuFour et al.'s (2004) *Whatever It Takes: How Professional Learning Communities Respond When Kids Don't Learn* and Kegan and Lahey's (2001) *How the Way We Talk Can Change the Way We Work.*

Challenged in particular by Kegan and Lahey, cohort participants explored how values, and often conflicting values they held personally, undergirded problems that they identified. A premise in the discussions was that, without understanding these underlying value issues, in the end efforts to change would fail. The facilitator explained it this way:

> We don't need to be "fix it" people, or people who are going to confession. I can tell you exactly what I said in confession for at least 12 years: "I was mean to my brothers and disrespectful to my parents." The priest would give me a rosary to say, to "fix" my sins. But I never changed my behavior; it was always the same.

Trying to get at why they did or did not behave differently led participants to rethink the values behind some of the assumptions they had held. For example, in working through exercises that required participants to note their beliefs about and challenges in their jobs, principals frequently recorded two common phrases. First, they believed that "Children have the right to a good education"; second, their common work challenge was that "There is not enough time to do what I need to do." During one session, principals discussed these statements for over an hour, finally agreeing that a sense of hurriedness can easily become an excuse for why children are not receiving a good education. To make such an excuse, however, would be to deny the value of providing quality education for all children. The group reworked these two statements into the following claim: "Children in my building have the right to most of my time." This revised statement carried important implications for how principals structured their days and focused their efforts.

The process of working with reading selections was often fluid, though facilitators generally began the discussions using a CFG protocol. Quickly, however, principals would move the discussion to personal situations, at which point the facilitator would seek to refocus the discussion within the context of the readings, helping principals make a clearer connection between the readings and their daily lives. In ways, just as the protocols were the structural mediator between principals' practice and developing a learning community, the facilitator was the conceptual mediator between research and practice.

The kind of learning evidenced during these sessions shared similarities with discussions using the protocols to address specific situations. However, in the conversations about readings, much of the discussion was less bounded by protocols, such that many voices found their way into the kinds of insights that "Joe" typified in the protocol experiences. Additionally, conclusions about any particular issue were most powerful for the individual who presented an issue, whereas other cohort members noted the power of the particular process in which they had participated. During reading discussions, principals equally shared in the learning from discussions and in the insights gleaned about the processes they used in dealing with the content.

Over the course of 2 years of data collection, it was apparent that principals' development occurred through a complex combination of engagement with readings, applying different protocols in focused ways to pressing issues, and continually building a professional learning community in which colleagues and facilitators were trusted. Throughout the cohort meetings, principals struggled with a range of topics, from staff morale about test scores to budget cuts, from teacher turnover to gang violence. Threaded through these discussions, three recurring themes were apparent within the data, generalized concepts that had far-reaching impact on principals' learning.

1. Leaders Can Hinder Learning by Judging Others. Among the most common dynamic in the groups was an exploration of principals' own preconceived notions of their staff. For example, one principal believed that a particular teacher encouraged students to be irresponsible because the teacher did not hold students accountable for bringing their own paper and pencils to class. Although, as was often the case, the principal cited the teacher's actions not because the issue was critical but only to illustrate a point brought out in a reading, the facilitator pressed the example as a broader learning opportunity. The summary of the following conversation captures the tenor of such cohort interchanges, with the italicized words representing the kinds of questions facilitators used to guide the conversations and the regular font capturing the place to which the group members progressed after an extended discussion:

> *Would there be any reason at all to believe the teacher acts purposefully to develop irresponsible students?* No, there was not. *Does anyone enter teaching hoping to be an instructional failure?* (Laughter.) *If we assume the teacher wants to do a good job and just doesn't understand his habit is counterproductive, what would it take to help him change?* Without a conversation to find out why he doesn't hold them accountable, there's no way to help him change. *Is it possible, too, that from that conversation you might find out the teacher encourages responsibility in other ways?* Yes, it's possible.

Over time, cohort members developed the capacity to question themselves and each other about the ways they viewed their own staff. One important lesson that participants regularly highlighted reflected such interchanges: They found that withholding judgment about fellow adults in the building could open doors for communication and problem solving.

2. School leaders have primary responsibility for facilitating and modeling behavioral changes.   A second type of learning suggested what a leader's responsibilities might be in schools that are trying to transform. Principals frequently voiced frustration that teachers didn't use their shared planning time well; they often "just chatted" or "complained." Facilitators quickly moved such comments to a new place by drawing on participants' own appreciation for the experiences they were having:

> *Is it fair to ask teachers, who don't have something like this cohort, to suddenly know how to have productive discussions instead of complaining?* (Contemplative silence.) *If it's not fair, how can we help them have similar experiences like ours so that their shared time has discussions like we have here?*

This particular type of interchange occurred regularly. Gradually, principals themselves began to express that they needed and wanted to help school staffs develop professional learning communities.

However, there was a chasm between the profound learning the participants experienced and the equally profound sense that they were not ready to lead their schools in these new ways. In fact, district personnel noted a lag between participants' professed learning and changes at school sites; project staff had heard superintendents voice questions about the ultimate impact of the cohort sessions. Facilitators handled such comments in the following way:

> *You tell us every month that this is the most important thing you do for your own professional development, but your district supervisors are not sure what this "professional learning community" is doing to help schools. What are you bringing back to your schools from these meetings that will help people understand why the time you spend here each month is a justifiable use of school resources?*

This area of questioning proved difficult because it required self-reflection to be translated into dramatically new actions, actions principals continued to feel they were not fully prepared to undertake, at least through the 2nd year of the project.

3. Leaders may inadvertently perpetuate hierarchical values that could be counterproductive to collegiality.   This third type of learning experience focused directly on the hierarchical nature of the traditional role of the principal. Often, principals voiced frustrations that teachers were not doing things they were asked to do. An implicit assumption within such comments is, of course, that teachers should do what they are asked to do, no matter what. In the principals' defense, many of the requests to teachers were in effect mandates, imposed by the district onto principals. However, such a "do as you are told" condition left little room for adults to interact in ways that demonstrated mutual professional respect or opened the door for communication and learning.

For example, one principal considered teachers who resisted filling out paperwork in a timely manner to be unprofessional. Facilitators pressed the issue:

> *It sounds like you would never turn in paperwork late. Does your frustration with people not turning in paperwork stem from your personal values system—how you would do your job—or is it about really moving the school forward?* Probably it's my own value system, but we also have to do it, and it could help us to move forward. *To the extent that it is about*

moving the school forward, do teachers see the paperwork in that light? Probably not. *How could you help them understand that the paperwork could help support learning in the school?* I'll have to think about that.

As was regularly the case, when principals became more conscious of how their personal biases—including their implicit acceptance of a hierarchical organization—influenced their interactions, they recognized the need to take the time to explore the relationship between those biases and their goals for school change.

Cultivating New School Cultures: The Evidence

The LeadNM discussions were highly effective in helping principals examine their assumptions within the context of the cohort. Evidence of drastically changed leadership practices within schools, however, was less pronounced: Principals spoke in ways that indicated a gradual cultivation of and movement toward new school cultures. Key to the shifts they sought was jettisoning the idea that the principal is the "head," the one who does and knows it all. The cohort helped principals realize that being the person responsible for "everything in the building" prevented them from attending "to the business of making a school community." The sense of being alone on an "island" changed to "seeing others on the island" who could share the work of changing the school. Several participants noted how they had come to appreciate that, rather than seeing their responsibility as doing things alone for the school, nothing meaningful would happen in a school "without collaboration and cooperation." One long-time principal captured both the historical sense of the principalship and the changing vision he was developing:

> I used to think that I had to make change, but now I realize that it is not "I" but "we." I realize that I am not the Lone Ranger, but part of the cavalry coming in to make positive change. I realize that without the support of peers, parents, teachers, etc., no matter how great my ideas may be, change won't occur in isolation.

The primary approach principals were taking to build collaboration was based on increased and effective communication. One participant captured this change as, "I'm going to listen to other people, instead of 'bam, bam, bam.'" Frequently, principals made multiple references to listening in the same sentence, for example, "listen and hear" or "listen with my ears to hear," as if to emphasize the importance of using listening to lead. Participants agreed that listening to teachers was not "typical" of past principal behaviors. One new principal noted that, on her arrival, "Teachers were afraid to express themselves. It was difficult." She continued by identifying another common theme among participants' efforts to change their schools: "If we as principals 'tell' what to do and don't 'work with' teachers to do it, change will not be sustainable. Nothing will change until it becomes a 'we.'"

Several principals shared stories of trying to enact this concept of "we." For example, one principal decided to become part of the "we" of instruction by asking students in the hallways what they had learned that day. In another school that had only one teacher per subject matter, the language arts teacher was implicitly held responsible for the whole school's scores in reading and writing. The principal explained her efforts to assist other teachers to realize that this was also their responsibility:

> In the area of reading and language arts, I really focused on building consensus and consciousness about shared responsibility. I said, "We're all going to work on this together; we're not going to leave one person out there on a tree limb by herself thinking, 'Gosh the state is going to kill me.'"

Building that "we" was an explicit target of the cohort experiences, with the goal of achieving what one leader stated as the ideal: "We're no longer I-You. It's Us." Another principal summed up the conceptual focus on collaboration this way:

> Aside from LeadNM, you don't have anyone helping you understand that it's all about the professional relationships. They don't teach you that when you're going through school, about the relationships. But if the relationship part of your work is lousy, it doesn't work.

In some cases, becoming part of the "we" of the school required principals to take personal responsibility for their own interaction styles. Principals sometimes shared very personal stories about how they were beginning to question themselves first, before blaming others. Said one, "I had a meeting with a teacher and the superintendent. The teacher had some negative comments about how I speak to her. I had to look at myself and thought, 'Maybe I do need to change that.' It was really hard because I think this teacher is pretty much off the wall, but on that point, maybe she was right." Another principal noted that a teacher had issues with his communication style. "I asked if she could tell me something to point out what she was talking about. She came in, and she did. I listened and then sent her a thank you note."

In some cases, the changes principals were able to realize through improved communications were significant enough that state and district personnel noticed. A superintendent of a district with several participants had this to say:

> LeadNM changed the way they approached their staff, how they organized staff meetings, their work in general. The teachers are more positive now. They are getting involved more; it's more of a collaboration, with the principal saying, "I'm the leader within your building, but all of us are working together as a team." Before LeadNM, it was more, "I'm it, and I'll tell you what to do." The change in attitude showed in the memos they write, and I think it's because of LeadNM.

One principal, located at a school that receives state department oversight because of its poor performance, shared that over the course of the year, state reviewers saw positive changes. From principals' and their supervisors' perspectives, in many cases the increasing goal of collaboration fostered important new cultures for schools to venture toward the road to learning for both staff and students.

DISCUSSION AND IMPLICATIONS

The LeadNM grant supported principals' professional development by cultivating new habits of thinking and communicating, habits that helped them rethink underlying causes to problems, moved their conversations away from blaming, and fostered a kind of tenacity in thinking and collaboratively working through the issues they faced at their worksites. In the beginning of the grant, conversations had a quality much like a series of proclamations, with each participant working in favorite insights or example issues. By the 2nd year of their interactions, however, principals had fostered the practice of probing and listening to assess the bigger picture surrounding those very same insights and examples. In all, the process at the individual level was an inspirational phenomenon to track over the period of the project.

As the LeadNM facilitator noted, "Folks don't get into this business hoping to fail," and we, as researchers and educators, anticipate that the changes brought about at the individual levels will continue to support important, if perhaps idiosyncratic and incremental, changes at school sites. Without in any way diminishing the importance of this work, we believe some larger lessons should be explored in an effort to bring the successes of this grant to a more systemic level. What follows is a set of implications from the grant as a whole, organized according to lessons gleaned from each of the five major subsections of the chapter.

Implications of Isolation

It appears as though isolation is a larger, and more universal, construct than was envisioned at the beginning of the LeadNM project. We began by seeing isolation as a dominant but purely physical manifestation, one of many critical variables hindering progress toward change. However, our work with principals revealed that the psychological and sociological aspects of isolation were, in fact, as problematic as physical distance. In particular, principals held traditional views of themselves as the "center" of school life, as the "heads" of highly structured hierarchical organizations, and as the critical decision makers in their schools. In every instance, these views reinforced a more isolated perspective of the principalship, increasing the distance between themselves and teachers, students, and community members. By assuming that these were the defining characteristics of their roles, principals had "accepted" a very traditional definition of who they were. As a result, they were trapped by this same structured role, effectively preventing themselves from engaging with their colleagues and students in anything other than a top-down approach to solving problems.

This broader conception of "isolation" increases the applicability of this rural research to other settings, including urban and suburban schools. In fact, isolation is likely a common characteristic in all principals' lives; it just has the disadvantage of an additional physical reality in the lives of rural principals. As such, breaking down the role-restricting dimensions of isolation may be one of the critical starting points for working with principals in this era of over-saturated professional development opportunities.

Implications for Professional Development Providers and Universities

Principals did not hesitate to fault program developers if they perceived their time not to be well spent; the initial summer institute provided a strong example of a vocal demand for changed professional development practices. Perhaps such demands are to be increasingly expected as pressures mount on principals for school performance.

The implication for professional developers and university programs working with principals is clear: We must be certain that professional development opportunities for principals are relevant and go directly to the heart of issues with which they deal.

Because the particulars of the LeadNM grant included deep involvement with University of New Mexico Educational Leadership faculty, the suggestion that research-based learning was inapplicable, or superfluous, proved troublesome. Faculty members did not want to accept such positions; nor did they want to be excluded or, perhaps worse, quietly tolerated when offering professional development opportunities for practicing principals. In fact, what faculty wanted was what the grant ultimately negotiated: a vibrant exploration of both theory and practice, in a way that blended the two for real experiences of praxis. The grant's approach—marrying principals' immediate needs with research-based learning through the use of structured protocols—offers one model for effectively addressing questions of praxis within large, multiyear projects and programs.

During the months of redesign of the grant, faculty came to appreciate that the issues the grant sought to address—isolation, building of professional community, and rethinking teaching and leadership practices—were also issues for the university. For the most part, faculty work alone in roles as isolated as those of principals and teachers; and though individual faculty constantly retool their teaching and leadership practices, the bureaucracies in which they work are much slower to do so. Thus, in similar ways that the grant supported principals to listen more deeply and rethink assumptions, faculty determined the Educational Leadership Program should also explore incorporating these practices.[2] We have come to believe that, to the extent that universities, colleges of education in particular, continue to be less than ideal models for reforming educational practices, conversations questioning the role of the university in educational preparation deserve serious consideration, regardless of the incompleteness of the arguments or the apparent partisan nature of the discussions (Levine, 2005; Orr, 2005; Young, Crow, Orr, Ogawa, & Creighton, 2005). Said another way, it is likely that we have much to learn from what we ourselves are trying to teach.

Implications for Development of Professional Communities

The cultivation of professional learning communities in the cohorts succeeded because of a constellation of factors. First, and initially most important to participants, discussions started with explicit exploration of the problems that were *real* problems and not abstractions or hypothetical illustrations. Principals were validated in their experiences because they were given the space to present their issues. Second, the cohort was a nonjudgmental context: no one was there to check up on how they presented things or whether they followed up on ideas that developed from the discussions. The cohort space was safe, and a key norm was that whatever was said in the room stayed in the room. Although principals were routinely professional in their speech, the assurance of confidentiality was key in freeing them to share their thoughts—particularly, we came to believe, their thoughts about themselves. Third, facilitators were not the keepers of in-

---

[2]The work discussing the program's development is in progress as of this writing; further information is available from the authors.

formation. They did not bring the problems to focus or tell principals what they needed to do; rather, they built a trusting, cohesive environment that allowed principals to find their way mutually to solutions that were cohort inspired and community based.

Fourth, and of overriding importance, the protocols supported cohort members in discussions that were at once both personal and universal, helping principals find ways to work through the individual issues they faced and to place these issues and their responses to them within the context of their broader goals. The protocol structures functioned in several ways to foster professional learning communities. They facilitated professionalism because they guided participants in respectful speech, listening, and questioning patterns. They facilitated learning by teaching participants to systematically probe issues deeply and from different perspectives. The protocols facilitated community by engaging all participants in the conversations and by creating a sense of shared responsibility for issues among cohort members. Although there are other approaches to accomplishing these goals, protocols offer a viable option for pursuit of such work at a system level, particularly when many groups are involved and limited contact possibilities are limited.

Implications for Fostering Deep Learning

The transition from a cynical, almost anti-intellectual, perspective on the part of the principals occurred gradually over the first 2 years of the project. It was a slow, incremental process that was facilitated by a combination of the readings, cohort meetings, careful guidance by facilitators, and interpersonal communications among the principals about the issues they faced. The facilitators were adept at helping principals explore complex reasons and conflicting values underlying their schools' situations. Said one participant, "LeadNM has helped me be open to the root causes of problems, the deeper picture. I'm better able to understand where people are coming from and to think of how to deal with them to solve the underlying problems."

LeadNM participants found that discussion and collective reflection focused on concrete problems proved key in permitting principals to see LeadNM not as a "silver bullet" but as a structured community that supported real work. They also saw that this work was improved by virtue of sustained, productive links to research and to other work brought in from outside the walls of principals' individual schools. As principals subsequently began to introduce these new ideas into their sites, the cycle of school change gathered momentum. To confirm this finding, one principal offered an insight, both sobering and promising, on his previous assumptions about being a principal: "I have learned so much this year—who would have thought that principals have to learn in order to become effective?"

Implications for Supporting Systemic Change

Although the literature on school leadership has promoted shared decision making since the popularization of site-based management in the 1980s, only one person among all the participants interviewed noted that she had been exposed previously to this particular leadership concept. That all others in the cohorts found these explorations to be unique in their professional development experiences raises a significant question about whether the theories in educational leadership research have found their way into practice. The dearth of understanding among these rural school principals about widely known leadership concepts also indicates that supporting change will require a significant time commitment to sustain the kind of work the grant supported. Absent long-term federal funding for such efforts, states and districts are left to their own resources, having to prioritize leadership development in light of other educational initiatives. Sadly, incentives weigh against long-term leadership development as a high priority for states and districts, with short-term pressures to raise individual student test scores being of such importance in the current policy context. Without a striking shift in the incentives of the system to value the long-term benefits of leadership work, the development of schools as rich learning communities is, ironically, likely to hinge in some way on isolated individuals who happen, through experience and will, to find the ways to foster such communities.

On a more hopeful note, we find the current discussions on educational leadership preparation programs (Levine, 2005; Orr, 2005; Young et al., 2005) to be a rare window of opportunity. All of the approaches and activities connected to the grant could be brought into a redesign of preparation programs, providing future principals with the kind of experience that the aspiring principals connected to the grant had. Such a focus might require faculty to retool in certain areas; a reconsideration of faculty workloads, revision of courses, and culminating program projects; and a renegotiation of the content and context of administrative internships. But if what we teach "theoretically" is, indeed, what should be acted on, perhaps the time is now to take some important steps to revisioning the work we do, so that future principals can more easily revision the work of leading schools.

ADDITIONAL RESOURCES

Professional Development and Professional Learning Communities

In addition to sources cited in the text, for insights on professional development and professional learning communities, the authors recommend Roland Barth's (2001) *Learning by Heart*, Linda Darling-Hammond's (1997) *The Right to Learn*, as well as David Hagstrom's (2005) *From Outrageous to Inspired: How to Build a Community of Leaders in Our Schools* and Thomas Serviovanni's (1999) *Building Community in School*. Other resources available include the following:

Annenberg Institute for School Reform (AISR).
http://www.annenberginstitute.org—As stated on its Web site, the Annenberg Institute for School Reform "develops, shares and acts on knowledge that improves the conditions and outcomes of schooling in America, especially in urban communities and in schools serving underserved children." The site contains a wealth of resources and access to resources from other organizations.

Coalition of Essential Schools (CES).   http://www.essentialschools.org—The Coalition of Essential Schools is a "network of schools, centers, organizations, and individuals working together to create and sustain personalized, equitable, and intellectually challenging schools." The Common Principles provide the philosophy behind the work of CES. The site provides hundreds of resources focused on school design, organizational practices, classroom practice, leadership, and community connections.

National School Reform Faculty (NSRF).   http://www.nsrfharmony.org—The Web site characterizes the NSRF as a type of professional development "that focuses on developing collegial relationships, encouraging reflective practice, and rethinking leadership in restructuring schools" for the purpose of increasing student achievement. This site provides practical information on Critical Friends Groups and the use of protocols.

National Staff Development Council (NSDC).   http://www.nsdc.org—The National Staff Development Council focuses on helping school personnel ensure "success for all students through staff development and school improvement." NSDC has publications, articles, and a variety of other resources to assist in providing staff development for teachers and principals. One particularly helpful resource is Dennis Sparks' 14 chapter book entitled *Designing Powerful Professional Development for Teachers and Principals*, which can be obtained free online at http://www.nsdc.org/library/leaders/sparksbook.cfm. This book provides several suggestions about how school systems can provide professional learning for their staffs.

Southwest Educational Development Laboratory (SEDL).   An early manuscript describing professional learning communities was written by Shirley Hord and published in 1997 by SEDL (*Professional Learning Communities: Communities of Continuous Inquiry and Improvement*). Since that time, SEDL has continued to have a major emphasis on professional learning communities as an important method through which "teachers and administrators can share decisionmaking, collaborate on their practice, and hone their skills to increase student learning." *Professional Learning Communities: An Ongoing Exploration* is available free from the SEDL Web site.

Isolation

In the area of isolation, a good starting point is the work of Robert Sternberg (2004), *Culture and Competence: Contexts of Life*. This book brings focus to a common problem researchers have about the study of "microworlds" in relation to the real dynamics of the "macroworld" in which we live. One of the earliest studies on the subject of isolation is found in the work of Helen Jennings (1955): *Leadership and Isolation: A study of personality in interpersonal relations*. Little's (1986) classic study reported in Liberman's *Rethinking School Improvement: Research, Craft, and Concept* describes how teachers replaced the norm of isolation through collegial discussions, critiquing, and working together. A year later Rosenholtz in *Teacher's Workplace: The Social Organization of Schools* described the differences between collaborative and isolated settings.

REFERENCES

Ackerman, R. H., & Maslin-Ostrowski, P. (2002). *Seeking a cure for leadership in our lifetime.* Paper presented at the American Educational Research Association, New Orleans, LA.

Barth, R. S. (1990). *Improving schools from within.* San Francisco: Jossey-Bass.

Barth, R. S. (2001). *Learning by heart.* San Francisco: Jossey-Bass.

Barth, R. S. (2002). The culture builder. *Educational Leadership, 59*(8), 6–11.

Beeson, E., & Strange, M. (2003). *Why rural matters 2003: The continuing need for every state to take action on rural education.* Arlington, VA: The Rural School and Community Trust.

Borger, J., Lo, C., Oh, S., & Walberg, H. J. (1985). Effective schools: A quantitative synthesis of constructs. *Journal of Classroom Interaction, 20*(2), 12–17.

Bottoms, G., & Moore, B. (2004). Principals can make a difference in improving science achievement. *Middle Matters, 13*(2).

Coalition of Essential Schools. Common principles. (n.d.). Retrieved July 22, 2005, from http://www.essentialschools.org/pub/ces_docs/about/phil/10cps/10cps.html

Darling-Hammond, L. (1997). *The right to learn: A blueprint for creating schools that work.* San Francisco: Josey-Bass Publishers.

Darling-Hammond, L., & McLaughlin, M. (1995). Policies that support professional teacher development in an era of reform. *Phi Delta Kappan, 76,* 597–604.

DeMoss, K., Winograd, P., & New Mexico Coalition of School Administrators. (2005). *Principal turnover in New Mexico schools.* Unpublished manuscript, Santa Fe, NM.

DuFour, R., DuFour, R., Eaker, R., & Karhanek, G. (2004). *Whatever it takes: How professional learning communities respond when kids don't learn.* Bloomington, IN: National Educational Service.

Educational Research Service. (2000). *The principal, keystone of a high-achieving school: Attracting and keeping the leaders we need.* Washington, DC: National Association of Secondary School Principals.

Elmore, R. F. (2002). Hard questions about practice. *Educational Leadership, 59*(8), 22–25.

Evans, P., & Mohr, N. (1999). Professional development for principals: Seven core beliefs. *Phi Delta Kappan, 80,* 530–532.

Farkas, S., Johnson, J., Duffett, A., Foleno, T., & Foley, P. (2001). *Trying to stay ahead of the game: Superintendents and principals talk about school leadership.* Retrieved July 25, 2005, from http://www.publicagenda.com/research/pdfs/ahead_of_the_game.pdf

Fullan, M. (2002). The change leader. *Educational Leadership, 59*(8), 16–20.

Glickman, C. D. (2002). *Leadership for learning: How to help teachers succeed.* Alexandria, VA: ASCD.

Hagstrom, D. (2005). *From outrageous to inspired: How to build a community of leaders in our schools.* San Francisco: Jossey-Bass.

Hancock, M., & Lamendola, B. (2005). A leadership journey. *Educational Leadership, 62*(6), 74–78.

Holloway, J. H. (2004). Mentoring new leaders. *Educational Leadership, 61*(7), 87–88.

Kegan, R., & Lahey, L. (2001). *How the way we talk can change the way we work: Seven languages for transformation.* San Francisco: Jossey-Bass.

Lambert, L. (1998). *Building leadership capacity in schools.* Alexandria, VA: ASCD.

Lambert, L. (2003). *Leadership capacity for lasting school improvement.* Alexandria, VA: ASCD.

Lashway, L. (2003). *Inducting school leaders.* (Eric digest 170) Retrieved from http://eric.uoregon.edu/publications/digests/digest170.html

Leithwood, K., Louis, K. S., Anderson, S., & Wahlstrom, K. (2004). *Review of research: How leadership influences student learning.* New York: Wallace Foundation.

Levine, A. (2005). *Educating school leaders.* Washington, DC: Education Schools Project.

National Center for Educational Statistics. (2003). *Overview of public elementary and secondary school districts: School year 2001–2002. Table 10. Number and percentage of public school students participating in selected programs, by state: School year 2001–02* (No. NCES 2003–411).

National Center for Educational Statistics. (2005a). *Digest of educational statistics, 2003. Table 54. Number and percent of children served under Individuals With Disabilities Education Act, part b, by age group and state or jurisdiction: Selected years, 1990–91 to 2001-02.* Retrieved from http://nces.ed.gov/programs/digest/d03/tables/dt054.asp

National Center for Educational Statistics. (2005b). *Digest of educational statistics, 2003. Table 124: Mathematics average scale score and performance and selected statistics on mathematics education for 4th-graders in public schools, by state or jurisdiction: 1992, 2000, and 2003.* Retrieved from http://nces.ed.gov/programs/digest/d03/tables/dt124.asp

National Center for Educational Statistics. (2005c). *Digest of educational statistics, 2003. Table 168: Total and current expenditures per pupil in fall enrollment in public elementary and secondary education, by function and state or jurisdiction: 2000-01.* from http://nces.ed.gov/programs/digest/d03/tables/dt168.asp

National School Reform Faculty. [Homepage] (n.d.). Retrieved July 22, 2005, from http://www.nsrfharmony.org/

Networks and clusters in the rural challenge: A special report to the Rural School and Community Trust. (2000). Cambridge, MA: Harvard University Graduate School of Education.

Newmann, F. M. (1996). *Authentic achievement: Restructuring schools for intellectual quality.* San Francisco: Jossey-Bass.

Orr, M. T. (2005). *Evaluating educational leadership preparation: A review of empirical, conceptual and methodological literature.* Unpublished manuscript.

Peterson, K. D., & Kelley, C. (2002). Principal in-service programs: A portrait of diversity and promise. In M. S. Tucker & J. B. Codding (Eds.), *The principal challenge: Leading and managing schools in an era of accountability.* San Francisco: Wiley.

Rogers, D. W., & Babinski, L. (1999). Breaking through isolation with new teacher groups. *Educational Leadership, 56*(8), 38–40.

Schmoker, M. (2004). Tipping point: From feckless reform to substantive instructional improvement. *Phi Delta Kappan, 85,* 424–432.

Sebring, P., & Bryk, A. (2000). School leadership and the bottom line in Chicago. *Phi Delta Kappan, 81,* 440–443.

Serviovanni, T. (1999). *Building community in schools.* San Francisco: Jossey-Bass.

Sparks, D. (2002). *Designing powerful professional development for teachers and principals.* Oxford, OH: National Staff Development Council.

Tucker, M. S., & Codding, J. B. (Eds.). (2002). *The principal challenge: Leading and managing schools in an era of accountability.* San Francisco: Wiley.

Wagner, T. (2001). Leadership for learning: An action theory of school change. *Phi Delta Kappan, 82,* 378–383.

Winograd, P., Feijoo, M., Thorstensen, B., Jacobus, K., & Hughes, S. (2004). *Accountability, teacher quality, & student success in northern New Mexico: Questions worth asking.* Paper presented at the Northern Network Education Summit, Santa Fe.

Young, M. D., Crow, G., Orr, M. T., Ogawa, R., & Creighton, T. (2005). *An educative look at "educating school leaders."* Retrieved June 18, 2005, from http://www.ucea.org/

8

Kentucky's Collaborative Model for Developing School Leaders for Rural High-Need Schools: Principals Excellence Program

Tricia Browne-Ferrigno
University of Kentucky

Jane Clark Lindle
Clemson University

Hard-to-staff schools—those with low accountability-test scores, limited resources, high staff turnover, poor school leadership—can be found in districts across America (Gates, Ringel, Santibanez, Ross, & Chung, 2003; Roza, Cello, Harvey, & Wishon, 2003). However, high-need schools located in isolated, economically distressed regions typically have "higher concentrations of poor and minority students, low per-pupil expenditures, and low principal salaries" (Roza & Swartz, 2003, p. 2). Such conditions create challenges when districts attempt to recruit and retain principals who will accept offers and remain long enough to make a difference in student outcomes (Arnold, Newman, Gaddy, & Dean, 2005). Twin challenges—sustaining effective school leadership in rural districts while simultaneously improving student learning—constitute the obstacles to refocusing schooling on learners in rural, high-need education systems.

Approximately 7.2 million of America's 45.1 million children and youth live in communities with populations of fewer than 2,500 residents. That means that one of every six P-12 students attends a rural school where opportunities to learn are different from those in urban or suburban schools (Arnold, 2004). Yet, the knowledge base about rural educational leadership issues—particularly how to recruit and retain adequately prepared principals for high-need schools—is nearly nonexistent (Arnold et al., 2005). Sadly, "there is a real problem finding people to serve as principals, in the very schools most in need of outstanding leadership" (Roza et al., 2003, p. 55). Addressing principal-candidate shortages in hard-to-staff rural schools requires unique strategies and determined efforts by districts desperately needing new administrative talent (Howley & Pendarvis, 2002; Miller, 2004). The increasing pressures of national and state accountability policies amplify rural schools' need for school leaders who understand and focus on learners and the conditions of learning. This chapter describes how one rural eastern Kentucky school district strove to meet its school leadership staffing issues as well as pressures for refocusing school leaders' work on student learning.

Since 1998, the current superintendent of Pike County School District (PCSD) has maintained a proactive stance in developing principals for its high-need schools. As a result of the superintendent's sustained commitment to improving learning, the PCSD and the University of Kentucky (UK) formed a partnership to reculture building-level school leadership. The goal of the program was to redirect the former district emphasis on school management into an expanded school leadership model that centered on learning as well as created a pool of well-prepared candidates ready to fill future open principalships.

This chapter describes that program using a four-part framework. The contextual circumstances that influenced the program's design and implementation are presented first, followed by a discussion of the program design. The evaluation design and pertinent results are presented in the third major section. The chapter closes with a discussion of policy issues and the potential for long-term sustainability.

LEARNER-CENTERED LEADERSHIP IN KENTUCKY: CONTEXTUAL ISSUES AND CHALLENGES

Comprehensive educational reform within the Commonwealth has been ongoing since passage of the Kentucky Education Reform Act of 1990 (KERA). This omnibus legislation restructured public school finance, curriculum, and governance and launched a demanding pace of high-stakes school accountability (Kannapel, Aagaard, Coe, & Reeves, 2000; Legislative Research Commission, 1990). The task force that designed the reform policy maintained the core belief that "all children can learn and most at high levels" (Pankratz & Petrosko, 2000, p. 3). KERA has been described as the "most comprehensive education legislation in modern American history" (Foster, 1999, p. 1) and as "the nation's most radical and far-reaching reform in a decade, [which] inspired school change initiatives throughout the United States" (Pankratz & Petrosko, p. 2). Kentucky educators at all levels were required to make "drastic change in nearly every aspect of schooling, all within a short period of time" (Guskey & Oldham, 1996, p. 3). Though comprehensive, the KERA changes were also systemic and conceptually coherent in refocusing Kentucky's public education system on student learning and aligning all aspects of schooling to student learning (Foster, 1999; Lindle, 2001a, 2001b; Steffy, 1993).

Education reform policy also changed the principalship in three significant ways. First, KERA increased emphasis on instructional leadership in schools to ensure acceptable student performance on the state's accountability system. To achieve desired outcomes of improved student learning, school leadership was expanded through mandated installation of local decision-making councils having legal authority over school matters directly related to "the ability of teachers to create an effective learning environment for all the children in their care" (Foster, 1999, p. 134). School-Based Decision-Making (SBDM) Councils are composed of three teachers, two parents, and the principal or a multiple of this configuration that must remain in a three-two-one ratio of representation (Lindle, 2001b; Required Adoption of School Councils, 1990). KERA also empowered school councils to make principal selections, drawn from a candidate pool screened by the superintendent. Because councils sustain the final hiring decision, superintendents are bound by council selection decisions, although superintendents retained control over principal supervision, evaluation, and termination (Lindle, 2001b).

Second, as part of the charge to the KERA-created Kentucky Education Professional Standards Board (EPSB) to set the requirements for educators' licensure, the EPSB established standards for new and experienced teachers and school administrators (Lindle, 2001a). Kentucky adopted—without modification—the Interstate School Leaders Licensure Consortium (ISLLC) *Standards for School Leaders* (Council of Chief State School Officers, 1996) as the blueprint for educational administration. EPSB joined with the Kentucky Department of Education, and the Council on Postsecondary Education in requiring alignment of preservice preparation, new-administrator induction, inservice professional development, and annual administrator evaluation to the ISLLC *Standards*.

Finally, in 2002 the Kentucky General Assembly enacted Reducing Achievement Gap legislation, which reasserted KERA's fundamental slogan that all pupils shall make progress in Kentucky's schools. The legislation identified five subgroupings of students for which performance data must be disaggregated and analyzed by schools. Four of the subgroups replicate the federal No Child Left Behind (NCLB) Act of 2001's listing of groups to be monitored for adequate yearly progress (AYP): (a) children in poverty, (b) students with disabilities, (c) racial and ethnic minorities, and (d) pupils for whom English is not their first language. Kentucky's law adds a fifth group to disaggregate and monitor for progress—males and females. The law cites specific tasks for principals and school councils to address and lists six categories that must be included in comprehensive school improvement plans (Lindle, 2004). Schools are evaluated biennially based on the KERA school accountability model, and Kentucky's policymakers give a nod to NCLB for providing teeth to educational policy on closing achievement gaps due to AYP requirements every year (Cibulka & Lindle, 2005; Goertz, 2005).

KERA was the catalyst for emphasis on learner-centered leadership in Kentucky: It charged school governance councils with ensuring that student achievement issues are recognized, planned and allocated for, monitored, and addressed. Kentucky adopted the ISLLC *Standards* as the framework for educational administration given the ISLLC emphasis on promoting the success of all students. Through recent gap-closing legislation, Kentucky policymakers not only addressed the NCLB requirement for evidence of annual learning progress by all students, but also expanded the KERA accountability model. These policy demands challenged all of Kentucky's school districts, particularly those high-need, rural districts located in the Appalachian region of eastern Kentucky.

Challenging School Leadership: High-Need Rural District

Pike County comprises the easternmost tip of Kentucky that borders Virginia and West Virginia, many miles distant from any metropolitan centers. During the mid-1700s the region began to be settled by Scotch-Irish and German clans that lived independently as yeoman-farmers and did not readily welcome newcomers (Clark, 1988; Drake, 2001). Remnants of the early culture persist today, particularly the deeply ingrained patriarchy. The rugged terrain of steep mountains and narrow hollows isolated settlements, creating distinctly different communities throughout the county. Residents often know the particular mountain, creek, or valley where individuals grew up or live based on their surnames.

Whereas the statewide population is approximately 90% "white persons, not of Hispanic/Latino origin" (United States Census Bureau [Census], 2000), in Pike County it is over 98%. Although two thirds of the county residents over age 25 are high school graduates, only 10% within that group completed a postsecondary degree despite the local availability of several institutions of higher education.

After decades of coal mining and logging during the 20th century, the abundant resources became depleted. Without employment opportunities, many residents left the region between 1940 and 1970. Those that remained often had to depend on welfare, and today reliance on governmental support is pervasive (Drake, 2001). Approximately 29% of the children under the age of 18, who comprise one fourth of the district's total county population, live in poverty (Census, 2000). The PCSD average rate for student participation in free and reduced price lunch programs is 69%; however, several schools in isolated communities have participation rates above 90%. Although Pike County does not have a diverse population based on race or nationality statistics, it is quite diverse when differences in socioeconomic status, level of education, residence location, work, life experiences, and cultural or familial history are considered.

Addressing School Leadership Challenges: Action Plan

By the late 1990s, PCSD had earned the dubious legal designation of an educational-system-in-default with a $1.5 million budgetary deficit due to long-term mismanagement.

KDE had identified several schools in the district as low performing, a pattern that persisted because many administrators and teachers were complacent about student learning. When the superintendent retired in 1998, the school board appointed the current superintendent, a lifelong resident of the county and highly respected educator with over 40 years experience. His appointment transformed the district.

After handling necessary fiduciary tasks required by the Kentucky Legislature's Office of Educational Accountability, the superintendent focused on improving student performance. First, he instilled a widespread, sustained commitment to the belief that all children can learn, a core tenet of KERA. In 1999, the school board adopted the superintendent-recommended slogan "Success For All" and then required district administrators and staff to reframe all policies and practices to serve at-risk children.

Immediately afterward, the superintendent and his leadership team began diligently shifting principals' roles from school management to school leadership focused on learners (Browne-Ferrigno & Allen, 2006; Browne-Ferrigno & Maynard, 2005). Although the district leadership team made considerable progress in the initial 4 years, they realized that they needed to actively attend to principal succession planning. The team also realized that it needed a catalyst to take their efforts to critical mass.

In the spring of 2002, the superintendent contacted UK faculty in the Department of Educational Leadership Studies for assistance in designing and delivering customized, intensive professional development for administrator-certified practitioners in the district. Shortly thereafter, the U.S. Department of Education announced its School Leadership Development Program authorized through enactment of NCLB. The collaborators submitted a proposal that was selected as one of the 20 original projects funded in September 2002. The grant award covered all expenses to design and deliver training for two cohorts during 2 calendar years and to evaluate program effectiveness during the third year. The monetary support launched the Principals Excellence Program (PEP).

STRATEGY FOR INNOVATIVE LEADERSHIP DEVELOPMENT: PROGRAM DESIGN

PEP was designed on the premise that becoming a principal requires more than completing preservice preparation. Rather, the "making of a principal" (Lane, 1984) is an intricate process of personal and professional transformation that often requires considerable time and support by others (Browne-Ferrigno, 2003; Crow & Glascock, 1995; Goldring & Rallis, 1993). Districts have vested interest in assuring that effective principals serve their schools, students, and communities (Institute for Educational Leadership, 2000). Beyond the traditional expectations of supervising, coaching, and evaluating principals, districts must also provide "continuous career-long professional development" (Kelley & Peterson, 2000, p. 20) intended specifically to improve administrative practice. At the time this program was designed, scant literature about innovative approaches to providing continuing professional development of school leaders was available (National Staff Development Council, 2000). PEP was modeled on a novel format: Provide advanced leadership development for cohorts composed of both practicing and aspiring principals.

To achieve the desired outcomes (i.e., reculturing the principalship, expanding candidate pool), the program designers selected socialization into a new community of practice as the theory of change for PEP. They used four theories of action—situated learning (Begley & Campbell-Evans, 1992; Lave & Wenger, 1991; Murphy, 1993), leadership mentoring (Capasso & Daresh, 2001; Crow & Matthews, 1998; Mullen & Lick, 1999), community building (Barnett, Basom, Yerkes, & Norris, 2000; Teitel, 1995), succession planning (Hart, 1993; Petzko & Scearcy, 2001)—to develop curriculum, learning activities, and performance assessments and to guide the required formative and summative evaluation. Cohort instructors used a variety of instructional and assessment strategies (e.g., inquiry learning, individual and small-group activities, participant-developed presentations, field-based projects, professional reflection) and adapted the curriculum to meet the learning needs of participants. PEP modeled learner-centered leadership.

CONTINUOUS EVALUATION OF PROGRAM IMPACT: STUDY DESIGN

The federal grant program that supported PEP required formative and summative evaluation; thus, data were collected regularly from the beginning of program implementation through program evaluation. The case study design was selected because the inquiry was bound by specific time periods and encapsulated in a particular structure (Creswell, 1998; Stake, 1995; Yin, 1994). Because case study research is essentially about exploration, a qualitative researcher can begin an inquiry with "a target of interest" and then describe "whatever emerges of significance" (Krathwohl, 1998, p. 26). The project director served as the principal investigator. A doctoral student was hired as the project coordinator to provide research assistance, and a professor from another research university assisted with program evaluation.

Primary Study Participants: Cohort Members

Fifteen educational practitioners were selected for each of the two cohorts. Cohort A included 8 women and 7 men whose ages ranged from 25 to 60 years when they begin their professional development in January 2003. At that time their total years of experience as educators ranged from 4 to 26 years. The group included five principals, three assistant principals, and six administrator-certified teachers and a media specialist. Tenures of the building-level administrators ranged from 6 months to 6 years. The superintendent selected four members from the first cohort to serve as mentor principals for the second cohort.

Within two years after completing the program, five teachers assumed school-administrator positions. In May 2004, a high school assistant principal was selected by KDE to serve as a Highly Skilled Educator, a position created through KERA to provide support for low-performing schools. He plans to seek an administrative position in PCSD after he completes his 3-year term. Sadly, the contract for one principal in the first cohort was terminated in June 2005 because she did not improve her school's academic performance, despite district efforts to assist her.

Cohort B membership included 5 women and 10 men whose ages ranged from 28 to 56 years when they began their professional development in January 2004. The group included four principals, three assistant principals, one teacher on special assignment as acting principal, and six administrator-certified teachers and a media specialist. When they began PEP, their years of experience as educators ranged from 4 to 25 years, whereas the tenure of participating principals spanned from 6 months to 7 years.

One year after completing their intensive professional development through PEP, four teachers (including the acting principal) now serve as principals or assistant principals. Those not yet working as school administrators have interviewed for principalships or plan to seek positions in the near future.

Methodology: Triangulated Perspectives, Qualitative Strategies

Data collection employed multiple strategies (e.g., surveys, reflections, focus-group interviews, observations) and gathered information from members of all key stakeholder groups (i.e., cohort members, mentor principals, district leadership team, cohort instructors) who voluntarily signed consent forms approved by the UK Institutional Review Board. The study intentionally focused on capturing the perceptions of cohort members at various times throughout their program experiences, rather than only at the beginning and end of their year-long professional development. Their responses sampled over time provided ongoing evaluation of implementation progress and guided the instructional team in adapting the curriculum to accommodate changing needs of the participants. The remaining study participants contributed assessments about program implementation through written reflections and group interviews; their contributions provided important contextual and historical information about the district.

Progressive data analysis was conducted concurrently with data collection to assess progress of participant learning and project implementation and to identify need for additional data collection. Analyses of questionnaire responses, interview transcriptions, and participant writing samples incorporated qualitative, grounded theory, and content analysis techniques (Kvale, 1996; LeCompte & Schensul, 1999; Miles & Huberman, 1994; Strauss & Corbin, 1998; Weber, 1990). The bulk of analysis was conducted during program evaluation using a qualitative data analysis software program that allows cross-case comparisons among various subgroups. Group authorship and member checking of in-progress and annual evaluation reports ensured authenticity and accuracy.[1]

PROGRAM IMPACT: SOCIALIZATION TO LEARNER-CENTERED LEADERSHIP

During the 2005 summer institute, the last program-sponsored event, two focus-group interviews were conducted. The 16 participants included 7 members of Cohort A, 7 members Cohort B, and 2 mentor principals who supported field-based activities for both cohorts. The interviewee groups included principals, assistant principals, and

---

[1] Various aspects of the Principals Excellence Program (PEP) have been disseminated through conference papers and journal articles. Topics include program design and participant experiences (Browne-Ferrigno, 2004, 2005; Browne-Ferrigno & Knoeppel, 2005; Browne-Ferrigno & Muth, 2004a, 2004b), rural education challenges and district efforts prior to PEP (Browne-Ferrigno & Allen, 2006; Browne-Ferrigno & Maynard, 2005), and sustainability potential (Browne-Ferrigno, Jackson, Allen, Maynard, & Stalion, 2005).

teachers. Both semistructured interviews opened with the question, *In what ways has PCSD changed since implementation of PEP in January 2003?*

Networking and collaboration were common responses. An assistant principal who began PEP as a teacher with 16 years experience asserted that "there's more collaboration" and "sharing of ideas" among schools. A new elementary principal noted that "administrators are networking across the district" and "discussing more education issues than in the past." A cohort peer agreed, "Networking among administrators has definitely improved the communication between the central office and building-level principals and that's been a result of PEP." The program's intentional combination of aspiring and practicing principals had the effect of lowering status and territorial issues to cement a common district focus on learners.

Several veteran principals who had just completed their 5th to 8th year as school administrators talked about longitudinal change. All three principals served as PEP mentors, and two participated as cohort members. An elementary principal described new district expectations.

> I have noticed a change in the programs that we implement because there was such a great emphasis on research with PEP. I've noticed that any time we mention any type of program now to [our district administrators], they want to know, "Is it research based? Does the research support the types of activities that we are looking at now?" I've been a principal now for 8 years, and I really don't recall that being brought into the discussion until after the inception of PEP.

Another veteran principal talked changed district practices:

> The district models PEP when we meet [for] leadership meetings (we don't call them principal meetings any more). … The superintendent commissioned each school to have a faculty meeting once a week and leadership teams within the school. We report back to him several times throughout the year on different activities or things that we are doing to improve [student learning]. … Every principal is expected to be an instructional leader, and we are reminded of that pretty much at every administrator's conference we have.

The third veteran principal concurred: "The focus is probably narrowed more towards instruction that what it ever has been before. And I think that's been a very positive outlook." PEP's focus on data-based deliberations about student performance increased leadership capacity focused on learning.

Reculturation of District Principalship

The focus of both interviews then narrowed with the first structured prompt about program outcomes: *One goal for PEP was the transformation of the principalship from an emphasis on school management to an expanded model that emphasizes instructional leadership. Has that goal been achieved?* One interview group included an assistant principal, a member of Cohort A, who said that her principal, a member of Cohort B, "has grown tremendously." When asked if he agreed, the principal replied,

> Yes, definitely. I had been a principal for 5 years prior to being involved in PEP. The things that I picked up on more than anything else was to become a stronger instructional

leader. ... My principalship training was more or less about managing a school. The two years that I've been involved with PEP, we focused on being instructional leaders.

Most interviewees agreed, either through comments or head nodding positively, that a change principalship had emerged. A few offered interesting perspectives about the change.

One mentor to both cohorts was asked by the superintendent to move to the district office as a supervisor of instruction in January 2005. The primary job responsibilities for this certified administrative position are to provide on-site assistance to teachers and principals in areas of curriculum, instruction, and assessment. She shared what she had observed during the previous 6 months.

> Not every person that's been in PEP is currently an administrator, but even those people who are in the classroom teaching are being used in an instructional leadership role. From the networking that has taken place between Cohort A and Cohort B and all the discussions that we've had, a focus point was definitely instructional leadership. As a result, even those individuals who may not be a principal [are] still playing a leadership role within the school.

A 1st-year principal, who often offered counterpoint positions during seminar-workshop discussions that reflected his earlier business career, decided he needed to offer "a dissenting opinion" about management and leadership.

> This isn't really popular in mainstream education, but I don't think principals can be one or the other. I don't think that we can be school managers or just instructional leaders. I think it has to be a combination of both. There are elements of the school that have to be managed. I think that you cannot help but be a manager in some respects.

A cohort peer who had completed his second year as a high school immediately responded that he believed being a school manager is a prerequisite to being a school leader.

> PEP broadened the understanding that we all had of the importance of being an instructional leader. Everybody already seems to have the concept that the principal is a manager from the get-go as he manages, supervises, oversees—that type of stuff. PEP gave me an understanding [that] the principal's job is not just limited to that. ... It broadened my understanding of what I should be doing.

The veteran middle school principal who moved to a high school principalship in July 2004 explained what he had learned about distributed leadership.

> I think probably the biggest thing that I gained from PEP was the understanding that you can't micromanage and be successful. I think that we still have administrators that feel like they have to micromanage everything. I still struggle with that sometimes myself. That's probably one of the areas of growth that I need to work on more than anything in order [for our high school] to reach a level that I want it to reach. I can't do it alone.

His struggle with micromanagement has been long term. During the 1st month he participated in PEP, he was anxious about what was happening back at his school and often left the training room to make or answer phone calls. The project director met with him privately and challenged him with two choices: drop out of the program or create a school culture that supported his weekly absences. He chose the second option, distributing responsibilities among his staff and assigning a teacher-in-charge. Eventually, he told his staff to call him only for dire emergencies. When he moved to another school in the district, the teacher who served as acting administrator was selected by the school council to be the principal.

Creation of Candidate Pool

The interview comments changed following this prepared question about program outcomes: *The second goal for PEP was the development of a candidate pool for future open principalships. Has that goal been achieved?* All heads nodded up and down, and several interviewees made affirmative comments simultaneously: "Absolutely!" "Beyond a shadow of a doubt." "Yes." A 3rd-year principal who participated in PEP during his 1st year then talked about hiring an assistant principal, a decision in which by law, councils have input, but not necessarily the final decision.

> I would see who was available out of PEP Cohort A or B that does not have [an administrative] job because of the training that they've received. Definitely, they're going to be an asset to a school. … I think that we have some outstanding candidates who deserve the opportunity to be a principal.

Another principal agreed that "being a PEP graduate would definitely have an influence." When hiring an assistant principal, "you've got someone who is trained, truly trained to be an instructional leader."

Another principal said that she did not "know of anyone that has been hired [recently as a PCSD administrator] that has not been part of the PEP." She believes the district is "now providing our own administrators" who are "much better trained." A teacher, who had submitted his application for a principalship the day of the interview, asserted that "the bar's been raised" because

> getting a leadership position in this district is a whole lot more competitive than it used to be. As a matter of fact, I think that unless you've gone through the program, you're at a disadvantage if you're going to try to get a principalship.

The new middle school principal agreed: "It should be. Yeah, it really should because what you get in PEP is a lot more advanced that what you get from books or theory classes."

The raised bar did not seem to worry another cohort member who had just completed his 2nd year as a high school assistant principal. He did not have plans to seek a principalship anytime soon, but he talked about the advantage he perceived that participating in PEP would give him.

> If I were being interviewed for a position, having gone through PEP, I'd feel a whole lot more comfortable about doing the interview. And I would think that I would do much better [in my interview] and therefore be a better candidate to a site-based council that is interviewing for a position.

Another perceived influence of the program implementation was expanded opportunities for women.

A teacher in the first cohort had been promoted to assistant principal in July 2004 and then selected as the principal of the same elementary school in January 2005. She asserted that more females were being selected as school administrators: "They [school councils] used to just choose males for principal. I've seen more females getting a chance to become principals." A cohort peer responded, "Well, that could have been because of the opportunity for females to get to participate in PEP." A female high school assistant principal reminded the group, "We don't have a lot of women [being selected as principals] but there's definitely a trend toward that."

These remarks attest to PEP's influence because the community's patriarchal culture surrounds the school district's professional culture. PEP participants perceive a shift in changing the patriarchal influences on the professional culture, but not necessarily vice versa.

Potential for Sustainability

The third prompt asked during the June 2005 interviews was about program sustainability: *The district leadership team viewed PEP as a necessary external catalyst to continue its efforts in developing principals. How will those efforts begun by PEP be sustained over the coming years?* The interviewees discussed among themselves who was responsible. A few believed that the superintendent was the key individual, whereas others asserted that program participants were. Then issues and concerns about principal selection arose.

An unintended consequence of the program appears to be the perception across the district of exclusivity. A principal who participated in Cohort A had tried to recruit a teacher at his school to participate in Cohort B. The teacher declined the nomination because his first child had just been born, and he wanted be with his family as much as possible. However, the teacher did express concern about his future career opportunities, according to the principal.

> His comment to me was, "I don't know if I'll ever get involved [in administration] because they say they're only going to select from the PEP group." And he was concerned that the fact that he hadn't participated in PEP might hurt his chances of getting an administrator's job in the county.

A few others confirmed that other individuals who had not participated in the program had similar perceptions.

Then a veteran principal, who believes that building leadership capacity is critically important, suggested the program created a "Catch 22." It "weeded out some people who seemed to have potential but did not" and advanced some who "might have been overlooked" that had become good principals through their participation in PEP. A colleague supported him by saying, "Everybody at this table knows the other person's strengths and weaknesses [although] it's not something that we ever talked about." The first principal responded by saying that program graduates needed to develop new leaders: "As you're leading, then you identify characteristics in people that you think will make them good leaders. You're able to [use] skills that [we] were taught to develop other leaders."

Through additional probing about exclusivity, the issue of differences in interactions among PCSD principals, between those who participated in the program and those that did, arose. The new middle school principal said,

> When I first started attending the administrators' conferences, I didn't feel like I was singled out [as a program participant], that I was any different than any of the other principals. I think principals that had been through PEP had always offered any support that they could. But I also felt that even those that haven't been through PEP were there to offer help. I didn't feel like there was any difference between being in PEP and not being in PEP.

His former principal agreed, "I didn't see any difference either."

The second issue about principal selection and its link to program sustainability was the KERA mandate that school councils hire new principals from pools of candidates screened by superintendents. Council members' lack of understanding about the training participants received was raised by a principal.

> I think one of the saddest things involved with this is that [council members] don't have the background to be able to look at truly qualified applicants in some cases because they don't have the training or the background in hiring principals. You know, they may know what to look for in personality, those types of things, but I'm concerned. Do they truly understand what being a part of PEP would mean to have that person as the administrator?

Interviewees discussed the required principal-selection training that the district must provide and brainstormed ideas within the framework of the law that the district needed to consider. An assistant principal suggested that "the district needs to do a better job communicating to the community." Another assistant principal offered a thoughtful insight about the issue.

> [S]upplying councils [with] strategic questions to ask so they are focused on important aspects of the principalship [would help because] the three teachers [on the council] have a limited perspective about the principal's role based on what their past principal did. The parents might have very limited ideas [about] the principal's job. ... [It would help to share with councils] things that they need to be looking for, suggestions of what would make a good principal, and questions that address different areas of the job so that they can see from the candidates who might be a better candidate. And that would be a benefit to those who've gone through the PEP training because they would be comfortable answering those questions.

Additional ideas were offered by the interviewees, including public-relations activities concerning PEP as well as educating the community toward a deeper focus on learners and learning. This need for ongoing communication about PEP mirrors the district's challenges to promulgate its mission of "Success For All" throughout the community since 1998.

LONG LEVER OF LEADERSHIP: LEADERS AT ALL LEVELS

PEP emerged from a high-need rural district's attempt to reframe the principalship into a contemporary model of school leadership focused on teaching and learning. This change was stimulated by Kentucky education reform policy and from the region's economic distress and geographic isolation. The district also faced a shortage of viable candidates for projected principalship openings. Socialization was the theory of change used in program design; four theories of action—situated learning, leadership mentoring, community building, succession planning—guided curriculum development and instructional activities.

Implications for Policy and Practice

The Kentucky law regarding principal selection has become more of an issue over recent years, particularly with the new requirement for not only schools, but also districts to close learning achievement gaps among specified student populations. District accountability had been integrated in the original school-performance evaluation model; however, in 2004 KDE implemented a separate district system. The issue of principal selection, particularly for low-performing schools, became a critical policy issue. The Kentucky Association for School Administrators (KASA) has lobbied the General Assembly since 1990 to change principal selection back to a responsibility for superintendents. Recently, KDE agreed to support KASA's efforts.

Findings from the PEP study suggest that the "making of a principal" (Lane, 1984) is indeed a career-spanning process. Perhaps a contributing influence in the problem of principal shortages (Gates et al., 2003; Roza et al., 2003) may be that graduates of preservice preparation need socialization opportunities to help them develop confidence and professional support networks for their roles as principals. Though districts can provide professional development for their school leaders, both PEP participants and the PCSD leadership team asserted that the partnership with UK was a key reason for the program's success. WestEd identified the program's innovative integration of theory and practice as a promising practice. Collaborative university-district partnerships formed for the purpose of advanced school leadership development can expand pools of viable candidates and transform the principalship to a focus on learners (U.S. Department of Education, 2005).

Points to Ponder

The authors offer questions for consideration and discussion about ways to prepare principals able to meet the complex demands for learner-centered leadership in this era of high-stakes accountability, changing student and community demographics, and hard-to-staff schools.

1. How are prospective candidates for educational administration identified and recruited? Should university-based programs offer open enrollment or should districts be involved in the selection process? If so, what criteria are most valuable in identifying leadership potential? What mechanisms can ensure that district participation in leadership development avoids exclusivity or cronyism? For a review of recommendations about careful selection of leadership candidates, see Browne-Ferrigno and Shoho (2004); Griffiths, Stout, and Forsyth (1988); Milstein (1992); and Stout (1973).

2. Because successful principal preparation requires individuals, typically classroom teachers, to experience personal and professional transformations to new role identification, how can part-time preservice preparation provide the necessary socialization experiences? For recommendations to improve socialization opportunities for aspiring principals, see Browne-Ferrigno (2003) and Browne-Ferrigno and Muth (2004a).

3. What other models of innovative leadership development have been implemented that may have found ways to address the challenges of developing contemporary principals? The Office of Innovation and Improvement within the United States Department of Education (2005) described six programs—both preservice preparation and inservice professional development, urban and rural—that were selected for their unique strategies in developing school leaders. Free copies of the booklet are available through the USDE Web site.

REFERENCES

Arnold, M. (2004). *Guiding rural schools and districts: A research agenda.* Aurora, CO: Mid-continent Research for Education and Learning.

Arnold, M. L., Newman, J. H., & Gaddy, B. B., & Dean, C. B. (2005, April 27). A look at the condition of rural education research: Setting a difference for future research. *Journal of Research in Rural Education, 20*(6). Retrieved April 30, 2005, from http://www.umain.edu/jrre/20–6.pdf

Barnett, B. G., Basom, M. R., Yerkes, D. M., & Norris, C. J. (2000). Cohorts in educational leadership programs: Benefits, difficulties, and the potential for developing school leaders. *Educational Administration Quarterly, 36,* 255–282.

Begley, P. T., & Campbell-Evans, G. (1992). Socializing experiences of aspiring principals. *Alberta Journal of Educational Research, 38*(4), 285–299.

Browne-Ferrigno, T. (2003). Becoming a principal: Role conception, initial socialization, role-identity transformation, purposeful engagement. *Educational Administration Quarterly, 39,* 468–503.

Browne-Ferrigno, T. (2004). Principals Excellence Program: Developing effective school leaders through unique university-district partnership. *Education Leadership Review, 5*(2), 24–36.

Browne-Ferrigno, T. (2005, January). Becoming principals. *LEAD Kentucky, 3*(2), 16–18.

Browne-Ferrigno, T., & Allen, L. W. (2006, February 10). Preparing principals for high-need rural schools: A central office perspective about collaborative efforts to transform school leadership. *Journal of Research in Rural Education, 21*(1). Retrieved February 12, 2006 from http://www.umain.edu/jrre/21~1.htm

Browne-Ferrigno, T., Jackson, J., Allen, L., Maynard, B., & Stalion, N. (2005, February). *Developing leadership capacity to sustain school improvement: Assessing impact of a university-district professional development initiative.* Paper presented at the annual meeting of the American Association of School Administrators, San Antonio, TX.

Browne-Ferrigno, T., & Knoeppel, R. C. (2005, Fall). Training principals to ensure access to equitable learning opportunities in a high-need rural school district. *Educational Considerations, 33*(1), 9–15.

Browne-Ferrigno, T., & Maynard, B. (2005). Meeting the learning needs of students: A rural high-need school district's systemic leadership development initiative. *The Rural Educator, 26*(3), 5–18.

Browne-Ferrigno, T., & Muth, R. (2004a). Leadership mentoring in clinical practice: Role socialization, professional development, and capacity building. *Educational Administration Quarterly, 40,* 468–494.

Browne-Ferrigno, T., & Muth, R. (2004b). On being a cohort leader: Curriculum integration, program coherence, and shared responsibility. *Educational Leadership and Administration: Teaching and Program Development, 16,* 77–95.

Browne-Ferrigno, T., & Shoho, A. (2004). Careful selection of aspiring principals: An exploratory analysis of leadership preparation program admission practices. In C. S. Carr & C. L. Fulmer (Eds.), *Educational leadership: Knowing the way, showing the way, going the way* (pp. 172–189). Twelfth Annual Yearbook of the National Council of Professors of Educational Administration. Lanham, MD: Scarecrow Education.

Capasso, R. L., & Daresh, J. C. (2001). *The school administration handbook: Leading, mentoring, and participating in the internship program.* Thousand Oaks, CA: Corwin.

Cibulka, J. G., & Lindle, J. C. (2005). *Four decades of performance evidence to reform k–12 education in two states: Measures and countermeasures.* Paper presented at the annual meeting of the American Educational Research Association, Montreal, Canada.

Clark, T. D. (1988). *A history of Kentucky.* Ashland, KY: Jesse Stuart Foundation.

Council of Chief State School Officers. (1996). *Interstate School Leaders Licensure Consortium: Standards for school leaders.* Washington, DC: Author.

Creswell, J. W. (1998). *Qualitative inquiry and research design: Choosing among five traditions.* Thousand Oaks, CA: Sage.

Crow, G. M., & Glascock, C. (1995). Socialization to a new conception of the principalship. *Journal of Educational Administration, 33*(1), 22–43.

Crow, G. M., & Matthews, L. J. (1998). *Finding one's way: How mentoring can lead to dynamic leadership.* Newbury Park, CA: Corwin.

Drake, R. B. (2001). *A history of Appalachia.* Lexington: The University Press of Kentucky.

Foster, J. D. (1999). *Redesigning public education: The Kentucky experience.* Lexington, KY: Diversified Services.

Gates, S. M., Ringel, J. S., & Santibanez, L., Ross, K., & Chung, C. H. (2003). *Who is leading our schools? An overview of school administrators and their careers.* Retrieved June 9, 2003, from RAND Web site: http://www.rand.org/publications

Goertz, M. E. (2005). Implementing the No Child Left Behind Act: Challenges to the states [Special issue]. *Peabody Journal of Education, 80*(2), 73–89.

Goldring, E. B., & Rallis, S. F. (1993). *Principals of dynamic schools: Taking charge of change.* Newbury Park, CA: Corwin.

Griffiths, D. E, Stout, R. T., & Forsyth, P. B. (Eds.). (1988). *Leaders for America's schools: The report and papers of the National Commission on Excellence in Educational Administration.* Berkeley, CA: McCutchan.

Guskey, T. R., & Oldham, B. R. (1996, April). *Despite the best intentions: Inconsistencies among components of Kentucky's Systemic Reform.* Paper presented at the annual meeting of the American Educational Research Association, New York.

Hart, A. W. (1993). *Principal succession: Establishing leadership in schools.* Albany: State University of New York Press.

Howley, A., & Pendarvis, E. (2002, December). *Recruiting and retaining rural school administrators.* Charleston, WV: AEL ERIC Clearinghouse on Rural Education and Small Schools. Retrieved April 30, 2005, from www.ael.org/eric

Institute for Educational Leadership. (2000, October). *Leadership for student learning: Reinventing the principalship.* Washington, DC: Author.

Kannapel, P. J., Aagaard, L., Coe, P., & Reeves, C. A. (2000). *Elementary change: Moving toward systemic school reform in rural Kentucky.* Charleston, WV: AEL.

Kelley, C., & Peterson, K. (2000, November). *The work of principals and their preparation: Addressing critical needs for the 21st century.* Paper presented at the annual meeting of the University Council for Educational Administration, Albuquerque, NM.

Krathwohl, D. R. (1998). *Methods of educational and social science research: An integrated approach* (2nd ed.). New York: Longman.

Kvale, S. (1996). *InterViews: An introduction to qualitative research interviewing.* Thousand Oaks, CA: Sage.

Lane, J. J. (Ed.). (1984). *The making of a principal.* Springfield, IL: Charles C. Thomas.

Lave, J., & Wenger, E. (1991). *Situated learning: Legitimate peripheral participation.* New York: Cambridge University Press.

LeCompte, M. D., & Schensul, J. J. (1999). *Analyzing and interpreting ethnographic data.* Walnut Creek, CA: Altamira.

Legislative Research Commission. (1990). *A guide to the Kentucky Education Reform Act of 1990.* Frankfort, KY: Author.

Lindle, J. C. (2001a). Curriculum reform, the Educational Professional Standards Board, and the Kentucky Department of Education. In J. M. Petrosko & J. C. Lindle (Eds.), *2000 review of research on the Kentucky Education Reform Act* (pp. 83–114). Frankfort, KY: Kentucky Institute on Education Research and the UK/UL Joint Center for the Study of Educational Policy.

Lindle, J. C. (2001b). School-based decision-making. In J. M. Petrosko & J. C. Lindle (Eds.), *2000 review of research on the Kentucky Education Reform Act* (pp. 245–276). Frankfort, KY: Kentucky Institute on Education Research and the UK/UL Joint Center for the Study of Educational Policy.

Lindle, J. C. (2004). *Handbook for School Based Decision Making* (Rev. ed.). Lexington, KY: University of Kentucky Interdisciplinary Human Development Institute. Retrieved April 20, 2005, from http://www.ihdi.uky.edu/iei/Files/Review%20Draft%20SBDM%20Rev%20Ed,3.pdf

Miles, M. B., & Huberman, A. M. (1994). *Qualitative data analysis.* Thousand Oaks, CA: Sage.

Miller, K. (2004, November). *Creating conditions for leadership effectiveness: The district's role.* Aurora, CO: Mid-continent Research for Education and Learning.

Milstein, M. M. (1992, October-November). *The Danforth Program for the Preparation of School Principals (DPPSP) six years later: What we have learned.* Paper presented at the annual meeting of the University Council for Educational Administration, Minneapolis, MN.

Mullen, C. A., & Lick, D. W. (Eds.). (1999). *New directions in mentoring: Creating a culture of synergy.* London: Falmer.

Murphy, J. (Ed.). (1993). *Preparing tomorrow's school leaders: Alternative designs.* University Park, PA: University Council for Educational Administration.

National Staff Development Council. (2000). *Learning to lead, leading to learn: Improving school quality through principal professional development.* Oxford, OH: Author.

Pankratz, R. S., & Petrosko, J. M. (Eds.). (2000). *All children can learn: Lessons from the Kentucky reform experience.* San Francisco: Jossey-Bass.

Petzko, V. N., & Scearcy, L. R. (2001, April). The recruitment of aspiring principals: A two-year follow-up study. *Connections: Journal of Principal Preparation and Development, 3.* [Online publication]. Retrieved March 26, 2005, from http://www.nassp.org

Reducing Achievement Gaps, Kentucky Revised Statute. KRS 158.649 (2002).

Required Adoption of School Councils, Kentucky Revised Statute, KRS 160.345 (1990).

Roza, M., Cello, M. B., Harvey, J., & Wishon, S. (2003, January). *A matter of definition: Is there truly a shortage of school principals?* Seattle, WA: Center for Reinventing Public Education, Daniel J. Evans School of Public Affairs, University of Washington.

Roza, M., & Swartz, C. (2003, April). *A shortage of school principals: Fact or fiction?* [Policy Brief]. Seattle, WA: Center for Reinventing Public Education, Daniel J. Evans School of Public Affairs, University of Washington.

Stake, R. E. (1995). *The art of case study research.* Thousand Oaks, CA: Sage.

Steffy, B. E. (1993). *The Kentucky education reform act: Lessons for America.* Lancaster, PA: Technomic Publishing Co.

Stout, R. T. (1973). *New approaches to recruitment and selection of educational administrators.* Columbus, OH: University Council for Educational Administration.

Strauss, A., & Corbin, J. (1998). *Basics of qualitative research: Techniques and procedures for developing grounded theory* (2nd ed.). Thousand Oaks, CA: Sage.

Teitel, L. (1995). Understanding and harnessing the power of the cohort model in preparing educational leaders. *Peabody Journal of Education, 72*(2), 66–85.

United States Census Bureau. (2000). *Pike County quickfacts from the US Census bureau.* Retrieved October 17, 2003, from http://quickfacts.census.gov/qfd/states/21/21195.html

United States Department of Education. (2005). *Innovative pathways to school leadership.* Washington, DC: Office of Innovation and Improvement.

Weber, R. P. (1990). *Basic content analysis* (2nd ed.). Newbury Park, CA: Sage.

Yin, R. K. (1994). *Case study research: Design and methods* (2nd ed.). Thousand Oaks, CA: Sage.

PART

IV

RESEARCH AND PRACTICE
ON SCHOOL LEADERSHIP
AND PROFESSIONAL DEVELOPMENT

9

LEADERSHIP FOR DATA-BASED DECISION MAKING: COLLABORATIVE EDUCATOR TEAMS

Jeffrey C. Wayman
The University of Texas at Austin

Steve Midgley
The Stupski Foundation

Sam Stringfield
University of Louisville

Principals and other school leaders have been given a difficult charge: Take an abundance of student data, mostly in the form of assessments, and turn this data into information to be used in improving educational practice. To read policy and news accounts, one might surmise that the mere act of providing student data is sufficient to create a school or district driven by this data. On the contrary, although many educators embrace the notion of becoming more reflective practitioners, few educators have the preparatory background to engage in such analysis and reflection.

Despite these potential difficulties, the use of student data to inform reflection on educational practice offers a concrete foundation from which to engage in learner-centered leadership as advocated in this volume: Though data use places clear focus on student learning, data use also provides important focus on educators' learning about their craft. In examining student data, teachers, principals, and other educators are afforded opportunities for reflection on practice, monitoring effectiveness, and participation in community learning. Further, by couching reflection in issues from day-to-day school life, educators are able to engage in action learning by applying new learning and practice to already-developed professional routines. These and other tenets of learner-centered leadership are well-supported in an efficient data initiative.

Although the research literature provides numerous case studies on individual schools or educators that have successfully used data to improve achievement, Stringfield, Reynolds, and Schaffer (2001) found the use of data at the school level to be an incredibly difficult task because school personnel often lack proper systemic supports for data use. Instead they often rely on the "hero model," so dependent on the heroic work of one or more individuals that the initiative is unsustainable after the hero leaves. Our observation is that data initiatives are replicable and scalable when they are built with proper supports at all levels to help educators in this learning endeavor. One such support is the establishment of collaborative data teams.

The goal of collaborative data teams is to form groups of educators that can work and learn together as they engage in the process of using student data to examine and improve their craft. These teams are typically established at the building level and can exist in a variety of forms: They can be made up entirely of teachers, or may also contain administrators, counselors, or other building personnel. These teams may be formed within or across subjects and grade levels. Regardless of their makeup, these teams all serve the same purpose: to support educators in conducting inquiry into practice, and make this inquiry efficient and fruitful.

Educator collaboration is supported by many researchers as an efficient way to improve education (Schmoker, 2004) and should be an effective method in placing a learner-centered focus on school data. The difficulties of educator collaboration have also been described (e.g., Gunn & King, 2003), so it is necessary to establish a firm research base on the implementation of collaborative educator data teams.

In this chapter, the experiences of four districts partnering with the Stupski Foundation to encourage data use within a larger reform context will serve as a backdrop to our discussion of collaborative data teams. This discussion will identify important elements and considerations that will help school leaders in the establishment of productive collaborative data teams, and will highlight practical difficulties in pursuing this endeavor.

RESEARCH BACKGROUND

Data Use

The use of data to inform school practice may seem new because of the increased attention brought about by NCLB, but this concept has received varied attention in school research literature for over 30 years. Many studies of positive outlier, "effective" schools demonstrating unusual academic gains have shown that the thoughtful use of student data positively correlates with a range of measures of student achievement (e.g., Edmonds, 1979; Stringfield, 1994; Teddlie & Reynolds, 2000; Weber, 1971).

Research on school improvement and school effectiveness has suggested that data use is central to the school improvement process (Chrispeels, 1992; Earl & Katz, 2002), and there are an increasing number of recently available case studies available describing ways in which data has supported educational decisions (e.g., Petrides, Nodine, Nguyen, Karaglani, & Gluck, 2005; Supovitz & Klein, 2003; Symonds, 2003; Wayman & Stringfield, 2006).

Inquiry into student data has been shown to be useful in improving overall school practice. Chrispeels, Brown, and Castillo (2000) demonstrated that data use can be a strong predictor of the efficacy of school improvement teams: Data use not only directly increased the efficacy of these teams, but served as a mediator for the positive effect of other factors. Lachat and Smith (2005) found data to be a useful and convenient vehicle for promoting faculty interaction with in-school coaches. Streifer and Schumann (2005) reported precise predictions of student achievement using complex data mining models. Chrispeels et al. (2000) noted the reciprocal nature of data use—the more their team learned about and used data, the more data informed important decisions.

Case studies and interviews suggest that data use may have a positive effect on the people involved in the educational process. Formal and informal research has suggested that schools involved in data use often evolve toward a more professional, collaborative culture (Chen, Heritage, & Lee, 2005; Feldman & Tung, 2001; Nichols & Singer, 2000; Symonds, 2003). Earl and Katz (2002) noted that school leaders involved in data use often consider themselves in charge of their own destiny, increasingly able to find and use information to inform their school's improvement. Data use can be helpful in changing educator views and attitudes toward educational practice and students: Administrators in Massell's (2001) study viewed data use as stimulating a search for new ideas, with data opportunities encouraging many to seek more professional development. Massell (2001) also found that increased communication and knowledge provided by data appeared to be positively altering educator attitudes toward the school capabilities of some underperforming groups. Armstrong and Anthes (2001) found the introduction of data use resulted in heightened teacher expectations of at-risk students, noting positive changes in teacher attitudes regarding the potential success of previously low-performing students.

Though accountability policies do not stress teacher involvement in data-based decision making, teacher involvement is a key element of a fully successful data initiative, particularly in a learner-centered environment. Researchers such as Black and Wiliam (1998) have argued for a classroom-focused policy for assessment because of the access teachers have to students and their performance. Preliminary evidence suggests that, though teachers are often critical of accountability initiatives, they will embrace such policy when it is soundly implemented, responds to the learning needs of their students, and helps them improve as teachers. Ingram, Louis, and Schroeder (2004) and Massell (2001) showed that, though teachers expressed concerns about the appropriateness of and importance assigned to assessments, they also recognized the new information afforded by assessments, along with the stimulus for new ideas brought about by inquiry. Other research has shown a variety of ways that teachers can realize improvement through involvement in a data initiative (Chen, Heritage, & Lee, 2005; Lachat & Smith, 2005; Murnane, Sharkey, & Boudett, 2005; Wayman & Stringfield, 2006).

Though not yet definitive, there is a growing research base to indicate that school data use can lead to a variety of educational improvements. However, this pleasant picture must be moderated by findings from Stringfield, Reynolds, and Schaffer (2001) that many schools have found the use of data for school improvement to entail a great deal of labor. Data are often stored in ways that frustrate flexible analyses, and lack of preparation places undue pressure and burden on a select few individuals. Still, as Earl and Katz (2002) noted, data use is suddenly not a choice for school leaders, but a must. Twenty-first century school leadership models will undoubtedly be heavy on the use of data to inform decisions. Consequently, it is incumbent on school leaders to identify structures and methods that support the use of student data and involve teachers and other staff. Collaborative teams that examine data and explore ways to improve practice are a promising support.

Collaboration for Data Use

In a learner-centered environment, leaders foster collaborative opportunities that offer shared learning, dialogue, and reflection from all members in the organization (Danzig, Blankson, & Kiltz, this volume). Not coincidentally, it has also been suggested that a data initiative will be most useful when it is characterized by widespread involvement among teachers and other faculty members (Wayman, 2005a; Wayman & Stringfield, 2006). Still, most accountability policies do not provide mechanisms for broad, effective involvement among educators and such policy omissions are often considered by researchers to be a hindrance to an effective data initiative (Massell, 2001; Porter, Chester, & Schlesinger, 2004; Stiggins, 1999). It is thus important to identify methods that can help leaders promote widespread collaboration among faculty involved in the inquiry into student data.

Collaboration is touted by many researchers as an effective general educational practice (Schmoker, 2004) and should be a particularly effective structure in promoting school data use. Copland (2003) described collaborative inquiry as one form of distributed leadership, a reculturation of schools and their organizations such that educators throughout the school take on formal and informal leadership roles. Mason (2003) described professional learning communities as the ideal organizational structure for data use.

In describing the administrator as a community builder, Murphy (2002) noted the importance of stretching leadership across different organizational roles to involve various players. Data use is an important component of promoting such leadership and the principal has been shown to be a key element in supporting and spreading data use among a faculty (Copland, 2003; Supovitz & Klein, 2003; Wayman & Stringfield, 2006). Still, there are barriers that make leadership of faculties problematic in a data initiative. Besides the aforementioned lack of preparation, principals often face faculty resistance because data initiatives often involve changes in school culture (Ingram et al., 2004). Also, although effective data use has been shown to be too burdensome for one individual (Stringfield et al., 2001), principals may be hesitant to pass off data exploration to others for fear of mistakes (Supovitz & Klein, 2003).

Solutions to these problems often lie in forms of collaboration that can help educators work together in exploring student data and crafting instructional solutions (Copland,

2003; Huffman & Kalnin, 2003; Mason, 2003). Though effective faculty collaboration can be difficult to achieve because of preexisting educator autonomy and implicit power relationships (Gunn & King, 2003), early evidence suggests that teachers are enthusiastic toward collaboration around data use. For instance, Mason (2003) described a school where teachers strongly expressed their desire for inquiry to be a collaborative process where learning and ideas were exchanged. Wayman and Stringfield (2006) described group meetings around analyses and data software to be a common component of successful data initiatives. Copland (2003) noted that engaging teachers in thoughtful, collaborative inquiry into practice is an empowering act that enables teachers to become equal partners in instructional improvement. Collaboration and data analysis help provide teachers input into important decisions, as illustrated by Schmoker (2004): "Effective teachers must see themselves not as passive, dependent implementers of someone else's script but as active members of research teams."

Even in a supportive, learner-centered environment, efficient data use is difficult to undertake without proper technology, so data systems that assist inquiry into student data are important supports in the creation of collaborative data teams. These systems promise fast, efficient delivery of student data in a user-friendly fashion (Wayman, Stringfield, & Yakimowski, 2004), and have been suggested to be a key element in eliciting and supporting teacher involvement in data use (Wayman, 2005a). These systems are just recently becoming more common in schools, and not coincidentally, much recent empirical evidence on data use comes from districts whose data initiatives include such systems (Brunner et al., 2005; Chen et al., 2005; Lachat & Smith, 2005; Murnane et al., 2005; Streifer & Schumann, 2005; Wayman & Stringfield, 2006).

A strong illustration of the attention required to foster effective data teams is given by Chen et al. (2005), who noted that collaboration for inquiry was a positive byproduct of a student data initiative supported by these systems, but also presented results that showed these collaborations were not ubiquitous and were sometimes unfocused. This contrast shows that, even in supportive environments, effective data teams are complex and difficult to foster. School leaders need information and research on practices that can help them cultivate effective data teams within a learner-centered environment, so in this chapter, we seek to discuss facilitators and challenges to the implementation and function of collaborative data teams. As an illustrative backdrop to this discussion, we draw on stories from four school districts currently partnering with the Stupski Foundation for school improvement. Through this discussion, we aim to offer practical information that school leaders and other educational professionals may use in establishing these teams to improve educational practice and student achievement.

THE STUPSKI FOUNDATION AND THE DISTRICT ALLIANCE PROJECT

Our points and suggestions are cast in terms of the experiences of four districts partnering with the Stupski Foundation in the District Alliance Project, a set of school reform partnerships focused on systemic improvements that develop high-performing schools and high student achievement. These four districts range in size from approximately 10,000 to 35,000 students and cover a range of ethnic makeups and economic classes.

The Stupski Foundation was founded in 1996 as a nonprofit operating foundation to help ensure that all children in America, regardless of race or income, have access to a high-quality public education. The Foundation believes that its most effective contribution to education reform will be through support at the district level, providing expert resources and financial investment in district partnerships. Resource teams working with school districts include former superintendents, educational leaders, and consultants who have led successful district reform initiatives, as well as organizational development, data analysis, and systems experts. The Foundation's District Alliance school reform partnerships began in 2001 with six small- to medium-sized urban, suburban, and rural districts on the West Coast (9,000–50,000 students). In subsequent years, larger and more geographically diverse districts were also added. All districts have been included on the basis of their demonstrated need regarding low student achievement in an environment including high poverty, high minority population, and often with English language acquisition problems.

District Alliance partnerships are expected to last from 2 to 5 years of active work, after which time the districts are expected to serve as a model of reform for other districts beginning the program. Partnerships are primarily with urban school districts and are focused on a systemic approach to school reform, with a goal of developing high-performing schools that provide high-quality educations for all students while closing the achievement gap between ethnical, racial, and socioeconomic populations.

The Stupski Foundation helps districts attain increased student achievement by supporting the use of research-based best practices in a strategic way, mindful of the unique needs of the district and its community. One of the key factors in this reform is a commitment to making equitable decisions and to consistently allocating its resources in ways that ensure all students achieve at high levels. The Foundation envisions equity not in the sense of treating all students equally, but in taking the necessary steps to guarantee that all students are successful.

Such a charge requires that school cultures be addressed. In the District Alliance project, cultural transformation is addressed through high expectations for focus on student achievement by all stakeholders of the district. This commitment is demonstrated by what people say and do, and their shared sense of responsibility for results. Transforming a district culture in this way requires relentless focus and strong, consistent leadership.

The Stupski Foundation has identified seven interrelated components it believes are essential to attaining cultural transformation and to accomplishing the goals of improved student achievement, equity, and social justice. All seven components must be present to bring about meaningful, long-term, systemic school reform. The seven core components of the Stupski Foundation's work are as follows:

- Strong, visionary results-oriented leadership.
- Alignment of action, resources, and results.
- Standards-based curriculum and powerful teaching.
- Effective and efficient processes.
- Active engagement of internal and external stakeholders.

- Employee and student accountability for results.
- Stellar teachers, board members, leaders, and support staff who are continuously learning and growing.

The four districts chosen as illustration for our discussion are ones where the use of student data is a focus within this larger reform context. Although collaborative data teams are not being implemented in these districts as a systemic initiative, collaboration is forwarded in each of these districts as a method for engaging in the thoughtful use of data to improve practice.

COLLABORATIVE DATA TEAMS

The benefits of educator collaboration are particularly valuable in involving faculties in data-driven inquiry into their teaching and practices. The use of data to improve educational practice is new to most educators, so the support and drive that results from group effort will serve faculties well. Wayman (2005a) noted that the relationship between data use and collaboration is reciprocal: Data initiatives are more likely to be successful if teachers are allowed to learn and work collaboratively and the use of data conversely helps foster constructive collaboration. Additionally, using data within a collaborative framework affords educators more opportunities to interact and share ideas across disciplines, and offers teachers opportunities to interact with and assume a variety of roles in the educational hierarchy.

In the following sections, we describe four important contexts regarding the establishment of collaborative data teams: (a) the exploration of standards and definitions for learning ("calibration"), (b) a focus on student data, (c) engagement of educators, and (d) technology to support data use. Following the discussion of each context will be an informal "Leadership Highlight" that offers practical information about the particular construct.

Calibration

Collaborative inquiry as described here demands a strong consensus regarding standards, definitions, and goals about schooling; without such consensus, this work can become fragmented and diffuse (Copland, 2003). This process is reciprocal because an inquiry-based approach builds a common vocabulary and focus (Copland, 2003; Murphy, 2002).

The establishment of common ground is not only important for leadership within collaborative teams, but at all levels of the system. From the top of the district down through the classroom, it is important to engage in the up-front work of defining what learning is, how instruction should be conducted for such learning, and how the assessment of such learning will take place. We refer to this process as "calibration" to remind ourselves that this work involves the dual duties of standardization and ongoing modification.

The calibration process allows stakeholders to explore personal positions on important questions such as, "what should students learn" and "how will we know learning has happened," with the stated aim of arriving at a group (e.g., team, school, or district) set of common standards and definitions. Much as a mechanic would calibrate the settings of an engine for maximum performance, so should school personnel calibrate the foundations and goals of schooling to produce positive learning experiences. At the building level, leaders may engage faculties in calibration activities (e.g., multiple grading of the same student work products by a number of teachers using a common rubric) that can provide a concrete process for schools or teams to identify areas of success, deficiency, and inconsistency.

Three of our illustration districts have experimented with calibration strategies and have shown positive anecdotal results with a few teacher teams. In these districts, we are observing initial progress regarding changes in teacher and principal practice, and in educator understanding of reform issues. As the calibration process continues to unfold in these districts, we anticipate this up-front work will serve these districts well in sensitive interpersonal issues at the school level, where calibration can serve to defuse potential conflicts due to the traditionally autonomous nature of teaching. In a case study of teaming in one school, Gunn and King (2003) described how an absence of shared educational orientation exacerbated conflict; conversely, Huffman and Kalnin (2003) reported teacher comments that team focus on data and goals enabled them to work on improvement in a nonblaming fashion. These results underline the importance of discussing and defining a shared vision–concept of teaching and learning—otherwise, everyone goes their own way.

Calibration is particularly important for classroom practitioners because of the frequent disconnect between policy definitions of success and individual educator definitions of success. Although accountability policies mandate that schools, teachers, and students be judged by external assessment data, Ingram et al. (2004) showed that teachers judge schools, themselves, and students by broader, less definite, and often less quantifiable criteria (e.g., behavior, grades). The calibration process is thus an important link between policy, which often ignores this aspect of school culture, and classroom reality, where educators operate autonomously. Although educators may eschew formal assessments as too narrow to be of much good, it is possible through the calibration process to engage educators in the process of identifying what information they find useful in mandated assessment and define what information should be collected to augment assessments.

The promising implementations of calibration in these districts are cause for optimism, but it is important to remember that even the best efforts of building leaders to foster calibration among their faculty will be difficult to maintain unless there is similar calibration that has occurred at the district level, aligning goals into objectives at the classroom level. Even the districts where we have observed calibration success have realized this only with sporadic faculty groups throughout the district, probably because these districts have not yet structured calibration into a larger district system of accountability and instruction.

Two of these three districts are moving toward this more systemic approach to calibration, creating district-wide accountability systems that direct schools to set local goals based on the success of their students. Although this in itself is a common practice (Reeves, 2004), these districts have additionally made substantial investments to ensure that the school goals are connected to regular collaborative meetings of teachers, and vice-versa. These meetings focus on student work, standards-based instruction and regular assessment. We hope to report on the progress of these measures in future work.

Leadership Highlight. There are a variety of activities leaders may engage their faculties in for calibration purposes. Examples of calibration activities include common grading, where multiple scorers independently evaluate a common set of student work, then come together to discuss similarities and resolve discrepancies, and professional observation and coaching, which provides constructive and designed ways for educators to simultaneously explore areas of success and improvement. Another interesting calibration activity for data use comes from the work of Doug Reeves, founder of the Center for Performance Assessment: The "Adult Science Fair."

In the Adult Science Fair, schools or instructional teams within a school build specific plans for improving teaching and learning. These plans include analysis of existing data to determine areas of strength and improvement, and strategies and measurement goals for targeted areas of improvement. Using these plans, the teams conduct their work (analysis, exploration, and goal setting) over some predetermined time interval (often 1 year). At the end of this year, every team prepares a simple, three-part "Science Fair Presentation." This presentation includes three main components: (a) analysis of existing data, as described in the plan; (b) evaluation of strategies and measurement (e.g., were strategies in plan implemented, what learning was measured based on these strategies); and (c) narrative and description of work to date. As in student science fairs, a common event hall is used to bring together all the teams and display their presentations. In addition to presenting their own work, teams examine the other presentations in the room, looking for accomplishments or successes that would assist in their work and planning. Opportunities for constructive critique may also be offered.

This activity has many positive implications. One is accountability: Peer review and public display creates motivation for high-quality analysis and proper execution of the research plan. Another is group learning and development: Professional learning is a shared experience among a large group of teams; educators are afforded the opportunity to learn from like-minded individuals working in a similar situation. Teams also have the opportunity to connect with other educators working on similar or identical problems.

Focus on Student Data

In building collaborative teams for school improvement, it is important that teams put student learning data at the center of their work and not waver from this focus. Over the years, all four of our districts have attempted a variety of collaborative techniques in an effort to build more effective practice throughout their systems. These prior efforts were marked by the same frustration: school personnel wanted to "go deeper," but had neither the tools nor the guidance to do so. It was not until these districts fully engaged in the thorough examination of student data, studying how well their students were meeting specific, time-bound learning objectives, that these districts began to feel their collaborations were yielding the deep information they had hoped.

The message that student data facilitates collaborative work is perhaps best described in a counterexample from one of our districts. In this district, faculties are meeting regularly about improving educational practice, but are not examining student work and assessments in a consistent and focused manner. Instructional progress in this district is impeded because the conversations in these meetings center on student learning only in the context of sharing techniques and materials, not on specific student learning progress. One current reform focus in this district is thus to help school leaders infuse data into these collaborations—to turn collaborative teams into collaborative *data* teams. If successful, these teams will still exchange materials and ideas as part of the teamwork, but will be supported by data examination. Collaborative conversations that center on topics such as "What did my students learn recently and how do I know this?" and "In what practices have I engaged that affect student learning?" make conversations around "I have these materials that might help you," or "have you considered this activity" much more meaningful.

There is a broad spectrum of student data that faculties will find useful, so leaders need not feel that they need to identify the perfect type of data. Common examples of available data include (a) summative assessments, such as state-mandated tests, that are used to document student achievement at the end of a quarter, semester or school year; (b) formative assessments that are given more frequently and are intended to guide planning, instruction, and daily practice; and (c) student data profiles, which provide information contained in a student's permanent record such as demographic information, test histories, and relevant family information (Wayman, Stringfield, & Yakimowski, 2004, provide a more thorough overview of various data forms). No single form of student data provides all learning information, so teams will find it useful to triangulate student information, using multiple forms of data to assess student learning.

In the four districts highlighted here, summative assessments have been in more frequent use than formative assessments. Summative assessments are frequently criticized because they do not provide up-to-the-minute information as do many formative assessments, yet summative data have served many uses in our districts. For instance, summative data have been used to define an agenda for upper level district administration and help build political support for a long-term strategic information plan. Summative data have been used to help teachers and principals identify specific groups of students for remediation and to provide a positive base for identifying areas of strength and improvement in educator practice. Summative data have also been used for capacity-building; one district in particular has successfully employed summative data to shift their analysis paradigm from a prevention focus to one of capacity-building. The success related to such a paradigm shift is common in other studies of capacity building (e.g., Brown, D'Emidio-Caston, & Benard, 2001) and particularly underscores the importance of a positive focus in using student data for school improvement.

Student data profiles are very popular with teachers because of the breadth of information provided (Wayman & Stringfield, 2006). These profiles lend themselves well to teaming because they provide an overall picture of the student's situation to educators from varied areas. When such profiles have been made available electronically, student data profiles have been used consistently in our districts. Still, lack of availability has rendered these profiles less popular in our districts than they potentially could be. Electronic versions of student profiles are sometimes difficult to produce, particularly with a homegrown student data system. Many commercial data systems offer student data profiles, and this feature is one where commercial vendors are placing increased emphasis and development (Wayman, 2005b).

Leadership Highlight. In building collaborative data teams, keeping the focus on student data serves a hardly surprising, but important, role: It gives team members something to talk about. Leaders should take care to ensure the work and conversations of the team are focused on data to provide a common, nonthreatening topic around which to establish collegiality and teamwork.

Focusing on data creates equality among a team because everyone works from a common starting point. By focusing on data, questions begin around topics such as "what do the data say," rather than, "who do we need to change." Once data are examined and the team moves to setting goals and directions, continued focus on data keeps improvement discussions centered around the numbers rather than centered around the successes or failures of specific people. These points are important toward keeping data examination a positive, nonthreatening experience for the educator. Educators are rightly suspicious of data initiatives, because data have been used to punish educators for so long. Focusing on data toward educational improvement enables practitioners to collaboratively and powerfully explore ways to improve their craft: this focus enables them to *use* data, rather than *be used* by data.

In focusing on data, it is important to remember that one source of information is educator judgment. Focusing on data does not replace educator judgment, but enhances it, because educator judgment is a data point, as may be assessment scores or student histories. All such data points are synthesized in decisions for improvement. In previous work (Wayman & Stringfield, 2006), we have termed this "nonthreatening triangulation" of data, highlighting the example of one principal who demands that all decisions be informed by at least three pieces of data—one of which must be educator judgment.

One final note on data focus: Many researchers correctly note the importance of real-time, ongoing assessment data. But for a faculty or team that is just beginning a data initiative, it is possible that members have never seen any available data on students. Consequently, "historical" data such as student profiles, student test histories, and the like often lend surprising amounts of information and may be an excellent place to start. Data use is a knowledge-building enterprise, so leaders should help their faculties build a good knowledge base about students before working up.

Engagement

In promoting effective teaming around data use, it is important to note that many teachers are understandably mistrustful of data initiatives. Ingram et al. (2004) found that some of this mistrust can be solved by involving teachers in the construction and implementation of a data initiative. Schmoker (2004) noted that instead of merely following directions, effective teachers must see themselves active members of research teams, an assertion backed up by data from Huffman and Kalnin (2003), who highlighted teachers taking ownership of the inquiry process.

It is our position that data initiatives built entirely around mandates are hard to sustain and are unlikely to yield widespread change in instructional practice. In building effective collaborative data teams, it is not only important to engage educators at all levels but to take care that compliance is not the focus of collaborative inquiry. Too much structure and mandate hinders deep, reflective thought, because team members are more engaged in following rules than in reflection and inquiry around this data.

We observed negative instances of this point in two of our districts. In both situations, a rigorous curriculum was implemented that initially helped improve achievement. However, the districts did not build on this success by encouraging input from all levels, and inquiry within this curriculum eventually deteriorated into a compliance system. Educators in these districts blamed subsequent achievement setbacks on the system rather than engaging in practical inquiry to explore further. We believe district educators may have pursued these questions had they felt ownership in the inquiry. Leadership can solve these problems by providing structure, but allowing inquiry and reflection to develop relevant to the particular context. This is a delicate balance, but achievable (Copland, 2003).

Striking a balance between the healthy, supportive pressure infused by mandates and the rich, contextual growth fomented by free inquiry is difficult. Administrators in one of our districts have addressed this problem after recognizing the inhibitions caused by a too-rigorous curriculum. The superintendent in this district has become very proactive in releasing some freedom back to the school level and creating two-directional communication and cooperation across levels of the school hierarchy. In such an environment, collaborative data teams can be a powerful player because they can serve to focus the opinions of educators from a wide range of backgrounds and provide a forum for educator engagement.

Our observations of other aspects of school reform within these districts provide further supportive evidence of the importance of faculty engagement in the health of collaborative data teams. We have observed many forms of engagement in systems planning in these districts, involving formation of accountability systems, selection of computer data systems, and the selection of program materials and assessment instruments. Districts who involved principals and teachers in these processes were generally able to make more rapid and effective use of data for school improvement.

Leadership Highlight.   Creating and fostering ongoing engagement and input from faculties can be tricky because context determines much of how engagement and collaboration operate. Besides serving as a *support* for collaborative data teams, faculty engagement can also be *accomplished* through collaborative data teams. Especially in the early stages of team development, leaders should look to create frequent opportunities for teams and individuals to weigh in on issues such as the functions of data teams, the way data are used to support instruction, and district alignment of data and curriculum. Leaders may structure these opportunities into the work of the team by creating time for building leaders to interact with the teams. Also, it may be important to create formal meetings between building teams and district personnel responsible for decision making about learning matters. Finally, in promoting engagement, leaders should remain aware of implicit power relationships and personal relationships that may hinder communication or present opportunities for growth.

Technology

Limited access to data is often a barrier to widespread school data use (Thorn, 2002; Wayman et al., 2004). Historically, there has been no shortage of school data, but these data have typically been stored in ways that were inaccessible to most educators. This situation is changing with the recent advent of user-friendly computer systems that offer efficient access to student data (Wayman et al., 2004).

Because of this powerful and flexible access, technology is often seen as a panacea for school data use. On the contrary, these systems must be implemented with proper leadership and support if they are to have the envisioned impact on educational practice—although such technology is a *necessary* condition for a scalable data initiative, it is not *sufficient* (Stringfield, Wayman, & Yakimowski, 2005). Educator teaming has been forwarded as an excellent method to help educators get the most out of these powerful tools (Wayman 2005a).

Wayman and Stringfield (2006) described districts that were proactive in involving entire faculties in the use of computer systems to explore student data. One particular school in their study noted the advancements their teams were able to make because district technology personnel were very responsive to team requests for support and training. In asserting the utility of student data to form a nonthreatening base from which to begin professional conversations, Wayman (2005a) noted that efficient student data systems help provide this data in the rapid fashion needed to build on early team successes. Although technology is a good support for data teams, it is also true that collaboration is a good support to help educators learn and grow in their use of these powerful tools. For instance, Zhao and Frank (2003) argued that positive teacher interaction is crucial to the survival of any new technology, demonstrating their teacher interaction construct to be a prominent factor in teacher use of technology.

The necessity of proper technical support for data use and data teams is well illustrated through a counterexample from Huffman and Kalnin's (2003) data. Educators in these data teams reported some difficulty and slowness in executing analysis plans because they had to first collect data, then construct analysis and presentation methods in packages such as Excel. If these teams had access to efficient technology, there would have been plenty of data already collected, organized, and at their disposal. Additionally, the system would have offered a variety of ways to explore, analyze, and represent their data. These teams described momentum and eagerness for more exploration that was built through their process; this momentum would have been far greater and the push for more knowledge much more fruitful with efficient supportive data technology.

In our districts, we saw contrasting examples of implementation and subsequent support of student data systems, with contrasting results. On the positive side, one district provided regular training sessions for principals, offering opportunities to work with data from their schools in these sessions. The district provided an established senior leader to act as a coach and advisor to help principals build skills and leadership capacity around data use with the system. This district also promoted the system at every opportunity, touting the power and potential held by this technology. In contrast, another district had implemented a similar system, but was not as proactive in supporting the technology. Use of the system was not championed, nor were plentiful opportunities provided. Consequently, the capacity of the first district to engage in data use was considerably higher than that of the second district and we anticipate a corresponding difference in the capacities of data teams in these districts.

Leadership Highlight.   Technology is among the most important supports for collaborative data teams. In the absence of proper technological support, even the best-trained team will continually encounter ceilings and hindrances, dampening the rich potential these teams hold for impacting teaching and learning. Still, today's technology world is a double-edged sword for school leaders: Although technology offers unlimited potential and unprecedented efficiency, the amount of technical options available can be daunting for most school leaders. Fortunately, there are resources to help; we highlight two such resources:

In a technical report on student data software for school improvement, Wayman et al. (2004) reviewed issues regarding software for data use, including discussion about choosing appropriate software and what good software might look like, and they also provided reviews of software packages that offered user-friendly access to existing student data. The authors also suggested that most districts would be better off buying systems than building them—they asserted this was no knock on local technical staff, but reflects the experience vendors bring to the problem and associated efficiency that can result in a greatly reduced time to implementation.

In acquiring student data technology, school leaders sometimes find themselves armed with little experience in negotiating business, technical, and legal details that will ensure the system is of the greatest use to their district. Help is available for schools through Contract Commons Project of the New York Law School. In partnership with The Stupski Foundation, the first area of focus of the project will be to produce a set of tools to help school leaders in technology procurement. These tools will be publicly available and will include technology contracts and contract language, a clearinghouse of vendor information, an expert contract drafting "wizard" to walk procurement officials through the business and legal issues necessary to consider when negotiating for technology, and a community forum to encourage debate, discussion, and collaboration among procurement officials and vendors. More can be found on the Contract Commons Project at http://www.contractcommons.org.

IMPLICATIONS

The use of student data to inform school improvement is increasing in popularity and importance, but is unfamiliar territory to most educators. The formation of collaborative data teams offers a positive environment for faculties to learn together and build an initiative they can call their own. Principals and other school administrators serve an essential role in leading, guiding, and organizing the work of collaborative data teams.

In this chapter, we have discussed four contexts that are important for school leaders in the establishment of collaborative data teams: (a) "calibration," (b) focus on student data, (c) engagement of educators, and (d) technology to support data use. Four districts partnering in school reform with the Stupski Foundation served as a backdrop for this discussion, lending practical illustrations for the discussion. The discussion set forth in this chapter has highlighted the potential that lies in collaboration around student data for school improvement, but has also highlighted the fact that educator collaboration and student data investigation are difficult endeavors to perform efficiently.

We have posited that the work of these teams will be most fruitful if the teams are led in forging a common understanding of teaching, learning, and measurement of learning. Calling this process "calibration," we have suggested that engaging in up-front conversations about what student learning is, how it will be achieved, and how it will be measured serve to build consensus and key foundations for teamwork. Data use and collaboration sometimes conflict with established school culture, so we have suggested that efficient teams will realize success by always keeping student data at the focus of discussions. This focus provides a nonthreatening atmosphere to engage in ongoing calibration and other activities involved in practical inquiry. Creating data initiatives can be tricky because of long-standing mistrust of the purposes of student data, so school leaders are well-served to ensure that faculties are engaged in the creation and maintenance of the data initiative and collaborative teams. Giving teachers and other educators a voice in this process helps build support and offers valuable feedback and professional insight that inform a healthy initiative. Finally, no data initiative is efficient, sustainable, or scalable without proper technology. Today's systems offer previously unimagined support for the collaborative work described here, but they in turn must be supported with proper educational training. These findings carry implications for policy and practice.

First, it is important to note the importance of ensuring that data use is grounded in inquiry. Accountability policies such as No Child Left Behind are largely responsible for the increased attention currently given to student data, but the architecture of these policies deal with reporting, thus giving school systems freedom in developing how they will use these data for school improvement. We believe that student data will be most useful when the data are used as tools to support inquiry into educator practice and student learning—learner-centered inquiry. The task thus falls to leadership to discern the best methods to enable this learning, and we believe one way leaders can realize success is to establish efficient collaborative data teams.

Such methods are not easily accessed. We have provided information that will be helpful to leaders looking to establish such teams, but the knowledge base on which leaders may draw is still unfortunately sparse. Thus, a second implication of this work is that it highlights the importance of rapidly establishing a sound research base specific to collaborative data teams, one that informs inform theory, policy, and practice. This void exists despite a fairly large amount of literature on collaboration and increasing attention to data use. That neither practice is independently in widespread use, much less combined into widespread use of collaborative data teams, underscores the need for expanding this body of research.

Third, we have cited evidence that suggests that collaborative data teams and technology may be mutually supportive means for inquiry. However, it is still unknown exactly how powerful these computer tools may be in this endeavor. More importantly, there is a strong need for an information base that provides leaders a variety of sound practices in using technology to support collaborative data teams and vice versa.

These and other implications lead to some important questions for consideration:

1. What scalable practices can be established for collaborative data teaming that are applicable in any educational context? What practices must vary according to context?
2. How may "calibration" prove most effective in establishing such teams? What varied forms of calibration activities may prove most useful?
3. What role may school culture play in determining effective teaming practices? How may existing school culture be both overcome and leveraged in fostering collaborative data teams?
4. What types and methods of principal involvement will prove effective in establishing efficient collaborative data teams? What practices and structures must leaders establish to support principals and engage teachers in collaboratively learning about their craft and increasing student achievement?
5. What role may computer technologies play in enhancing the work of collaborative data teams (and vice versa)? What features and capacities will prove most useful in this endeavor?

Through these and other forms of questioning and research, we hope to witness and contribute to the development of a knowledge base that results in a variety of effective practices in collaborative use of data for educational improvement. Ultimately, we hope that these practices are useful in furthering knowledge about educational improvement and student learning.

REFERENCES

Armstrong, J., & Anthes, K. (2001). How data can help. *American School Board Journal 188*(11), 38–41.

Black, P., & Wiliam, D. (1998). Inside the black box: Raising standards through student assessment. *Phi Delta Kappan, 80,* 139–148.

Brown, J. H., D'Emidio-Caston, M., & Benard, B. (2001). *Resilience education.* Thousand Oaks, CA: Corwin.

Brunner C., Fasca C., Heinze, J., Honey, M., Light, D., Mandinach, E., et al. (2005). Linking data and learning: The Grow Network study. *Journal of Education for Students Placed At Risk, 10*(3), 241–267.

Chen, E., Heritage, M., & Lee, J. (2005). Identifying and monitoring students' learning needs with technology. *Journal of Education for Students Placed At Risk, 10*(3), 309–332.

Chrispeels, J. H. (1992). *Purposeful restructuring: Creating a climate of learning and achievement in elementary schools.* London: Falmer.

Chrispeels, J. H., Brown, J. H., & Castillo, S. (2000). School leadership teams: Factors that influence their development and effectiveness. *Advances in Research and Theories of School Management and Educational Policy, 4,* 39–73.

Copland, M. A. (2003). Leadership of inquiry: Building and sustaining capacity for school improvement. *Educational Evaluation and Policy Analysis, 25,* 375–395.

Edmonds, R. (1979). Effective schools for the urban poor. *Educational Leadership, 37,* 15–27.

Earl, L., & Katz, S. (2002). Leading schools in a data-rich world. In K. Leithwood & P. Hallinger (Eds.), *Second international handbook of educational leadership and administration* (pp. 1003–1022). Dordrecht, The Netherlands: Kluwer.

Feldman, J., & Tung, R. (2001). Using data-based inquiry and decision making to improve instruction. *ERS Spectrum, 19*(3), 10–19.

Gunn, J. H., & King, B. (2003). Trouble in paradise: Power, conflict, and community in an interdisciplinary teaching team. *Urban Education, 38,* 173–195.

Herman, J. L., & Gribbons, B. (2001, February). *Lessons learned in using data to support school inquiry and continuous improvement: Final report to the Stuart Foundation* (CSE Tech. Rep. No. 535). Los Angeles, CA: Center for the Study of Evaluation (CSE), University of California, Los Angeles.

Huffman, D., & Kalnin, J. (2003). Collaborative inquiry to make data-based decisions in schools. *Teaching and Teacher Education, 19,* 569–580.

Ingram, D., Louis, K. S., & Schroeder, R. G. (2004). Accountability policies and teacher decision making: Barriers to the use of data to improve practice. *Teachers College Record, 106,* 1258–1287.

Lachat, M. A., & Smith, S. (2005). Practices that support data use in urban high schools. *Journal of Education for Students Placed At Risk, 10*(3), 333–349.

Massell, D. (2001). *The theory and practice of using data to build capacity: State and local strategies and their effects.* In S. H. Fuhrman (Ed.), *From the capitol to the classroom: Standards-based reform in the states* (pp. 148–169). Chicago: University of Chicago Press.

Mason, S. A. (2003, April). *Learning from data: The role of professional learning communities.* Paper presented at the 2003 Annual Meeting of the American Educational Research Association, Chicago IL.

Murnane, R. J., Sharkey, N. S., & Boudett, K. P. (2005). Using student assessment results to improve instruction: Lessons from a workshop. *Journal of Education for Students Placed At Risk, 10*(3), 269–280.

Murphy, J. (2002). Reculturing the profession of educational leadership: New blueprints. *Educational Administration Quarterly, 38*(2), 176–191.

Nichols, B. W., & Singer, K. P. (2000). Developing data mentors. *Educational Leadership, 57*(5), 34–37.

Petrides, L., Nodine, T., Nguyen, L., Karaglani, A., & Gluck, R. (2005). *Anatomy of school system improvement: Performance-driven practices in urban school districts.* San Francisco: Institute for the Study of Knowledge Management of Education.

Porter, A. C., Chester, M. D., & Schlesinger, M. D. (2004). Framework for an effective assessment and accountability program: The Philadelphia Example. *Teachers College Record, 106,* 1358–1400.

Reeves, D. B. (2004). *Accountability in action: A blueprint for learning organizations.* Englewood, CO: Advanced Learning.

Schmoker, M. (2004). Tipping point: From feckless reform to substantive instructional improvement. *Phi Delta Kappan, 85,* 424–432.

Stiggins, R. L. (1999). Assessment, student confidence, and school success. *Phi Delta Kappan, 81,* 191–198.

Stringfield, S. (1994). Outlier studies of school effects. In D. Reynolds, B. Creemers, P. Nesselrodt, E. Schaffer, S. Stringfield, & C. Teddlie (Eds.), *Advances in school effectiveness research* (pp. 73–83). Oxford, England: Pergamon.

Stringfield, S., Reynolds, D., & Schaffer, E. (2001, January). *Fifth-year results from the High Reliability Schools project.* Symposium presented at the meeting of the International Congress for School Effectiveness and Improvement, Toronto, Canada.

Stringfield, S., Wayman, J. C., & Yakimowski, M. (2005). Scaling up data use in classrooms, schools and districts. In C. Dede, J. P. Honan, & L. C. Peters (Eds.), *Scaling up success: Lessons learned from technology-based educational innovation.* San Francisco: Jossey-Bass.

Streifer, P. A., & Schumann, J. A. (2005). Using data mining to identify actionable information: Breaking new ground in data-driven decision-making. *Journal of Education for Students Placed At Risk, 10,* 281–293.

Supovitz, J. A., & Klein, V. (2003). *Mapping a course for improved student learning: How innovative schools systematically use student performance data to guide improvement.* Philadelphia: Consortium for Policy Research in Education.

Symonds, K. W. (2003). *After the test: How schools are using data to close the achievement gap.* San Francisco, CA: Bay Area School Reform Collaborative.

Teddlie, C., & Reynolds, D. (2000). *The international handbook of school effectiveness research.* London: Falmer.

Thorn, C. A. (2001). Knowledge management for Educational Information Systems: What is the state of the field? *Education Policy Analysis Archives, 9*(47). Retrieved June 22, 2006, from http://epaa.asu.edu/epaa/v9n47/

Wayman, J. C. (2005a). Involving teachers in data-based decision-making: Using computer data systems to support teacher inquiry and reflection. *Journal of Education for Students Placed At Risk, 10*(3), 295–308.

Wayman, J. C. (2005b). *Technology that facilitates school improvement through data-informed practice.* Presentation at the 10th Annual K-12 School Networking Conference of the Consortium for School Networking (CoSN), Washington DC.

Wayman, J. C., & Stringfield, S. (2006). Technology-supported involvement of entire faculties in examination of student data for instructional improvement. *American Journal of Education, 112*(4), 549–571.

Wayman, J. C., Stringfield, S., & Yakimowski, M. (2004). *Software enabling school improvement through analysis of student data* (CRESPAR Technical Report No. 67). Baltimore: Johns Hopkins University. Retrieved June 22, 2006, from http://www.csos.jhu.edu/crespar/techReports/Report67.pdf

Weber, G. (1971). *Inner city children can be taught to read: Four successful schools* (Occasional Paper No. 18). Washington, DC: Council for Basic Education.

Zhao, Y., & Frank, K. A. (2003). Factors affecting technology users in schools: An ecological perspective. *American Educational Research Journal, 40,* 807–840.

10

LEARNER-CENTERED LEADERSHIP IN "URBAN" CONTEXTS: KEY ELEMENTS TO CONSIDER FOR PROFESSIONAL DEVELOPMENT

Bruce A. Jones
Nathan D. Jackson
University of South Florida

Since the emergence of the effective schools movement in the 1970s, enormous and critical attention has been given to the role of the school leader as *instructional leader*. In the role of instructional leader, school leaders focus less on leading schools in a "business" sense and more on teacher evaluation and efficacy in the classroom. More recently, with the emergence of the *learner-centered community school* concept, there is a realization that school principals must do more than just focus on teacher evaluation and efficacy in the classroom to be effective leaders (DuFour, 2002). This is particularly true for school leaders who are employed in urban environments, which are replete with a web of social, political, economic, and cultural issues that are significantly less characteristic of suburban and rural environments. Urban school principals who naively operate from a narrow instructional leadership framework may be eaten, chewed, and swallowed up by the social, political, economic, and cultural phenomena that are embedded in the urban environment.

This chapter contends that professional development for urban school leaders must take into account the uniqueness of the urban environment, or else such professional development will be viewed as irrelevant and a waste of time by school leaders who are genuinely committed to improving the academic and sociocultural environment of their schools and school districts. The chapter is informed by studies on school leadership that were underway in the St. Louis and Kansas City school districts through the Urban School Leadership Consortium (USLC).

USLC

The USLC was launched in April 2003 with the formalization of a partnership between the St. Louis and Kansas City, Missouri, school districts. The USLC is the first and only such partnership in the United States that involves two large urban school districts in one state working to jointly improve professional development for practicing school leaders in coordination with leadership development for aspiring school leaders at the higher education level. More specifically, the goals of the USLC are as follows:

- Identify conditions of leadership that support and/or inhibit highly effective urban school leadership.
- Develop strategic alliances that foster nontraditional collaboration between urban school districts, higher education, community, and state-level partners focused on preparation and development of school leaders in the urban centers.
- Actively engage key stakeholders in urban school leadership through the development of a statewide national advisory council committed to strong leaders and academic achievement in urban districts.
- Share best, tested, and promising leadership practices with university partners, local urban districts, and state-level policy makers to advance the field and impact a critical mass of aspiring and practicing school leaders.

Under the auspices of the USLC, during the 2004 and 2005 school years, the author engaged in site visits to the St. Louis School District to collect quantitative and qualitative data that focused in part on understanding the professional development needs of the school leaders. In addition, during a biannual USLC School Leadership Summit, a sample of school leaders (principals, teacher leaders, and central office administrators) from the St. Louis[1] and Kansas City school districts were surveyed to gain their perspectives on how professional development improvements may occur in each district and how curriculum in schools and colleges of education can be enhanced to better prepare aspiring school leaders for employment in the urban environment.

---

[1]Some of this work began under the auspices of the Project LEAD initiative in St. Louis. Project LEAD is an initiative funded by the Wallace Foundation that aims to improve the effectiveness of school principals as a chief method for bringing about high teacher efficacy and student achievement.

ONE SIZE DOES NOT FIT ALL

As with most education reform initiatives, the history of educational administration reform is characterized by fads regarding what school leaders need to know and practice. In the mid-19th century, principals acted more as teacher leaders who focused on pedagogy and instruction. With the rise of the scientific management movement at the turn of the century, the principal became viewed as more of a manager than an academic leader. During the 1970s, the pendulum moved back to an emphasis on the role of the principal as an academic (instructional) leader (Edmonds, 1982; Grogan & Andrews, 2002).

None of the reform initiatives refer to "context," such as how such reform would manifest in an urban versus rural versus suburban environment. The implication is that school leaders face the same set of issues and challenges regardless of where they practice. The author disagrees with this implication. It makes no conceptual or practical sense to believe, for example, that the professional development needs of a school principal in the large, urban New York City Public School system are the exactly the same as those of a school principal in small, rural Chilocothe, Missouri. In urban areas, according to Cororan, Walker, and White (1988), "Teaching and leadership efforts take on a different and debilitating scale given the resource problems, the bureaucracy, and the special needs of children" (p. 127). Sachs (2004) expressed a similar sentiment when he documented his research on effective teaching:

> The impact of the urban context has been historically and consistently overlooked in the research on effective teaching. Yet the sociocultural identities of teachers and students and the factors that differentiate urban from suburban and rural settings characterize a unique urban context for examining teacher success. (p. 178)

Population Density

According to the U.S. Census Bureau, "urban" is defined as a metropolitan statistical area of at least 50,000 inhabitants with a total metropolitan population of at least 100,000. Typically, an "urban" area contains five or more dwellings per acre. There are approximately 261 metropolitan areas in the United States.

The inherent population density of urban areas presents urban school leaders with a unique set of challenges that are not faced by their colleagues in suburban and rural settings. Larger schools that house student populations of 2,500 or more present leadership challenges associated with building maintenance, overcrowding, high teacher turnover, low parent involvement, and lack of teacher–student interpersonal relationships that are fundamentally important to student development and learning.

Economic Poverty

Between 1950 and 1970, urban areas across America suffered tremendous population losses largely through white flight. As white flight occurred, the economic infrastructure of the urban inner city was ripped out. Urban communities suffered significant business losses and corporate disinvestment. Through an array of tax incentives, loans, and strategic partnerships, city and county governments worked systematically with the business sector to steer private investment out of the city and into the outlying metropolitan (suburban) regions (Monti, 1990; Rist, 1973).

Socioeconomic status is often cited as the most significant correlate to academic achievement. Numerous studies reveal that, the higher the poverty, the lower the student achievement (Stuart Wells & Crain, 1997). Table 10.1 illustrates that urban school leaders bear the brunt of leading schools with high concentrations of children and families in poverty. In urban settings, 40% of all children attend "high poverty schools" compared with 25% in rural areas and 10% in suburban areas (National Center for Education Statistics, 2000). Without question, urban school leaders are presented with significantly higher challenges when working to improve student achievement in their schools (Kantor & Brenzel, 1993).

Jones (1994a) distinguishes between two different types of poverty that exacerbate the challenges faced by school leaders in urban environments. *Traditional* poverty is characteristic of groups that are at or below the poverty line but still view the political system with credibility. Groups in a state of traditional poverty are more likely to ascribe their status to personal attributes that they themselves hold. For these groups, education remains a viable option or means to move out of poverty. For these groups, the community's political institutions (i.e., the police department, court house, local banks, city hall, and the local university) are comparatively accessible and, overall, remain legitimate venues for addressing citizen concerns. Additionally, groups in traditional poverty hold on to the belief that *if I do not achieve economic security in this generation, then my children will in the next generation.*

In contrast, groups that are in a state of *structural* poverty have lost faith in the political system largely because the system (political institutions) has never worked for them. Groups in a state of structural poverty are more likely to attribute their status to the indifferent, deeply embedded, racist, and paternalistic character of the political institutions in the community. In this instance, schools, the police, banks, city hall, and the university are the enemy. Schools as institutions are viewed as *a waste of time* and irrelevant because they do not reflect a concern or understanding of the groups that are in a state of structural poverty. Hodgkinson (2002) reports many more African American and Hispanic American children live in poverty (37%) compared to European American children (16%). With these statistics, urban school leaders are more apt to be faced with communities that are African American or Hispanic American who live in a state of structural poverty, as opposed to the traditional poverty faced by their counterparts in rural and suburban settings. In the urban school leadership position, it

TABLE 10.1

Children in Poverty by Geographic Type

Geographic Type	Attendance High Poverty Schools
Urban	40% of Children
Rural	25% of Children
Suburban	10% of Children

Vail (2003: source, NCES).

can often be an uphill battle to create credibility around a school mission in a community of perceived illegitimate institutions.

Student Diversity

Without question, school leaders across the nation are faced with the challenges and opportunities associated with an increasingly diverse student population (Fix & Passel, 2003; Hodgkinson, 2002). Nowhere is this more evident than in urban school systems. According to the Council of Great City Schools (1992), which represents 47 of the largest urban school systems in the country, 42% of the students in these urban systems are African American, 26% are Hispanic American, 25% are White, 6% are Asian American, and 0.5% are Alaskan or American Indian. Furthermore, the report reveals that there are growing numbers of immigrant children and families from Central and South America, the Caribbean Islands, East Asia, and Russia entering the United States. Overall, approximately 54% of all teachers in the United States have English learners in their classrooms and only one fifth reportedly feel well-prepared to serve them (Romo, 2003).

With these trends, it is urban school principals who will have to be uniquely prepared to effectively work with possibly 64 different racial combinations of students who represent over 200 national-ethnic origin categories and multiple languages, according to the U.S. census data (Hodgkinson, 2002).

Mobility and Youth Homelessness

In a study of 247 high schools in the United States, the highest mobility rates occurred in urban settings where there was high economic poverty and large numbers of African American and Hispanic American students (Rumberger & Thomas, 2000). In another urban study, Vail (2003) provides an example of a family that moved 11 times in 1 year because, "that's how many times the rent was due." Dillon (2004) wrote about the concerns that teachers in schools have when "one new student can change a classroom's entire dynamics." Another teacher reported:

> I spent six weeks on fractions—adding them, dividing them—and then I get new students in and they haven't done fractions, so I have to slow down and catch them up ... I didn't know teaching was going to be like this, I'm 48 and I'm supposed to work until I'm 60. But I can't do this for 10 more years.

High student mobility rates in urban areas are exacerbated by youth and family homelessness. According to the U.S. Department of Education (2004), homeless children and youth fall into the following categories:

- Sharing the housing of other persons due to loss of housing, economic hardship, or a similar reason (sometimes referred to as doubled up).
- Living in transient motels, hotels, trailer parks, or camping grounds due to lack of alternative adequate accommodations.

- Living in emergency or transitional shelters.
- Abandoned in hospitals.
- Awaiting foster care placement.

As poverty rates continue to grow in America, more children are thrown into the streets (Knowlton, 2004). The National Law Center on Homelessness and Poverty (2003) reveals that 67% of the homeless in 27 cities are single parent families and 40% are families with children. On any given night, 750,000 homeless people are in need of housing and or shelter with only 250,000 spaces available. The negative impact on children who are homeless is intensified by movements in at least 80 cities to criminalize activities associated with homelessness, such as sleeping and/or camping in public areas.

The youth homeless crisis, coupled with the frustrations surrounding student and family mobility, serve as examples of what urban school leaders must deal with as they work to become effective leaders and develop effective strategies on student retention, dropout prevention, teacher efficacy and retention, and parent–guardian relations. These issues are nowhere near to being as intense or existent in suburban and rural settings.

"URBAN" AND LEARNER CENTERED

Based on the USLC research data, Fig. 10.1 provides a conceptual model for the implementation of the professional development programming that was developed for a joint cohort of school principals in the St. Louis and Kansas City school districts. Three major themes emerged out of the USLC research that are consistent with the learner centered model, and NCATE and ELCC standards for school leaders with respect to the professional development needs of the urban school leaders:

1. Professional development that gives particular attention to the notion of *educational entrepreneurship*.
2. Professional development that gives particular attention to the field of leadership, communications, and working effectively with *multiple constituency groups*.
3. Professional development that entails hands-on uses of *technology* to advance the school academic and operational mission.

People Development and Entrepreneurship

A study by Henson (2004) revealed that principals in both highly effective and highly ineffective schools were adept at understanding and engaging in instructional leadership strategies. The principals in both types of schools knew how to evaluate teachers and understood the differences between classrooms where learning was occurring and classrooms that were devoid of learning. However, the major difference between the highly effective leaders and highly ineffective leaders was that the former possessed leadership attributes that went well beyond a narrow focus on instructional leadership. The highly effective leaders were charismatic and inspirational. They possessed skills that enabled them to motivate teachers, staff, and students to do well. These principals

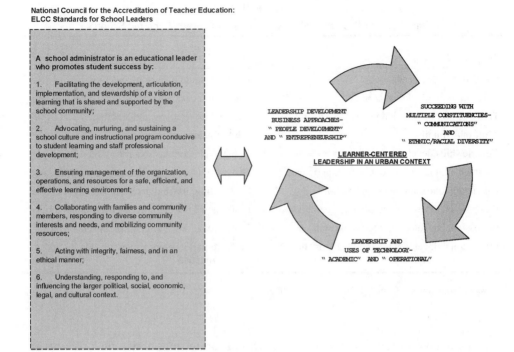

National Council for the Accreditation of Teacher Education:
ELCC Standards for School Leaders

A school administrator is an educational leader who promotes student success by:

1. Facilitating the development, articulation, implementation, and stewardship of a vision of learning that is shared and supported by the school community;

2. Advocating, nurturing, and sustaining a school culture and instructional program conducive to student learning and staff professional development;

3. Ensuring management of the organization, operations, and resources for a safe, efficient, and effective learning environment;

4. Collaborating with families and community members, responding to diverse community interests and needs, and mobilizing community resources;

5. Acting with integrity, fairness, and in an ethical manner;

6. Understanding, responding to, and influencing the larger political, social, economic, legal, and cultural context.

LEADERSHIP DEVELOPMENT
BUSINESS APPROACHES—
" PEOPLE DEVELOPMENT"
AND " ENTREPRENEURSHIP"

SUCCEEDING WITH
MULTIPLE CONSTITUENCIES—
" COMMUNICATIONS"
AND
" ETHNIC/RACIAL DIVERSITY"

**LEARNER-CENTERED
LEADERSHIP IN AN URBAN CONTEXT**

LEADERSHIP AND
USES OF TECHNOLOGY—
" ACADEMIC" AND " OPERATIONAL"

Figure 10.1.   Conceptual model.

developed school teams to facilitate learning in the schools, and practiced strong distributive leadership through what Kellerman (2004) and James (2003) would characterize as a transformational, as opposed to transactional, leadership style. Transformational leaders use a system of rewards and incentives to bring about organizational change. This is in stark contrast to transactional leaders, who lead through a system of transactions—*I'll scratch your back if you scratch mine.* Those who fail to engage the leader in this way may be subject to sanctions, retribution, or some form of punishment (Jones, 2004; Peters & Williams, 2002).

The findings in the Henson study are consistent with the articulated needs of the school leaders who served as members of the USLC cohort. School principals recognize the complexity of leading and managing urban schools and recognize the need to develop teams, engage in distributive leadership, and adopt transformative as opposed to transactional management styles. Effective professional development for school leaders must reflect this recognition. Table 10.2 provides the elements of a learner centered school in contrast to a more traditional school regarding professional development approaches.

Since the 1980s, there has been a steady and ongoing public and private sector retrenchment in support of public education. Now more than ever, school leaders need to become entrepreneurial in how they conduct the affairs of schooling. This is particularly true for practicing school leaders in urban school settings, which have been hit hardest by this retrenchment. In short, professional development for urban leadership and entrepreneurship focuses on the acquisition of skills that are necessary for understanding when opportunities exist and when to seek community investments

TABLE 10.2

A Paradigm for Professional Development in Learner-Centered Schools

Traditional School	*Learner-Centered School*
Focus on teacher needs	Focus on student learning outcomes
Focus on individual development	Focus on individual and system Development
Transmission of knowledge, skills, and strategies	Inquiry into teaching and learning
"Pull-out" training	Job-embedded learning
Generic skills development "One size fits all"	Content and content-specific skill building
Fragmented, piecemeal, one-shot experiences	Driven by clear, coherent, long-term strategies
District direction and decision making	School direction and decision making
Professional development as some people's job	Professional development as everyone's job
Professional development for some staff	Professional development for all school staff
Professional development as a "frill" or" luxury"	Professional development as a necessity and routine practice

Note. From Loucks-Horsley (1995) and Seller (1993).

(i.e., monetary support, voluntary support, corporate donations, etc.) for the advancement of the school mission.

Furthermore, action that is associated with entrepreneurship is grounded in the need for school leaders to (a) know who their students are regarding academic, sociocultural, and economic needs, because the success of school programming will center around these needs; (b) engage teachers and staff in the planning, development, and design of staffing plans that are appropriate to the needs of the school—this concerns how staff selections occur and how departments and committees are structured in the school; (c) develop school schedules that are consistent and realistic with the mission of the school. How schedules develop may vary from school to school depending on student needs; and (d) select instruction and curriculum materials that are relevant to the student population. These materials must result in actual improvement in student performance and teacher efficacy (Cooke, 2002; Ouchi, 2003; Sergiovanni, Kelleher, McCarthy, & Wirt, 2004).

Table 10.3 provides a framework for guiding professional development for urban school leaders who articulate a need for gaining leadership skills that are associated with entrepreneurial behavior. The table distinguishes between organizations that are entrepreneurial and those that lack entrepreneurial elements.

Communications and Multiple Constituencies

In complex urban school environments, leaders must be adept at communicating and working effectively with multiple constituencies inside and outside the school and school district. A prerequisite for doing this is to have an understanding about multiple constituent agenda and how these agenda may conflict or overlap with the school mission (Jones, 1994b; Stoll & Fink, 1996). Figure 10.2, *Table Top Theory in Urban Set-*

TABLE 10.3
Comparisons of Traditional and Entrepeneurial Educational Organization

ORGANIZATIONAL CHARACTERISTICS	Traditional Educational Organization	Entrepreneurial Educational Organization
External Environmental Scanning	Identify threats to traditional and educational system.	Identify opportunities. Seek out change that can create new initiatives.
Strategy	Defensive protection of traditional educational system.	Proactively seeking new initiatives created by change and competition.
Control Systems	Budgets are only means of control.	Budgets used for short-term control. Forecasts and business plans used for entrepreneurial planning.
Structure	Formal lines of authority, centralized, and highly specialized.	Empowered staff that is willing to "do what it takes."
Communication	Formal lines of communication	Informal communication that focuses on getting information to those who need it when they need it.
Creativity	Belongs only in the classroom.	Fostered, supported, and developed throughout the organization. Is pervasive.
Organization Culture	Serves to protect the traditional education system.	Serves to support and foster innovation and entrepreneurship.
Information	Performance data not used, not shared, not disseminated.	Data is open and select/strategic level of public transparency.

Brown & Cornwall: modified (2000)

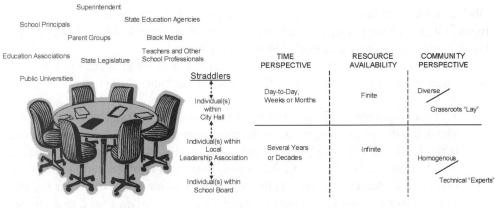

Figure 10.2.   Jones (2006).

tings, provides a professional development framework for understanding how multiple constituents communicate and relate to a school mission in an urban policy setting. The theory allows for a critical examination of power in decisionmaking settings—who has said power and how this power manifests in an urban education arena. The theory allows for a critical discussion of race, ethnicity, and the influence of community and culture on communications in an urban educational arena. Additionally, issues concerning urban poverty, homelessness, student mobility, employment, and housing can be discussed within the framework for urban school leaders who face the reality of these issues on a daily basis.

Poor communications was expressed as a major concern by the USLC principal cohort. This concern was expressed in the broadest sense, with particular regard to the lack of consultation that occurs with school principals around school reform planning, development, and implementation. One principal, for example, remarked that this was the first time in the many years of his professional career that someone took the time to ask him what he thought. Evidently, this sentiment is felt across the nation by school leaders. Elmore (2002) and Jones (1994b, 2004) lament how traditional models of school reform often rely too heavily on so-called "experts" and "consultants" to define truth and tell others how to perform their jobs. Gooden (2002) discussed the failure of education reform as this relates to the problem of forcing "recipe-like" recommendations for education reform down the throats of urban school leaders that fail to address many of the unique challenges they face.

Using Fig. 10.2 as a conceptual guide, in St. Louis clear distinctions emerged between constituencies who comprised the public sector and those who comprised the private sector about decision making around school reform. In the figure, public officials are labeled on "top" of the table because of their visibility around engagement in education reform. In other words, the lay public knows the names of the mayor, school superintendent, and legislative representatives. In contrast, private organizations and individuals—such as business, philanthropy, nonprofit think tanks, private institutions of higher education—are labeled "under" the table, largely because these individuals and institutions hold enormous influence on the strategic direction of the City of St. Louis and the school system, but they and their actions are largely hidden from public view.

According to the figure, three dimensions emerged that provided examples of how constituencies on "top" of the table differed from those "under' the table:

> 1. There was a tendency for private constituents under the table to hold different views about *time* in comparison to the public constituents who are on top of the table. The former (private group) tended to engage in planning around education and the future of the St. Louis education system in an intergenerational fashion, that is, in increments of 10, 15, or 20 years. Constituents in the latter (public group) tended to think of strategies day by day—"What do I need to do to get through this day?" There did not seem to be an understanding that much of what was going on with the strategic direction of the school district (and the City of St. Louis) was planned and methodically developed by individuals "under" the table several years (in some instances decades) earlier.

> 2. Private constituents who are under the table appeared to have unlimited resources to accomplish whatever was needed to carry out an education reform or

citywide agenda. For example, no money was spared for the implementation of the recent reform initiative in St. Louis that took place during the 2003–2004 academic year. This reform initiative was being driven, at its source, by the corporate community. On the other hand, principals, teachers, and other public constituents on top of the table scrambled to get by day to day on meager resources.

3. There was a tendency for the private constituencies under the table to define "community" differently from public constituencies on top of the table. For the latter, "community" means grassroots community and someone who reflects the social and ethnic makeup of the community. With the former, "community" means the person with a PhD in community affairs from Harvard University who invariably is European American and has a limited and "academic" understanding of "urban." This difference in definition led to heated arguments during school board meetings over the course of the 2003–2004 academic school year in St. Louis.

This scenario is somewhat explicated, in a general sense, by Cibulka (2000), who reports,

> Elites within the private sector have in recent decades become increasingly involved in education and education reform. This involvement has posed the most significant challenge to the established order of public schooling. … These elites, if anything, pose more of a challenge than the mass protest challenges of the 1960s and 1970s because they come from a power base of their own and wield wide influence in a variety of other institutions (such as the corporate sector, city hall, state governors and legislators and the mass media—which they may own). (p. 17)

The clashing of multiple constituencies is heightened when said constituencies fail to recognize that all schools are not equal and all individuals do not hold the same level(s) of power. For example, Kowalski (2004) reported,

> Often members of the dominant culture, in an effort to ensure a non-biased approach to people from other cultures, attempt to stress so-called color-blindness, or an inability to recognize a cultural difference. … In most cases, treating everyone the same means treating everyone as if they were members of the dominant cultural group. Problems arise from the fact that not everyone is the same and that engaging everyone from a single cultural perspective will place some cultural groups at a distinct disadvantage. (p. 6)

School leaders in urban settings should not have to acquire basic understandings about working with multiple constituencies and communication phenomena in a serendipitous fashion—after they have been repeatedly blind-sided by the media, business sector, or constituents in the public sector. Professional development for school leaders in urban settings that avoids systematic and ongoing discussion of communications and how to work with multiple constituency groups is woefully inadequate. Furthermore, school leaders cannot be expected to engage themselves, teachers, and students in their own learning, as emphasized by the learner centered model[2] of schooling, if they lack an understanding of the environment in which they work and the communication skills that are necessary for working with multiple constituencies.

---

[2]On this note, see McCombs (1997); Thorton and McEntee (1995).

Technology and the Digital Divide

A third concern for the USLC principal cohort was in the area of technology—its availability, application, and maintenance for school academic programs and administrative operations. Urban school leaders need to be prepared to understand the persistence of the *digital divide* in America and how to systematically act on this divide. According to the National Center for Education Statistics (NCES, 2000), only 23.5% of African American and 23.6% of Latino households had Internet access in comparison to 41.5% of all households nationwide. At the school level, the National Educational Technology Standards for Administrators (2004) reports that only 60% of classrooms in low-income communities were connected to the Internet during the 2000–2001 academic year in comparison to 82% in high-income communities. Moreover, the future of funding for technology in education looks grim. In referencing an Education Testing Service report, Landgraf (2004) wrote,

> The decreased availability of resources for technology in schools will leave students under-prepared for the technology-saturated world they face in higher education, the workplace, and daily life. Most alarming, this is especially true in poor, urban schools that are already behind in technology spending and use.

Given the circumstances described here, school leaders in urban settings must be more proactive and aggressive about garnering support for technology in school academic and business operations. In this way, the earlier foci on (a) *communications*, (b) *people development*, and (c) *entrepreneurship* become more important. The essential conditions for meeting the National Educational Technology Standards (NETS) for administrators can be categorized under these foci.

From a *communications* standpoint, urban school leaders will need to articulate a shared vision for technology in their schools and school districts in collaboration with multiple community constituents. These standards must be consistent with a vision that is communicated as student centered and connected or aligned with education content and curriculum standards. From a *people development* standpoint, these leaders will need to ensure that teachers and staff are integral to the planning, design, implementation, and internal assessment of technology in their buildings and that access to technology and related services are equitable and credible. In an *entrepreneurial* sense, urban school leaders will need to be adept at securing resources through, for example, grant development and community-partnership venues to support the technology needs and mission of their schools and school district. Ongoing community support is integral to these endeavors (National Educational Technology Standards for Administrators, 2004).

CONCLUSION

School leaders who work in urban settings are faced with extenuating circumstances that require them to deal with and work through sociopolitical, cultural, and economic issues that are not faced by their counterparts in suburban and rural settings. These issues relate to dire fiscal, material, and human resource limitations, high population concentrations, structural economic poverty, large numbers of limited English profi-cient students, and youth and family mobility and homelessness.

Given these issues and the complex nature of urban environments, it is imperative that school leaders create schools that are learner centered as a conceptual and prac-tical method for operating in urban contexts. It follows that the professional devel-opment for school leaders must reflect this imperative. Through professional development, urban school leaders must acquire the skills that are necessary to be entrepreneurial and people oriented. This is particularly true today given the unre-lenting retrenchment in public support of public education. This truth means that school leaders must not retreat but rather must aggressively reach out to seek oppor-tunities that advance their schools and school districts.

Consistent with the learner-centered concept, urban school leaders must become *transformational* in their leadership style. Transformational leaders engage in distrib-utive forms of leadership, which means that they develop leadership teams to govern schools and they view professional development and ongoing adult learning as a ne-cessity as opposed to a luxury.

Finally, the complex nature of the urban school environment will require school leaders to be adept at communicating and working effectively with multiple (individ-ual and institutional) constituencies outside the school and school district. In their role as transformational leaders, they must develop the skills that are necessary to motivate and move people toward a shared community vision of schooling.

REFERENCES

Brown, R. J., & Cornwall, J. R. (2000). *The entrepreneurial educator.* Lanham, MD: Scarecrow.

Cibulka, J. G. (2000). Contests over governance of educational policy: Prospects for the new cen-tury. In Jones, B.A. (Ed.), *Educational leadership: Policy dimensions in the 21st century* (pp. 3–20). Stamford, CT: Ablex.

Cooke, G. (2002). *Keys to success for urban school principals.* Arlington Heights, IL: Skylight.

Cororan, T. B., Walker, L. J., & White, J. L. (1988). *Working in urban schools.* Washington, DC: In-stitute for Educational Leadership.

The Council of Great City Schools. (1992). *National urban education goals: Baseline indicators, 1990–91.* Washington, DC: Author.

Dillon, S. (2004, July 21). When students are in flux, schools are in crisis. *New York Times,* p. 9B.

Dufour, R. (2002, May). The learning-centered principal: Beyond instructional leadership. *Educa-tional Leadership, 59*(8), 12–15.

Edmonds, R. (1982). Programs for school improvement: An overview. *Educational Leadership, 40*(3), 4–11.

Elmore, R. (2002, January). Building capacity to enhance learning. *Principal Leadership,* 7–9.

Fix, M., & Passel, J. S. (2003). *U.S. immigration – Trends & implications for schools.* Washington, DC: The Urban Institute.

Gooden, M. A. (2002). Stewardship and critical leadership: Sufficient for leadership in urban schools? *Education and Urban Society, 35*(1), 133–143.

Grogan, M., & Andrews, R. (2002). Defining preparation and professional development for the fu-ture. *Educational Administration Quarterly, 38*(2), 233–256.

Henson, M. (2004). *Characteristics of highly effective urban school leaders.* Unpublished disserta-tion, St. Louis, MO: Webster University.

Hess, F. (2004). Treating principals like leaders. *American School Board Journal, 191*(5), 32–35.

Hodgkinson, H. (2002). Dealing with diversity. *Principal, 82*(2), 14–16.

James, C. (2003). Designing learning organizations. *Organizational Dynamics, 32*(1), 46–61.

Jones, B. A. (2006) Informal dynamics of educational policy in St. Louis. Paper presented at the annual meeting of the American Educational Research Association. San Francisco, California.

Jones, B. A. (2004, September 15). As I see it: Reform schools from inside, *Kansas City Star*, p. B6.

Jones, B. A. (1994a). Schools in the community and "urban" context: Incorporating collaboration and empowerment. In B. A. Jones & K. M. Borman (Eds.), *Investing in U.S. schools: Directions for educational policy* (pp. 5–16). Norwood, NJ: Ablex.

Jones, B. A. (1994b). The multiple constituency concept of collaboration: Influences of race, class, gender and ethnicity. *Theory Into Practice, 33,* 227–234.

Kantor, H., & Brenzel, B. (1993). Urban education and the "truly disadvantaged": The historical roots of the contemporary crisis, 1945–1990. In M. Katz (Ed.), *The "underclass" debate: Views from history* (pp. 366–402). Princeton, NJ: Princeton University Press.

Kellerman, B. (2004, January). Leaders: Warts and all. *Harvard Business Review*, 40–45.

Knowlton, B. (2004, August 26). More Americans are living in poverty, Census Bureau says. *New York Times*.

Kowalski, T. (2004). *Public relations in schools*. Upper Saddle River, NJ: Pearson.

Landgraf, K. M. (2004). *Digital divide: Without visionary leadership, disparities in school district budgets increase*. Princeton, NJ: Educational Testing Service.

Loucks-Horsley, S. (1995). Professional development and the learner centered school. *Theory Into Practice, 34,* 265–271.

McCombs, B. (1997, March). Self-assessment and reflection: Tools for promoting teacher changes toward learner centered practices. *Bulletin*, 1–14.

Monti, D. J. (1990). *Race, redevelopment and the new company town*. Albany: New York State. University of New York Press.

National Center for Education Statistics. (2000). *Internet access in U.S. public schools and classrooms, 1994–1999*. Washington, DC: United States Department of Education.

National Law Center on Homelessness & Poverty. (2003). *Homelessness and poverty in America*. Washington, DC: National Law Center on Homelessness & Poverty.

National Educational Technology Standards for Administrators. (2004). *NETS news: Essential conditions for implementing NETS for administrators*. Retrieved from http://cnets.iste.org/administrator/

Ouchi, W. G. (2003). *Making schools work*. New York: Simon & Schuster.

Peters, R., & Williams, C. (2002). The demise of Newt Gingrich as a transformational leader: Does organizational leadership theory apply to legislative leaders. *Organizational Dynamics, 30,* 257–268.

Rist, R. (1973). *The "urban" school: A factory for failure*. Cambridge, MA: MIT Press.

Romo, H. (2003). Issues of teacher preparation: Implications for urban minority students. *Educators for Urban Minorities, 2*(2), 9–23.

Rumberger, R., & Thomas, S. (2000). The distribution of dropout and turnover rates among urban and suburban high schools. *Sociology of Education, 73*(1), 39–67.

Sachs, S. K. (March/April 2004). Evaluation of teacher attributes as predictors of success in urban schools. *Journal of Teacher Education, 55*(2), 177–187.

Seller, W. (1993). New images for the principal's role in professional development. *Journal of Staff Development, 14*(1), 22–26.

Sergiovanni, T. J., Kelleher, P., McCarthy, M. M., & Wirt, F. M. (2004). *Educational governance and administration* (5th ed.). Boston: Pearson.

Stoll, L., & Fink, D. (1996). *Changing our schools*. London: Open University Press.

Stuart Wells, A., & Crain, R. L. (1997). *Stepping over the color line*. New Haven, CT: Yale University Press.

Thorton, L., & McEntee, M. (1995). Learner centered schools as a mindset, and the connection with mindfulness and multiculturalism. *Theory Into Practice, 34,* 250–257.

U.S. Department of Education. (2004). *Education for homeless children and youth program*. Washington, DC: Author.

Vail, K. (2003, December). The social challenge. *American School Board Journal, 190*(12), 15.

Villani, C. J., & Lyman, L. L. (2001). Strengthening communication skills. *The American Association of School Administrators (AASA) Professor, 24*(3), 2–5.

11

MANAGING POLICY ISSUES IN CARRYING OUT SYSTEMIC REFORM: LESSONS FOR PRINCIPALS FROM CHICAGO, EL PASO, MEMPHIS AND MIAMI

Kathryn M. Borman
Theodore Boydston
William Katzenmeyer
University of South Florida

In carrying out our study of the impact of the National Science Foundation's Urban Systemic Initiative (USI) in four cities, a major focus concerned how national, state, and district policies supported or constrained the day-to-day roles and responsibilities of the 46 school principals participating in our research. The questions we addressed in our work included several examining the implementation at the school level of policies related to systemic reform including assessments, standards, and professional development. In addition, we explored how resources were mobilized among various constituencies such as schools, universities, business and industry, and community-based institutions and agencies. Finally, we sought to determine community and district contextual characteristics that were particularly important in affecting student outcomes. Concentrating on aspects of policy implementation, achievement gains, and school culture at the school level, this article analyzes data from interviews with 44 principals as well as data gathered at the school level from teachers and other staff members to understand characteristics of the school culture related to student achievement outcomes.

Our assumption is that principals influence policies that contribute to school culture. We believe that vibrant school cultures are associated with positive outcomes for students and that learner-centered principals are an important element of this mix. Our perspective draws from Danzig's view that

> Learner-centered leadership suggests an ability to frame educational issues from multiple perspectives and minimize the damages stemming from simplistic views that all kindergarten children should be reading, misguided views that learning is synonymous with test scores, self-defeating views of and about children who think they can't or don't need to learn, and self-interests of educators in maintaining the status quo. (Danzig, 1999b)

During the 1st year of our 3-year project in addition to interviewing principals, we also asked faculty members to complete short surveys investigating their perceptions of factors contributing to the quality of the school culture. Other data included student achievement in mathematics as measured by student performance on norm-referenced tests such as the Stanford-9 and on high stakes tests such as the Texas Assessment of Academic Skills (TAAS).

In this article we seek to address the question: What can we learn from principals whose schools, in addition to providing evidence of increased student achievement, are also exemplary workplaces? Our findings have direct implications for the policies governing professional development of principals. The article provides case examples from our project to show how this can be accomplished and why it is important. We next turn to a brief description of the National Science Foundation's efforts in carrying out systemic reforms in math and science.

THE NATIONAL SCIENCE FOUNDATION'S ROLE IN SYSTEMIC REFORM

The resources and leadership of the National Science Foundation (NSF) have been critical in providing both the support and the conceptual rubric for institutionalizing systemic reforms. According to the NSF,

> *Systemic reform* occurs when all essential features of schools and school systems are engaged and operating in concert; when policy is aligned with a clear set of goals and standards; when forthcoming improvements and innovations become intrinsic parts of the ongoing educational system for all children; and when the changes become part of the school system's operating budget. (NSF, 2000)

Initially, NSF provided support to 25 states through its Statewide Systemic Initiatives program (SSI). The goal of the SSI is to assist the states in developing the capacity to move from independently devised science and mathematics educational reform measures to state-developed efforts. Coordinating reforms in teacher preparation, standards-driven instructional materials, and the assessment of student performance comprise the range and scope of the SSI to date (Westat* McKenzie Consortium, 1998, p. 6). Although large numbers of teachers received curricular and instructional materials, and schools of education undertook some degree of curriculum change in teacher preparation programs, these programs failed to reach urban schoolchildren in the most difficult circumstances.

To address this need, NSF established the Urban Systemic Initiatives (USI) program in 1993. Funding under the USI program was made available to the urban school districts in the U.S. with the highest rates of poverty among their school-aged children according to the 1990 census. Of the 28 eligible school districts, 22 successfully applied for and received a total of 15 million dollars each over a 5-year period to carry out systemic reforms in math and science (Westat*Mckenzie, 1998). The funding provided by NSF was considered a medium for developing, expanding, or sustaining reform through partnerships with businesses, educational institutions, and community organizations. The University of South Florida's 3-year evaluation project completed in 2001 targeted four district sites receiving funding under the USI: Miami, Memphis, El Paso and Chicago.

Principals and Systemic Reform

City and state officials as well as parents have become increasingly concerned with how well schools are promoting student achievement. Because principals are held accountable for the success of their schools, their responsibilities have come to include much more than an emphasis on management and discipline. Principals must create the conditions in the school that best promote outstanding teaching and student achievement outcomes. This is a considerable responsibility under the guidelines of the No Child Left Behind Act requiring schools to make adequate yearly progress or suffer the threat of closure. In an earlier analysis of our principal interview data (Kersaint, Borman, & Boydston, 2001), we determined that principals in each of our four participating USI sites were preoccupied with three major issues that beset them in their day-to-day work in implementing USI reforms. First, principals perceived a mismatch between the goals of the reforms and the objectives of state and school district accountability practices. Put another way, principals perceived a poor fit between the NSF reform curriculum and pedagogical strategies and state-mandated student assessments. In truth, NSF does not sanction a particular approach; however, a constructivist orientation to student learning following from the national standards is at the heart of the reforms. Though NSF reform emphasizes hands-on problem solving approaches to math and science, in contrast high-stakes testing can promote rote learning and regurgitation of facts. In Linda McNeil's terms, testing and standardization also foster defensive teaching of "fragmented and narrow information on the test which comes to substitute for a substantive curriculum in the schools of poor and minority youth" (McNeil, 2000, p. xxvi).

A second, more mundane issue is that principals confront the practical concern of finding substitutes for classroom teachers who attended professional development sessions off campus. Though this may seem to be a trivial issue, for principals faced with managing instructional resources, facilitating the professional growth of their teaching staff, and enhancing student learning, it presents a major challenge in implementing reform. Professional development is the cornerstone of most large-scale instructional reform, and USI reforms are no exception.

Finally, principals were concerned about the press to take on new entrepreneurial responsibilities in funding reform. Several talked about using Title I funding to augment NSF resources in purchasing new computers and other technology. All were burdened by pressure to create working capital to supplement allocations from the school district and other sources.

THE IMPORTANCE OF SCHOOL CULTURE
IN SUPPORTING A STRONG PROFESSIONAL COMMUNITY

In addition to gaining insight into how principals interpreted their challenges in undertaking school-wide reform in math and science, we also learned from related analyses that schools with the highest scores on a measure of school culture (The School Culture Quality Survey) were also those schools with the greatest math score gains over the duration of the reform. In the earlier study (Katzenmeyer, Uekawa, Borman, & Lee, 2001), the School Culture Quality Survey (SCQS) was used as the measure of professional community. Schools were divided into high, average, and low math gain groups. Multivariate analysis of variance was used to determine whether there were differences in the quality of professional community among the high, average, and low math gain groups. Professional community scores were significantly higher in the high math gain group than in either the average and low math gain groups. Effect sizes for these comparisons ranged from .33 to .41. The largest effect sizes were found on the Shared Vision and Learning Community scales of the SCQS. No significant differences were found between SCQS scores of schools in the average and low math gain groups. A set of assumptions regarding learning community formation and leadership underlie the items comprising the SCQS. We consider these next.

Learner-centered leadership in part rests on the ability of the principal to nurture the capacity of school organization members to surface, critique, and apply mental models that people bring to the world (Senge, 1999, 2000). The SCQS defines "professional community" in terms of four core concepts adapted from the quality movement and the work of Peter Senge et al. (1999, 2000). The SCQS defines a desirable professional community as including the following:

- Shared vision: A collective awareness of an organization future members would like to share.
- Facilitative leadership: The capacity to actively facilitate the work of organizational members.
- Teamwork: The capacity to work together productively toward common goals.
- Learning community: A cadre of colleagues who are actively seeking and learning together the new skills and knowledge needed to achieve the desired organizational future.

These qualities were included as indicators in the SCQS survey administered to principals and school staff to evaluate the school culture in each site. The results from these surveys were examined in combination with multiple data sources to identify trends and themes tied to math achievement score gains.

Professional Community/School Culture

The overarching rubric framing the four components of professional community is synonymous with school culture. Culture, according to Peterson and Deal, is "the underground stream of norms, values, beliefs, traditions, and rituals that has built up over time as people work together, solve problems and confront challenges" (1998, p. 28). A strong, nurturing culture within a school fosters the development of teacher leadership, and in turn produces positive results in student outcomes (Anderson & Ronnkvist, 1999).

Given the importance of relationships, Hargreaves and Fullan (1998) suggested that highest priority be placed not on restructuring, but rather on "reculturing" the schools. The goal of reculturing the school is to engage teachers and other stakeholders to work together differently by creating more collaborative work cultures. In their guidelines for principals, they suggest attention to emotional management "which is ultimately about attending to the relationships within the school properly" (p. 119).

Evidence from several studies including those undertaken by Newman and Wehlage (1995) and Louis, Kruse, and Marks (1996) supports the notion that students learn more productively when principals and teachers work collaboratively within a professional learning community. According to Bryk and Schneider (2002), the act of working collaboratively is captured best by the concept of relational trust. Relational trust is reflected in the nature of the social dynamics of the school as workplace and is critical to the success and well-being of all. Relational trust is a "complex mix of considerations: instrumental concerns about achieving valued outcomes; hedonic concerns about self-esteem, social status, and institutional identification; and moral-ethical concerns about advancing the best interests off children" (p. 21). Relational trust can be diminished if a critical mass of individuals in the organization—teachers, students, and parents in the case of schools—believe members of the organization are not "doing the right thing." We would expect to find that lower performing schools would display organizational characteristics associated with diminished relational trust whereas higher achieving schools would not.

Shared Vision.   After studying many of the most successful business organizations, Senge (1990) identified five characteristics they held in common. Two of them— "shared vision" and "team learning"—are ongoing processes, involving leaders and team members. Leaders are responsible for facilitating the continuing development of the vision with team members, and serving as custodians of the vision, articulating and rearticulating its evolving message to the members. Effective leaders must not only hold visions and ideals of an organization's possibilities; they must also inspire others in the organization to carry the vision forward in action (Kouzes & Posner, 1987).

Facilitative Leadership.   Leaders at the school site have a significant bottom-up role to play in making changes in teaching and learning (Anderson & Ronnkvist, 1999). Principals set the cultural context within the school. If a positive culture exists in a school and fosters teacher leadership, possibilities that strong student achievement outcomes are produced are enhanced. Resnick and Hall (1998), working with schools adopting a nested learning community approach, determined that while teachers find their primary community of learners among their peers, it is the inter-action between role groups that constitutes the nesting feature of nested learning commu-nities ... Thus the orchestrator of the school-based learning community for teachers is the school principal. (pp. 89–118)

This conceptualization underscores the important work of the principal in facilitat-ing interaction across boundaries of grade-level or subject matter. Facilitative leader-ship is critical in successful systemic reform because everyone in the system must pull in the same direction if student learning is to be supported.

Teamwork

Teamwork, as separate from learning community or team learning, has not been exam-ined extensively. In our factor analytic studies of the items gathered in the development of the SCQS, a cluster of items that looked related to the concept of teamwork appeared as a separate cluster from those identified with learning community, the construct we discuss next. Teamwork reflects the capacity to work together well in the interests of stu-dents apart from the capacity to learn together as an organization or community.

Learning Communities

The term "learning community" has become well established in the educational re-search literature. In the organizational research literature, emphasis has been given to the importance of developing teachers' collective engagement in sustained efforts to im-prove practice (Louis, Marks, & Kruse, 1996). Resnick and Hall (1998) advocate nested learning communities where "not only students but also all education professionals are learners" (p. 6). In this model of organizational development, teachers, principals, and central office administrators form communities of adult learners focused on improving their practice. Boyd and Hord (1994) found that building a learning community in the school reduces isolation, increases staff capacity, and provides a caring, productive en-vironment. Over time, schools become sites for learning as the work of both students and professional educators. In these sites, reform is likely to be systemic throughout the or-ganization with all perceiving educational improvement as the norm.

In the related literature on in-service teacher education, Lieberman (1996) described a learning community as "teachers and administrators sharing and discussing their work experiences, contributing to and gaining access to learning that solves immediate prob-lems of practice as well as grappling with problems in greater depth and complexity" (p. 6). Lieberman (1992) cited powerful effects on students, on the culture of the school, and on teachers' sense of efficacy when they are part of a learning community.

Involvement in teacher learning communities moves the locus of control for change in the school into the purview of teachers (McLaughlin, 1995). Teachers no longer spend time blaming the "kids" for the lack of learning and begin to recognize the con-trol rests with them—by changing the way they teach, they have control over how well students will learn. Membership in a learning community expands the repertoire of teachers' practices; seeds are planted for alternative instructional practices.

Principals can have a great impact on the creation and maintenance of learning communities within their schools, particularly through their formal and informal policies of instructional support. As both members of the learning community and administrators in the school hierarchy, principals occupy a role that allows them unique access to influence their school's learning community. In sum, the presence of a strong professional community or school culture, though not a guarantee of positive academic outcomes for all students, will likely help to foster and sustain strong and positive results. Though each of the components comprising professional community–school culture is important, the culture of the school is most enhanced when all are working in concert.

METHOD

Participants

The 44 school principals included in this research had served in their current schools an average of 6 and one half years with one principal having 20 years of continuous service in the same school. These principals had, on average, 2 additional years as principal in a different school and had taught for an average of 14 years. They reported diverse teaching backgrounds such as music, business education, mathematics, and science. Thirty-nine percent were former elementary school teachers.

As shown in Table 11.1, these school principals were an ethnically diverse group: 36% Black, 21% Hispanic, and 43% White. Slightly more that half are females (51%). Six principals held doctoral degrees, two held master's degrees in addition to supervision certification, and 17 held master's degrees. The length of each principal's tenure in role differs somewhat by city with Miami principals having served longest—on average 10 years. The average length of service was 9.5 years in Chicago, 8.7 years in Memphis, and 5.3 years in El Paso. Same-school tenure as principal is highest in Memphis (7.6 years), followed by Miami (6.3 years), Chicago (6.0 years), and El Paso (4.4 years). Chicago, Memphis, and Miami each have at least one principal whose tenure is over 20 years whereas the longest serving principal in El Paso is in his or her 10th year. Principals in Chicago have the most years as teachers (16.8), whereas El Paso principals' have the least experience, averaging 5.7 years.

Data Collection and Analysis

Data were collected during the first 18 months of our project. During that time, we carried out structured interviews with principals of the 44 schools in the four cities participating in our study using a principal interview protocol that consisted of 13 multipart items. In addition, we administered the SCQS to members of the school staff and also began to assemble student achievement data at the school level in each of our participating district sites.

In calculating math gains during the course of the reform, gains were represented as a standardized residual residualized regarding math score at year 1, percent of free and reduced lunch, and mobility rate. Those schools with a residual less than $-.5$ were placed

TABLE 11.1

Principal Demographics

	Chicago District (n = 8)		El Paso Districts (n = 10)		Memphis District (n = 8)		Miami-Dade District (n = 16)		Total District (n = 42)	
	N	%	N	%	N	%	N	%	N	%
Assistant Principal	1	8.3	0	0.0	1	7.7	1	6.7	3	5.8
Principal	12	91.7	10	100.0	12	92.3	14	93.3	48	94.1
Gender										
Female	6	50.0	7	70.0	8	61.5	10	62.5	31	60.8
Male	7	50.0	3	30.0	5	38.5	6	37.5	20	39.2
Race/ethnicity										
Black	8	66.7	0	0.0	7	53.9	6	37.5	21	41.1
Hispanic	2	16.7	4	40.0	0	0.0	4	25.0	10	19.7
Caucasian	2	16.7	6	60.0	6	46.2	6	37.5	20	39.2
Years in position										
1 or less	2	16.7	3	30.0	1	7.7	2	12.5	8	15.7
2 to 4	4	33.3	2	20.0	2	15.4	5	31.3	13	25.5
5 to 8	4	33.3	4	40.0	7	53.8	6	37.5	21	41.1
9 to 12	2	16.7	1	10.0	2	15.4	2	12.5	7	13.7
13 to 20	0	0.0	0	0.0	1	7.7	1	6.3	2	3.9

into the low group (low gain group) those between −.5 and .5 (inclusive) were placed in the medium group, and those above .5 were placed in the high group. Following these calculations, we standardized schools' SCQS scale and determined overall standardized scores (z scores) and separated schools into groups using the same procedure. Next we considered the rank order of schools in light of the principal interview findings.

RESULTS

Our analyses of the SCQS data were aimed at identifying those schools and their principals with the highest ratings on all SCQS scales and overall as well as the highest math gains over the duration of the reform. Schools were split equally between low and high math gains with 14 schools in each of these categories. Eight schools fell in the "Medium gains" category. The remaining analyses will examine characteristics of schools and their cultures associated with high and low math gains, relying primarily on data from our principal interviews conducted with those principals whose schools showed either the highest or the lowest math score gains.

With few exceptions, the 14 high math gain schools in our sample had no SCQS scores lower than "medium." Conversely, only four low math gain schools had any "high" ratings. Lows and highs are fairly evenly spread among elementary, middle, and high schools. Miami has four high math gain schools and six low math gain schools. El Paso has four high math gain schools and only two low math gain schools whereas the remaining cities fall in between.

The school with the highest math gains also had high SCQS scores across the board. An elementary school in Miami (Mi110), the Memphis high school (Me320), Chicago middle school (Ch230) and elementary school (Ch110), and Miami elementary school (Mi160) clustering near the upper end of the spectrum each has a principal who is either Black or Hispanic, experienced in the role of principal, serving at least 7 years in their current schools, and holds strikingly similar views of their roles as principals as shown in Table 11.3. Schools with high math gains exhibited high SCQS scores, and the principals' statements of their roles underscore parallels between the SCQS indicators and principals' perceptions of their responsibilities. Conversely, schools with low math gains were less likely to be rated highly on SCQS indicators; however, the principals of those schools also stressed the importance of responsibilities similar to principals in high gain schools.

As demonstrated in Table 11.2, principals saw their roles as diverse, but many described their roles as containing aspects of "instructional leadership" (47.7%), "professional development" (31.8%), "community collaboration" (27.3%), or "collaboration and facilitation" (22.7%). Table 11.3 shows the percentages of principals in each city who stated that their daily role included these responsibilities. In most cases, principals' views of their roles line up with staff perceptions of components on our school culture measure.

Table 11.3 illustrates the stated roles and responsibilities of principals at each site. For example, the principal's description of his role at Ch110, an elementary school in Chicago showing high math gains and correspondingly high SCQS scores, emphasizes his responsibilities in coordinating people and resources:

> [T]he principal is one that helps to put the pieces in place for that vision to come about and become a reality, whether that is … helping to put your hands on the resources be they money or grants, getting the parents together to help out in whatever capacity that you

TABLE 11.2
Daily Responsibilities and Roles Stated by Principals in Each Site

Daily Responsibilities and Roles	Chicago (n=8)	El Paso (n=8)	Memphis (n=12)	Miami (n=16)	Total (n=44)
Instructional Leadership	25%	62.5%	66.7%	37.5%	47.7%
Professional Development	50%	50%	25%	18.7%	31.8%
Community Collaboration	37.5%	62.5%	16.7%	12.5%	27.3%
Facilitation	50%	0%	16.7%	25%	22.7%
Policy Implementation	12.5%	12.5%	33.3%	12.5%	18.2%
Diverse Roles	12.5%	12.5%	16.7%	18.7%	15.9%

Note: Some principals mentioned more than one role.

TABLE 11.3

Principals' Role in Reform

School Code	Math Gains	SCQS Score (Overall)	Principals' Statements
Mi110	High	High	Diverse. Have to work well with staff, community and district. Need to know the community and its needs. Need to have a clear vision of what needs to be done.
Me320	High	High	I think my role as principal is found in my personal mission statement which is simply to provide all the necessary resources and an environment where students and teachers engage in learning where the end result will be a highly competitive and functional student ready to fulfill the needs of the community.
Mi160	High	Medium	I would define my role as principal as the instructional leader, work in a team oriented approach with faculty.
Ch110	High	High	So I think the principal is one that helps to put the pieces in place for that vision to come about and become a reality, whether that is . . . helping to put your hands on the resources be they money or grants, getting the parents together to help out in whatever capacity that you feel comfortable in, and making them feel welcome once they get here. And of course the principal has to be in the classroom to see what's going on.
Mi210	High	High	The role is in two large categories. Education is a regulated government service. The principal's job is to make sure the rules and regulations are implemented as best you can with available resources. The other role is leadership -- enabling people to maximize their own potential, build a learning community, help guide to where it is trying to go.
EP120	Low	High	First and foremost [my role is as] an instructional leader. And that is something I don't take lightly. That means being in there working with teachers. It means leading grade level meetings, talking about what good instruction looks like.[These include] practices of how we interact with kids, how we access kids' learning, what good instruction looks like, and then how do we know we are getting it basically. And then I think next would be your public relations skills, your ability to bring people together. And I mean teachers, staff, the community…

Me240	Low	Medium	Well, I am, for all practical purposes, the instructional leader. That's you know, what the role has been defined to be. And I guess I'm manager as well. The management activities sometimes get in the way of the instructional duties.
EP130	Low	High	I really believe that the role of principal has changed so much and I think that the challenge . . . is making bridges between community, teachers and students and always factoring to the equation where the students are.
Ch120	Low	Low	I am of the opinion that the principal is the instructional leader in the school, and it is, I see a large part of my job, the majority of it, as being that of facilitator, coach and mentor to my staff. [. . .] the only thing that I would add is that administrators must be careful because there is a limited amount of funds that one would have to purchase programs or just so many free services that one can get. We are prolific grant writers at this school. That has helped us to finance some of our initiatives.[I am also] an implementor. I regard myself as an advocate for my student, staff and parents. And if these things are good for students, I am about the business of implementing.
Mi150	Low	Low	A facilitator, listen to what's going on, sending teachers to workshops, selecting the best, and presenting the faculty to what's expected of us.
Mi320	Low	High	I would define it as being a leader. The buck stops with me from academics to the environment of the school, the safety of the school. I set the tone. I set the table.

Note: The school codes were devised using a two letter combination to indicate city (Mi-Miami, Me-Memphis, Ch-Chicago, EP-El Paso), a corresponding school number showing the school grade levels (100-elementary, 200-middle school, 300-high school) and an identifying number to track individual schools within the research sites by level (20, 30, etc.).

231

feel comfortable in, and making them feel welcome once they get here. And of course the principal has to be in the classroom to see what's going on."

Similarly, the principal of the Miami elementary school (Mi110) with the highest math gains of any participating school saw her role as complex and varied in the following ways:

> [The roles a principal enacts are] diverse. [You] have to work well with staff, community and district. Need to know the community and its needs. Need to have a clear vision of what needs to be done.

Principals of schools with high math gains and high SCQS scores emphasized their roles as both local school leaders and facilitators of collaborations between community, parents, students, and teachers more often than principals of schools with low gains and low SCQS scores. The principal of a high achieving elementary school in Chicago saw his ability to help promote teamwork among his staff as a key to students' success:

> I define my role, really, as a facilitator. I see myself being the principal teacher in the school, not just the principal person in charge. But I also try to stress the last syllable in principal and be a "pal" to the staff as well as to the teachers … of the students. I believe in teamwork. Our theme is "Teamwork makes the train work." And our dream is for the students to become the best they can be in the 21st Century. So I try to develop my leadership by sharing [it] with others but also, not where I'm the focal point but I'm like … I prefer myself to be like a facilitator … to just help out wherever I can … Because I basically send the teachers out to look at the different kinds of programs that the board has offered or that's out there and then they bring them back to me. And I kind of let them kind of go for it … more … more so. Because I think they may show more ownership that way. I'm not too involved in that aspect of it. (CH150)

This principal sees teamwork as a complex set of relationships and responsibilities. To get the "train to work" this principal actively engages the teachers in the school in making critical decisions about their work and working conditions as he stands back and facilitates by supplying the necessary resources.

Principals of high achieving schools were also more likely to mention the need for maintaining a clear vision emphasizing student learning and remaining flexible in their approach to the role. A Chicago principal (Ch110) of a high-achieving elementary school in Chicago's South Side offered this account of the importance of both having a vision and understanding one's particular strengths in fulfilling the role of the principal:

> So I think the principal is one that helps to put the pieces in place for that vision to come about and become a reality, whether that is … helping to put your hands on the resources be they money or grants, getting the parents together to help out in whatever capacity that you feel comfortable in, and making them feel welcome once they get here. And of course the principal has to be in the classroom to see what's going on.

Among principals whose schools displayed low SCQS scores and low math gains, length of time in role is a major explanatory variable. For example, at the time of her interview, the principal of Coolidge Elementary School in Chicago (Ch120) had served as principal only 2 years. She had grown up in the neighborhood and attended the school as a youngster, began her teaching career at Coolidge, obtained her doctor-ate, and also served as principal elsewhere for 7 years. In addition, she served as mas-ter teacher, assistant principal, and district-wide coordinator for state Chapter One programs. When asked about the impact of NSF reforms, she responded,

> I would rate it a two (Moderate impact). Because we are certainly not where we want to be. There is a beginning, as our CSI coordinator mentioned, we have a new team in place and that team has the responsibility of serving as a resource I have just completed two years here. And some experts say that it can take as long as seven years. I think James Comer says that it may take up to seven years to show true school wide improvement. I don't think I have the luxury of waiting seven years, but two years might not be enough to give a true evaluation.

This principal understands the difficulty of making change and seeing results in 2 years. Staff turnover and the arrival of younger, inexperienced but bright teachers in ad-dition to a large special education student population complicated the situation further. However, her optimism and faith in teachers, students, and neighborhood resources sug-gest a forthcoming turnaround in both climate factors and student achievement. Time in role is also a factor in explaining low math gains and high SCQS scores.

The principal at Reed Beach Elementary School in Miami, Mi150, had been a teacher for 20 years but had served only 4 years as principal. In her interview, although she stressed leadership and facilitation as major parts of her role, she acknowledged that time allocated to preparing for FCAT testing eroded learning opportunities for students. Unfortunately, standardized tests may place pressure on teachers to focus on a narrow set of topics that they understand will be a major focus of the high-stakes test. A director in El Paso sees this as the case in her district.

> I think the districts have been very good in implementing … in prioritizing mathematics, beginning now, I would say, and science, but primarily mathematics, because what gets tested gets done. (EP02)

This district administrator saw gaps in the implementation of reform as a result of emphasizing math over science in carrying out the changes and restructuring associ-ated with the USI. This director approved of the district's overall plan of implementa-tion, but emphasized that "what gets tested gets done." This view was commonly held by district officials who, while recognizing the usefulness of student test performance in deploying resources including opportunities for professional development, also recognized that total reliance on these scores might undermine the success of the re-form especially if teachers "taught to the test" through drill and practice. The pressures of standardized testing on the schools are twofold. Though principals are asked to im-plement reforms that rely more on "hands-on" and "exploratory" learning, those skills may not be reflected in the standardized tests. An associate superintendent for instruc-tion in Miami believed that, because standardized tests were used both as a measure of student performance and school performance, the test was emphasized at the cost of other important educational experiences.

> I think the bigger danger is the emphasis on standardized testing. Because there are many things that tell me that a student has an understanding of a subject besides their perfor-

mance on a standardized test. A standardized test can never, in my estimation, be the sole measure of a student's learning. There are just too many other things. And the risk, as I see it, is that, when the standardized test drives an accountability system that labels schools and kids that the pressure becomes such, on teachers in schools, and administrators, that there is an over-emphasis on "the test," as opposed to a rich instructional experience. (MI14)

The idea that a student can have an understanding of subject matter that standardized tests will not assess accurately led district administrators to support alternative means of assessment. In Chicago, a director suggested forms these alternative assessments might take:

> It could be a paper pencil assessment. It could be an interview. It could be a group discussion in class, where the teacher is standing there and processing, very quickly, all of the information that you are gaining from the general conversation that you're having with the students, okay. And of course, it could be artifacts such as a portfolio. (CH07)

Interviews, group discussions, and portfolios were all mentioned as assessment tools that could be used by teachers, but some principals (and their district administrator counterparts) were skeptical about relying on portfolio assessments because such practices ran counter to their state's focus on high stakes testing. In El Paso, students take the TAAS, a standardized test that is used to rank and reward schools.

A strikingly successful way to improve students' scores on high stakes assessments is to invest in programs for low-achieving students. A total of 61.4% of school principals reported the use of special academic programs to increase student achievement focused on the lowest achieving students as shown in Table 11.4. These programs relied almost exclusively on academic tutoring, with only 6.8% addressing economic concerns and 4.5% addressing social concerns. Chicago was an exception with 25% of the principals interviewed emphasizing the importance of their social programs for low achieving students. Economic programs such as free and reduced lunch were often referred to as well even though these are not specifically aimed at improving student achievement.

Overall, 93.2% of the principals interviewed agreed that standardized testing influenced their policies and instruction. In addition, because of the school's large immigrant population, staff development in areas such as Teaching English as a Second Language was emphasized in in-service activities for teachers, with 39 days of professional development. Math and science-related in-service opportunities took a back seat with only six designated professional development days available to teachers. Thus, in this case, priorities in a subject area other than math affected both teacher

TABLE 11.4
Programs for Low Achieving Students to Reduce Achievement Differentials

Program Type	Chicago (n=8)	El Paso (n=8)	Memphis (n=12)	Miami (n=16)	Total (n=44)
Academic	75%	62.5%	66.6%	50%	61.4%
Economic	0%	12.5%	16.7%	0%	6.8%
Social	25%	12.5%	0%	0%	4.5%

in-service time and student achievement. Though teachers may be part of a learning community in the school, the emphasis is not on math, the likely reason for students poor achievement in this area.

A high reform implementation elementary school in El Paso, EP130, reported similar trends, exhibiting both low gains in math and high SCQS scores on all indicators. The students in this school evidenced high math achievement on standardized tests during the course of reform, but less gain in math scores during the reform period. Looking to the principal's role, in this case, the principal had been in office for 3 years and previously had taught 6 years at the elementary level and was extremely familiar with his school community, current educational research, and reforms he stressed the importance of collaboration as a team. In his time as principal, he had instituted a number of reforms, including an emphasis on vertical teaming between the teachers in the school. As the principal of a school designated as high implementation, he expressed a number of concerns regarding the continuation of the amount of funding for training and materials that had been available for the first 3 years of his principalship. The emphasis on teamwork and collaboration may help to explain high SCQS scores. Another plausible reason is that many teachers were handpicked by this principal with the reform designs in mind.

> I hired 10 new teachers by the way this year and every single one of them are fantastic I hired experience teachers that is not to say that they are not great new teachers but all things being equal because our district doesn't say this person is going to cost more because he has more years of experience and this one isn't. I go for the one with more experience.

Because principals in this and indeed in all of our studied districts were accorded decision-making power through site-based management, hiring and firing decisions were his to make.

With evidence of teamwork, high SCQS scores overall, and high reform implementation in this school, one wonders why the student math gains remain low. The principal mentions issues such as teaching in bilingual classrooms, high student mobility, and low socioeconomic status in the surrounding community as areas of concern. Both the 2001–2002 school improvement plan and the principal mention raising attendance rates, which the 1999–2000 school report card reports at 96.6% during the 1998–1999 school year. It appears that building blocks are in place for successful reform and increased student math gains, from teacher training to classroom materials. Though this school did not evidence the highest gains in math achievement, high levels of achievement as measured by the skills-based test were in fact in place.

CONCLUSION/POINTS TO PONDER

Under the mandates of No Child Left Behind, all principals are now responsible for demonstrating adequate yearly progress for all students in the school and for each student subgroup to address the issue of the achievement gap that separates underserved from "overserved" students. Failure to attain adequate yearly progress over a 3-year period results in a school's being labeled "low performing" and subject to "reconstitution," a process that involves replacement of the entire school staff; in addition, students are eligible to attend another school of their choice. This legislation is dramatic and sweeping and because it was a bipartisan effort, seen by many of its supporters as an extension of the government's involvement to ensure the civil rights and equal access to educational opportunities of all students. Others hold less sanguine views, seeing it as an unfunded mandate that punishes schools unfairly. In any case, principals will now have to consider strategies for improving their "failing" students' academic outcomes. Addressing student needs through learner-centered leadership resulting in improved school culture and ultimately in increased student engagement and student learning outcomes is the major task facing all principals. It is especially daunting in the case of those working in high-poverty school environments such as those we studied during our research. It is our hope that lessons from this research can provide opportunities–guides for principals in high poverty–mobility–minority schools undertaking reform to enhance student outcomes.

These case studies reveal the importance of particular issues in ensuring reform implementation and success. Each of these cases highlights particular circumstances that principals of schools with high mobility, high percentages of minority students, and students with low socioeconomic status may find familiar as reflections of their own schools. The principals we interviewed agreed that certain factors influenced the success of reform implementation in their schools. Among the factors identified by principals were:

1. The importance of professional development.
2. Demographic factors such as ethnicity, language, and socioeconomic status.
3. School vision, attitudes, and guiding principles that support a culture of reform.

These areas were also reflected in the findings from the SCQS, which supported the need for a school environment that stresses the cooperative aspects of school leadership and reform responsibility. This suggests that principals can reinforce reform efforts in their schools by fostering a school culture that values the contributions of teachers and students while supporting teamwork and instruction. In practical terms, this research suggests that principals who are rated positively by their staffs in leadership and cooperative areas are better able to incorporate reform ideals into their schools' day-to-day activities. These issues of school culture were seen as key in determining the success of program implementation and reform adoption within each school as determined by student gains in math achievement scores.

Based on our findings, we have the following recommendations for principals whose schools are implementing systemic reform programs:

1. Be aware and try to build a supportive school culture that includes high levels of teamwork, facilitative leadership, a shared vision, and a strong learning community.
2. Understand the different aspects of the roles played by the principal, faculty, and staff in reform efforts and offer support to areas of special need.
3. Take into consideration and involve the school's community of teachers, students, parents, and community residents in important school decisions.
4. Note and adjust program requirements based on situations that are unique to your school, such as high bilingual or ESOL rates.

Translating policy requirements and reform objectives into the daily school routine can be a daunting task for principals, particularly in schools serving high-risk populations. A commitment to reform and to improving collaboration in the school community is a first step toward reaching those goals. Principals who embody a strong vision of excellence and cooperation in their schools have the opportunity to encourage teachers, students, and community members to support reform efforts and, in turn, to see successful programs coalesce. We also strongly recommend reading, and if possible discussing the links between school culture and student engagement (and, we think, achievement) with others who have similar responsibilities as teachers, principals, and the like. Most pertinent here is a classic in the field by T. Sergiovanni (1994) entitled Building Community in Schools, a key reading for those who wish to understand both the importance of these concepts but also strategies for putting community in place in schools. Finally, we would also recommend the full-length story of our study in four cities entitled: Meaningful Urban Education Reform: Confronting the Learning Crisis in Mathematics and Science (2005). Both of these works emphasize the importance of building strong communities of practice and emphasize the critical importance of school culture in influencing processes and outcomes including student engagement and academic achievement.

REFERENCES

Anderson, R., & Ronnkvist, A. (1999). *"The Presence of Computers in American Schools."* *1998 National Survey. Report #2.* Retrieved from http://www.crito.uci.edu/TLC/findings/Internet-Use/startpage.htm

Boyd, V., & Hord, S. M. (1994). *Principals and the new paradigm: Schools as learning communities.* Paper presented at the Annual Meeting of the American Educational Research Association. New Orleans, LA.

Borman, K., et al. (2005). *Meaningful urban educational reform: Confronting the learning crisis in mathematics and science.* Albany: State University of New York Press.

Bryk & Schneider (2002). *Trust in schools: A core resource for improvement.* New York: Sage.

Danzig, A. (1999a). How might leadership be taught? The use of story and narrative to teach leadership. *International Journal of Leadership in Education: Theory and Practice, 2,* 117–131.

Danzig, A. (1999b). The use of stories in the preparation of educational leaders. *International Studies in Educational Administration, 27,* 11–19.

Hargreaves, A., & Fullan, M. (1998). *What's worth fighting for out there.* New York: Teachers College Press

Katzenmeyer, W., Uekawa, K., Borman, K., & Lee, R. (2001, April). *The relationship between school culture and mathematics achievement in USI school in Chicago, El Paso, Memphis, and Miami.* Paper presented at the meeting of the Systemic Initiative Conference of Key Indicators, Evaluation, Accountability, and Evaluative Studies of Urban School Districts, Tampa, FL.

Kersaint, G., Borman, K. M., Lee, R., & Boydston, T. (2001). Balancing the contradictions between accountability and systemic reform. *Journal of School Leadership, 11,* 217–240.

Kouzes, J. M., & Posner, B. Z. (1987). *The leadership challenge: How to get extraordinary things done in organizations* (pp. 3–14). San Francisco: Jossey-Bass.

Lieberman. (1996). Learning communities. *Educational Leadership, 54*(3), 51–55

Louis, K. S., Kruse, S., & Marks, H. (1996, Winter). Teachers' professional community and school reform. *American Educational Research Journal,* p. 8.

McLaughlin, M. (1994). *Urban sanctuaries: neighborhood organizations in the lives and futures of inner-city youth.* San Francisco: Jossey-Bass.

McLaughlin, M. (1995, December). *Contexts for professional development.* Speech delivered at the annual conference of the National Staff Development Council, Front Royal, VA.

McNeil, L. M. (2000). *Contradictions of school reform: Educational costs of standardized testing.* New York: Routledge.

Newmann, F. M., & Wehlage, G. G. (1995). *Successful school restructuring: A report to the public and educators.* Madison, WI: Center on Organization and Restructuring of School, Wisconsin Center for Educational Research, University of Wisconsin.

National Science Foundation. (2000). *Six critical drivers.* Retrieved from http://www.ehr.nsf.gov/ EHR/ESR/driver.asp

Peterson, K. D., & Deal, T. E. (1998, September). How leaders influence the culture of schools. *Educational Leadership,* 56(1). p. 28.

Resnick, L., & Hall, M. W. (1998). Learning organizations for sustainable education reform. *Daedalus, 27*(4), 89–118.

Senge, P. (1990, Fall). The leader's new work: Building learning organizations. *Sloan Management Review,* 7–23.

Senge, P., et al. (2000). *Schools that learn: A fifth discipline for educator, parents, and everyone who cares about education.* New York: Doubleday.

Senge, P., Roberts, C., Ross, R., Smith, B., Roth, G., & Kleiner, A. (1999). *The dance of change: The challenges of sustaining momentum in learning organizations.* New York: Doubleday.

Sergiovanni, T. (1994) *Building community in schools.* San Francisco: Jossey-Bass.

Westat*McKenzie Consortium, W. M. (1998, October). *The National Science Foundation's Urban Systemic Initiatives (USI) Program: Models of reform in K-12 science and mathematics education.* Washington, DC: Division of Educational System Reform of the National Science Foundation.

SOCIAL JUSTICE AND URBAN REFORM ISSUES IN PROFESSIONAL DEVELOPMENT FOR LEARNER-CENTERED SCHOOL LEADERS

V

12

Leadership in Border Rural Areas: A Pedagogical Awakening of a Principal Preparation Program

Elsy Fierro
María Luisa González
New Mexico State University

Recent research studies have confirmed the critical role principals play in improving instruction for all students (Cotton, 2003; Davis, Darling-Hammond, LaPointe, & Meyerson, 2005; Leithwood, Jantzi, Coffin, & Wilson, 1996; Sebring & Bryk, 2000). Other studies have identified leadership practices of successful principals in addressing curricular and systemic change in schools, in meeting the annual yearly progress of underserved subgroups established by NCLB (Anderson, 2004; Brewster & Klump, 2005). As a result, current literature on the essential features of principal preparation programs suggest the need for curricular and structural changes that reflect current research in leadership, instruction, and management as well as a link between theory and practice through field based internships (Davis et al., 2005). In addition, few studies on leadership practices or principal preparation address how principals develop the capacities and skills to address curricular and systemic change in schools (Davis et al., 2005).

That is, how do effective principals acquire the skills necessary to adapt their leadership to address the context-specific needs of students, teachers, and other members of the school community (Davis et al., 2005; Waters & Grubb, 2004; Waters, Marzano, & McNulty, 2003)? Though the literature on principal preparation programs has been informed by the studies of successful principals (Knapp & Copland, 2003; Murphy & Vriesenga, 2004), few of these examples address school communities with cultural and linguistic differences, poverty, and immigration issues. As a result, the pedagogical content of principal preparation programs has few examples of successful principals leading culturally and linguistically diverse school communities and do not address the educational needs and implications on student learning of these communities. This takes place in spite of the fact that research studies indicating students of color and low socioeconomic status continue to score lower on achievement tests than their White middle-class counterparts (Brown, 2004).

The challenge for principal preparation programs is not only one of recognizing the existence of these unique needs and their implications on student learning, but one of preparing principals to be cognizant and reflective of the school system's role in perpetuating student failure (Valenzuela, 1999) and inequality (Nieto, 2000). In meeting this challenge, principal preparation programs must equip aspiring principals with the skills and knowledge of how to redress these systemic failures and improve schools for culturally and linguistically diverse students (Brown, 2004).

A fundamental question then is "What must preparation programs include that will change people from what they are to what they must become (Brunner, Hammel, & Miller, 2003, p. 73)?" The answer to this question is a pedagogical awakening of the principal preparation program where issues of equity, race, class, language, sexual orientation, and power relationships are integrated into all courses and their content (Brown, 2004; Shields, Larocque, & Oberg, 2002).

A pedagogical awakening of the way courses are taught and the type of content offered in these courses. This pedagogical awakening supports and agitates aspiring administrators to act and address equity issues affecting all involved in the school's learning community (Cambron-McCabe & McCarthy, 2005; Marshall, 2004)—in other words, preparation programs with a social justice orientation where all entities (faculty included) develop vocabulary, knowledge, and skills to debate and dialogue on issues of equity and justice (Brown, 2004).

PEDAGOGICAL AWAKENING

Several writers have posited that social justice initiatives are important elements of educational leadership preparation programs (Lyman & Villani, 2002; Marshall, 2004; Marshall & McCarthy, 2002; Marshall & Ward, 2004) to create long-term systemic reform. Other writers insist that only preparation programs with a social justice orientation can instill in aspiring administrators the urgency for their moral and ethical obligation to foster equitable and socially responsible learning for all students (Brown, 2004).

LEADERSHIP IN BORDER RURAL AREAS

The purpose of this chapter is to describe practices of a principal preparation program designed from a social justice perspective, which created a pedagogical awakening in both the program and the aspiring principals. These pedagogical approaches provided curricula that scaffolded issues of race, ethnicity, gender, class, language, culture, poverty, and immigration throughout the program of study (Brown, 2004). All principal preparation courses addressed these issues and agitated students to reflect and act on the social, economic, and educational inequities perpetuated in our schools. This agitation of students was done by infusing each course with activities that provided for bridging theory through practice, dialogue with debate, critical reflection through journal writing, and social identity papers of self (Brown, 2004).

Leadership in Border Rural Areas (LIBRA) began as collaborative project between Las Cruces Public Schools (LCPS) and New Mexico State University (NMSU). The aim was for Project LIBRA to become a new model for preparing educational leaders in addressing the educational needs of all students along the Mexico and U.S. border by focusing on issues of poverty, culture, and linguistic diversity. The goal of Project LIBRA was to provide a collaborative, comprehensive, and sustained leadership program for the preparation–training of principal candidates to become school leaders who promote long-term gains in the academic achievement of all students with a focus on English language learners (ELLs). Because the majority of ELLs along the U.S.–Mexico border in the Las Cruces, New Mexico, area are of Mexican descent, Project LIBRA emphasized the issues related to the Hispanic population.

Project LIBRA consisted of two components aimed at the preparation of aspiring principals and the professional development of current principals in Las Cruces public schools. The first component of the project included the preparation of 34 aspiring principals through rigorous course work that addressed the learning needs of students along the Mexico and U.S. border by focusing on issues of poverty, culture, and linguistic diversity.

The second component provided professional development for current principals in Las Cruces Public Schools on issues of poverty, culture, and linguistic diversity. The professional development provided these learning opportunities for the current principals through speaker series, site visits of successful schools along the border, and mentoring from the principals of these successful schools.

Addressing the learning needs of students along the U.S.–Mexico border was a critical feature of Project LIBRA for both aspiring principals and current principals. Project LIBRA emphasized the learning needs of all students; yet, the proximity of New Mexico State University and Las Cruces Public Schools to the U.S.–Mexico border necessitated an emphasis on ELLs and issues related to the Hispanic population.

THREE-WAY MENTORING
WITH EXPERIENCED PRINCIPALS/ASSISTANT PRINCIPALS

Scaffolding of key concepts was accomplished through a three-way mentoring component that used a dialectal theory approach (Darder, 1991) that "seeks to uncover the connections between objective knowledge and the norms, values, and structural relationships of the wider society" (p. 80). Aspiring principals and current principals were engaged in a series of activities and assignments that examined the social, political, and economic contexts of their lives. Through the three-way mentoring component, participants were challenged to analyze their lives for contradictions and limitations that have prevented them from advocating and creating change for all students (Nieto, 2000).

FIELD EXPERIENCES

LIBRA participants were provided field experiences for observing their mentoring principal and other principals in schools along the U.S.–Mexico border. The intent of the field experiences was to provide various perspectives for Project LIBRA participants to analyze and interpret their observations and readings of the research. Aspiring principals were provided opportunities to observe their mentoring principal make decisions related to leading and managing a school. They also visited schools on both sides of the U.S.–Mexico border, in El Paso, Texas, Sunland Park, New Mexico, and those in Juarez, Chihuahua, Mexico to further their understanding of educational needs along the border and to observe various leadership styles of school administrators. During these field experiences, participants were asked to observe and reflect on the curriculum, assessment, and instructional practices of teachers and administrators. The authentic settings and observations of principals addressing and in some cases solving problems contributed to Project LIBRA's emphasis on critical self-reflection.

COURSE CONTENT

All professional development and course content focused on issues of race, ethnicity, gender, class, language, poverty, immigration, and healthcare. Traditional course content that would emphasize management skills and basic leadership skills incorporated a discussion and a critical analysis of these issues within the realm of instructional leadership as well as opportunities for praxis (Brown, 2004; Freire,1990). Brown (2004) posits the need for preparation programs to include opportunities for "critical reflection, rational discourse, and policy praxis to increase awareness, acknowledgement, and action" (p.91), in addition to having a commitment to rethink the type of content, delivery methods, and assessment used. Figure 12.1 illustrates the components that each Project LIBRA course contained. Courses also emphasized leadership through the use of literature that defined parent engagement, critical pedagogy, program and student assessment models, and strategic planning procedures.

The course work for project LIBRA participants combined the required courses and New Mexico competencies for administrator licensure with the goals and objectives of the project. The intent of Project LIBRA was to go beyond the traditional course content and provide opportunities for aspiring principals to explore personal attitudes and beliefs as well as become both culturally and professionally aware of the inequities that exist in our schools. This was accomplished through course content that provided opportunities for problem based learning, reflective journaling, and field experiences that linked theory and practice (Brown, 2004).

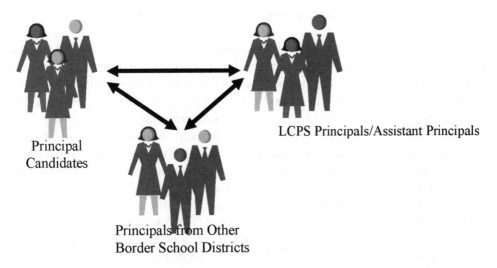

Principal Candidates

LCPS Principals/Assistant Principals

Principals from Other Border School Districts

Figure 12.1. Three-way mentoring.

Coursework Development

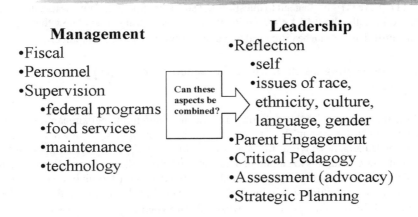

Figure 12.2. Course development components.

REFLECTIVE JOURNALS

Aspiring principals in Project LIBRA were provided numerous opportunities for critical self-reflection. LIBRA participants submitted weekly written reflections related to their field experience observations–activities and responses to the assigned readings. Participants submitted weekly reflective journals that asked the students to reflect on the following statements:

- The most important thing that I learned this week was:
- The aspect of leadership that I feel the best about this week was:
- The aspect of leadership that I feel uncomfortable with this week was:

- One incident that stands out in my mind from this week was:

In their initial reflections, the student responses to these statements clearly detailed their level of awareness regarding border schooling issues. Although some students reflected on the "need to take notes during staff meetings," others reflected on how "we are not aware of the unfairness in schools when it comes to Hispanic students" and the need for "parents to be an integral part of the curriculum."

As students took course work emphasizing language acquisition and critical pedagogy theories and best practices for educating ELLs and children of poverty, the gap in their reflections narrowed. By the Fall 2004 semester, their reflections showed what Paulo Freire (1990) referred to as "conscientizacao." According to Freire (1990), conscientizacao "refers to learning to perceive social, political, and economic contradictions, and to take action against the oppressive elements of reality."

Examples of conscientizacao were found in the following student reflections. Student A on participating in the child study team meeting:

The experience that made the biggest impact on me was when the person in charge of the child study team committee stated that "unlike Ray Elemtary School where parents referred their children because they all feel their children were gifted, not at John Elemtary School parents are all referring students to special education to get social security checks." This comment showed how pervasive stereotypes are. I discovered that I need to stand up for what I believe is right. In need to question and speak up. So I did. I am passionate about children, especially about ELLs and giving them a voice, letting others know that stereotypes are hurtful, ELLs can be gifted and language diversity is good. (September 10, 2003)

Student B on visiting a school where the principal believes in parent and community engagement:

The thing that was overwhelmingly obvious was how much one person can lose when going up against the system. If someone is not organized and surrounded with other like-minded leaders, it's obvious that a person could lose everything. Most importantly I discovered how crucial it is to gather leaders that can help instigate change. Without help it would be a lonely fight for change. I also discovered that I don't think I've ever been so passionate about something so as to put my career on the line. I would consider myself an advocate for bilingual education but at what point do you throw in the towel?

Student C on her learning experience attending the UCEA conference:

Prejudice exists in every being and James Banks the presenter in this conference said it best when he said that we all need each other because without the other we can not exist. In every session, the theme was the same, social justice was the key in the evaluation, creation and reevaluation of universities and schools. The marginalized need from the so called mainstream and the mainstream needs from the marginalized. The awareness of needing each other was clearer to me when my roommate and classmates in this conference confronted the issue of social justice. We had continuous discussions … and it made me feel that these issues must be discussed even if it makes us uncomfortable. Honest discussions need to be had because prejudice is sometimes an unconscious act and people need to be asked and confronted about their statements and actions.

Student D on visiting schools in a low-income neighborhood:

I'm embarrassed to say this, but this is the kind of neighborhood I would be afraid to be in by myself. I know that comes from stereotypes about neighborhoods that are old and run-down. I discovered I do still have fears based on stereotypes. What I did find in that neighborhood was a lot of strength, warmth, and pride. I know I will have to continue to examine my beliefs so that I can positively impact the communities I work in. I particularly enjoyed the conversation about why people are color blind. It made me realize that I often don't want to discuss race because I feel guilty that others have been oppressed by my race. It also made me think that not talking about these issues openly is a form of oppression. I think I will always have areas of "color-blindness," but I think I have to keep confronting it.

Social Identity Papers

Another activity that encouraged participants to further reflect on their experiences was the writing of social identity papers. Aspiring principals submitted three social identity papers, written at the beginning, middle, and end of their participation of the project.

At the beginning of the project, aspiring principals were asked to write a social identity paper about their experiences that contributed to their development as individuals. In this paper they discuss the social forces of gender, culture, language, social class, race, and ethnicity. The social identity paper was the initial paper that emphasized critical self-reflection by encouraging LIBRA participants to begin to understand the social forces that have shaped who they are as individuals, in their roles as brother–sister, mother–father, aunt–uncle, and so on, as well as in their role as professionals, teachers, and administrators. According to Huddy (2001), how we view and function in our multiple roles and relationships is shaped by the social forces of gender, culture, language, social class, race, and ethnicity. Ultimately, it is these social forces that become part of our work as teachers and administrators. The recognition of these social forces in one's life is essential in beginning the process of self-discovery, social consciousness, and acceptance of others (Banks, 1994; Brown, 2004).

Problem-Based Learning

Problem-based learning activities focused on problems of practice and required aspiring principals to problem solve and reflect with their mentoring principal–assistant principal as well as their cohort peers (Bridges & Hallinger, 1993; Davis et al., 2005). For example, regarding an assignment for the course entitled Instructional Leadership, aspiring principals were asked to collaborate with cohort members in analyzing student achievement data and to develop an instructional plan for an identified instructional area of need for ELLs.

Aspiring principals reviewed either math or reading test results. Data were used from one of their internship schools and aspiring principals consulted with their mentoring principal–assistant principal on activities to address the identified instructional need. Data analysis consisted of comparing all subgroups and graphing results. Questions related to achievement gaps and instructional practices were part of the dialogue among aspiring principals and their mentors.

Consultation Groups

LIBRA participants also participated in weekly seminars to continue their reflection of problems they encountered during their internship–field experiences. Within these weekly seminars, aspiring principals were involved in consultation groups that consisted of other LIBRA participants and a current principal. The purpose of these consultation groups was to further the participants' understanding of leadership, social system dynamics, and strategy for developing collaboration. In this vein, participants brought actual problems of practice, challenges of leadership, to the consultation group sessions. Participants discussed the actual problems, applying theory and insights from lectures and readings to address the identified problems of practice.

In presenting their problem of practice, participants prepared an outline of their experience and listed one or two questions that the group needed to help them answer. This provided the discussion a frame of reference for the consultation. Participants also needed to describe in their outline any underlying assumptions that perhaps clouded their perception of the problem. The role of the current principal was one of mentoring by facilitating the discussion and providing insights from his or her experiences as a principal. Brown (2004) described this type of dialogue as rational discourse where "conversations evolve over time into a culture of careful listening ... richer understandings of our own biases as well as where our colleagues stand on their understanding of the issues" (p. 95).

Pedagogical Awakening of Preparation Programs

The pedagogical activities presented in this chapter are suggestions on how a principal preparation program may equip aspiring principals with the skills and knowledge of how to redress systemic failures and improve schools for culturally and linguistically diverse students (Brown, 2004). The pedagogical activities offer an example of how a principal preparation program can experience a pedagogical awakening of the way courses are taught and the type of content offered in these courses. Project LIBRA participants and LIBRA faculty were agitated to act and address equity issues affecting a school's learning community (Marshall, 2004; Cambron-McCabe & McCarthy, 2005).

REFERENCES

Anderson, W. (2004). *Making sense of adequate yearly progress.* Portland, OR: Northwest Regional Educational Library.

Banks, J. (1994). *Multiethnic education: Theory and practice.* Needham Heights, MA: Allyn & Bacon.

Brewster C., & Klump, J. (2005). *Leadership practices of successful principals.* Portland, OR: Northwest Regional Educational Laboratory.

Bridges, E., & Hallinger, P.(1993). Problem-based learning in medical and managerial education. In P. Hallenger, K. Leithwood, & J. Murphy (Eds.), *Cognitive perspectives on education leadership* (253–267). New York: Teachers College Press.

Brown, K. (2004). Leadership for social justice and equity: Weaving a transformative framework and pedagogy. *Educational Administration Quarterly, 40*(1), 79–110.

Brunner, C. C., Hammel, K., & Miller, M. D. (2003). Transforming leadership preparation for social justice: Dissatisfaction, inspiration, and rebirth—an exemplar. In F. C. Lunenburg & C. S. Carr (Eds.), *Shaping the future: Policy, partnerships, and emerging perspectives. National Council of Professors of Educational Administration*. Lanham, MD: Scarecrow Education.

Cambron-McCabe, N., & McCarthy, M. M. (2005). Educating school leaders for social justice. *Educational Policy, 19*(1), 201–222.

Cotton, K. (2003). *Principals and student achievement: What the research says*. Alexandria, VA: Association for Supervision and Curriculum Development.

Darder, A. (1991). *Culture and power in the classroom*. Westport, CT: Bergin & Garvey.

Davis, S., Darling-Hammond, L., LaPointe, M., & Meyerson, D. (2005). *School leadership study: Developing successful principals*. Stanford, CA: Stanford Educational Leadership Institute.

Herrity, V. A., & Glasman, N. S. (1999). Training administrators for culturally and linguistically diverse school populations: Opinions of expert practitioners. *Journal of School Leadership, 9,* 235–253.

Huddy, L. (2001). From social to political identity: A critical examination of social identity theory. *Political Psychology, 22*(1).

Jacobsen, D. (2001). *Doing justice: Congregations and community organizing*. Minneapolis, MN: Fortress.

Knapp, M. S., Copland, M. A., & Talbert, J. E. (2003, February). *Leading for learning: Reflective tools for school and district leaders*. Seattle, WA: Center for the Study of Teaching and Policy.

Leithwood, K., Jantzi, D., Coffin, G., & Wilson, P. (1996). Preparing school leaders: What works? *Journal of School Leadership, 6,* 316–342.

Lyman, L. L., & Villani, C. J. (2002). The complexity of poverty: A missing component of educational leadership programs. *Journal of School Leadership, 12,* 246–280.

Marshall, C., & McCarthy, M. (2002). School leadership reforms: Filtering social justice through dominant discourses. *Journal of School Leadership, 12,* 480–501.

Marshall, C. (2004). Social justice challenges to educational administration: Introduction to a special issue. *Educational Administration Quarterly, 40*(1), 3–13.

Marshall, C., & Ward, M. (2004). "Yes, but ...": Education leaders discuss social justice. *Journal of School Leadership, 14,* 530–563.

McNeil, L. M. (2000). *Contradictions of school reform: Educational costs of standardized testing*. New York: Routledge.

Murphy, J., & Vriesenga, M. (2004). *Research on preparation programs in education administration: An analysis*. Monograph prepared for the University Council for Educational Administration, University of Missouri-Columbia.

Nieto, S. (2000). Placing equity front and center: Some thoughts on transforming teaching education for a new century. *Journal of Teacher Education, 51*(3), 180–187.

Nieto, S. (Ed.). (2005). *Why we teach*. New York: Teachers College Press.

Sebring, P. B., & Bryk, A. S. (2000). School leadership and the bottom line in Chicago. *Phi Delta Kappan, 81,* 440–443.

Shields, C. (2004). Dialogic leadership for social justice: Overcoming pathologies of silence. *Educational Administration Quarterly, 40*(1), 109–132.

Shields, C., Larocque, L., & Oberg, S. (2002). A dialogue about race and ethnicity in education: Struggling to understand issues in cross-cultural leadership. *Journal of School Leadership, 12*(2), 116–137.

Valenzuela, A. (1999). *Subtractive schooling: US-Mexican youth and the politics of caring*. Albany: State University of New York Press.

Waters, T., & Grubb, S. (2004). *The leadership we need: Using research to strengthen the use of standards for administrator preparation and licensure programs*. Aurora, CO: Mid-continent Research for Education and Learning.

Waters, T., Marzano, R. J., & McNulty, B. (2003). *Balanced leadership: What 30 years of research tells us about the effects of leadership on student achievement*. Aurora, CO: McREL.

13

USING STORY AND NARRATIVE TO ENHANCE THE PROFESSIONAL DEVELOPMENT OF LEARNER-CENTERED LEADERS

Arnold B. Danzig
Arizona State University

William F. Wright
Northern Arizona University

As schools and school districts struggle to implement federally and state-mandated accountability systems, educational leadership has become a critical component to ensuring improved student learning. It is our contention that for these efforts to be successful, school administrators need a firm understanding of their own role as learners and the ways in which learning connects to instructional practices and curricular content. Success will require principals and other school administrators to engage in new efforts at personal growth and professional development. As Rick DuFour notes, "When learning becomes the preoccupation of the school, when all the school's educators examine the efforts and initiatives of the school through the lens of their impact on learning, the structure and culture of the school begin to change in substantive ways" (2002, p. 13). In this chapter, we argue for a more individual view of learning, informed by personal narratives, as the basis of professional development for school administrators.

Increased accountability and pressures from high-visibility student testing outcomes have resulted in fewer principals in the pipeline. "In 1998, 50% of 400 superintendents surveyed reported trouble filling principal vacancies. The challenge of meeting the immediate need for quality principals (is) compounded by a forecasted turnover of at least 40% of our nation's principals in the next ten years" (U.S. Department of Education, 2002, p. A-3). New challenges embedded in the work of school administrators and changing demographics of the field, provide opportunities for school administrators to focus on learning in their schools, their own learning as well as student learning.

This alternative framing, one in which leaders are learners (Danzig & Wright, 2002; 2003; DuFour, 2001; Murphy, 2002a, 2002b) is central to this research. The professional development activities that are facilitated by collaborative mentoring reflect the focus on leaders as learners. The expected outcomes of the professional development are specific leadership actions that are implicit in a learner-centered approach and include (a) the leader translates guiding ideas into educational practices that engage all members of the community; (b) the leader designs effective learning processes so that individuals and organizations learn; (c) the leader provides relevant school data that can be used as a tool for developing a learning community that strives to improve; (d) the leader surfaces mental metaphors and identifies strengths and weaknesses of these metaphors; (e) leadership embraces a deeper understanding and learning about one's own work and practice.

This view of learning implies that leaders commit to their own learning and the learning of others. Leaders who are learners must therefore have the intrinsic motivation to personally improve along with the necessary time to question and reflect on experience and to apply what they have learned to their performances as school leaders. Learner-centered leaders ask questions that challenge current practices and beliefs embedded in management administration. Crafting narratives provides a process to reorient administrators from learning managers to learning leaders.

A LEARNER-CENTERED APPROACH TO PROFESSIONAL DEVELOPMENT

Earlier chapters have explored the concept of learner-centered leadership, in which attention is given to the primary role of teaching and learning in the development of school leadership expertise. This view implies a change in the source of inspiration for educational leadership, a view away from management and toward teaching and learning. Murphy (2002) proposed a role for leadership, which entails developing a learning community, one in which greater attention is needed to promote an atmosphere of inquiry with greater focus on collaboration and shared decision making. In this new role, leaders will need to develop the capacity for reflection and promote self-inquiry among the entire school community.

Learner-centered leadership also involves a balance between the professional norms and personal dispositions of educators, with the larger good as defined by a learning community. Without a focus on learning, Murphy argues that there is considerable risk that the daily press of management tasks and a crisis mentality will override the school leader's attention. This enlarged role of leadership also implies a movement away from bureaucratic models to a 21st-century model of schooling with the expanded responsibility of successfully educating all students. These changes result in two challenges: (a) to reorient the principalship from management toward a more broadly defined view of learner-centered leader; and (b) to refocus the principalship from administration and policy toward teaching and learning. According to this view, understanding and valuing teaching and learning provide the basis for development of leadership in schools.

The best examples of professional development reflect a method of embedding new knowledge into the existing roles, processes, and structures of schools (Guskey, 2000). Our approach fosters individual and collective learning through a collaborative process that includes stories and narratives, constructed by individual school administrators.

Spillane and Seashore Louis (2002) argued that school administrators can promote instructional capacity in their schools by building a professional community of learners. The development of professional communities in schools creates the foundation for systemic change. A key factor in creating professional community is social trust, which provides a "foundation on which collaboration, reflective dialogue, and deprivatization of practice can occur" (p. 94). In a community of learners, no single person is expected to master everything. The entire school or institution, rather than a single person, works to build what might be described as collective and collaborative expertise. Developing social trust, a prerequisite for professional community, is also built around the time to talk with others. Ongoing conversations about teaching and learning are also part of the development and cultivation of professional networks that go beyond a particular school.

The narrative approach described in this chapter also draws from the research base on legal and medical education by using problem-based learning (PBL) to support the professional development of school leaders. Medical educators, for instance, found that when participants studied patients' medical records, group focus shifted from isolated facts to an emphasis on meaningful information (Aspy, Aspy, & Quinn, 1993). In PBL, learners use ill-structured, "real world" problems as a context to learn critical thinking and problem solving skills, and acquire knowledge of the essential concepts at work in the problem (Stepien & Gallagher, 1993).

When school leaders' professional development activities focus on real life problems of practice, and is coupled with educational research literature related to learner-centeredness, teaching, curriculum, and student learning, school leaders are equipped to lead efforts to improve academic outcomes for all students. By embedding a problem-based approach in an environment consistent with adult learning theoretical principles, school administrators learn from and solve real problems in community, and learn to apply what they learned in their work, and develop a collective wisdom gleaned from the collective learning experience. This is, in part, what we are describing as a narrative approach to professional development.

USING STORIES AND NARRATIVES TO EMPHASIZE LEARNING IN PROFESSIONAL DEVELOPMENT

One way to explore and reflect on one's learning is through story and narrative. Many scholars and practitioners have explored the use of story and narrative to show the way this form enhances the opportunity for individual learning (Ackerman & Maslin-Ostrowski, 2002; Bruner, 1996; Coles, 1989, 2000; Gardner, 1996). The narrative form can also be used to promote organizational learning by building competence (Danzig & Harris, 1996), understanding tacit knowledge associated with professional practice (Clandinin & Connelly, 1991, 2000; Schön, 1991), exploring the organization's and institution's identity (Czarniawska, 1997; Schön, 1991), understanding leadership and decision making (Bennis, 2000; Danzig, 2001), and promoting professional growth based on a moral basis for professional practice (Clandinin & Connelly, 2000; Coles, 2000; Cooper, 1995; Danzig, 1999a, 1999b).

Narratives and stories serve are a way for professionals to reflect on practices, to challenge value structures, and to resolve dilemmas. These stories can also be used to teach other leaders through analysis, reflection, and action. Life and career experiences of administrators are presented as an entry route to understanding the key values expressed by leaders, and the central vision that they operationalize in their organizations. De Pree (1989, 1993) wrote more autobiographically while focusing attention on the value commitments of his father, and how his own experiences growing up shaped his philosophy and ultimately the organization's values and mission. Gardner (1995) suggested that leaders communicate key values to followers through stories, especially stories that resonate with followers.

The narrative approach also taps into the theory and research on adult learning to build learning communities that work to improve student achievement. The process of professional development is interactive in nature with each participant given the space and opportunity to share mental models related to experiences pertinent to urban education (Palmer, 1998). The process is not a hierarchical model where one person disseminates information to the rest of the participants. Instead, real world challenges or problems are presented, and used as the subject on which participants share knowledge, beliefs, and assumptions and as a way to examine multiple perspectives with several solutions.

The narrative approach that is discussed in this chapter provides evidence of how school leaders in urban districts develop collective wisdom regarding practice. The importance of learning to leadership practice, the significance of language and culture, and the availability of community resources are part of the wisdom to be tapped to ensure that all students are included in the mix. Narratives assist school administrators to become better learners, collaborators, and problem solvers by encouraging them to tap into community resources and think systemically about how to manage challenges associated with urban, diverse schools; ultimately, it is hoped that these administrators take actions that result in better learning outcomes for all students.

If leadership itself is learned rather than innate, then the processes by which these skills and dispositions are learned deserve greater attention. Stories and narratives are one way to illustrate the complexities and complications related to school administration and leadership. Narratives and cases illustrate some of the ways in which administrators work through challenges and make decisions regarding complicated issues using tacit and personal knowledge. Through stories and narrative reflections, educational leaders are able to gain greater insight regarding the skills and characteristics of leadership.

Using a Narrative Approach to Leadership Development With a District Leadership Team: An Example

During the 2000–2001 school years, the authors worked with the leadership team from a county accommodation school district in a major urban center in the southwestern United States. The goal of the professional development was to assist the leadership team in accomplishing high-quality work, while paying attention to the underlying moral purposes of administration in a school district that serves homeless children, incarcerated children, and children who have been largely unsuccessful in their prior school experiences.

The narrative approach asked the principals and administrators in the district to explore their own stories, their workplace experiences, and professional dilemmas, as they crafted stories of their leadership and practice. The authors met weekly with the leadership team of the district beginning early in September 2000, and continuing through June 2001, and included district superintendent, four principals, four assistant principals and site directors, directors of curriculum, business services, and personnel and computer services. The researchers met with this group every Monday for approximately 3 hr in addition to site visits and individual conversations.

Methodological Considerations in the Crafting Stories of Practice. The methodology for writing and analyzing stories of practices involved multiple steps. Participants read and analyzed education-related stories and narratives of others. They worked in pairs to collect and craft each other's stories. Interviews among team members were taped, transcribed, and crafted into accounts or stories of self, with consideration for how personal background, experience, and training contributed to administrative practice. The stories often led to larger conversations about the motivations and commitments of school leaders, teaching and learning processes, professional commitments and administrative standards, and testing and curricular standards.

Data Sources. The leadership stories were constructed during the year by the researchers and district leadership team. Each participant was given a list of suggested questions to begin the interviews and guidelines for what the final story should look like. (For details and examples of see Danzig, 1997a; Danzig 1997b; Danzig, 1999a; Danzig 1999b; Danzig & Harris, 1996.) The administrators were invited to talk about their own personal biographies and entry into their respective fields. In a subsequent interview, they were invited to talk about a specific problem or situation in which they had played a leadership role. The problem was to be discrete rather than ongoing, and involve others inside and outside their respective organizations. The resolution, if any, was also to be discussed. All interviews were audiotaped and transcribed into written text.

There were multiple steps in the preparation and crafting of the stories. Step one involved introducing the assignment and giving out a list of preliminary prompts or questions. In subsequent sessions, each member of the leadership team told his or her story to one other person, and reciprocated by hearing that person's story. These stories were audiotaped, transcribed, and returned to the original listener. Step two required the listener to take the transcription and craft the conversation into a more sequenced story, removing the prompts, hesitations, and sidebars. The stories usually included two distinct parts: (a) a general biographical background of the administrator up to and including discussion of his or her current leadership position; (b) a detailed discussion of a problem or situation at work in which the leader was asked to play a leadership role—handling of a problem or an issue at work, discussion of outcomes, and reflection on what might be done differently next time. The listener then crafted the conversation into a story form. The end product was a 2000- to 3000-word leadership story, in the actual words of the teller. Tellers reviewed an initial draft of the story to ensure accuracy and provide an opportunity to edit the written story.

The final step was the presentation of the story. Written copies of the story were distributed to all members of the group. The stories were read aloud by either the crafter or person whose story was being told. Discussion of general themes, story dilemmas, problems inherent in the story, leadership themes, recipes for actions, and multiple strategies and considerations were all part of the conversations that ensued.

The initial conversation or telling of the story provided an opportunity for both the storyteller and listener to reflect on the experience. Listener and teller inevitably raised different questions and concerns, as both become more aware of what is important about the story. Crafting the story from transcripts required the story crafter to think about how someone else's experiences compared with his or her own experiences; it provided the opportunity to consider how the problem or situation was handled, what options considered, what opportunities were missed

Self-Disclosure—The Researchers' Stories

As part of the process, we crafted own narratives of experience. Wright had been a superintendent and his story draws on his experiences as coach and school administrator. Danzig had been a teacher, administrator, and college professor and his story presents a few of the dilemmas faced in finding services for a chronically ill child. A brief excerpt from each of their stories is presented below and the complete stories can be found in Danzig and Wright, 2002.

Wright's Story.   Wright's story relates his own experiences growing up. He presents the story of someone growing up without a father, who challenges authority, and fights for the underdog. His first jobs as teacher and coach in rural and urban settings raise questions about who goes unserved by the system and why. His movement into school administration is almost immediate and as principal and then superintendent, he reflects on the dilemma raised by a strong work ethic and personal belief in hard work and the recognition that some children just don't fit the school or system and unless the system becomes more flexible, these children fail and drop out. He recalls,

So, I remember thinking that I'm the guy that believes in self-help. Here I was the guy that believed that if you want something out of this life, you've got to work hard to get, because that's the way I grew up. Do what's right and be responsible for your own success. So now, I was arguing for is let's make it easier and I was being told. "You're trying to give things away." I did not want to give things away, rather wanted to come up with some kind of a program where every kid could at least get a high school diploma. We weren't very sophisticated in those days, but I felt I was talking about something important. I was talking about making adjustments for kids that can't adjust. So, out of that whole discussion came, I think, came a philosophy that said **we're going to work with every child**. In spite of the fact that almost everybody says they believe in it, almost nobody did anything about it.

Wright describes his own evolution and recognition that school betterment requires changes to the deeply held and personal beliefs of individual teachers and administrators about children, curriculum, testing, and what it means to be educated. Self-scrutiny is a prerequisite to developing competence, as learner, teacher or administrator. Professional development is also enhanced through guided practice and reflection.

Danzig's Story.   Danzig's story highlights dilemmas of balancing professional responsibilities and family life. Danzig's experiences as a teacher, administrator, and college professor are informed by not only his education and professional experiences, but also his experiences as a parent raising four children and negotiating for services for a profoundly handicapped daughter. Danzig's story brings the personal into the professional realm, by exploring how his learning as a parent becomes part of his teaching, research, and service. Having to negotiate complex arrangements and boundaries among public and private schools, social service agencies, medical, and long-term care provides Danzig with first-hand experience making decisions about the educational, social, psychological, medical, and legal services. Danzig's evolution is from a naive college student being surprised at how newspaper reports of student protest differ from first-hand accounts to recognition of the human and institutional barriers that prevent services from being provided. Danzig also reframes professional development in ways that professionals, individually and collectively, learn to change themselves.

We went through lots of administrative hearings to get services, and sometimes, we'd leave those administrative hearings where people were telling us what was best for one of our children, and we would cry in frustration. As you walked out, you would have to tell yourself to absolutely not listen to the words or accept the recommendations. You quickly learn that it is almost impossible to change the ways others define situations. Sometimes it is personal, "we don't want to do it your way." Other times it is system driven, "we don't have the resources to do it your way." So you leave, you seek out new organizations and providers to get help, to provide services. When you go against the recommendations of professionals who are part of a system of providers, you realize pretty quickly that you have to leave, find other systems, because the system will work against you. Consciously or not, the system wants to take credit for its successes and blames others for its failures. And once you go against institutional norms, the system has someone to blame.

At particular points we had to make decisions about our children even though we didn't have enough information to make the right decision. You learn to make decisions, on limited knowledge. You look for people who seem to understand, who take for granted that what it is that you are looking for is best. Conventional wisdom does not take you to the right place. Conventional wisdom is block because it looks for solutions or answers to situations that can't be solved. But you still must do something, even though it may not be the best thing. Doing nothing sends a message that nothing can be done. If it's a wrong decision, change the wrong decision, but keep moving.

The two stories adopt a similar perspective, with primacy on the personal rather than organizational; the stories prioritize individual integrity and responsibility as prerequisites for institutional commitment and betterment.

Leadership Stories From the Participants

There were three critical issues that may have influenced the quality of participation, contributions, or attitudes of the administrators toward becoming seriously engaged in the professional development activities employed by the researchers, including the degree to which the participants were honest with themselves, fellow participants, and researchers in the development and sharing of their respective stories. The specific issues were researchers relationship with the district superintendent, the district superintendent's relationship with the administration, and the motivation of the administrators to share stories openly and honestly.

Researchers' Relationship With the Superintendent. One of the researchers and the district superintendent enjoyed a long-term professional relationship. They worked to promote state policies beneficial to education and collaborated on the development of a consortium involving multiple districts that created a comprehensive K–12 curriculum. The district superintendent also engaged one of the researchers to conduct a search for a top administrator and help revise board policies during the same time period that the project was underway. Knowing of the professional relationship that existed between the researchers and the district superintendent may have caused some of the participants to be less than candid during discussions, and especially during the development and sharing of individual stories.

Superintendent's Relationship With the Administration. The school district was a county accommodation school district with an elected superintendent of schools who also served as a one member governing board. All of the district administrators are appointed and serve at the pleasure of the governing board. There was casual talk that several of the district administrators were selected on the basis of personal relationships and/or political connections in the district. The remaining administrators were outsiders with no particular connection to the district superintendent other than the traditional employer–employee relationship. There appeared to be two perceptions held by the administrative team. One perception was that the county superintendent favored certain administrators, based on personal allegiances, and political considerations rather than educational administrative competence. A second and related perception was that elected officials care more about political considerations and positive publicity than about the education of children. Some administrators believed that producing good educational results was less important to their work evaluations, and the avoidance of poor publicity determined one's future in the district. The political focus of the county superintendent seemed to reinforce these perceptions, whether accurate or not.

Motivation of Administrators to Participate in the Story Crafting Project: Pros and Cons.   The motivation of administrators to participate in the professional development project varied:

- Wanting to develop their respective administrative skill and knowledge to perform better on the job, and/or move to a better position in the district or elsewhere.
- Participating in the project because of the potential to curry favor with the county superintendent by appearing to be seriously engaged in the project.
- Others may have believed that they could somehow damage their future in the district by making negative, or critical remarks, even where critique may have been warranted. Some administrators shared the view that the county superintendent would not tolerate criticism of district programs or the superintendent.
- Still others may have believed that if they revealed a lack of professional knowledge or discussed professional shortcomings that it might be reported to the county superintendent.
- Two of the administrators had also applied to the doctoral program led by the researchers and may have been motivated by a desire to enhance their doctoral applications and candidacy.

The researchers tried—to the extent possible—to provide a safe harbor in which the members of the administrative team would feel free to share their respective stories without fear of political reprisal, rejection, or peer criticism, as well as retribution from the county superintendent. To achieve that outcome the researchers took care to make their intentions clear, provide relevant research, and guide the participants through training sessions, activities, and discussions. They also took care to deal ethically and honestly with the participants, and to demonstrate respect for the individuals and their ideas. Finally, the researchers took care to assure the administrators that their points of view, opinions, remarks, and their stories would be held in strict confidence and would not be shared without the written permission of the participants.

We begin with selections from these stories, with limited comment or annotation. At the end of the chapter, we comment on the extent to which administrators reflected on story themes and were able to characterize the normative filters and knowledge that was embedded in their leadership stories. Some participants were able to make explicit the relevance of personal experience to decision making and subsequent actions. Some were also able to explicitly capture the multiple perspectives that were part of the stories. Others were able to characterize situations in which personal values and institutional values conflict, and how they manage the gap between the two.

Learning From Crisis: A Superintendent's Story

The first excerpt is from the governing board appointed superintendent of schools, whose major responsibility included the day-to-day operation of schools. He shared his story with us even though he knew that his contract was not being renewed. His story provides insight into his own background and experiences as student, teacher, administrator, and superintendent. This is followed by narratives of some of the participants in the year-long professional development activities.

Learning From Crisis: The Superintendent's Story

Probably the most difficult thing that I ever did in my educational career was when I was the principal at CS High School. I think it was about my third year in the district, and it was right after the new high school had opened. It was a new and beautiful school that we had planned and put together. On the first day of school, one of the alternative kids, one of the gangster kids, one of the kids that thought that he was a gang-wannabe type, which was unusual for that community, beat-up one of the high profile kids in this school. He beat him up in the lunchroom and beat him up badly, just smacked him up real bad. The kid who got beat up was a member of the football team and so several members of the football team took on this other group up, who were basically skateboard kids, into rock music and that type of thing. The kids from the football team then beat up a couple of the skateboard kids and then a couple of days later some of the skateboard kids found this football player by himself and beat him up. Within the first week of school we had had several fights, bad fights in that kids were hurt, and kids who needed to be stitched up, kids in the hospital.

A group of parents called me up and said that they wanted to meet with me. Two of the parents said that they had heard of these fights going on, that they were concerned about it, and that they were going to invite some other parents. They wanted to have a meeting with me, the principal. So, we set a time of 8 o'clock in the evening. I had been doing whatever on the campus that day and I told them that I would meet them in the cafeteria. I had a guard in the cafeteria and people were alarmed, and I was just totally shocked. Basically I went in and I said I would like to hear your concerns. The parents went on and on—schools were unsafe, that I hadn't done my job, that the kids were out of hand and they were going to demolish the school, that kids were afraid to go to classes and kids weren't going to school, that I had let it get out of hand, that I had been too strict with these kids and not strict enough with these other kids. The parents had a whole list of things that I had done wrong. So I just listened to it all and I was taken aback by all of it because I had been so consumed with it that I just hadn't been seeing all of the concerns that had been there. I just didn't know what to say and I told them that I was going to get a microphone so that I could talk to them. So I walked down to the gym, got a microphone, and as I was getting the microphone, I was kind of putting my thoughts together.

Basically I just told them that there were some things that I was going to do and laid out a plan of things that I was thinking of while I was getting the microphone. I quickly came up with a plan of action and certain activities I was going to do to stop this gang fighting that was going on, and the things that I could do to make the school safer. I said that we would have a meeting within one week and they would evaluate whether or not I was doing an effective job or not. I couldn't think of anything else to do. After I recommended all of these things, it was two weeks later when I met with parents again. At that meeting only two people showed up, the original two parents. They just told me that the parents liked what I was doing and that I was carrying through and what I had promised.

We found out that there other issues on the campus that I hadn't been aware of and that we needed to work on. Some of the things came from the discussions that I had with the kids. I'd call on different groups of kids and we'd have an open forum and they would just talk to me. Then we would try to do something about it. There were a few kids that were doing different things that I was not aware of. For instance one of the major issues was the fact that the males, the boys, were treating the girls very poorly. They were saying things to the girls, they were playing sexual games, harassment things, abuse things, just bad stuff that was going on. I would never have learned about these things if the fights hadn't happened and if we hadn't had these open forums. We found professional staff, and other people to work with the student body and by end of the school year I think we had approached issues that needed to be approached; it took a full year probably to get everything to do with those incidents resolved and handled. That time, less than nine months, was probably the most difficult situation that I had ever faced as an administrator. We needed to have some type of vehicle to find out what is going on in the school because on the surface, it wasn't always observable. Uncovering these issues and problems are now considered a normal part of our efforts to find out what was going on with the kids.

I think that the reason why I was able to deal with all those issues and other stuff is because I had the conviction that I could solve the problem and I was able to solve them. If you had heard the attacks, the things that were being said that night by the parents, you would just say the problems were just too big, too difficult. It never entered my mind that we were not going solve these problems. I just thought we could solve them. I promised the people that I could and we did. So I think that you need to have the confidence to go ahead and approach problems and hit them head on and to be up front with the people, communicate with the people.

The kind of things that I would have done differently has to do with communicating with others. I was communicating with student counsel, I was going to the PTA meetings, I was going to the booster club meetings. But I wasn't talking to a cross-section of the student body and that's what I needed to do. There was a group of students that felt disenfranchised, was disenfranchised and I needed to affirmatively go after that group. I needed to identify who they were, identify who the leaders of these different groups were, subgroups, cliques, or whatever you want to call these social groups. I needed to identify them, bring them in, talk to them, and communicate with them. That's what I did not do prior to this whole set of events. After that, we would take different social groups on campus and identify the kids in the skater group, the Hispanic group. I would have faculty and staff identify these kids and then we would go on retreats and work out issues and come back and work together as a group. That's what I would do. My educational experiences, while difficult in many ways, didn't prepare me for being at the center of all things. While I was principal at the high school, all problems centered on me, on the principal. The principal has to solve everything. And my first reaction was I can't solve it, I can't do everything. But instead of saying that, I began to bring in all of these people. And then I brought in all of these people and we would solve problems together.

The superintendent's story provides insight into his learning, and how learning from experience shaped his handling of events and school-related crisis. One idea that comes from this story is consideration of how leaders anticipate problems and how anticipation results in subsequent crisis (or problems) being averted (Forester, 1991). This raises a secondary question of how others will recognize this skill as leadership expertise, when the preferred outcome is that nothing or nothing bad happens (as opposed to problems or crisis happening). In this story, there are examples of both lack of anticipation (the superintendent's surprise at finding a crowd of angry parents in the cafeteria) and his application of prior learning (the importance of giving the media access and to their concerns for news and information). The fact that his contract was not renewed during the year that we were working there may speak to his inability to anticipate what was expected of him by the county superintendent/board and/or his willingness to do something about it.

Entering School Administration From Special Education Experiences

The next story is by a member of the administrative team with the most years of experience with the District. Her story is raises issues of gender and the requisite experience for entry into school administration through her background in special education.

Serving Special Education Children as Entry Into School Administration

Administrative Preferences

I give a great deal of importance, as far as my administrative style to being organized and personable. I believe it's important for people to be able to get along with each other. I do not like to work with haughty or arrogant people, and I therefore try not to be haughty or arrogant myself. I appreciate the classroom teacher's role, the role of the special educator, because I've done all those things. But I'm not a classroom teacher. I've never been a classroom teacher. So, it's important to me to be able to understand all the demands and the needs that they have. Something that had an effect on my professional practice or my career, I would have to say was the Effective Schools Movement and also the professor from California, where you did the Effective Teaching Skills, Madeline Hunter. Those two things were very useful to me and I have, I think, incorporated them, as far as being an effective teacher, an effective principal, and trying to accomplish the things that happen in an effective school.

I enjoy being an administrator. I do not wish to go back to the classroom. I like doing what I do. I think my organizational skills are quite good and I'm able to accomplish things, even on a long time line. I can plan. I'm very careful with my calendar and I'm dependable, as far as following a timeline and keeping on schedule with assignments that I'm given. My first superintendent that was my mentor for a number of years has positively influenced me in this district. Dr. Arthur Parker, who was, I think, an extremely effective personnel manager for our district for a long time, has influenced me positively. He used to spend a lot of time talking to me, sharing his insights and his background. I think I have profited from a lot of the things that he shared with me and talked to me about.

I have a couple of other skills too. I communicate well in both verbal and written expression. I have very limited, marginal computer skills and very, very poor math. But, I am learning and I appreciate the technology. I actually enjoy the things that I'm able to do with the computer. I have, I think, a very rich and varied background, both as a person and a teacher, therapist, and an administrator. I enjoy working with the Accommodation School, and I like working with the kids with special needs. I've always done that. I enjoy working as an administrator in the detention schools, perhaps more than any other assignment I've had with the regional school district. I was apprehensive at first, and I was really surprised to find that I liked working in the detention centers. I like working with detention staff members and I have no fears or problems in working with the population. The teachers are good to work with and the kids, students for the most part, are appreciative of what we do. I plan to work for approximately another eight to ten years. This, by the way, is the only district I've ever worked for in Arizona. I've worked for the district for 23 years. I've enjoyed the work that I do and I think I've been appropriately compensated and rewarded for the things that I've done, so I'm happy to be in the district and I have a very positive feeling about the future of our district and our programs.

In presenting her story, Diane relates her early travel as part of a military family, and a conservatism born out of Depression-era parents. She indicates that she is a good student (except for math) and her entry into special education is based on considerations of the job market of the 1960s rather than zeal to work with a particular population of children. She leaves the workforce to raise her own family and presents a view toward balance and health in one's personal and professional life, just as she has balanced family and profession. As an administrator, she defines herself as a negotiator and peacemaker, a good colleague and team player. She is mostly supportive of the work of teachers, though she has never been a teacher. In the telling of her story, Diane told us that she "tries to make life and the job as pleasant and comfortable for people as possible." Diane's story draws heavily on the moral lessons of her parents, where leaders are organized, make good use of available resources, and conserve time and money. There is less room for conflict in this style, and Diane told us that, in her many years as a school administrator, she has never fired anyone. She sees her leadership as more personal, with the goal of getting people to enjoy their lives.

Rural Work Ethic and Moving Up the Ladder

The next excerpt is about growing up in a rural community. It is a story that relates to gender, ethnicity, and work ethic.

An Administrator's Story: Moving Up the Ladder

Entering School Administration

I interviewed at MP District for an assistant principal's position, the superintendent asked my viewpoint regarding bilingual education. I told him I did not believe in it, stating students should go through immersion in order to be more successful. He did not hire me as an assistant principal, but he did offer me a teaching position. I accepted and he assigned me to a third grade bilingual classroom. I had no experience teaching bilingual children, I remember staying up nights researching effective strategies and methodologies for teaching these children. During that year the superintendent came to visit my classroom several times to see how I was doing. The beginning of the second year in the district, he came in to see me and asked me how I felt about Bilingual Education, I responded that it was the toughest thing I had ever done, but I was a believer, and understood how imperative it was for children to learn foundational skills in their own language before attempting to learn English. In November, he assigned me as interim principal. At the end of the school year, he asked me if I would take the principalship at the same elementary school. I stayed at the district for a total of four years. The superintendent has remained my friend and mentor throughout my professional career.

I was hired in the DI Unified School District as an assistant principal for a new middle school. The district advertised for planning principals. Opening up a school was the best experience I have ever had. Luckily, Phoenix Preparatory had just opened and the principal there at the time would share some of the problems they were facing, simple things like beginning school and forgetting to order clocks for the classrooms. Furniture, equipment, and supplies were not delivered on time. The principal and I got to hire our own staff, which was in tune with a true middle school philosophy. The school was divided into four pods with seven classrooms, seven teachers and 200 students in each pod. Each grade level shared a common patio, where they constructed a bird aviary and raised cockatiels and lovebirds, assembled a greenhouse and learned about propagations, and built a fishpond. The eighth grade curriculum called for Life Science. The seventh grade science curriculum physical science, the patio had a simulated outer space project that displayed different backgrounds for studying the characteristics of outer space.

Class scheduling incorporated different clubs. Clubs included yearbook, school paper, school council, National Junior Honor Society, Jr. ROTC, ham radio, dance, art, woodshop, etiquette, culture, writing, sewing, cooking. There were after school sports and clubs would meet for activities after school as needed. The idea was to keep students to busy to get into trouble. My experience at Dysart Middle School was very valuable and very rewarding. It was very hard work and very long hours.

Shortly after that, the school was running so smoothly that I soon felt that there was no challenge, so I applied for a central office position and was promoted to that, to the position, without a problem. I worked in tandem with the assistant superintendent as the academic support director. I was very fortunate to work with a person who placed no restraints on me or my abilities. I learned so much from this position. I traveled all over the United States, and was given the opportunity to visit schools with effective programs. My job was to come back to the district, report my findings to the cabinet and to the teachers and principals. I did a lot of teacher training and staff development. I trained principals, also.

I resigned from that position in 1998 to move to Alaska. I traveled to Alaska in April and applied for a principalship at Northern Lights Elementary School in the Anchorage district. I was offered a contract. My sister, a registered nurse, and I made plans to move to Alaska together. I sold my home and, as we were preparing to make the move, actually, she suffered a serious heart attack. I could not leave her by herself. She's my little sissy, so I stayed. I had no home, no job, nor any job prospects at this time.

However, I was looking through the paper one day and I did find a job advertisement for a principalship in the County Regional School District. I applied, interviewed, and was hired in August of 1998. I started my career in the East Valley, at a middle school. I was transferred at the end of the year to an elementary school serving a homeless population of children, and transferred again in March to the district office. I must say, working for County Regional School District has given me a multitude of educational experiences.

Administration and Oppositional Behaviors—
The Principal of an Alternative School

The next story concerns the principal at one of the "alternative schools" that serves children that have been excluded or self-selected out of traditional school environments. Her story is one of her own opposition to authority.

Personal and Political Power in Becoming a School Principal

I preach the Golden Rule to my students. You treat people the way that you want to be treated and I do believe good things will happen to those that do their best to become positive role models. I do see a lot of goodness in my students especially when they help each other. We have new students coming in and out all the time and the veteran students help the new students and it's very touching. And I do see a tremendous amount of empathy among them. And they're very lovely children. It's unfortunate that because we're in an alternative school, a lot of people associate those students as being bad children. But there are no bad children. They're children that made a few poor choices. And who hasn't? I was very much a late bloomer so I think I have a tremendous amount of empathy.

Being that I'm a young administrator, people sometimes get the wrong idea of why I'm an administrator. But, I was always that type of person that you couldn't tell me no. You couldn't say no to me or tell me that I couldn't do that. When they told me I couldn't be an administrator because I was too young, so don't even bother trying, I tried, and I became a principal. When they told me at Loyola that I was too young to go into a doctoral program, to take my superintendent certificate, and to take those classes that went along with it, they said that they expected me to do very high on some type of a test and I said,

"Oh, I can do that." And I did it. And they said I would never finish because it would be too grueling because I hadn't had that many life experiences. And I graduated with a 4.0 and I was one of the first to graduate from the licensure program, even though I'm still ABD. And I told them I would do that. I told them that I would be one of the first to finish and that I would graduate with a 4.0 because I was committed and I wanted it. And I was one of the youngest certified superintendents in the nation, especially with a 4.0 GPA. I think I might be one of only ones from such a prestigious university. I was one of the stellar students and I'm proud of it. I worked hard and I always had to work a little bit harder because of my age. I deserved it.

You know I'm proud of what I accomplished. I guess, as I get older, I won't have to worry as much. Every year I get fewer and fewer questions about "Are you really an administrator?" And if I can accomplish what I achieved, anybody can accomplish if your mind and your heart and your soul are with it. That's what I preach to these at risk children, that they can to whatever they want to do and if I can help them reach that goal, it's mutually reinforcing. If they achieve, if they win, I win. And that's the advantage of working with an at-risk group and I wouldn't have it any other way. You know, people say, "Why don't you go to school now that you have all this experience and work for one of the wealthier districts?" To me, that's not as challenging. Those kids have things handed to them, even though I know they have issues. It's not as challenging as helping homeless or helping those that have had a really bad experience at the former school. Now you have them and you want to make it a positive experience for them. Sometimes I'm hard on these kids. Maybe they will go off to college, but maybe that's not their goal. But I want to have the resources for them, so that they can become productive members of society.

You know, a lot of the kids think that it's academics that should be stressed. To me, it's more important that they grow up to be good people, giving people in the community. Grades are not everything. I mean, how good is it to be a straight "A" student and murderer? I would rather have someone that works really hard, and maybe obtains "Cs," but gives back to the community and makes a difference in someone's life. And so, if I can affect someone's life in a positive manner, maybe they can take what they've learned from me and from their teachers, who are phenomenal, and do that for somebody else. And I see a lot of that going on at East Valley. I see that the kids are helping each other and I see a lot of good energy at the school and my future will always be like I was once told, if you just help someone once every day and just do something nice for them, you know, it'll come back. And I find that when I am working; it is my goal to continue doing good and at least attempting to do good and attempting to make a positive impact on someone's life.

Allison shares her own anti-authority sentiments growing up and in school. Her schooling experience raises the issue her own sensitivity to criticism and the damaging effects of a culture of criticism that pervades many schools. Her resistance helps to salvage her own reputation and self-esteem. Her subsequent achievement allows her to beat "them" at their own game. Not by accident, the student population that she works with in the alternative school displays the very same behaviors that she exhibited while growing up. The difference, perhaps, was a supportive father, with resources to minimize the damage and penalties of her youth, while providing opportunities for future successes.

The next story is a brief excerpt from a principal that was relieved of his responsibility as principal at the end of the school year. His story considers the importance of mentoring in a career as a teacher, doctoral student, and school administrator.

Leadership and Mentoring

My first years in the profession were great. DF, Teacher of the Year, mentored me. Dale was my next door neighbor teaching math, and was always helpful and helped my maturity in the profession on a nearly daily basis. I still say today that anyone who can be a success in middle school can probably be successful at any level. When I had the chance to transfer and be a part of a new high school, I did so eagerly. I taught at that high school and another high school and to this day I can say that I enjoyed the experience, and the experiences I had in the district.

In 1987 I went through a difficult and messy divorce that still in some ways haunts me. I was fortunate however to meet a wonderful woman in 1988, and began a relationship and marriage that still lasts and prospers today. After marrying in 1988 I was encouraged by my new wife to finish a doctoral program. It would require me to leave the school and that took no small amount of courage. However, I made the decision, relocated, and began work as a lecturer at the College of Education and be a full time doctoral student. At the university, a number of interesting and provocative individuals influenced me. All these folks had a positive influence on my program in someway. For example, when writing comprehensive examinations one of my exams was on the sociology of education. Four other people wrote on the sociology of education as well, but took the class the semester before I did. I had no background on the question I received, but somehow, I passed that part of the comprehensive exam. I was either lucky, or perhaps others were taken in with my charming personality. (Earlier I mentioned I had poor vision. I had RK surgery done, and for more than 10 years I was able to go without glasses. Though I now wear the darned things again, my vision is no where as bad as it once was.)

I successfully defended my dissertation in April of 1993. Realistically my dissertation is probably gathering dust in some corner of the library, but I was proud of finishing it, and being able to put letters after my name. In June of 1993, Ann and I began a fairly long sojourn as gypsies, We moved to Oregon, then the Navajo reservation, then the western slope of Colorado, back to beautiful Gila Bend, Arizona and finally now as a Regional Principal for the County Regional Schools. My position as a Regional Principal is due significantly to the encouragement and help provided by mentors. That help is now recognized and thanks offered. If I stretch, I can say that my career as a school administrator has been average. Prior to being regional Principal the schools I worked at were either troubled schools, or schools that were less the gems of desire for other administrators. I don't know what the future holds and perhaps that is the best. I am still not sure what I want to be when I grow up, and maybe the best thing is to just take one day at a time, and do the best I can.

This story is also about personal growth and resilience. Graduate work and doctoral degree represent major events in life. The entry into school administration seems less based on commitment to serve than on continuation of his own growth and learning that begins in college and continues through his graduate training and doctoral degree. However, his strengths may lie more in the intellectual arena concerning the study of schools and society than in the administrative practice domain, which requires a different set of skills, temperament, and energy.

The next story also looks at an administrator who spent years in the classroom prior to entry into administration. Her commitment to be an administrator and to learning is based on a service ethic; she connects professional development with her own personal growth as teacher and administrator.

Learning by Doing: Work Ethic and Administration

Learning to Be a School Administrator

One thing I learned more quickly as an administrator was that politics affects just about every single thing you do as an administrator. That's been my struggle. It's taken an enormous amount of discipline to learn to separate what happens on a district level from the school level, keeping what happens at a district level from falling into the classroom; not letting it affect the quality of teaching; not letting it affect morale. It means sometimes being the bad guy. Instead of saying, "Well, so and so told me we have to do this and that," you have to say, "I decided we're going to do this and that." Everybody gets to be mad at you. But, number one, I believe in this district and number two, whether my staff knows it or not, I protect them. It's a hard role, leadership, because sometimes you are alone, a lot of time actually. It is a middle management position. You are stuck in the middle. You try to marry the expectations of one level with the needs of another level and it's a hard match, a really hard match. I think the beauty of the struggle, though, is that it made me a stronger person. It allowed me to develop my self-confidence and be willing to stand up to any kind of criticism. Leadership means developing a vision and doing everything possible to make that vision come true. It means getting into the politics. It means climbing over the gossip. It means protecting yourself and your staff, empowering your faculty and your staff and giving everybody what they need to be successful. I've learned that from being a principal. Until you've experienced it, no one can teach it to you.

I think education is like being a parent. I take my role and my responsibilities very seriously. You need to assess the needs of the students at your particular school and then meet those needs. I am a proponent of holistic education. I think we have to educate the whole child. In order to educate the whole child, you have to have the whole picture. That means setting up partnerships, getting a nurse, going to an agency and begging for dental care, providing snacks, etc. I deal with a population that suffers from diabetes, so I bring in nutrition specialists. You do whatever you need to do so that you clear any obstacle that prevents students from learning. My philosophy is back to basics. I believe in reading, math, and writing. I believe in students being given the opportunity to achieve to their highest ability. Those three subjects should be integrated into whatever we are teaching—social studies, science, etc. I want all kids to have the opportunity to learn.

I haven't really had another career except education. I worked while I went to college from 2pm to 10pm every night allowing me to go to school in the mornings. I worked for an awesome guy, an ordained Pentecostal minister. He allowed me to study in a hole-in the-wall room for a couple of hours helping me pull through work and school. I was very fortunate. Because of this job, I drive my custodians crazy. I can tell if something hasn't been mopped in three days because of the way the circles form. Crazy stuff. Outside of that job, I have only been in education.

When I retire I am going to travel. Hopefully I will travel internationally. I am also a big believer in volunteering. Where, I don't know, but I will continue to volunteer. Maybe in a dog shelter, working in schools, but wherever, I will be volunteering. Oh and my ten thousand dogs will be with me too! Actually, I only have 9 dogs, all the homeless ones I found out and around the reservation, while working at my school!

J's story reveals some of her early experiences and socialization as a teacher. These experiences contribute to her perspective of administration as service, and her own growth in appreciating what it takes to best serve the needs of children. Her sensitivity to children, especially those who have been placed at a disadvantage by traditional schools and life circumstances, gives her a mental toughness that allows her to manage the clearly difficult politics at the district in which she works.

REFLECTIVE AND UNREFLECTIVE STORIES: SOME PRELIMINARY DISCUSSION

One criticism of the narrative form is that it is "inherently uncritical, partaking of a script composed elsewhere, by others, with the purpose of maintaining the maldistributions of power within the larger culture" (Barone, 2001, p. 169, citing Goodson, 1995). Stories that are not subject to questioning and scrutiny risk presenting an uncritical account of personal and professional experiences that fail to recognize the structures of power and privilege present in the story. These criticisms imply that analysis and interpretation of story and events are important components of experiencing a narrative. Story discussions and analysis provide opportunity to scrutinize multiple themes related to power, culture, class, race, and gender, which are part of the story. Without analysis and reflection, important elements of the story are likely to go unnoticed and important actions or possibilities missed.

Goodson's (1995) caution points to a need for sharing stories with others and hearing multiple interpretations and meanings of stories. Schön (1991) referred to this reframing of experience as the *reflective turn*, the moment where inquirers explicitly look inward, look at themselves engaged in the action, to understand how biography and experience contribute to which questions are asked, what perspectives are noticed, valued, and/or disputed. Reflection allows for a reconstruction of events in which embedded values, overlooked consequences, alternative meanings, and interpretations are made explicit. Discussing an actual story provides the opportunity to reflect on actions and to reframe one's understanding of actions and decisions.

The extent of reflection and reframing of events is affected by multiple factors: (a) How detailed is the narrative? Does it include details of decisions, motives, actions, and behaviors? (b) How safe is the environment? Are individuals and the group willing to confront major issues and values in the stories? Are they willing or able to express views which are critical or unflattering? Stories that include greater details about experiences and actions allow for greater scrutiny. Stories that detail hardship and resilience, relationships with others (parents, siblings, and peers), experiences in school, experiences with authority, and entry into the leadership domain provide a pathway to consider leadership and the development process. One hoped for outcome of group discussion is that the values and assumptions of both teller and listener will become more explicit. This is not so different from what Senge et al. (1999) called "surfacing mental models" to bring to the surface some of the underlying concerns, expectations, and values that people use to make decisions and take actions. This inquiry was seen as a central part of the story process as well as central to the study and practice of leadership.

Tacit Knowledge and Practical Knowhow Embedded in the Stories of Leadership

Stories provide a basis for understanding how people think and act in the world, of how expertise is gained in the real world. Stories allow practitioners to consider and inspect the informal systems in the workplace, which exist side by side with the more formal systems, which are used to define expertise and practice. Stories provide an opportunity for practitioners to share their experiences. Stories are a way for practitioners to move from superficial to deeper issues embedded in practice; they allow professionals to identify some of the difference between how they might have constructed a problem and how other practitioners constructed the situation. The story leads both novices and experienced practitioners to consider their own choices in what to select as important and what is peripheral to the story. A good story permits the listener to examine her own filters, or biases, to reach a more complete understanding of what is important to the story. The story elicits reflection on how problems are defined, specific situations are handled, and actions are taken. Stories encourage the sharing of knowledge, from expert to novice, as both reflect on the strengths and limits of experience (Barone, 2001; Coles, 1989; Danzig, 1999a, 1999b).

SUMMARY AND QUESTIONS
FOR FURTHER CONSIDERATION AND DISCUSSION

Crafting and sharing stories raises four important questions for readers to consider when viewing the importance of narrative to professional development for learner-centered leaders: (a) What is the power of personal biography to leadership and decision making? (b) What are some of the multiple perspectives people bring to the workplace and why is this important? (c) What are the expert processes in which leaders engage during situations with limited knowledge and ambiguously defined problems? (d) How do school administrators map the formal and informal organizations to anticipate potential hazards and separate relevant details?

   The narrative experience that is described in this chapter indicates that education leaders need a safe harbor, away from the politics and conflicting demands of district and schools, to talk, reflect, and learn. Such a setting would allow school administrators to discuss and reflect on issues of concern and problems of practice. Though the story-based professional development allowed some opportunities for open discussion, it does not automatically provide a safe environment to discuss many of the very issues needing attention. One goal of professional development, along with coaching and mentoring, would be to develop such a safe harbor for school administrators to turn for help. Particularly in places with a strong press for academic accountability, the opportunity for leaders to adopt postures in which they are more vulnerable, such as those required for learning, may require special nurturing. Otherwise, school leaders may find themselves vulnerable to many pressures from within and outside the school and district.

   A related understanding that comes from the stories and story discussions is the need for administrators to develop some sort of critical event review. Particularly regarding serious situations, there is need to review what the problem was, what actions were taken, how effective these actions were, and what might be done to improve performance, assuming the possibilities of subsequent occurrences. In this sense, the stories also serve as case studies of administrative actions or performances and allowed for nonthreatening discussions of prior administrative behaviors and actions.

These stories model how knowledge is constructed and communicated and the participants developed a clearer understanding of how other administrators talk about and approach problems in ways similar or different ways to their own ways. Crafting and then reflecting on stories helped school leaders develop a more expert understanding of how they learn and how knowledge is shared. The stories model how knowledge is constructed and communicated and the participants developed a clearer understanding of how other administrators talk about and approach problems in ways similar to or different from their own ways. Crafting and then reflecting on stories helped school leaders develop a more expert understanding of how they learn and how knowledge is shared.

Does story-based professional development make someone a more effective leader? The power of stories is something we have witnessed and there is no debate about the impact of stories on learning. Crafting stories has many functions for the individual and the organization, yet organizational decisions often reflect the belief that the time and space necessary are not worth benefits. People make sense of their past. They place themselves in a tangible present. Within written or verbal communication they draw others into a narrative and a deeper sense of their point or purpose. They also learn from their mistakes in-practice and learn to reflect on-practice. Professional communities are built in the learning that is created in these personal and professional conversations. Through sharing stories, people reveal the unseen in a common lived experience, the rules and artifacts of a system (Halverson, 2003; Huber & Whelan, 1999; Quong, Walker, & Bodycott, 1999; Robillard, 2003; Rust, 1999).

For experience to become more than war stories, however, a form of critical scrutiny and written inspection is necessary. Looking at leadership stories of Australian headmasters, Quong et al. (1999) argued that, even when stories are often left unexamined or even unnoticed, they present a framework for taking advantage of the learning opportunity represented in the stories. Stories provide insight into system structures. The basic structure of stories provides for understanding how people give context, how they become aware of and use intuition, and how values and beliefs impact leaders' decision making.

In his report to the National College for School Leadership in Britain, Weindling (2003) reviewed programs for school leader development in the United States and the United Kingdom. The leadership development program from NCSL New Visions Programme for Early Headship was an example of a new approach. "Most noticeable is the combination of features (drawn from a body of theory and good practice), which are integrated around an explicitly constructivist theory of learning that emphasizes dialogue, reflection and the use of learning sets" (Weindling, 2003, p. 16). The program recruits approximately 300 new heads each year who work in 20 regional groups of 8–12 people with a facilitator and a consultant. Over the year, the groups meet for a 2-day retreat followed by eight single sessions. Narrative forms and storytelling form an integral part of this development program through the use of journaling and case studies. Storytelling is a beginning to having professional conversation. Weindling makes further comments: "Probably the most prevalent concept that runs through leadership programmes is the use of reflection in a variety of forms" (Weindling, 2003, p. 18).

If professionals are expected to learn from experience, they must learn ways to capture and reflect on these experiences. Learning from prior experience requires discussion and reflection, of what happened, what it meant, and what to do about it in the future. This learning does not necessarily come from breaking down into a set of component parts. Practitioners must also learn to recognize how actions are connected to cultural norms, to initial experiences growing up, to institutional histories, and to professional socialization on the job. Leadership is learning to tell one's story in a way that is understandable to others and learning that there are other stories that are equally powerful determinants of actions.

SUGGESTIONS FOR FURTHER READING ON NARRATIVE, LEARNING, AND PROFESSIONAL DEVELOPMENT FOR SCHOOL LEADERS

This chapter argues that learning to lead a school is not the same as applying universally generalizable principles. Reading and discussing abstract theories of leadership need to be combined with opportunities to experience what leaders do and how it feels to be a leader (Bridges & Hallinger, 1997; English, 1995). Practice and experience are fundamental to the development of expertise in the area of complex problem solving. Situating learning in a real world context makes the new knowledge more meaningful and usable (Hallinger, Leithwood, & Murphy, 1993; Leithwood & Steinbach, 1995). These understandings point to the importance of blending theory with careful consideration of its meaning in practice. Professional development must ensure that beginners will learn from their experiences (and mistakes) on the way to achieving expert status.

Recent literature on cognitive psychology extends understanding of how reflection functions in the learners' route toward expertise. Expertise develops as the result of "reflective skills," the ability to think more deeply about a problem, and the ability to take action or make adjustments accordingly (Bransford, Brown, & Cocking, 2000). Short and Rinehart's (1993) research on the reflective activities in a leadership training program concludes that learners are able to move from a lower level of expertise, always describing the surface features of a situation or problem, to a higher level of expertise. They are more likely to see the underlying patterns and deep structure of problems, resort to more extensive knowledge base, react more quickly, and offer more alternatives.

It is also important to situate reflection and knowledge acquisition in practical contexts so learners recognize when and how to use knowledge properly (Bridges & Hallinger, 1997; Clandinin & Connelly, 2000). Expert practice includes a relevant knowledge base *and* the circumstances in which it is applied. Expertise is part of a complex performance rather than a discrete piece of information (Shulman, 1986). Experts take action and make adjustments during the act. They also reconsider these actions after the fact. Similarly, administrative practice is a complex art, which combines thinking abstractly, weighing prior experience, and taking action. No two performances are ever exactly the same because no two sets of conditions are ever exactly alike. Expertise comes from this combination of action and reflection. Expertise is enhanced as one learns to adjust one's performance based on these key factors and one's experiences with them. Learning from one's prior actions is basic to the development of expertise.

The emphasis on leadership stories (in training and development programs) requires a practitioner to develop a more accurate understanding of context (Glasman &

Glasman, 1997). Therefore, learners must have explicit opportunities to reflect in- and on-action (Bennis, 2003; Clandinin & Connelly, 2000; Schön, 1991). Reflection is the very process of learning and practitioners engage in a dialogue of thinking and doing both during an event and afterward. Tacit knowledge becomes manifest; the internal, implicit route toward expertise is externalized and the foundation of new knowledge acquisition is set in place.

Leadership requires action in the face of dynamic situations involving complex and interwoven themes (Gardner, 1995; Hallinger et al., 1993; Heifetz, 1994; Heifetz & Linsky, 2002). If leaders are to learn from experience and not make the same mistakes over and over again, there must be opportunities to reflect on these actions. Narratives and stories provide one opportunity to reflect on practice.

Narratives and stories are designed first to externalize the otherwise internal and autonomous expertise process. The emphasis on self-knowledge and learning from experience requires the learner to examine closely how one moves from novice to expert (Bennis, 2003; Clandinin & Connelly, 2000; Hallinger et al., 1993). That is, what prior knowledge do experts need, and how do they adjust themselves to different practical situations and learn from experience? The process toward expertise is not linear with clear-cut starting and ending points, but an ongoing circle where reflection, application, and growth occur again and again. School life is increasingly complex and school leaders are facing ambiguous and ill-defined situations. School leaders need to examine their own beliefs about the complexity of teaching, learning, and school leadership, which combines abstract thought processes, concentrated study, and practice.

REFERENCES

Ackerman, R., & Maslin-Ostrowski, P. (2002). *The wounded leader: How real leadership emerges in times of crisis.* San Francisco: Jossey-Bass.

Aspy, D., Aspy, C., & Quinn, P. (1993). What doctors can teach teachers about problem-based learning. *Educational Leadership, 50*(7), 22–25.

Barone, T. (2001). *Touching eternity: The enduring outcomes of teaching.* New York: Teachers College Press.

Bennis, W. (2003). *On becoming a leader: Updated and expanded with a new introduction.* Cambridge, MA: Perseus.

Bennis, W. (2000). The leader as storyteller. In W. Bennis (Ed.), *Managing the dream: Reflections on leadership and change* (pp. 273–282). Cambridge, MA: Perseus.

Bransford, J., Brown, A. L., & Cocking, R. R. (Eds.). (2000). *How people learn: Brain, mind, experience, and school: Expanded edition.* Washington, DC: National Academy Press.

Bridges, E. M., & Hallinger, P. (1997). Using problem-based learning to prepare educational leaders. *Peabody Journal of Education, 72*(2), 131–146.

Bruner, J. (1996). *The culture of education.* Cambridge, MA: Harvard University Press.

Burton, J. (1990). *Conflict: Resolution and prevention.* New York: St. Martin's.

Clandinin, D. J., & Connelly, F. M. (2000). *Narrative inquiry: Experience and story in qualitative research.* San Francisco, CA: Jossey-Bass.

Clandinin, J., & Connelly, F. M. (1991). Narrative and story in practice and research. In D. Schön (Ed.), *The reflective turn* (pp. 257–282). New York: Teachers College Press.

Coles, R. (1989). *The call of stories.* Cambridge, MA: Harvard University Press.

Coles, R. (2000). *Lives of moral leadership.* New York: Random House.

Cooper, J. (1995). The role of narrative and dialogue in constructivist leadership. In L. Lambert, D. Walker, D. Zimmerman, J. Cooper, M. Lambert, M. Gardner, P. J. Slack (Eds.), *The constructivist leader* (pp. 121–133). New York: Teachers College Press.

Czarnaiawska, B. (1997). *Narrating the organization: Dramas of institutional identity*. Chicago: University of Chicago Press.

Danzig, A. (1997a). Leadership stories: What novices learn by crafting the stories of experienced administrators. *Journal of Educational Administration, 35*(2), 122–137.

Danzig, A. (1997b). Building leadership capacity through narrative. *Educational Leadership and Administration, 9,* 49–59.

Danzig, A. (1999a). How might leadership be taught? The use of story and narrative to teach leadership. *International Journal of Leadership in Education: Theory and Practice, 2*(2), 117–131.

Danzig, A. (1999b). The contribution of stories to leadership development. *International Studies in Educational Administration, 27*(1), 11–19.

Danzig, A., with the assistance of D. Beckel, L. Harrison, B. Marsh, K. Rolle, S. Rossow, N. Sebring, B. Spaulding, and M. Treviño. (1996). *Educational leadership stories with implications for a standards-based education system: Report to the Colorado Commission on Higher Education.* ERIC Clearinghouse on Educational Management. (ERIC Document Reproduction Service No. ED401615)

Danzig, A., & Harris, K. (1996). Building competence by writing and reflecting on stories of practice. *Journal of Educational and Psychological Consultation, 7*(2), 193–204.

Danzig, A., & Wright, W. (2002). *Science versus service: Narrative and story-based professional development with school administrators at a county regional school district.* Paper presented in Division A—Symposium, New Models of Professional Development for Learner-Centered Leadership at the annual meeting of the American Educational Research Association, April 1–5, 2002, New Orleans, LA.

De Pree, M. (1989). *Leadership is an art.* New York: Dell.

De Pree M. (1993). *Leadership jazz.* New York: Dell.

DuFour, R. (2002, May). The learning-centered principal. *Educational Leadership, 59*(8), 12–15.

English, F. W. (1995). Toward a reconsideration of biography and other forms of life writing as a focus for teaching educational administration. *Educational Administration Quarterly, 31*(2), 202–223.

Gardner, H. (1995). *Leading minds: An anatomy of leadership.* New York: Basic Books.

Glasman, N. S., & Glasman, L. D. (1997). Connecting the preparation of school leaders to the practice of school leadership. *Peabody Journal of Education, 72*(2), 3–20.

Goodson, I. (1995). The story so far: Personal knowledge and the political. In J. Hatch & R. Wisniewski (Eds.), *Life history and narrative* (pp. 89–98). London: Falmer.

Hallinger, P., Leithwood, K., & Murphy, J. (1993). *Cognitive perspectives on educational leadership.* New York: Teachers College Press.

Halverson, R. (2003). Systems of practice: How leaders use artifacts to create professional community in schools. *Education Policy Analysis Archives.*

Heifetz, R. (1994). *Leadership without easy answers.* Cambridge, MA: Belknap Press of Harvard University Press.

Heifetz, R., & Linsky, M. (2002). *Leadership on the line.* Cambridge, MA: Harvard Business School.

Huber, J., & Whelan, K. (1999). A marginal story as a place of possibility: Negotiating self on the professional knowledge landscape. *Teaching and Teacher Education, 15,* 381–396.

Jaworski, J. (1996). *Synchronicity: The inner path of leadership.* San Francisco: Berrett-Koehler.

Johnson, M. (1992). *Redefining leadership: A case study of Hollibrook Elementary School.* University of Illinois at Urbana-Champagne, Urbana, IL: National Center for School Leadership. (ERIC Document Reproduction Service No. ED360687)

Kiltz, G., Danzig, A., & Szescy, E. (2004). Learner centered leadership: A mentoring model for the professional development of school administrators. *Mentoring and Tutoring: Partnership in Learning, 12*(2), 135–153.

Leithwood, K., & Steinbach, R. (1995). *Expert problem solving: Evidence from school and district leaders.* Albany, NY: SUNY Press.

McDrury, J., & Alterio, M. (2003). *Learning through storytelling in higher education: Using reflection & experience to improve learning.* Sterling, VA: Routledge.

Murphy, J. (2002). Reculturing the profession of educational leadership: New blueprints. *Educational Administration Quarterly, 38*(2), 176–191.

Oakes, J., Quartz, K. H., Ryan, S., & Lipton, M. (2000). *Becoming good American schools: The struggle for civic virtue in education reform.* San Francisco: Jossey-Bass.

Polkinghorne, D. (1995). Narrative configuration in qualitative analysis. *International Journal of Qualitative Studies in Education, 8*(1), 5–24.

Putnam, R. W. (1991). Recipes and reflective learning. In D. Schön (Ed.), *The reflective turn* (pp. 145–163). New York: Teachers College Press.

Quong, T., Walker, A., & Bodycott, P. (1999). Exploring and interpreting leadership stories. *School Leadership & Management, 19,* 441–453.

Riessman, C. (1993). *Narrative research.* Thousand Oaks, CA: Sage.

Robillard, A. (2003). It's time for class: Toward a more complex pedagogy of narrative. *Class English, 66*(1).

Schön, D. (Ed.). (1991). *The reflective turn: Case studies in and on educational practice.* New York: Teachers College Press.

Senge, P. (1990, Fall). The leader's new work: Building learning organizations. *Sloan Management Review,* pp. 7–23.

Senge, P., Kleiner, A., Roberts, C., Ross, R., Roth, G., & Smith, B. (1999). *The dance of change.* New York: Doubleday.

Short, P., & Rinehart, J. (1993). Reflection as a means of developing expertise. *Educational Administration Quarterly, 29,* 501–521.

Shulman, L. (1986). Paradigms and research programs in the study of teaching: A contemporary perspective. In M. C. Wittrock (Ed.), *Handbook of research in teaching,* (3rd ed.). New York: Macmillan.

Shulman, J., & Mesa-Bains, A. (1993). *Diversity in the classroom: A casebook for teachers and teacher educators.* Philadelphia: Research for Better Schools & Lawrence Erlbaum Associates, Inc.

Slater, R., & Teddlie, C. (1992). Towards a theory of school effectiveness and leadership. *School Effectiveness and School Improvement, 3*(4), 242–257.

Stepien, W., & Gallagher, S. (1993). Problem-based learning: As authentic as it gets. *Educational Leadership, 50*(7), 25–28.

Vickers, G. (1995). *The art of judgment: A study of policy making.* Thousand Oaks, CA: Sage.

Weindling, D. (2003). *Leadership development in practice: Trends and innovations.* (Full Report Summer 2003—A review of programme literature carried out for National College for School Leadership.) National College for School Leadership.

Welch, J. (1998). *Jack Welch speaks: Wisdom from the world's greatest business leader* [compiled by Janet C. Lowe]. New York: Wiley.

Wortham, S. (2001). *Narratives in action: A strategy for research and analysis.* New York: Teachers College Press.

Moral Issues in a Test-Driven Accountability Agenda: Moral Challenges for Learning-Centered Leadership

Robert J. Starratt
Boston College

This chapter will address important moral issues in the context of state mandated high-stakes tests and the moral responsibilities of school leaders to respond to these moral issues. Initially through a case study and then through a more elaborate analysis, we will address the moral responsibility of school leaders to prevent harm—in the case, the harm that falls with particular severity on various segments of student learners as a result of high-stakes testing. The case presents several implications for those designing Learner-Centered Leadership (LCL) programs. We then push the analysis further to explore the intrinsic morality of the learning process itself, connecting that process with the moral agenda of students to become authentic persons. Learner-centered leaders will find themselves challenged to correct the all-too-pervasive promotion and acceptance of inauthentic learning as "the real thing." A proactive, moral leadership response that offers a beginning balance to the current curriculum and pedagogy of the high-stakes accountability agenda is suggested toward the end of the chapter.

PART I: THE FIRST MORAL CHALLENGE TO LEARNING-CENTERED LEADERSHIP

Let us begin by exploring the moral plight of a school principal who is struggling to do the right thing. This principal, as is true of many principals in the United States, is supposed to be "leading" a school in which more than half of his student body have failed the state test. Of those who failed the test, 30% were special needs students; 30% were second language learners, children from recently immigrated families; 28% were children living in "the projects"—the low-cost public housing where neighborhoods struggle with gangs, drugs, dysfunctional families, and large members of unemployed adults; the remaining 12% were an amalgam of learners who had a variety of deficits, either physical, emotional, attitudinal, motivational, poor learning skills, or poor test taking skills.

All of these children are now required to attend after-school remediation programs, Saturday classes, or summer school. Given budgetary restrictions, there are no opportunities for smaller classes, no concentrated professional development programs during the normal school day, and no additional support staff such as counselors, social workers, teacher aides, or specialists such as reading and math teacher coaches. By and large, veteran teachers are appointed to the extra paying jobs in the remediation programs, but they tend to repeat the same, ineffective teaching methods employed in their regular classrooms.

The principal feels that the failing students, already in at-risk circumstances, are being unfairly victimized by the imposition of high stake tests. As part of the administration of a school system that collaborated in the imposition of these high-stakes tests with the subsequent imposition of both punitive and ineffective consequences for these at-risk pupils, the principal feels that somehow he has a moral responsibility to protect these students from the harm being inflicted on them by these high-stakes assessments.

As the principal struggles to understand what he intuitively feels to be a moral issue, he remembers being struck by a phrase in the initial legislation on high-stakes testing, namely that students should only be held accountable for what they had an "opportunity to learn." As he reflected on the plight of many of his students that were failing the test, he began to question whether they had been given a reasonable opportunity to learn the material on which they were being tested. Many teachers in his school would claim that the failing students had been exposed to the same curriculum material as those who passed the test. The principal questioned whether simple exposure within a one-size-fits-all time frame constituted a true opportunity to learn for students whose learning disabilities, language deficiencies, or chaotic home and neighborhood environments affected their readiness to learn in a fast-paced pedagogy (Resnick & Hall, 1998).

He now begins to question the expectation that many second-language learners can master curriculum materials in the same time frame as students studying that material in their native languages. Furthermore, those second-language learners have to decode the language of the test itself, and then express their understanding of the material in a language that they had only partially mastered—and to do this under the same time constraints as their English language peers. He remembers his own struggles in ninth grade initially to understand Algebra; "Imagine studying algebra in a partly mastered foreign language!" he muses.

He also begins to realize that special needs children are also placed in jeopardy by the testing demands. These learners experience a variety of challenges—physical, emotional, intellectual—to their ability to master a curricular similar to their nonchallenged peers in the same learning time frame. Although some assessment formats and time frames for completing the tests are altered, the testing framework is more or less the same. Thus, they are being denied not only an adequate opportunity to learn the material being assessed, but in many cases an adequate opportunity to express their learning in the relatively rigid assessment formats and time frames.

The principal becomes convinced, further, that many of the children living in the housing projects are coping with a variety of circumstances—family poverty, family disorder, fear of violence from gangs, drug addictions, shake-downs, and bullying from older children—as to affect their motivation, their ability to focus, as well as to connect with a curriculum that represented a different world, a different culture, a different value orientation, and differing assumption about life chances and adult roles. These circumstances are bound to severely affect their opportunity to learn the material being assessed. Furthermore, many of these students perceive the values and culture reflected in the daily life of the school are assumed to be superior to and even antithetical to the values and culture of their own immediate environment (Popkewitz, 1998). This perception easily leads to a resistance to comply with the demands of school that they conform to the school's cultural norms.

For many underperforming students, a one-size-fits-all daily and weekly schedule is a large part of the problem. The principal recalls from his university courses that *time to learn* the material in the curriculum had been shown again and again in the research to be a crucial variable in student achievement. Benjamin Bloom's (1981) research on mastery learning had demonstrated that, given adequate time to work with the material, the large majority of students could achieve a grade of A or B. With no flexibility in the school's time schedule for low-performing students to have the additional time they needed to master the material to be tested, these students were being victimized and then punished by the school system (Resnick, 1999). Furthermore, provision for specialists and flexible curriculum material were extremely limited. When these factors were added to an inadequate support for home–school partnerships with parents of these students—another variable highly correlated with student achievement gains—it becomes increasingly clear that the school is implicated in the failure of these children. His reflections conclude with a baseline criteria for labeling the punishment of these students unjust: whether these students had experienced a reasonable "opportunity to learn" the material on which they were being tested. The school was failing these children before the testing, and then accepting their failure with a fatalistic resignation.

The principal began to see that as an educator and, more fundamentally, as a human being, he had a moral responsibility to protect these children from harm, from a system that punished them for not being able to achieve a passing score on tests for which they had not been adequately prepared. The principal recognized that he was having difficulty looking at himself in the mirror each morning as he prepared to go off to work in a role that placed him "in charge" of a public institution that was failing its own responsibilities and then blaming the victims of their failure and punishing them for a situation over which they had minimal control.

Let us pause at this point and internalize the plight of this principal—a plight experienced by many school leaders in many urban centers—and reflect on the moral issues embedded in this situation and their implications for learning-centered leadership. We can easily discern three important lessons for those concerned with developing learning-centered leaders and for those aspiring to become learning-centered leaders. (a) Some view moral leadership exclusively within a perspective of interpersonal morality. This view looks at how leaders treat individual persons on the staff or in the student body. Are the leaders truthful, respectful, supportive, or, on the contrary, manipulative, arrogant, and arbitrary in their dealings with others. This view of moral leadership as interpersonal misses the institutional context, which may be structured in such a way as to advantage some and disadvantage others. That institutional perspective may call for—in addition to interpersonal moral leadership—a much more proactive transformation of structural arrangements that disadvantage many students in the school. (b) Some view learning-centered leadership as the exercise of leadership techniques, strategies, or skills that will improve test scores as their sole or primary indicator of school effectiveness. However, this view is often coupled with a superficial or exclusively instrumentalist view of learning that equates learning with the production of right answers to someone else's questions. Such learning is often transitory and superficial, simply considered an essential ingredient of playing school. This view ignores a potentially much richer, and indeed more authentic practice of learning (Freid. 1995; Hawkins, 2002; Sarason, 2004; Starratt, 2005; Wenger, 1998). (c) Some view learning-centered leadership as focused primarily on the learning of adults in the system, without first examining the quality and authenticity of student learning and what that implies for teaching strategies, teacher–student relationships, and institutional arrangements or resources.

The case takes us beyond these limited views of learning-centered leadership to a level of moral leadership. The principal began to see that he had to move beyond a concern for interpersonal moral leadership—that leadership that attended to interpersonal moral issues such as truth telling, respect, caring, and opposing their opposites such as lying, cheating, and disrespect in dealings with individual staff, students, and parents. The principal began to see that the institution he was leading was not morally neutral—that it treated some students unfairly and not simply in one incident–situations, but *systematically*. The principal began to see more clearly that schools were organized to serve children who were already advantaged, and reward them for achieving what their privileged cultural, physical, economic, linguistic, and social background already supported and promoted. Those who were different from this "mainstream" group were already classified as at risk (thereby assigning an inferior status to their culture, their physical condition, their economic and linguistic communities). The standard of "success" would be their ability to become like mainstream people and eradicate or minimize or camouflage whatever circumstances placed them "at risk" (Apppel, 1993; Popkewitz, 1998).

The second lesson the story communicates is that LCL should not be limited to learning "leadership-skills" (how to run effective meetings; how to be a good listener; how to measure the results of direct versus indirect teaching on test scores) or to leading the learning of teachers (how to map instruction to curriculum standards; how to improve students' test-taking skills, etc.). These skills, though not unimportant, do not answer students' questions such as "Why are we studying this stuff anyway?" "What does this stuff we're studying have to do with real life?" "What difference does this stuff make in my life?" These are questions about meaning and meaning making. There are substantive questions about the *what*, *why*, and *how* of learning. The questions suggest that, if students could find a reason to learn "this stuff," they might actually want to try. They are asking for a personal connection to the realities of their lives. Teachers and school leaders often ignore these substantive questions and focus primarily on learning as a technical matter, as learning how to perform better in a prescripted drama that is simply assumed to be legitimate or morally justifiable. Without asking more basic questions of the learning promoted in the classroom of the school, many educators simply continue to refine the techniques of a dysfunctional system.

The third lesson flows from the second. LCL has to attend first to what students are learning or not learning in school. They need critically to uncover what institutional processes and structures actually disadvantage some students while favoring others. They need to explore more fully the various ways children learn, the complexity and particularity of the learning process itself on any given day for any given student. They need to examine the assumptions behind one-size-fits-all practices—one 50-min instructional episode fits all; one group learning activity fits all; one textbook fits all; one test fits all; one rubric fits all; one semester's learning outcomes fit all.

The implications for LCL development programs from these three lessons include the following: (a) Participants need a generous exposure to the various critiques of schools as sites of institutional injustice contained, for example, in the writings of James Seurich (1998), Beverly Tatum (1992), Jonathon Kozol (1992), Michael Apple (1993), John Ogbu (1992), William Pinar and associates (Pinar, Reynolds, Slattery, & Taubmen, 1995), Patrick Shannon (1998), and Joel Spring (2004). Exposure to these critiques, and others, helps to sensitize prospective school leaders to the systemic, structured ways schools favor some and disadvantage others, irrespective of individual teachers' attempts to attend to specifically disadvantaged children.

Beyond developing a critical presence to institutional injustices in the way schools are run, LCL development programs need to explore a variety of ways of refocusing the schooling process and the systemic support required for "narrowing the achievement gap" and attention to "quality learning for all children." Although these explorations will include some current "best practices" such as reducing class size, creating schools within schools, cross-disciplinary projects, effective reading and writing programs in early childhood centers, they will look beneath the surface of such programs to understand why and how they increase quality learning for all children (Resnick & Hall, 1998; Sarason, 2004; Wenger, 1998).

A second implication for LCL development programs is that leadership requires more than technique and skills. Leaders lead through inspiration, through example of a deep and rich humanity, through a visible commitment to values embedded in the authenticity of teaching and learning, through clearly articulated purposes that energize the public mission of the school, its orientation toward free democratic and participative society based on a foundation of equity and social justice. Preparation programs, therefore, need to provide a generous attention to the cultivation of these more substantive qualities of leadership and to a consistent leadership platform committed to these purposes of schooling (Day, Harris, Hadfield, Tolley, & Beresford, 2000; Hawkins, 2002).

A third implication for LCL development programs is that they attend much more to student voices. Their learning-centered leadership should start with the primary learners in the school, namely the students (Maehr & Midgley, 1996). That includes a greater understanding of child and adolescent development as well as cognitive development. Major influence on many school initiatives currently comes from the field of cognitive psychology, whether that has to do with research on brain-based learning, information processing, abstract logical thinking, short- and long-term memory development, or higher order thinking skills. This influence on pedagogy is easily married to a view of curriculum as the preparation of novice experts in academic scholarship (Wiske, 1998). These influences have by and large ignored the scholarship in the psychology of human development. This has resulted in a bifurcation between cognitive achievement and self-development. In schools that deal with self-development in any publicly intentional way, it would tend to be found in the counseling center and the office of student support services, although some would still claim a place for it in K–4 elementary classrooms. Were we to ask youngsters in school settings where they experience life, almost all will refer to their experiences outside of school, and within the school, outside of the classroom—on the playground, in the cafeteria, playing intermural or varsity sports. If real learning is to hold any interest for students it has to be connected to their life-world, to what it means to own themselves, to their significant relationships (Starratt, 2004; Wenger, 1998).

These connections with human development should take account both of mainstream and nonmainstream understandings of development—that is, the influence of culture, gender, social class, disability, sexual orientation, and religion as contextualizing that development, as suggesting differing approaches to designing learning activities and alternative approaches to the curriculum (Kincheloe & Steinberg, 1995). With a deeper understanding of the plurality of backgrounds and learning potentials that children and youth bring to the daily work of learning, learning-centered leaders will understand the need for a variety of responses to this plurality to ensure quality learning for all. Furthermore these leadership development programs should systematically expose participants to actual student voices—to seminars in which students talk about what helps and what hinders their learning in school.

A fourth implication for LCL is that it should be grounded in a sophisticated understanding of learning itself. LCL preparation programs should expose participants not only to research on learning science and math (Pelligrino, Chudowski, & Glaser, 2001), but also to research on the learning potential in imaginative and creative learning tasks (Egan, 2005), on effort based learning and learnable intelligence (Resnick, 1995, 1999; Resnick & Hall, 1998), on multiple intelligences (Gardner, 1999), on the scaffolding of the zone of proximal development (Vygotsky), on learning within communities of practice (Wenger, 1998), and on experience-based, expeditionary, and service learning (Eyler & Giles, 1999; Weinbaum, Gregory, & Wilke, 1996). In other words, if programs are concerned to develop learning-centered leaders, then they ought to provide a heavy concentration on what they mean by learning (Sarason, 2004).

PART II: THE LARGER CHALLENGE OF LEARNING-CENTERED LEADERSHIP

The preceding analysis has suggested ways to lead the learning process within the current policy agenda of school renewal. The previous analysis of the case argued that certain students—second-language learners, special needs learners, racially and culturally classified minorities, and learners at risk due to poverty and unstable home environments—do not enjoy a reasonable opportunity to learn the material they would be tested on and therefore were victimized and punished by high-stakes testing practices. Learning-centered leadership, it was argued, should attend to necessary institutional changes that would provide them a more reasonable opportunity to learn the material being tested, as well as a more reasonable diversity of deadlines for being tested and a variability of formats and time frames of the testing process itself so that students could actually demonstrate what they know. This attention to the opportunity to learn should be seen not only as a technical managerial leadership task, but as an obligatory moral exercise of educational leadership.

This previous analysis, however, only lightly questioned the assumptions about the nature and purpose of learning embedded in the current policy agenda of schooling. That policy agenda is driven by an economic ideology that channels the educational enterprise primarily, if not exclusively, toward economic purposes, namely to supply employers with trained workers who posses the skills for the 21st century workplace as well as the dispositions of hard work and obedience to workplace rules (Apple, 1993; Shannon, 1998). This economic orientation tends to communicate a competitive view of learning as the sure road to well-paid employment in which competition for high grades is the dominant motivation. Producing right answers on tests and the repetition of predetermined formulae, classifications, vocabularies, cognitive frameworks, and problem-solving processes constitutes the learning agenda. This learning agenda is individualistic, competitive, decontextualized from personal experiences as well as pressing issues in public life, and assumes a subject–object mastery and control of the world as property. Within this view of learning, students absorb information uncontaminated by public dispute and personal value. Knowledge is what one accumulates as personal property to be used to further one's own self-interest, one's competitive journey up the economic ladder. To fail in this agenda means to diminish one's "life chances," to consign oneself to the periphery of the good life, to choose a future at the bottom of society. The school is set up, moreover, to contribute to this sorting task of a competitive economy: namely to identify the successes and the failures. The school shapes the failures' self-blame, labeling their failures as their own fault, and affirms the successes' self-congratulation, labeling success as due to obvious hard work and purposeful devotion to high goals of achievement.

Connecting the Moral Agenda of the Learner to the Academic Agenda

Rather than grounding the purposes of schooling exclusively in an economic rationale, I want to suggest a perspective that is grounded much more in the fully human development of learners. That full human development involves physical, emotional, aesthetic, intellectual, and moral development. Among those I want to assign a priority of place to moral development because it provides a vantage point for integrating all the other aspects of human development within the schooling process. Furthermore I want to argue that, unless the learning of school curriculum is seen as intimately tied to the students' moral agenda, schools will fail to generate that rich kind of learning that issues in a fuller human growth. This argument has been more fully stated in other venues (Starratt, 2005, 2004, 2003) and is summarized briefly here.

Charles Taylor (1991) has proposed that all humans have a basic moral agenda, one that encompasses most other specific moral dimensions of their lives, and that is the moral responsibility to be and to seek to be authentic. He suggests that there is a "certain way of being human that is *my* way. I am called upon to live my life in this way, and not in imitation of anyone else's" (Taylor, 1991, p. 28). This provides a moral imperative to be true to oneself. Not to be true to oneself would be to miss the whole point of one's life. Because I am a once-occurring being in the whole history of the universe, my originality is something only I can discover, author, perform, define, and authorize. Only I can realize a potentiality that is properly my own. If I refuse this most basic human privilege and opportunity, then I violate my destiny and myself. I prostitute my eternally unique inheritance, my possibility. My possibility is like my child, the *me* to be born. I either bring it to birth—albeit gradually—or I gradually abort it. As Anton (2001) commented, authenticity is a matter of "how passionately one takes the whole of one's participations in a once-occurrent existence" (p. 155).

To bring myself to birth, however, is not solely my act. I bring myself to birth through others. My authenticity is ontologically relational. As Taylor says, "We define (our identity) always in dialogue with, sometimes in struggle against, the identities our significant others want to recognize in us" (1991, p. 33). Authenticity is also something we create through and with our culture. Our culture provides not only a rich human language of self-expression and value through which we perform and define ourselves, but also a storehouse of exemplars of virtue and vice who teach us the necessary moral lessons about life.

Here we are very close to the basic meaning of freedom. Our authenticity is "grounded in a self-determining freedom" (Taylor, p. 39). Our freedom to determine ourselves is seen within a culture that believes that there is something noble and courageous and inescapably decisive in giving shape to one's life. What it means to be human is precisely to have this freedom and bear this burden, to enjoy this journey and brave its challenges. To be a human being in this sense requires the most decisive moral choice or continuum of choices.

We do not work out our authenticity in a closet or on a desert island. We shape our lives as unique human beings in a family, in neighborhoods, with friends. We recognize (re-cognize, that is, come to know again in a new light) ourselves in the dialogical recognition that occurs between parent and child, between siblings, between friends. Loving relationships are crucial to our authenticity for we experience ourselves therein as loveable, as precious, as of great worth. For the infant, totally dependent on the mother for everything, being alive means being loved. Withdrawal of that love is literally life threatening. In the family, young children begin to learn the lesson that their freedom to be themselves is dependent on the tacit agreement that everyone in the family is free to be themselves as well. Somehow the family arranges its life so that everyone learns how to be free and at the same time limits the extent of that freedom to preserve the freedoms of the other members of the family. Rules about who gets to use the one bathroom in the morning—first, second, third, or fourth—provide a daily lesson in the communal exercise of freedom. Gradually it sinks in to the self-centered child: Mutuality is the way of the world; it is the way I can be assured of some exercise of my freedom; playing by the rules benefits everyone in the game (Davidson & Youniss, 1995; Youniss, 1981). This is true for individuals, for corporations, for nations (Erikson, 1964).

Bonnet and Cuypers (2003) offered a helpful analysis of the active and passive process of becoming an authentic person, an argument originally developed by Taylor (1991). The active process involves the constructing of the self, sometimes even in opposition to societal and cultural rules and authorities. The passive process, equally influential in becoming an authentic person, involves attending to how others respond to our expressions of ourselves. The self appraises itself in terms of the feedback provided by the other. That feedback expresses either acceptance or rejection of the active self. Through the ongoing socialization process, youngsters hear evaluations of their words and actions as truthful or distorting, courageous or cowardly, appropriate or inappropriate. In this way they learn how to negotiate relationships with parents, siblings, friends, and enemies in the unfolding drama of their self-construction (Becker, 1971). Moreover, Taylor posited the "larger horizon of significance" (1991, p. 66) as influencing both the self's and the others' definitions of meaning and significance. In the very activity of defining oneself, one uses the larger culture's meanings and values to articulate that definition or what in the culture one resists in that definition, for example, women and men resisting cultural and political definitions of themselves according to traditional gender and racial categories. As we will see, this active and passive side to becoming an authentic person suggests a model for authentic learning.

Sharing a common life that recognizes the legitimacy of differences *brings with it the burden of sustaining the common life.* Taylor here links the ethics of authenticity with the ethics of social responsibility. Authenticity is grounded in community and in the activity of sustaining community. "Authenticity points us toward a more self-responsible form of life" (Taylor, 1991, p. 74).

When we say that authentic persons are real we mean that they attempt to get at the insides of things—not to control or use them—but to dialogue with them as they really are. Of course, that is a lifelong task because getting to the really real means peeling back or penetrating layer after layer of the exterior complexity to the simpler elements, which themselves are enormously complex in their micro-universe—as we have discovered in the human genome project. Likewise, authentic persons come to realize that their own authenticity is made up of layers and layers of culturally and spiritually constructed "stuff"—all those things that some recent philosophers point to in their "deconstruction of the self." Oddly enough, however, authentic persons become more, not less, in the process of such deconstruction, aware of where they came from, how they came to be. They discover in that process the much greater freedom to choose to be some or all of that self, with all or some of these culturally and spiritually constructed layers of themselves.

Authenticity as a virtue is always a relative achievement, always at risk, always in dialogue with the other in actualizing itself, always amplifying or diminishing in the face of daily circumstances. We also see how essential a virtue it is to living a moral life. One is tempted to say that the more authentic one is, the more moral will the whole tenor of one's life be in all its many daily activities.

We can conclude, therefore, that not only is the choice to be ourselves the most fundamental moral choice we daily make, but we can now appreciate how richly textured that choice is as it is acted out over years. The choice to be oneself is a choice to adventure into the real, an adventure of a lifetime, an adventure into discovery of who one is and who the other is and how the dialogue between the emerging real self and the emerging real other is both enormously gratifying and enormously humbling at the same time, because the real is all gift, not mine to possess, but mine to share and to share in.

All students arrive every day at school with this moral agenda. The school is the daily public arena for 13 or more years of their lives where they construct themselves, for better or worse. What drives that daily adventure is a tacit quest to become real, to become an authentic player in the social drama. When teachers do not connect the work of the classroom with that adventure, then it is difficult, if not impossible for the student to connect to the curriculum (Fig. 14.1). The question often asked, either tacitly or explicitly, is "Why are we studying this stuff?" After enduring lame responses from the teacher, the question is finally reduced to "Is this stuff going to be on the test?" The assumption behind the question is that (a) if it is not going to be on the test, then it obviously holds no value, and (b) if it is going to be on the test then it had better be learned in its "correct" form, with no personal connections interjected, no questions asked, no imagination or whimsy.

The question, "Why are we studying this stuff?" has an answer that connects to the students' moral agenda. "You are studying this stuff so you can find out who you are, and so

---

The Essential Connection

**The Primary Moral Character of Learning
is connected to
The Primary Moral Agenda of Learners**

such that

**The Moral Activity of Learning Speaks To
and Challenges the Moral Agenda of Learners
and
The Moral Agenda of Learners Activates and Energizes
The Moral Character of Learning**

Figure 14.1.

you will be able to explain yourself to yourself and to others. You are studying this stuff because this stuff reveals aspects of the worlds you belong to, aspects of what it means to be a member of these worlds, aspects of the adventure we are all engaged in as members of these worlds. If we don't learn this stuff well, then we won't be able to enjoy and take pride in these worlds, participate in them as full members with others, carry our load in sustaining and improving those worlds. If you want to be a zombie, a robot, a sleepwalker in life, then this stuff is not important. If you want to be a somebody, a player in the drama, a contributor to the community, a maker of history, then it's important to learn this stuff." The response, of course, can get more specific about why it is important to read and perform Shakespeare, why it's important to study the genetics of fruit flies, why the algebraic slope-Y-intercept formula is valuable in the human adventure.

The question, "Why do we study what we study in schools?" is asking, "What difference does attention to these subjects have to do with who we are, how we define ourselves, how we live our lives, what we should value?" and conversely, "What do these studies tell us about the mistakes, pitfalls, habits, perspectives, attitudes, self-understandings that are self-destructive, harmful, foolish, repugnant—that is, contrary to what it means to be human?" The answer to those questions is that these studies have much to do with those basic human concerns. These studies can (though not necessarily will) help us understand who we are as physical beings, as social beings, as cultural beings, as historical beings, and cumulatively as human beings (Nussbaum, 1997). These studies gradually and cumulatively tell us how we are in relationship to these various worlds, how these worlds construct us, and how we construct the intelligibility of these worlds so that we can act responsibly and authentically within those worlds (Fig. 14.2).

The Moral Agenda of Learners as Human Beings

* To Find Themselves...To Be a Somebody

* To Create/Construct themselves...To Be a Person

* To be True to Themselves... Being Real, Being Authentic, Being Present

* To Own Themselves...Being Responsible

Figure 14.2.

Our school studies can (again, not necessarily) gradually and cumulatively engage us in a conversation, both personal and public, with those worlds in which we can ask, "How do you work? How do you help me (us) understand how I (we) work? How is my (our) immediate 'life world' like your world? What do you teach me (us) about my (our) possibilities, my (our) limitations, my (our) responsibilities?" With capable teachers, these studies can develop into ongoing conversations between the worlds expressed and interpreted through the academic disciplines that comprise the curriculum, conversations where the learners listen to those worlds talk back to them. Through those conversations learners can become more fully present to those worlds and thus to the various relationships that come to be seen as increasingly complex and demanding. Within these newly discovered relationships learners continue to shape their self-understanding both individually and communally.

Based on these deep and rich understandings of themselves as human individuals and human communities, learners may then very legitimately and explicitly turn to the economic world of work and national economic policy and to the political world of power relationships and communal self-governance. Exposure to the worlds of economics and politics is thus not carried out in isolation from, but in dialogue with those other worlds of nature, society, culture, and history. One's economic and political life and responsibilities can be brought into some kind of harmony or balance that contains and recognizes tensions and obstacles across these worlds, but can hold out hope for an increasing integration among the way one inhabits those worlds.

Such a justification for engaging the school "subjects" is lacking in the current articulation of the learning agenda of schools. Furthermore, the understanding of learning as a dialogue with the various worlds humans inhabit, a dialogue in which the integrity of the learner and the integrity of those worlds is maintained, each listening to the other, each disclosing itself to the other as the other, becomes more authentically present in the activity of learning—this understanding of the moral character of learning seems lacking in the current articulation of school policy.

Instead, we hear other metaphors: The curriculum is "delivered" by teachers to students, who in turn "master" the curriculum, the mastery of which is revealed by identifying or producing preordained "right answers," which are then tallied in numbers and percentages that reveal what the student has "achieved." Clearly this is a one-way appropriation of prefixed menu of abstracted right answers that are presumed to be objectively factual and uniformly and universally appropriate. There appears to be no concern in this process with either the self-knowledge about one's humanity in relationship to these studies, nor the learning of responsibility toward these worlds. Achieving right answers seems an end in itself, a sign of hard work, self-interest, obedience, and conformity to a dominant adult world that has constructed this artificial obstacle course of puzzles, riddles, problems, formulae, vocabularies, and definitions, the mastery of which is supposed to predict successful performance in adult work either at the next level of academic test taking, or in a corporate career.

From this deeper view of learning, school subjects ground our humanity and emancipate it from the corrupting influences of society's prejudices, vanities, and injustices. This deeper view of learning acknowledges that the process of learning is fluid and dialogical, necessarily both personal and social. To force learning into a uniform time frame for all learners to "learn" a specific skill or understanding is not only artificial, but it leads to a wholly mistaken notion of learning. Furthermore, it forces learners to hurry up, to scramble for some scrap of what it is the teacher expects them to have learned, to parrot out a phrase or a definition just in time before the class or the test period runs out, to guess at a right answer without having any clue as to why this constitutes a "right" answer. More often than not, learners are forced to make believe that they know what they know they do not know (Freid, 1995). Once programmed into this attitude, they will argue with the teacher after a test is graded that they should get partial credit for having a piece of the answer, even though that piece is not connected to any real understanding of the material under study. Neither, perhaps, were their answers that were graded as "correct" (Fig. 14.3).

Even for those students who are quick to learn how to study for tests and classroom recitations and identify what it is the teacher and the textbook expect for the right answer, the learning imposed by the current testing and standard movement should be critiqued as distorting any kind of authentic learning. The current learning agenda promotes a view of learning as an acquisition to be recorded in one's portfolio of private property (Freire, 1972), as a manipulable commodity to be used for self-serving purposes, imposing no obligation on the learner either during or after the leaning activity.

This agenda promotes unethical learning, learning that is inauthentic, irresponsible, and domineering toward all knowledge and the worlds of relationships that knowledge is intended to reveal. Schooling currently promotes a dominant and exclusive form of learning that is not only inappropriate and misguided, but, more impor-

AUTHENTIC LEARNING	INAUTHENTIC LEARNING
*Personal Appropriation of Intelligibility Translated into Meaning	Impersonal Appropriation of Information Categories, Formulas, Definitions
*Personal grasp of Mutual Relationality between the Self and the Subject/Object of study	Impersonal Appropriation of Decontextualized , Prepackaged Knowledge
* Respect for the Integrity of the Subject/Object of study	No Concern for or with the Integrity of of the Subject/Object of study
* Concern for Meaning in Relationship to Self and the Trajectory of One's Life	Concern for Right Answers to the Teacher's questions in order to get a passing grade
*Can Perform a Rich Understanding of the Subject/Object of Study	Can Perform a Superficial, Formulaic, Make-Believe Understanding of the Subject/Object of Study

Figure 14.3.

tant, *morally harmful*. In actuality, we are looking at a situation in schools where the currently classified at-risk students are not the only ones at risk. Possibly the most "successful" ones are more at risk because they have been most thoroughly programmed to approach their world in such a thorough-going self-referential and exploitative learning process. This kind of learning lends itself to economic, environmental, and geopolitical policies and practices where the winners take all and, in the process and in its consequences, lose all.

Implications for LCL

Obviously, this dominant form of learning and its assessment will not evaporate with the publication of this essay. The current paradigm of learning is rooted in various elements of the culture and traditions of the United States, such as the stress on individualism, an understanding of democracy as the freedom to consume and compete; freedom understood as the pursuit self-interest unburdened by minimal social and political obligations; a practice of learning as individualized competition for grades; and a view of learning as private property and self-promoting capital, and as a tool for domination and control of natural and social forces. Collectively, the "achievement of learning" in the nation's schools is explicitly promoted to further the nation's global economic hegemony, with the international comparisons of students' scores on standardized tests suggesting a direct connection with global economic competition. In other words, this approach to school learning is supported by powerful political and economic traditions and interests.

Nevertheless, many educators attempt to balance these exclusive views of the purpose of schools with a more encompassing view of educating complete human beings. Though powerful interest groups promoting a market view of schooling currently appear to hold the upper hand, there remain groups of educators, parents, and concerned citizens opposing such a dominant and exclusive use of schools. These groups provide a continuing source of support for a deeper, more moral pursuit of learning. Indeed, it would appear that the coalition promoting LCL want a greater balance in the type of learning promoted in schools.

What practical steps might learning-centered leaders take in their school, given the saturation of current school policies by economic rationalism? Certainly they can use the bully pulpit of their position as leaders to articulate and advocate more humanizing approaches to learning. They can remind their colleagues of their ideals in joining the profession, the ideals of expanding the souls and spirits of their students as well as their minds. Going beyond verbal advocacy, these leaders can encourage their teacher colleagues to choose, for example, one or two curriculum units per semester that would be taught in this more authentic way. By that I mean that the teachers would design learning activities that would promote dialogue between the worlds represented in the curriculum unit and the learner. Concrete issues of membership in those worlds and the skills and understandings required for the exercise of responsible membership could be stressed. Students would be encouraged to ask how membership in these worlds clarifies or challenges their sense of themselves. Assessments would not only seek to ascertain the academic vocabulary and logic of the unit, but promote a personal and perhaps creative expression of the student' relationship to the topics under study.

LCL, therefore, should, at the very least, explore ways of introducing more authentic, dialogical, and progressive approaches to some learning units in the curriculum. The aim is not the immediate, wholesale replacement of the current view of learning, but rather to challenge its *exclusive* claim to legitimacy. What is sought is a growing balance between the two approaches. A healthy tension between the two views of knowledge and learning provide a corrective and prevent the extremes of either view becoming a new orthodoxy. My hunch is that the learners, not the pedagogues, will decide the issue as they experience the alternatives of competing perspectives about which worlds of learning offer them a more humanly satisfying future.

University programs focused on developing LCL can also challenge their students to evaluate their own understanding of authentic learning and the ways their schools support or inhibit this kind of learning. Besides exposure to the authors mentioned earlier and their challenge to the unjust cultures and structures of schools, these programs need to probe the kinds of proactive leadership that will support and promote a greater balance between the instrumentalist approaches to learning as preparation for high-stakes tests, and the more authentic approaches to learning that respect the integrity of the worlds under study as well as the integrity of the learning process itself. This reappraisal of the learning process, of course, should be turned on these programs' own courses and the authentic quality of the learning they are promoting or inhibiting.

ACKNOWLEDGMENT

The predicament of the principal was earlier described in Starratt, 2003 and 2004.

REFERENCES

Apple, M. (1993). *Official knowledge: Democratic education in a conservative age*. New York: Routledge.

Bloom, B. (1981). *All our children learning: A primer for parents*. New York: McGraw-Hill.

Day, C., Harris, A., Hadfield, M., Tolley, H., & Beresford, J., (2000). *Leading schools in times of change*. Buckingham, UK: Open University Press.

Eyler, J., & Giles, D. E., Jr., (1999). *Where's the learning in service learning?* San Francisco: Jossey-Bass.

Freid, R. L. (1995). *The passionate teacher*. Boston: Beacon.

Gardner, H. (1999). *Intelligence reframed: Multiple intelligences for the 21st century*. New York: Basic Books.

Hawkins, D. (2002). *The informed vision: Essays on learning and human nature*. New York: Algora.

Kincheloe, J. L., & Steinberg, S. R. (Eds.). (1995). *Thirteen questions: Reframing education's conversations* (2nd ed.). New York: Peter Lang.

Kozol, J. (1992). *Savage inequalities*. New York: Harper Perennial.

Maehr, M. L., & Midgley, C. (1996). *Transforming school cultures*. Boulder, CO: Westview.

Maturana, H. R., & Varela, F. J. (1992). *The tree of knowledge: The biological roots of human understanding* (R. Paolucci, Trans.). New York: Random House.

Nussbaum, M. C. (1997). *Cultivating humanity*. Cambridge, MA: Harvard University Press.

Ogbu (1992). Understanding cultural diversity and learning. *Educational Researcher, 21*(8), 5–14.

Pelligrino, J., Chaudowsky, N., & Glaser, R. (Eds.). (2001). *Knowing what students know*. Washington, DC: National Academy.

Pinar, W. F., Reynolds, W. M., Slattery, P., & Taubmen, P. M. (1995). *Understanding curriculum*. New York: Peter Lang.

Popjewitz, T. (1999). *The struggle for the soul.* New York: Teachers College Press.

Porter, A. C. (1995). The uses and misuses of opportunity-to-learn standard. *Educational Researcher, 24*(1), 21–27.

Resnick, L. B. (1995). From aptitude to effort: A new foundation for our schools. *Daedalus, 24*(4), 55–62.

Resnick, L. B. ((1999). Making America smarter. *Education Week Century Series, 18*(40), 38–40.

Resnick, L. B., & Hall, M. W. (1998). Learning organizations for sustainable educational reform. *Daedalus, 27*(4), 89–118.

Scheurich, J. J. (1998). Community: The grave dangers in the discourse on democracy. *International Journal of Leadership in Education 1*(1), 55–60.

Scheurich, J. J., & Skrla, L. (2003). *Leadership for equity and excellence: Creating high-achievement classrooms, schools, and districts.* Thousand Oaks, CA: Corwin.

Shannon, P. (1998). *Reading poverty.* Portsmouth, NH: Heinemann.

Starratt, R. J. (2003). Opportunity to learn and the accountability agenda. *Phi Delta Kappan, 85*(4), 298–303.

Starratt, R. J. (2004). *Ethical leadership.* San Francisco: Jossey Bass.

Starratt, R. J. (2005). Cultivating the moral character of learning and teaching: A neglected dimension of educational leadership. *School Leadership and Management, 25,* 399–411.

Tatum, B. D. (1992). Talking about race, learning about racism: The application of racial identity development theory in the classroom. *Harvard Educational Review, 62*(1).

Vygotsky, L. S. (1997). *Educational psychology* (R. Silverman, Trans.). Boca Raton, FL: St Lucie.

Weinbaum, A., Gregory, L., & Wilke, A. (1996). *Expeditionary learning/outward bound: Summary report.* New York: Academy for Educational Development.

Wenger, E. (1998). *Communities of practice: Learning, meaning and identity.* Cambridge: Cambridge University Press.

Wiske, M. S. (Ed.). (1998). *Teaching for understanding: Linking research with practice.* San Francisco: Jossey-Bass.

AUTHOR INDEX

A

Aagaard, L., 172, 185
Ackerman, R. H., 151, 153, *169*, 254, *272*
Aladjem, D., 3, *18*
Alexander, D., 79, *99*
Alexander, K., 79, *99*
Allen, D., 81, 82, *100*
Allen, L. W., 175, 177, *184*
Allensworth, D., 82, 84, *99*
Allensworth, E., *129*
Allington, R., 81, *101*
Alterio, M., *273*
Alvy, A., 64, *71*
Ames, C., 80, *99*
Anderson, C., 82, *99*
Anderson, R., 225, *237*
Anderson, S., 113, *129, 152, 169*
Anderson, W., 241, *248*
Andrews, R., 209, *219*
Anthes, K., 191, *204*
Anton, 282
Apple, M., 78, 79, 90, *99*, 278, 279, 281, *289*
Archibald, S., 88, *105*
Armstrong, J., 191, *204*
Arnold, M. L., 87, *99*, 172, *184*
Aspy, C., 253, *272*
Aspy, D., 253, *272*

B

Babinski, L., 152, 153, *170*
Bacharach, S., 89, *99*
Baer, G., 81, 83, *99*
Bagin, D., 87, *102*
Baker, S., 81, *102*

Bamberger, P., 89, *99*
Bangert-Drowns, R., 81, *99*
Banks, J., 247, *248*
Baratta-Lorton, M., 139, *147*
Barnett, B. G., 176, *184*
Barnhardt, V., 89, 91, *99*
Barone, T., 268, 269, *272*
Barth, R. S., 13, *24, 38, 49*, 90, *99, 144*, 149, 153, 167, *169*
Bascia, N., 85, 91, *104*
Basom, M. R., 176, *184*
Battistich, V., 78, *106*
Bauer, D., 86, 87, *99*
Bauer, S., 89, *99*
Baumrind, D., 92, *99*
Beane, J., 78, *99*
Beck, L., 7, *19*, 83, 90, 91, *99, 104*
Becker, 283
Beeson, E., 150, *169*
Begley, P., 90, 99
Begley, P. T., 176, *184*
Bellamy, T., 4, *18*, 76, *74, 98, 99*, 104
Benard, B., 198, *204*
Bennis, W., 5, *18*, 254, *272, 272*
Bensman, D., 27, *49*
Bereiter, C., 78, 79, *99*
Berends, M., 91, *99*
Beresford, J., 279, *289*
Biklen, S., 79, *99*
Birman, B., 53, *70*, 90, *102*
Bista, M., 113, *128*
Black, P., 81, *99*, 191, *204*
Blasé, J., 88, 90, *100*
Bloom, B., 277, *289*

291

Blythe, T., 81, 82, *100*
Bodily, S., 91, *99*
Bodycott, P., 270, *274*
Bolman, L., 89, 90, *100*
Bonnet, 283
Borger, J., 152, *169*
Borman, K. M., 3, *18*, 223, 224, *237*
Bosker, R., 88, 91, 95, 96, 97, *106*
Boskers, R., 97, *107*
Bote, L. A., 143, *148*
Bottoms, G., 113, *128*, 152, *169*
Boudett, K. P., 192, 193, *205*
Boyatzis, R., 94, *102*
Boyd, V., 226, *237*
Boydston, T., 223, *237*
Boyer, E., 83, *100*
Boyle, C., 54, *70*
Boyle, J., 93, *100*
Boyles, D., 9, 10, *18*
Bracey, G. W., 9, *18*
Bransford, J., *70*, 78, 79, 80, *100, 271, 272*
Bredekamp, S., 26, *49*
Brenzel, B., 210, *220*
Brewer, D., 79, *100*
Brewster, C., 241, *248*
Bridges, E. M., 247, *248,* 271, *272*
Brooks, B., 78, *102*
Brooks, G., 94, *100*
Brophy, J., 81, *102*
Brown, A. L., *70*, 78, 79, 80, *100,* 271, *272*
Brown, D., 86, 87, *100*
Brown, F., 68, *70*
Brown, J. H., 191, 198, *204*
Brown, K., 242, 243, 244, 247, 248, *248*
Brown, R. J., 215, *219*
Browne-Ferrigno, T., 175,177, 183, *184*
Bruner, J., 26, *49,* 254, *272*
Brunner, C., 193, *204*
Brunner, C. C., 242, *248*
Bryant, D., 145, *147*
Bryk, A. S., *129,* 152, *170,* 225, *237,* 241, *249*
Burden, P., 81, *100*
Burnette, J., 84, *100*
Burton, J., *272*

C

Caffarella, R., 89, 90, *104*
Cambron-McCabe, N., 83, *104,* 241, 242, *248*
Cameron, J., 78, *100*
Campbell, E., 80, *100*
Campbell-Evans, G., 176, *184*
Canady, R., 86, 88, *100*
Capasso, R. L., 176, *185*
Carini, P., 26, *49*

Carnine, D., 79, *101*
Carpenter, T. P., 137, *147*
Carter, K., 3, *18,* 113, *128*
Casella, R., 84, *100*
Castaldi, B., 88, *100*
Castillo, S., 191, *204*
Cello, M. B., 171, 183, *186*
Chapman, C., 113, *129*
Chaudowsky, N., 280, *289*
Chavkin, N., 93, *100*
Chen, E., 191, 192, 193, *204*
Chenoweth, K., 8, *18*
Chester, M. D., 192, *205*
Chiang, *147*
Chrispells, J. H., 114, *128,* 191, *204*
Chung, C. H., 171, 183, *185*
Cibulka, J. G., 9, *18,* 79, 84, 92, *100,* 174, *185,*
    217, *219*
Clandinin, D. J., 254, 271, 272, *272*
Clark, D. C., 113, *128,* 114, *129*
Clark, R., 92, *100*
Clark, S. N., 113, *128*
Clark, T. D., 174, *185*
Cochran-Smith, M., 89, 91, *104*
Cocking, R., *70,* 78, 79, 80, *100*
Cocking, R. R., 271, *272*
Cockrell, D. H., 113, *129*
Cockrell, K. S., 113, *129*
Codding, J. B., 149, *170*
Coe, P., 172, *185*
Coffin, G., 241, *249*
Cohen, J., 94, *100*
Cohen, S., 90, *104*
Coleman, P., 93, 94, *100*
Coles, R., 254, 269, *272*
Commins, N., 81, 82, *104*
Conley, S., 89, 90, 91, 99, *101*
Connelly, F. M., 254, 271, 272, *272*
Cooke, G., 214, *219,*
Cooney, S., 113, *128*
Cooper, J., 79, *105,* 114, *130,* 254, *272*
Copland, M. A., 192, 193, 195, 200, *204,* 242, *249*
Corbin, J., 177, *186*
Corcoran, T., 8, *18*
Cornwall, J. R., 215, *219*
Cororan, T. B., 209, *219*
Cotton, K., 241, *248*
Covington-Clarkson, L. M., 115, *128*
Crain, R. L., 210, *220*
Creemers, B., 81, *101*
Creighton, T., 165, 167, *170*
Cresswell, A., 90, *104*
Creswell, J. W., 176, *185*
Crow, G., 68, *70,* 165, 167, *170,* 175, 176, *185*
Cuban, L., 7, *18, 49*

Cunningham, P., 81, *101*
Cushner, K., 83, *101*
Cuypers, 283
Czarnaiawska, B., 254, *273*

D

Damico, J., 82, 84, *101*
Daniels, H., 81, *107*
Danielson, C., 80, 90, *101*
Danzig, A., 54, 59, 68, *70,* 222, *237,* 252, 254,
     255, 256, 269, *273*
Darder, A., 243, *248*
Daresh, J. C., 68, *70,* 176, *185*
Darling-Hammond, L., 27, 38, *49,* 167, *169,* 241,
     242, 247, *248*
Davidson, 283
Davis, S., 241, 242, 247, *248*
Day, C., 279, *289*
Deal, T. E., 83, 89, 90, *100, 101,* 105, 225, *237*
Dean, C. B., 172, *184*
Delpit, L., 82, 83, *101*
D'Emidio-Caston, M., 198, *204*
DeMoss, K., 150, *169*
DePree, M., 254, *273*
Desimone, L., 53, *70,* 90, *102*
Dewey, J., 26, *49*
Diamond, J. B., 113, *129*
Dillon, S., 211, *219*
Desimone, L., *114, 128*
Donmoyer, R., 74, *101*
Doyle, W., 78, 81, *101*
Drake, R. B., 174, *185*
Driscoll, M., 145, *147*
Duckwork, E., 26, *49*
Duffett, A., 151, *169*
DuFour, R., 90, *101,* 149, 159, *169,* 207, *219,* 252,
     273

E

Eaker, R., 90, *101,* 149, 159, *169*
Earl, L., 91, *102,* 191, 192, *204*
Eccles, J., 80, 82, *107*
Edmonds, R., 83, *101,* 191, *204,* 209
Egan, 280
Eiler, A., 84, *101*
Eisner, E., 78, 79, *101*
Elmore, R., 216, *219*
Elmore, R. F., 159, *169*
Emery, K., 8, 9, *18*
Engleman, S., 79, *101*
English, F. W., 271, *273*
Epstein, J., 91, 92, 93, *101*
Erikson, 283
Erlickson, B., 11, *18*

Essex, N., 91, 93, *101*
Evans, P., 156, *169*
Evans, R., 89, 91, *101*
Evertson, C., 81, *101*
Eyler, J., 280, *289*

F

Farkas, S., 151, *169*
Fasca, C., 193, *204*
Feijoo, M., 150, *170*
Feldman, J., 191, *204*
Fennema, E., *147*
Fenwick, L., 54, *70*
Fink, D., 214, *220*
Fiore, D., 93, *107*
Firestone, W., 86, 87, 101
Fischer, L., 83, 84, 88, 90, *101*
Fisler, J., 87, *101*
Fix, M., 211, *219*
Flanary, R., 68, *70*
Flores, A., 141, *147*
Foleno, T., 151, *169*
Foley, P., 151, *169*
Forester, 261
Forsyth, P. B., 74, *101,* 183, *185*
Foster, J. D., 172, 173, *185*
Frank, K. A., 201, *206*
Franke, M., 115, *128*
Frasier, B., 95, 96, *101*
Freid, R. L., 278, 287, *289*
Freire, P., 244, 246
French, N., 86, 88, *101*
Froebel, F., 26, *49*
Fullan, M., 24, *49,* 91, *102,* 112, 113, *129,* 153,
     169, 225, *237*
Fulmer, C. L., 4, *18,* 74, 76, 98, *99, 104*
Fyans, L., 82, *104*

G

Gaddy, B. B., 80, *102,* 172, *184*
Gallagher, D., 87, *102*
Gallagher, S., 253, *274*
Gameron, A., 79, *102,* 146, *147*
Garden, K., 82, 84, *102*
Gardner, H., 254, 272, *273,* 280, *289*
Garet, M., 53, *70,* 90, *102,* 114, *128*
Garman, M., 90, *106*
Gates, S. M., 171, 183, *185*
Gay, *81*
Gersten, R., 81, *102*
Gilbert, T., 75, *102*
Giles, D. E. Jr., 280, *289*

Girard, D., 93, *102*
Glascock, C., 175, *185*
Glaser, R., 280, *289*
Glasman, L. D., 272, *273*
Glasman, N. S., *113, 128, 248,* 272, *273*
Glatthorn, A., 79, *102*
Glickman, C. D., 90, *102*, 149, *169*
Gluck, R., 191, *205*
Goble, F., 78, *102*
Goertz, M. E., 8, 11, *18*, 174, *185*
Goldring, E. B., 175, *185*
Goleman, D., 94, *102*
Good, T., 81, *102*
Gooden, M. A., 216, *219*
Goodlad, J., 79, 86, 87, 91, *102*
Goodson, I., 268, *273*
Gordon, S., 90, *102*
Gorman, T., 94, *100*
Gorn, S., 84, *102*
Granovetter, M. S., 39, *49*
Grant, C., 80, *106*
Greene, M., 26, *49*
Greeny, J., *105*
Gregory, L., 280, *290*
Grenny, 91
Gribbons, B., *204*
Griffiths, D. E., 73, 74, *102*, 183, *185*
Grimes, J., 84, *107*
Grogan, M., 209, *219*
Grouws, D. A., 137, *147*
Grubb, S., 242, *249*
Guba, E. G., 74, *103*
Gunn, J. H., 190, 193, 196, *205*
Guskey, T. R., 51, 53, *70,* 173, *185*, 253
Guthrie, J. W., 8, *18*, 87, *102*

H

Hackmann, D., 114, *129*
Hadfield, M., 277, *289*
Haertel, G., 78, 80, *107*
Hagstrom, D., 167, *169*
Hale, J., 92, *102*
Hall, G., 89, 91, *102*
Hall, M. W., 225, 226, *237,* 276, 279, 280, *290*
Hall, W., 80, *102*
Hallinger, P., 113, *129*, 247, *248, 271,* 272
Halverson, R., 88, *102,* 113, *129,* 270, *273*
Hammel, K., 242, *248*
Hammond, O., 91, 93, *105*
Hancock, M., 152, 153, *169*
Hannum, J., 113, *129*
Hansman, C. A., 51, *70*
Hanson, M., 92, *103*
Harachiewicz, J., 80, *103*

Hargreaves, A., 24, *49*, 89, 91, *102, 103*, 225, *237*
Harkins, P., 64, *70*
Harman, J., 94, *100*
Harris, A., 113, *129*, 279, *289*
Harris, K., 254, 255, *273*
Hart, A. W., 89, 90, *106*, 176, *185*
Hart, B., 92, *102*
Harvey, J., 171, 183, *186*
Hattie, J., 95, 96, *101*
Hawkins, D., 278, 279, *289*
Hay, J., 64, *69*
Heck, R., 113, *129*
Heifetz, R., 272, *273*
Heinze, J., 193, *204*
Henderson, A., 92, *102*
Henson, M., 212, *219*
Heritage, M., 191, 192, 193, *204*
Herman, J. L., 86, 87, *103, 204*
Herrity, V. A., *248,*
Hersh, R., 83, *103*
Hess, F., 7, *18*, 113, *129, 219*
Hevinson, J., 92, *107*
Hewson, P., 91, *103,* 144, *148*
Hidi, S., 80, *103*
Hill, *74*
Hills, J., 73, 74, *103*
Hodgkinson, H., 210, 211, *219*
Hoeffer, T. B., 114, *129*
Holcomb, J., 87, *103*
Holland, H., 53, *70*
Holloway, J. H., 152, 153, *169*
Honey, M., 193, *204*
Hord, S. M., 89, 91, *102,* 226, *237*
Horner, R. H., 82, 83, *106*
Howley, A., 172, *185*
Hoy, A., 90, *103*
Hoy, W., 90, *103,* 113, *129*
Huber, J., 270, *273*
Huberman, A. M., 177, *185*
Huddy, L., 247, *248*
Huffman, D., 193, 196, 199, 201, *205*
Hughes, S., 150, *170*
Hutchinson, D., 94, *100*
Hyde, A., 81, *107*

I

Ingersoll, R., 90, *103*
Ingram, D., 191, 192, 196, 199, *205*
Inhelder, B., 26, *49*

J

Jackson, J., 177, *184*
Jackson, M., 92, *102*

Jacobsen, D., *249*
Jacobus, K., 150, *170*
James, C., 213, *219*
Jantzi, D., 241, *249*
Jaworski, J., *273*
Johnson, H., 64, *69*
Johnson, J., 151, *169*
Johnson, M., *273*
Johnson, R., 91, *103*
Jones, B. A., 7, 9, 10, *18,* 210, 214, 216, *219, 220*
Joyce, B., 83, *103*
Judson, E., 137, 140, 143, 146, *148*

K

Kalkman, D., 51, *70*
Kalnin, J., 193, 196, 199, 201, *205*
Kannnapel, P. J., 172, *185*
Kantor, H., 210, *220*
Karaglani, A., 191, *205*
Karhanek, G., 149, 159, *169*
Kathak, L. M., 114, *129*
Katz, S., 191, 192, *204*
Katzenmeyer, W., 224, *237*
Kaufman, R., 86, 87, *103*
Kazemi, E., 115, *128*
Kegan, R., 159, *169*
Kelleher, P., 214, *220*
Kellerman, B., 213, *220*
Kelley, 7, *19*
Kelley, C., 150, *170*
Kelly, A., 7, *18*
Kelly, C., 83, 84, 88, 90, *101,* 175, *185*
Kendall, J., 78, 79, *104*
Kennedy, M. M., 132, *147*
Kersaint, G., 223, *237*
Kiltz, G., 54, 59, *70, 273*
Kincheloe, J. L., 280, *289*
Kindred, L., 87, *102*
King, B., 190, 193, 196, *205*
King, R., 87, *106*
Kirby, S., 91, *99*
Kirtek, *92*
Klaghoz, 10, *19*
Klein, V., 191, 192, *205*
Kleiner, A., 5, *19,* 224, *238, 274*
Klump, J., 241, *248*
Knapp, M. S., 242, *248*
Knoeppel, R. C., 177, *184*
Knowles, M., 51, *70,* 89, 90, *103*
Knowlton, B., 212, *220*
Koch, S., 93, *102*
Koellner, K. A., 143, *148*
Kohn, A., 78, *103*
Koki, S., 91, 93, *105*

Kouzes, J. M., 225, *237*
Kowalski, T., 88, *103*, 217, *220*
Kozol, J., 279, *289*
Krathwohl, D. R., 176, *185*
Kritek, W., *100*
Kruger, M., 97, 107
Kruse, S., 90, *103,* 113, *129,* 225, 226, *237*
Kulic, J., *99*
Kulik, C., 81, *99*
Kvale, S., 177, *185*

L

Lachat, M. A., 191, 192, 193, *205*
Lahey, L., 159, *169*
Lambert, L., 149, *169*
Lamendola, B., 152, 153, *169*
LaMorte, M., 83, 88, 90, *103*
Landgraf, K. M., 218, *220*
Lane, J. J., 175, 183, *185*
LaPointe, M., 241, 242, 247, *248*
Larocque, L., 242, *249*
Larson, C., 91, *103*
Lashley, C., 80, *103*
Lashway, L., 152, 153, *169*
Lave, J., 51, 70, 176, *185*
Lawler, E., 89, *104*
Lawrence, E., 90, *103*
Lawson, E., 82, 84, *99*
Leake, B., 90, *103*
Leake, D., 90, *103*
LeCompte, M. D., 177, *185*
Lee, J., 191, 192, 193, *204*
Lee, R., 223, 224, *237*
LeFloch, K., 3, *18*
Leithwood, K., 86, *103*, 113, *129,* 152, *169,* 241, *249,* 271, 272, *273*
Levine, A., 165, 167, *169*
Levine, D., 83, 88, 94, *103*
Lezotte, L., 83, 88, 94, *103*
Lick, D. W., 176, *18*
Lieberman, 226, *237*
Lieberman, A., 40, *49*
Liebermann, J., 82, 84, *102*
Light, D., 193, *204*
Lincoln, Y. S., 74, *103*
Lindle, J. C., 173, 174, *185, 186*
Lindsey, R., 81, *103*
Linsky, M., 272, *273*
Lipsey, M., 91, 93, 94, 96, 97, *103*
Lipton, M., 4, *19,* 115, *129, 274*
Little, J., 89, *103*
Lo, C., 152, *169*
Loef, M., *147*
Lomotey, K., 82, 83, *103*

Lopez, G., 93, *103*
Loucks-Horsley, S., 90, 91, *103,* 144, *148*, 214, *220*
Louis, K. S., 89, 90, *103,* 113, 114, *129, 130*, 152, 169, 191, 192, 196, 199, *205,* 225, 226, *237*, 253, *274*
Love, N., 91, *103,* 144, *148*
Lovely, S., 64, *70*
Lucas, S., 114, *129*
Lyman, L. L., *220*, 242, *249*
Lynch, E., 92, *103*
Lytle, S., 89, 91, *104*

M

Maehr, M., 82, *104*
Maehr, M. L., 280, *289*
Mahitivanichcha, K., 93, *103*
Mandinach, E., 193, *204*
Manning, S., 91, *102*
Marks, H., 77, 90, *103, 104*, 113, *129,* 225, 226, *237*
Marrett, C. B., 143, *147*
Marshall, C., 242, *249*
Martella, R., 83, *105*
Martin, G., 68, *70*
Martin, K. J., 114, *128*
Marzano, R., 78, 79, 80, 71, 91, 95, *102, 104,* 242, *249*
Maslin-Ostrowski, P., 254, *272*
Mason, S. A., 192, 193, *205*
Massell, D., 191, 192, *205*
Matsumoto, C., 90, *103*
Matthews L. J., 68, 70, 176, *185*
Maturana, H. R., *289*
Maynard, B., 175, 177, *184*
McCarthy, M. M., 83, *104*, 214, *220,* 241, 242, *248, 249*
McClain, K., 141, *148*
McClelland, A., 83, 101
McColl, A., 9, 19
McCollum, H., 78, 80, 106
McCombs, B., 217, *220*
McDonnell, L., 79, 104
McDrury, J., *273*
McEntee, M., 217, *220*
McGreal, T., 90, 101
McKee, A., 94, 102
McKibben, M., 83, 103
McLaughlin, M. W., 38, 40, 49, 84, 85, 91, *104,* 226, *237*
McMillan, R., 91, 105
McNamara, C., 164, *148*
McNeil, L. M., 223, *237, 249*
McNulty, B., 242, *249*

McTighe, J., 79, *81,* 107
Meier, D., 88, 104
Merriam, S., 51, 70, 89, 90, 104
Merton, R. K., 74, 75, 104
Mesa-Bains, A., *274*
Meyers, R., 87, 104
Meyerson, D., 241, 242, 247, *248*
Middleton, J. A., 132, 133, 137, 140, 141, 142, 143, 147, 146, *148*
Midgley, C., 280, *289*
Miles, M. B., 113, *129,* 177, 185
Miller, K, 172, 186
Miller, L., 82, 84, 104
Miller, M. D., 242, 248
Milstein, M. M., 183, 186
Miramontes, O., 81, 82, 104
Mohr, N., 156, *169*
Mohrman, A., 89, 90, *104*
Mohrman, S., 89, 90, 91, *104, 107*
Moles, O., 93, *107*
Molnar, A., 79, *104*
Monti, 210
Moore, B., 113, *128,* 152, *169*
Moore, S., 91, *102*
Moore, W., 114, *129*
Moos, R., 82, *104*
Morgan, M., 81, *99*
Morrow, L., 94, *104*
Moyers, P., 82, 84, *104*
Muijs, D., 113, *129*
Mullen, C. A., 176, *186*
Murnane, R. J., 192, 193, *205*
Murphy, J., 4, 7, *19,* 90, 91, *104,* 112, 113, 126, *129,* 176, *186,* 192, 195, *205,* 242, *249,* 252, 271, 272, *273*
Murphy, M. J., 4, *18,* 74, 76, 90, 91, 98, 99, *104*
Murtadha, K., 91, *103*
Muth, R., 4, *18,* 74, 76, 98, 99, *104*, 177, *184*

N

Nadeau, A., 81, 82, *104*
Nee-Benham, M., 79, *105*
Nelson, J., 83, *105*
Newmann, F., *129*
Newmann, F. M., 112, *129*, 152, *170*, 223, *237*
Newmann, J. H., 172, *184*
Nguyen, L., 191, *205*
Nicely, R., 90, *102*
Nichols, B. W., 191, *205*
Nicholson, L., 82, 84, *99*
Nieto, S., 242, 244, *249*
Noddings, N., 79, 83, 91, *105*
Nodine, T., 191, *205*

Nori, J., 114, *129*
Norris, C. J., 176, *184*
Nussbaum, M. C., 285, *289*

O

Oakes, J., 4, *19, 27, 29, 49,* 86, 88, *105,* 115, *129,* 274
Oberg, S., 242, 249
Odden, A., 87, 88, *105*
Ogawa, R., 165, 167, *170*
Ogbu, J., 279, *289*
Oh, S., 152, *169*
Ohanian, S., 8, 9, *18*
Oja, S., 89, 90, *105*
Olban, 27
Oldham, B. R., 173, *185*
Onikama, D., 91, 93, *105*
Orr, M. T., 165, 167, *170*
Osanloo, A., 54, *70*
Osborne, W., 89, *105*
Oser, F., 80, *105*
Osterman, K., 83, *105*
Otterbourg, S., 9, *18*
Otto, L., 82, 83, *105*
Ouchi, W. G., 214, *220*

P

Palmer, 254
Pankratz, R. S., 172, 173, *186*
Passel, J. S., 211, *219*
Patterson, J. L., 24, 49
Patterson, K., 91, *105*
Payne, R., 79, 81, *105*
Pelligrino, J., 280, *289*
Pendarivs, E., 172, *185*
Pennell, J., 86, *101*
Peters, R., 213, *220*
Peterson, K. D., 83, 89, 90, *101,* 105, 150, *170,* 175, *185,* 225, *237*
Peterson, P. L., *147*
Petrides, L., 191, *205*
Petrosko, J. M., 172, 173, *186*
Petzko, V. N., 114, *129,* 176, *186*
Piaget, J., 26, *49*
Pickering, D., 81, *104*
Picus, L., 83, *105*
Pierce, J., 51, 70
Pierce, M., 54, *70*
Pierce, W., 78, *100*
Pinar, W. F., 279, *289*
Playko, M., 68, *70*
Polanyi, M., 73, *105*

Polkinghorne, D., *274*
Pollard, D., 79, *99*
Pollock, J., 81, *104*
Popham, J. W., 8, *19*
Popjewitz, T., 277, 278, *290*
Poplin, M., 24, *49*
Porter, A. C., 53, *70,* 79, 90, *102,* 114, *128, 192,* 205, 290
Posner, B. Z., 225, *237*
Pounder, D., 113, *129*
Powell, B., 81, 82, *100*
Pratt, C., 26, *49*
Putnam, R. W., *274*

Q

Quartz, K. H., 4, *19,* 115, *129, 274*
Quinn, P., 253, *272*
Quong, T., 270, *274*

R

Rallis, S. F., 175, *185*
Rasher, S., 82, *107*
Rasinski, K. A., 114, *129*
Reeves, C. A., 172, *185*
Reeves, D. B., 196, *205*
Reid, W., 78, 79, 91, *105*
Reiman, A., 89, 90, *105*
Resnick, L. B., 27, 49, 225, 226, *238,* 276, 277, 279, 280, 280, *290*
Reynolds, D., 113, *130,* 191, 192, *192, 205*
Reynolds, W. M., 279, *289*
Rich, D., 92, *105*
Richardson, V., 78, *105*
Riessman, C., *274*
Rinehart, J., *274*
Ringel, J. S., 171, 183, *185*
Risley, T., 92, *102*
Rist, R., 210, *220*
Robbins, D., 81, *103*
Robbins, P., 64, *71*
Roberts, C., 5, *19,* 224, *238, 274*
Roberts, K., 5, *19*
Robillard, A., 270, *274*
Rodriguez, D., 80, 82, *107*
Rogers, D. W., 152, 153, *170*
Romberg, T. A., 120
Romo, H., 211, *220*
Ronnkvist, A., 225, *237*
Rosenholtz, S., 81, *106*
Rosenshine, B., 81, *106*
Ross, K., 171, 183, *185*
Ross, R., 5, *19,* 224, *237, 274*

Ross-Gordon, J., 90, *102*
Roth, G., 5, *19*, 224, *238, 274*
Rothstein, L., 79, *106*
Rowan, B., 89, *106*
Roza, M., 171, 183, *186*
Rumberger, R., 211, *220*
Rury, J., 114, *129*
Russ, J., 113, *129*
Rust, 270
Ryan, S., 4, *19,* 115, *129, 274*

S

Sachs, S. K., 209, *220*
Sadker, D., 78, 80, *106*
Sadker, M., 78, 80, *106*
Safford, P., 83, *101*
Sahl, K., 115, *130*
Santibanez, L., 171, 183, *185*
Sarason, S., 78, 80, 89, *106,* 114, *129,* 278, 279, 280
Sawada, D., 137, 140, 143, 146, *148*
Scardemalia, M., 78, 79, *99*
Scearcy, L. R., 176, *186*
Schaffer, E., 190, 192, *205*
Scheerens, J., 88, 91, 95, 96, 97, *106*
Scheffler, I., 79, *106*
Schensul, J. J., 177, *185*
Scheurich, J. J., 279, *290*
Schimmel, D., 82, 83, 88, 90, *101*
Schlechty, P., 77, *106*
Schlesinger, M. D., 192, *205*
Schmoker, M., 159, *170,* 190, 192, 193, 199, *205*
Schmuck, R., 90, *106*
Schneider, 225, *237*
Schon, D., 5, *19*, 254, 268, 272, *274*
Schonfield, W., 92, *107*
Schroeder, R. G., 191, 192, 196, 199, *205*
Schumann, J. A., 191, 193, *205*
Scott, E., 78, 80, *106*
Scribner, J. P., 93, *103*, 113, *129*
Sebring, P., 152, *170*
Sebring, P. B., 241, *249*
Secada, W. G., 143, *147*
Seller, W., 214, *220*
Senge, P., 5, *19*, 224, 225, *238, 268, 274*
Serbiovanni, T. J., *49*
Sergiovanni, T. J., 8, *19*, 24, 74, *106*, 167, *170,* 214, *220,* 237, *238*
Shannon, P., 279, 281, *290*
Shapiro, J., 91, *106*
Sharkey, N. S., 192, 193, *205*
Shavelson, R., 73, *106*

Shea, G., 64, 69, *71*
Shields, C., 242, *249*
Shockley-Zalabak, P., 89, 90, *106*
Shoho, A., 183, *185*
Short, P., *274*
Shulman, J., *274*
Shulman, L., 271, *274*
Simon, R., 78, *106*
Singer, K. P., 191, *205*
Singh, R., 82, *107*
Skelton, K., 86, 88, 106
Skrla, L., *290*
Slater, R., *274*
Slattery, P., 279, *289*
Sleeter, C., 80, *106*
Smith, B., 5, *19, 129*, 224, *237, 274*
Smith, S., 191, 192, 193, *205*
Smithson, J., 79, *102*
Smylie, M., 89, 90, 106
Smyth, J., 90, *106*
Solomon, D., 78, *106*
Sorenson, G., 84, 88, *101*
Sparks, D., 149, *170*
Spillane, J. P., 113, *114, 129,* 253, 274
Spring, J., 80, *106,* 279
Springer, M. G., 8, *18*
Stafkovich, J., 91, *106*
Stake, R. E., 176, *186*
Stalion, N., 177, *184*
Starratt, R. J., 64, *71,* 278, 280, 282, *290*
Stasz, C., 79, *100*
Staub, F., 81, *107*
Steffy, B. E., 173, *186*
Stein, N., 83, *106*
Steinbach, R., 271, *273*
Steinberg, L., 77, 82, 83, 92, *106*
Steinberg, S. R., 280, *289*
Stepien, W., 253, *274*
Steven, R., 81, *106*
Stewart, M., 83, *106*
Stiegelbauer, S., 113, *129*
Stiggins, R. L., 192, *205*
Stiles, K. E., 91, *103*, 144, *148*
Stoll, L., 113, *129,* 214, *220*
Stout, R. T., 183, *185*
Strahan, D., 114, *129*
Strange, M., 150, *169*
Strauss, A., 177, *186*
Streifer, P. A., 191, 193, *205*
Stringfield, S., 190, 191, 192, 193, 198, 201, 204, *205, 206*
Stuart Wells, A., 210, *220*
Su, Z., 79, *102*

Sugai, G., 82, 83, *106*
Supovitz, J. A., 130, 191, 192, *205*
Swanson, A., 87, 106
Swartz, C., 171, *186*
Switzer, A., 91, 105
Symonds, K. W., 191, *205*
Szecsy, E., 54, *70, 273,* 271, *273*

T

Talbert, J. E., 38, *49,* 85, 91, *104*, 242, *249*
Tallerico, M., 74, 101
Tangri, S., 93, 107
Tanner, D., 78, 107
Tate, W. F., 114, *130*
Tatum, B. D., 279, *290*
Taubmen, P. M., 279, *289*
Taylor, C., 282, 283
Teddlie, C., 113, *130,* 191, *205, 274*
Teitel, L., 176, *186*
Terrell, R., 80, *103*
Thomas, A., 84, *107*
Thomas, S., 83, *104*, 211, *220*
Thompson, R., 82, 84, *107*
Thompson, S., 73, 74, *107*
Thorn, C. A., 201, *206*
Thorstensen, B., 150, *170*
Thorton, L., 217, *220*
Tilton, L., 81, *107*
Tizard, J., 92, *107*
Tolley, H., 279, *289*
Toole, J., 89, *103*
Towne, L., 73, *106*
Tschannen-Moran, M., 113, *129*
Tucker, M. S., 149, *170*
Tung, R., 191, *204*

U

Uekawa, K., 224, *237*

V

Vachon, M., 90, *103*
Vail, K., 210, 211, *220*
Valentine, J. W., 113, *114, 129*
Valenzuela, A., 242, *249*
Varela, F. J., *289*
Vickers, G., 6, *19, 274*
Villani, C. J., *220,* 242, *249*
Vriesenga, M., 242, *249*
Vygotsky, L. S., 26, *49,* 280, *290*

W

Wagner, T., 152, 153, 159, *170*
Wahlstrom, K., 113, *129,* 152, *169*
Walberg, H. J., 78, 80, 82, 95, 96, *101, 107*, 152, *169*
Walker, A., 270, *274*
Walker, L. J., 209, *216*
Wang, M., 78, 80, *107*
Ward, M., 114, *129*, 242, *249*
Warner, C., 86, 87, *107*
Waters, T., 95, 96, 97, *107,* 242, *249*
Watson, M., 78, *106*
Watters, K., 86, 87, *103*
Wayman, J. C., 191, 192, 193, 195, 198, 199, 201, 204, *205, 206*
Webb, N. L., 132, 133, *148*
Weber, G., 191, *206*
Weber, R. P., 177, *186*
Wehlage, G. G., 12, *129,* 225, *237*
Weick, K., 5, *19*
Weinbaum, A., 280, *290*
Weindling, D., 270, *274*
Weishaar, M., 93, *100*
Welch, J., *274*
Welch, W., 9, 96, *101*
Wenger, E., 51, *70,* 176, *185, 278,* 279, 280, *290*
West, L., 81, *107*
Whelan, K., 270, *273*
Whitaker, T., 93, *107*
White, J. L., 209, *216*
White, P., 79, *102,* 115, *130*
Wigfield, A., 80, 92, *107*
Wiggins, G., 79, 81, 82, *107*
Wiggins, T., 89, *105*
Wiley, T., 54, *70*
Wiliam, D., 81, *99,* 191, *204*
Wilke, A., 280, *290*
Wilkin, A., 94, *100*
Williams, C., 213, *220*
Wilson, D., 91, 93, 94, 96, 97, *103*
Wilson, P., 241, *249*
Windschitl, M., 115, *130*
Winograd, P., 150, *169*
Wirt, F. M., 214, *220*
Wishon, S., 171, 183, *186*
Wiske, M. S., 280, *290*
Witziers, B., 97, *107*
Wohlstetter, P., 91, *107*
Wong, H., 81, *107*
Wong, R., 81, *107*
Wortham, S., *274*
Wright, W., 68, *70,* 252, 256, *273*

Wyche, J., 82, 84, *99*

Y

Yakimowski, M., 193, 198, 201, 204, *205, 206*
Yerkes, D. M., 176, 184
Yin, R. K., 176, *186*
Yoon, K., 53, *70*, 90, *102*
Young, J., 94, *104*

Young, M. D., 165, 167, *170*
Youniss, 283

Z

Zemelman, S., 81, *107*
Zepeda, J., 64, *71*
Zhao, Y., 201, *206*

SUBJECT INDEX

A

Abbott v. Burke (NJ), 10–11
Accountability agenda, 17, 275
Achievement, *see* Student achievement
Action learning, 52, 54, 61, 190
    plans, 58–59, 61, 174–176
Adequate yearly progress (AYP), 8–9, 173
Administrative dilemmas, 5–6
Administrator development, 13, 53–54, 133
    leadership, ix, 6, 3, 112, 126–127
    motivation, 53, 258–259
Adult learner autonomy, 51, 53
Adult learning theory, 51
Alternative school
    narrative, 264–265
America 2000, 8–9
Assessment, 11, 13–16, 27, 32, 38–40, 47, 64, 66,
    78, 82, 121–125, 128, 132, 137–138,
    141, 146, 176, 179, 191, 195–200, 218,
    222, 234, 244, 277, 288
Assumptions, 4, 6, 14, 28, 52–53, 114, 134–135,
    144, 150, 156, 158–160, 162, 165, 224,
    248, 254, 268, 279–281
Autonomy, 4, 6, 51–53, 68–69, 193

B

Book discussions, 60
Border rural areas, 242–243

C

Calibration, 195–197, 202–204

Center for Collaborative Education (CCE)
    schools, 25, 39–40
    challenges, 34–39
    core values, 28–34
Central Park East Elementary School (CPE),
    27–28, 31
    descriptive review, 32–34
Change, viii, 14, 24–25, 47, 89, 111–121,
    134–140, 146, 162, 166–167, 173, 178,
    183, 200, 213, 223, 226, 233, 241, 246
    organizational change, 85, 89, 91
Charter schools, 47–49, 121
Child-centered education, 27
    children's needs, 31–32
Choice, 27, 47–48, 52–53, 85, 192, 236, 282, 284
Classroom management, 13, 53, 55
Collaboration, 5–6, 15, 24, 37, 46, 54–56, 61,
    68–69, 114, 158, 162–163, 178, 190,
    192–193, 195, 200–203, 208, 218, 229,
    235, 248, 252–253
    collaborative teams, 15, 192, 195–198,
        199–200, 203
Communication patterns, 118
Community, 89–92, 133, 155–156, 165–166, 253
    community elite involvement, 9
    community importance, 5
    community values, 5, 39–40, 74–76
    leadership, 10, 13, 40, 114, 143–144, 146, 225
    learner-centered community, 10, 207
"Community of practice" (case study), 14
Contradictory values, 38–39, 43
Contexts, 5, 15, 24, 26, 38, 48–49, 51–52, 85, 113,
    150–153, 168, 195, 202, 207, 243, 271

Craft knowledge, 4, 12, 73–74, 86
Critical Friends Groups (CFG), 156, 159
Critical thinking skills, 6
Cultural diversity, *see* Diversity
Culture cultivating, 162–163
Curriculum
    change, 111–127, 223
    development, 132, 136, 183
    standards, 218, 278
    math curriculum studies, 115–126
Curriculum reform, 13, 111–112, 114–121

D

Data use, 189–193, 199–204
    collaboration, 192–193, 195–196
    decision making, 14, 189, 191
    student data, 14, 15, 189–199, 201–204
Decision making, 4, 6, 9, 40, 94, 115, 125, 141,
    166, 173, 189–191, 214, 216, 235,
    252–254, 259, 269–270
Deep learning, 166
Digital divide, 218
Dilemmas, 5–6, 12, 17, 65, 135, 140, 156,
    254–257
Direct reflection, 52
District Alliance Project, 193–195
District leadership, 14, 143–147, 175, 177, 181,
    255
District level meetings, 62
District principalship, 178–180
District support, 65
Diversity, 4, 24, 30–31, 33–34, 37, 40, 42, 52,
    54–56, 62, 116, 211, 281
    linguistic, 243, 246

E

Education
    formal, 7, 127
    higher, 13, 36, 133, 135, 144, 208, 216, 218
    mathematics, 131, 135–138, 140, 145
    public, 7–8, 47, 135, 154, 173, 194, 213, 219
    rural, 14, 151
    special, 17, 28, 61, 82, 84, 96, 233, 246, 262
    teacher, 143, 226
    urban, 61, 111, 216, 237, 254
Educational leadership, 6, 16, 91, 142, 151, 165,
    167, 172, 175, 242, 251–252, 281
Efficacy, 10, 15, 85, 94, 126, 191, 207, 212, 214,
    226
Elementary and Secondary Education Act
    (ESEA), 8
Empowering others, 37–38
English Language Learners (ELLs), 17, 136, 243

Entrepreneurship, 212–214, 218
Environment for learning, 76–77, 85, 89, 98
Environment for teaching, 77, 85, 89, 98
Ethical issues, 17, *see also* Moral challenges
Experience
    learning experience, 53, 63, 134, 161, 246,
        253, 276
    mentoring experience, 58, 64

F

Family, 30–34, 42, 56, 61–62, 77, 85, 89, 92–96,
    116–118, 122, 128, 133, 181, 198,
    211–212, 219, 257, 262–263, 277,
    282–283
Federal involvement, 8
    "coercion", 9
    financial consequences, 9
    state standards, 8, 56, 122, 125, 128
Formative assessments, 198
Framework for School Leadership Accomplish-
    ments (FSLA), 76–77, 94–95

G

Goals 2000, 8–9
Graduates, 7–8, 143, 174, 181, 183
Grantsmanship, 139–140

H

Homelessness, 211–212, 216, 219

I

Income discrepancy, 7
Instruction, 6, 78–82
    effective, 13, 55
    guided, 135, 137, 140
    individualized, 95
    math, 114, 119, 122, 125–126, 137
Instruction reform, 9–11, 112, 241
Instructional leader, 143, 178–180, 207, 209,
    230–231
Intrinsic motivation, ix, 52, 252

K

Kentucky Education Reform Act of 1990
    (KERA), 172–176, 182

L

Leadership
    administrator, ix, 3, 6, 112, 126–127

community, 10, 13, 40, 114, 143–144, 146, 225
distributive, 10, 113, 213
district, 14, 143, 146–147, 175, 177, 181, 255
educational, 6, 16–17, 142, 151, 165–167,
        172, 175, 242, 251–252, 281
effective, 64
facilitative, 224–226, 236
in math, 138–141
in schools, 4, 7, 12, 14–18, 24–25, 37, 47, 54,
        74–75, 98, 113, 133, 152, 155, 166,
        171–175, 182–183, 192, 208, 210,
        236, 252, 270, 272
instructional, 4, 13, 16, 51, 114, 173,
        178–179, 207, 212, 229, 244
moral, 275, 278
participatory, 115, 128
preparation, 51, 167, 242
principal, 7, 12, 74, 78, 82, 94, 112
professional culture, 42, 46–48, 181
teacher, 10, 114, 143–146, 225
Leadership change, 115–121
Leadership development, 4, 7, 12–15, 132–135,
        141, 143, 167, 175, 183–184, 208, 255,
        270, 280
assumptions, 134–135, 158–160
Leadership in Border Rural Areas (LIBRA) case
        study, 16–17, 243–248
consultation groups, 248
course content, 244–245
problem-based learning, 247
self-reflection, 245–246
social identity papers, 247
Leadership sources, 113–114
Learner-centered community, 10, 207
Learner-centered leadership (LCL), 3, 11, 41,
        49–51, 112, 149, 151, 174, 176, 183,
        189–190, 207, 222, 224, 236, 252–253,
        275
administrators, ix, 3, 6, 112, 126–127
and schools, viii, 6, 11, 41
Learner-centered schools, 23, 25, 36–40, 42, 48,
        150, 214
corridor advisors, 26
in the 1970s, 23, 26–27
Learner-centered values, 37, 41, 43–44, 49
case study, 41–44
Hi Tech Hi, 44–46
Learning, *see also* Student learning
action plans, 58–61
adult learning, 26, 51, 53, 89, 140, 156, 219,
        253–254
autonomy, 6, 52–53
community, viii–ix, 27–29, 47–48, 226–227,
        253
deep learning, 166
hinderances, 160–162
opportunities, 36–37, 28, 53, 112, 155, 233,
        243
organizational learning, 4, 5, 254
principles, 4, 51, 53, 156
social aspect, 4, 52–53
Learning goals, 77–78, 82, 95
curriculum, 78

M

Master's LCL certification education program,
        54–66
accomplished administrators, 63–64
course relevance, 65
district support, 65
in urban settings, 54–56
promotions, 65–66
prospective administrators, 56–57
rising administrators, 57–58
Mathematics initiatives (case studies), 13, 131
Math curriculum studies, 112, 115–126, 132
Math education, 131, 135–138, 140, 145
Math instruction, 114, 119, 122, 125–126, 137
Math leadership, 131–147
teacher-leaders (MTLs), 138–145
Mentoring, 6, 12–13, 17, 53–54, 57–58, 63–64,
        68–69, 132, 139, 176, 183, 243–248,
        252, 265–266, 269
Mobility, 133–134, 146, 152, 211–212, 216, 219,
        227, 235–236
family mobility, 212, 219
student mobility, 211, 216, 235
teacher mobility, 133
Moral agenda, 275, 282–285
authentic persons, 275, 283–284
Moral challenges, 275–289
Moral leadership, 275, 278
Motivation, ix, 4, 40, 52–53, 80, 82, 85, 94, 111,
        197, 258–259, 277
intrinsic, 9, 52, 252
Multiple constituencies, 15, 214–217

N

Narratives, 17–18, 252, 254–270, 272
administrator motivation, 259
alternative school, 264–265
data sources, 255–256
leadership development, 255
perspectives, 254, 259, 268–269
self-knowledge, 272, 286
special education, 262–263
National Science Foundation (NSF), 13, 113,
        115, 140, 146, 222–223, 233

Urban Systemic Initiative (USI) case study, 16, 221, 223, 233
Nation at risk report (1983), 8
NCTM standards, 113, 125–126, 128, 137
No Child Left Behind Act (NCLB), 5, 7–8, 126, 173–174, 190, 203, 223, 235

O

Open corridor initiative, 26–27
Organizational change, 85, 89, 213
Organizational learning, 4–5, 51, 254
Outcomes, *see* Student outcomes

P

Pedagogy, 6, 116, 120, 126, 131, 135, 137, 147, 209, 242, 244–246, 275–280
Perspectives, 31, 42, 61, 75, 89, 98, 112, 154, 156, 163, 166, 177, 179, 208, 244, 248, 285, 289
    critical perspectives, 78–79, 86–87
    multiple perspectives, 18, 151, 222, 254, 259, 269
Policy issues, 15, 172, 221–237
Policymakers, 6–7, 94, 114, 173–174
Political leadership, 6
Poverty, 16–17, 112, 136, 141, 150, 173–174, 194, 209–212, 216, 219, 223, 236, 242–243, 244, 246, 277, 281
Pragmatism (pragmatic theory), vii–viii
Principal development, 150
Principal involvement, 95, 117, 120–121, 204
Principal leadership, 5, 7, 12, 73–77, 82, 94, 112, *see also* School leadership
    criticisms, 73–74
    effort, 94
    professional knowledge, 74, 82, 98
    systemic reform, 222–224
Principal preparation program, 16, 241–242
    field experiences, 244
    mentoring, 243–244
Principals Excellence Program (PEP) case study, 14, 175–183
Problem-based learning, 247, 253
Professional community, 14, 43, 46, 48, 158, 165, 224–227, 253
Professional culture, 42, 46–48, 181
Professional development
    administrator development, 53–54
    mentoring, 57–58, 63–64, 68–69, 243–244
    narratives, 254–255
Professional effort, 77, 85, 92, 94
Professional knowledge, 3, 37, 74–78, 82, 86, 89, 98, 259

Promotions, 65–66
Psychological principles, 51–52, 69

R

Reflective inquiry, 54
Resources, 13, 26, 28, 33–34, 47, 61, 69, 78, 82, 112, 135, 139, 151, 161, 167–168, 174, 194, 202, 216–218, 221–224, 229, 232, 257, 263, 265, 278
    community, 16, 254
    limited, 39, 43, 171
    material, 39, 85
Revolving door administrators, 133
Role definitions, 66, 153
Rural contexts, 153
Rural schools, 13, 149–151, 171–172, 174–175
    action plan, 174–176
    border rural areas, 242–243
    isolation, 151–154, 164
    Lead NM, 151–154
    principal needs, 154–155
    study, 176–177, 180–181
Rural work ethic, 263–264

S

School accomplishments, 74–75, 97–98
    success criteria, 75
School betterment, 4, 257
School culture, 6, 33, 44, 113, 128, 134, 144, 192, 196, 203–204, 221–222, 224–229, 236–237
School leadership, 4, 7, 12–18, 37, 47, 54, 62, 73–76, 98, 113, 133, 152, 155, 166, 171–175, 182, 192, 204, 208, 210, 236, 252, 270, 272
School operations, 15, 86, 88, 96
    staff support, 86–87
School reform, 6–11, 16, 28, 112–113, 156, 167–168, 193–194, 200, 202, 216
    funding, 8, 10, 75, 85–86, 131–133, 140, 147, 160, 223–224, 235
    packages (CSR), 10–11
School renewal, 89, 91, 97, 281
Self-knowledge, 18, 272, 286
Self-reflection, 54, 161, 245–247
Social interaction, 52–53
Socialization, 175–178, 183–184, 267, 271, 283
Special education, 17, 28, 61, 82, 233, 246
    narrative, 262–263
Standards
    NCTM, 113, 125–126, 128, 137
    state, 8, 56, 122, 125, 128
Stories, *see* Narratives

Student achievement, 5, 9, 11, 13–16, 61, 85, 113, 132, 136, 141–142, 168, 174, 190–194, 198, 204, 208, 210, 222–227, 233–235, 247, 254, 277
gap, 7, 114, 218
Student climate, 75, 82, 95
Student data, 14–15, 189, 197–199, 202–204
Student effort, 77, 85, 92
Student learning, 24, 26, 36, 43, 53, 75–77, 94, 98, 111, 132, 138–143, 156, 168, 178, 190, 197–198, 203–204, 214, 223, 226, 232, 242, 278
improving, 172–173, 251
Student outcomes, 15–16, 29, 48, 115, 149, 221, 225, 236
Student testing, *see* Testing
Stupski foundation, 193–195
Success for All (SFA), 10
Summative assessments, 198
Superintendents, 14–15, 54, 62, 133, 150, 161, 173, 182–183, 194, 252
Sustained reform, 133
Systemic reform, 15–16, 133, 142, 166–167, 221–226, 236, 242
and principals, 223–224
study, 227–235

T

Teacher-directors, 24, 28, 35, 37, 41
Teacher education, 143, 226
Teacher-leaders, 24, 25, 132, 135–136, 138, 142–146
in math (MTLs), 138–145
resistance, 145
Teachers
efficacy, 15, 208, 212, 214
leadership, 10, 114, 143–146, 225
learning opportunities, 36–37, 53, 112, 155, 243
supporting growth, 35–36

Technology, 10, 15, 153, 193, 195, 201–203, 212, 218, 224, 262
digital divide, 218
Territorialism, 6
Testing, 7, 9, 17, 38, 44, 56, 61, 116, 122, 126, 218, 223, 233–234, 252, 255, 257, 275–277, 281
Training and Educational Leader Self-Assessment (TELSA), 66–67

U

Universities, 12–13, 16, 74, 135, 140, 143, 149, 164–165, 221, 246
Urban contexts, 15, 207–214, 219
school leaders, 10, 15, 208–219
Urban reform, 131, 135–141
Urban School Leadership Consortium (USLC)
case study, 15, 208, 212–213, 218
Urban Systemic Initiative (USI), 16, 221, 223, 233
U.S. Census Bureau, 7, 209

V

Values
centered, 37, 41, 43–44, 49
community, 5, 39, 74–76
contradictory, 38, 43, 159, 166
core values, 28, 41–43, 49
Vision, 5, 14, 34–37, 41, 44, 65, 131, 135, 162, 219, 229, 232, 237, 252
empowerment of others, 37–38
shared vision, 13, 196, 218, 224–225, 236
Vocational skills, 45

W

Workshops, 7, 12–14, 53–54, 59–65, 68–69, 139, 143, 155